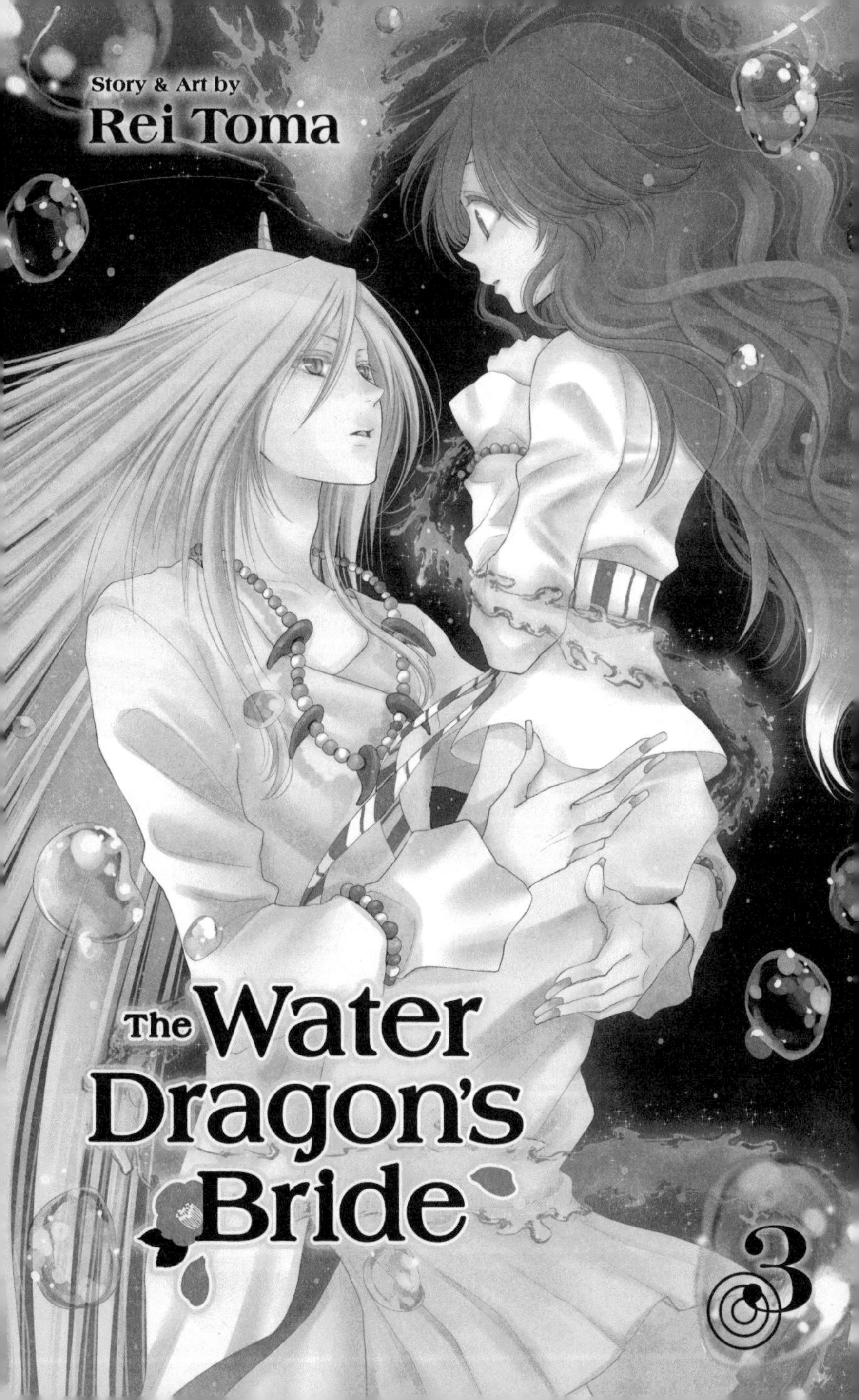
Story & Art by
Rei Toma
The Water Dragon's Bride
3

The Water Dragon's Bride CHARACTER INTRODUCTIONS

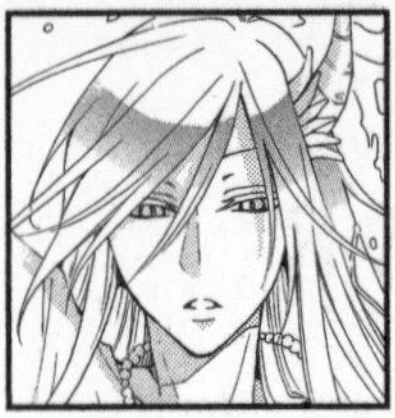

The Water Dragon God

The god who rules over the waters. Though he hates humans, he seems to be intrigued by Asahi and feels compassion for her.

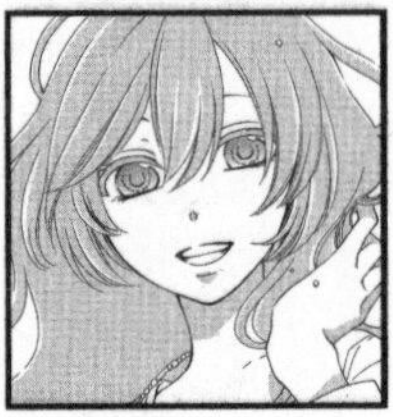

Asahi

A girl who was transported to another world when she was young. She was sacrificed to the water dragon god by Subaru's mother.

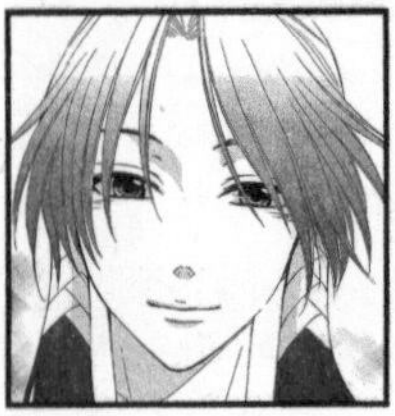

Subaru

He is drawn to Asahi and has resolved to protect her from his mother and the water dragon god.

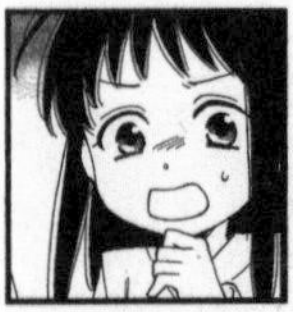

Shiina

Subaru's sister. She thinks Asahi is weird and frightening.

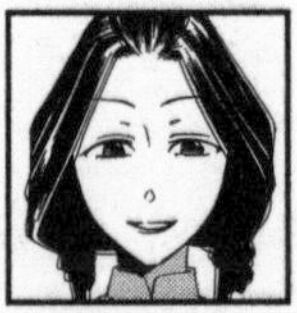

Subaru's Mother

She hates Asahi and has attempted to have her killed.

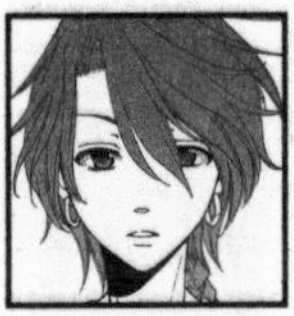

Tsukihiko

Asahi's caretaker. He has the ability to sense people's thoughts and emotions.

STORY THUS FAR

◎ Asahi is living a normal, sheltered life when she suddenly gets pulled into a pond and is transported to a strange new world. She meets Subaru, the son of the most prominent family in his village, and he helps her and brings her home. Subaru's mother dislikes Asahi, however, and plots to sacrifice her as a bride to the water dragon god in the Great Lake.

◎ The water dragon god decrees that Asahi will become his wife and takes her voice from her. Subaru rescues Asahi and safely returns her to his village, but since his mother hates Asahi, she convinces the villagers that Asahi has been touched by the god's anger and must be killed.

◎ The water dragon god's rage is finally aroused by the selfishness and insolence of the humans, and he reacts explosively. Asahi and Subaru are washed away in the ensuing flood, but the water dragon god rescues them. The water dragon god begins to have feelings, including compassion, for Asahi, and he gifts her with strange powers. Because of this, the villagers begin to revere Asahi as the water priestess.

◎ Asahi finds out that there was a priestess whose situation was the same as hers, and she despairs when she hears that this priestess died without ever being able to return home. Stranded in this strange world, Asahi grows up into a lovely young woman...

The Water Dragon's Bride

3

CONTENTS

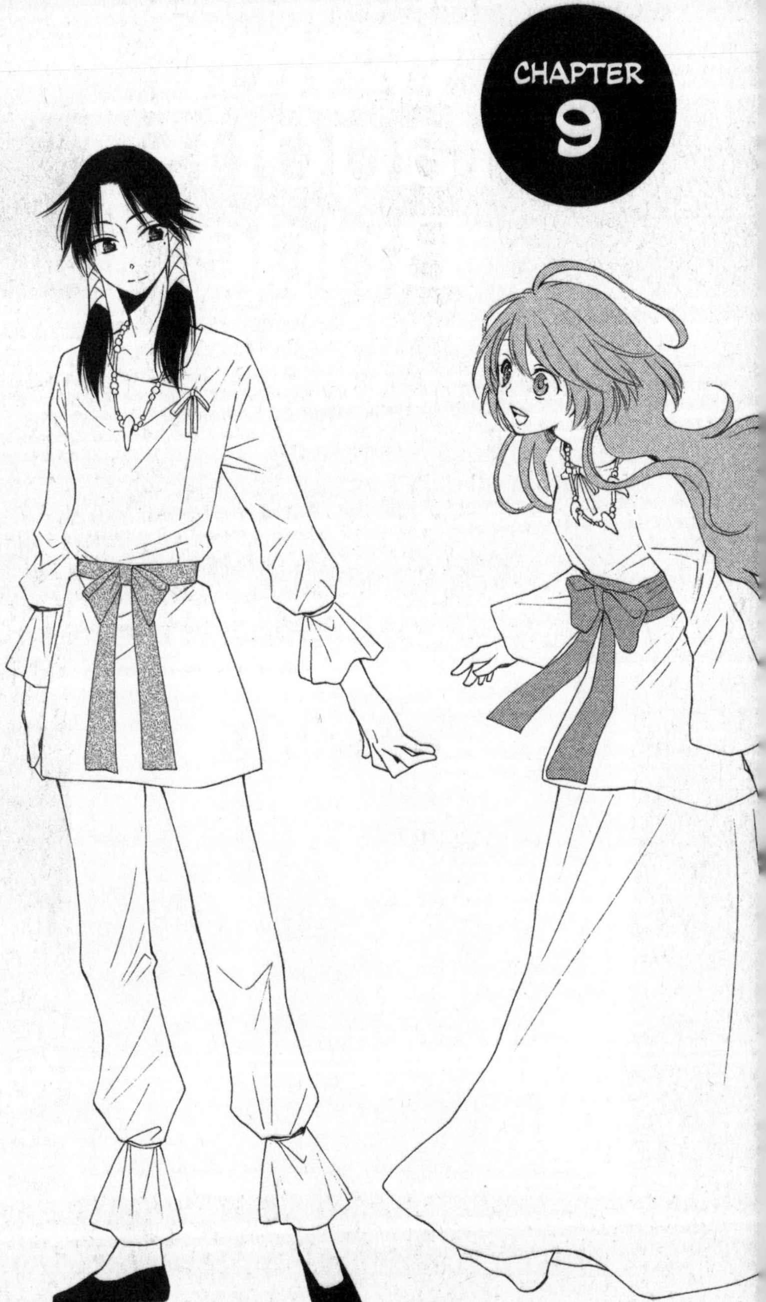
CHAPTER
9

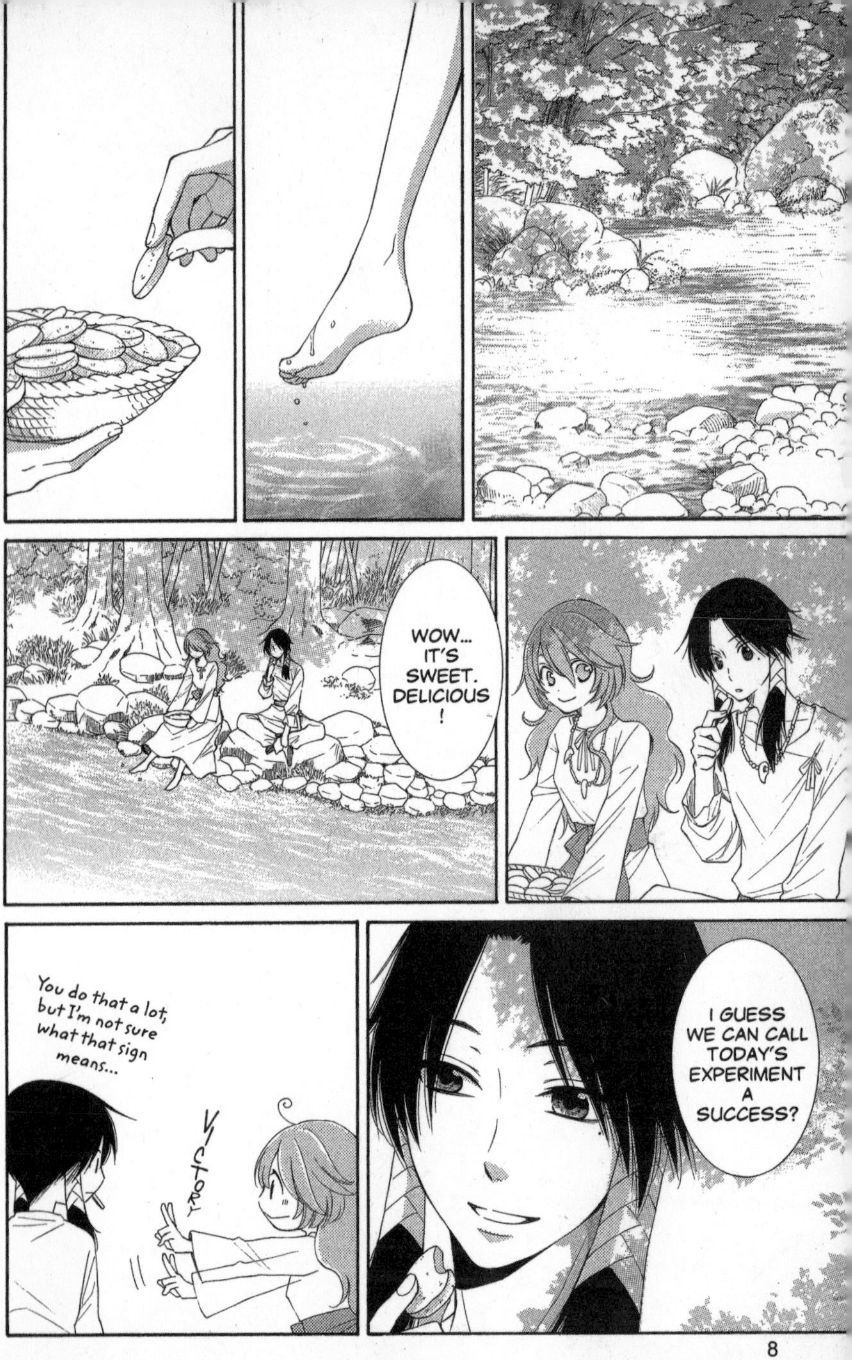
WOW... IT'S SWEET. DELICIOUS!
I GUESS WE CAN CALL TODAY'S EXPERIMENT A SUCCESS?
VICTORY
You do that a lot, but I'm not sure what that sign means...

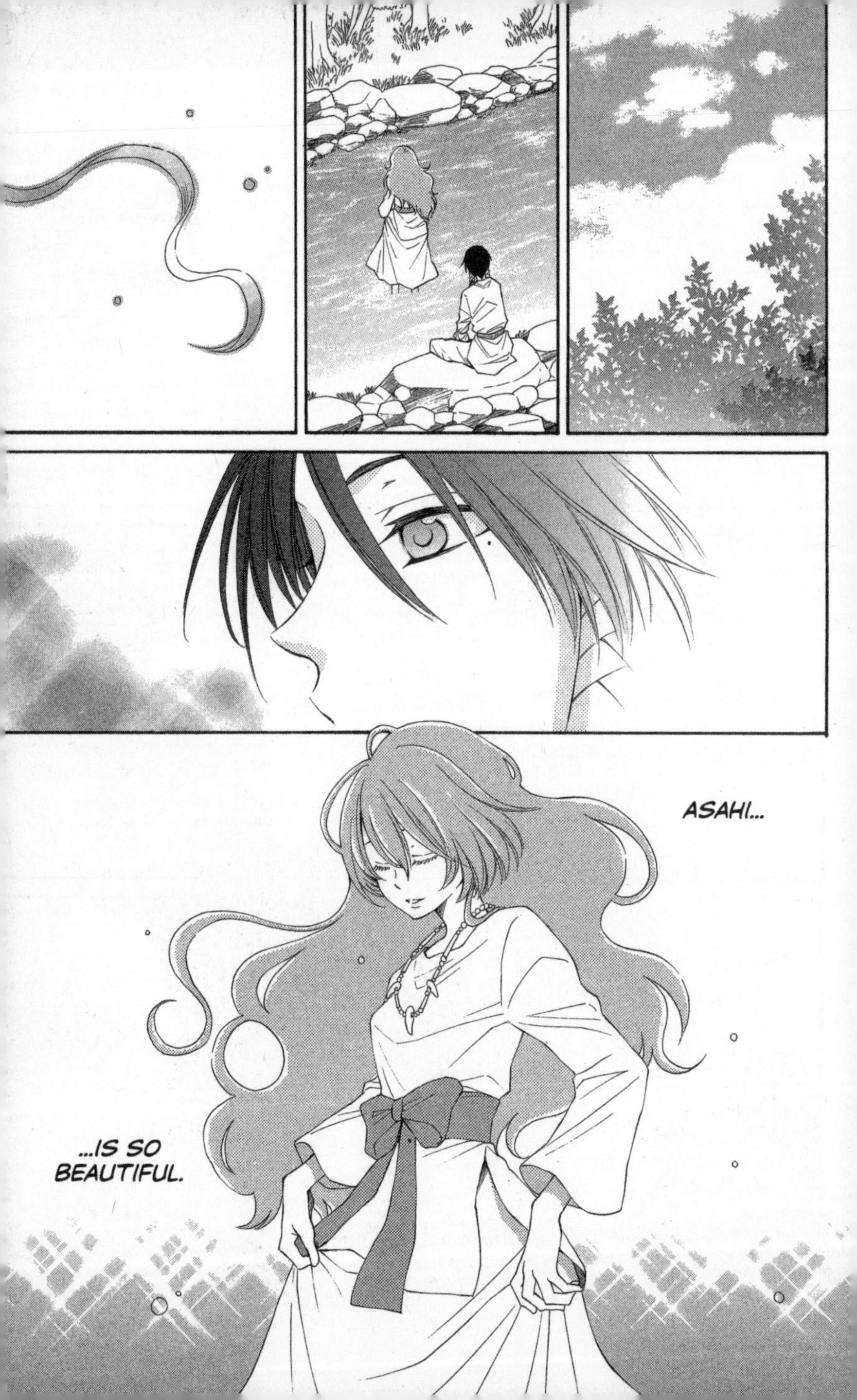

ASAHI...
...IS SO BEAUTIFUL.

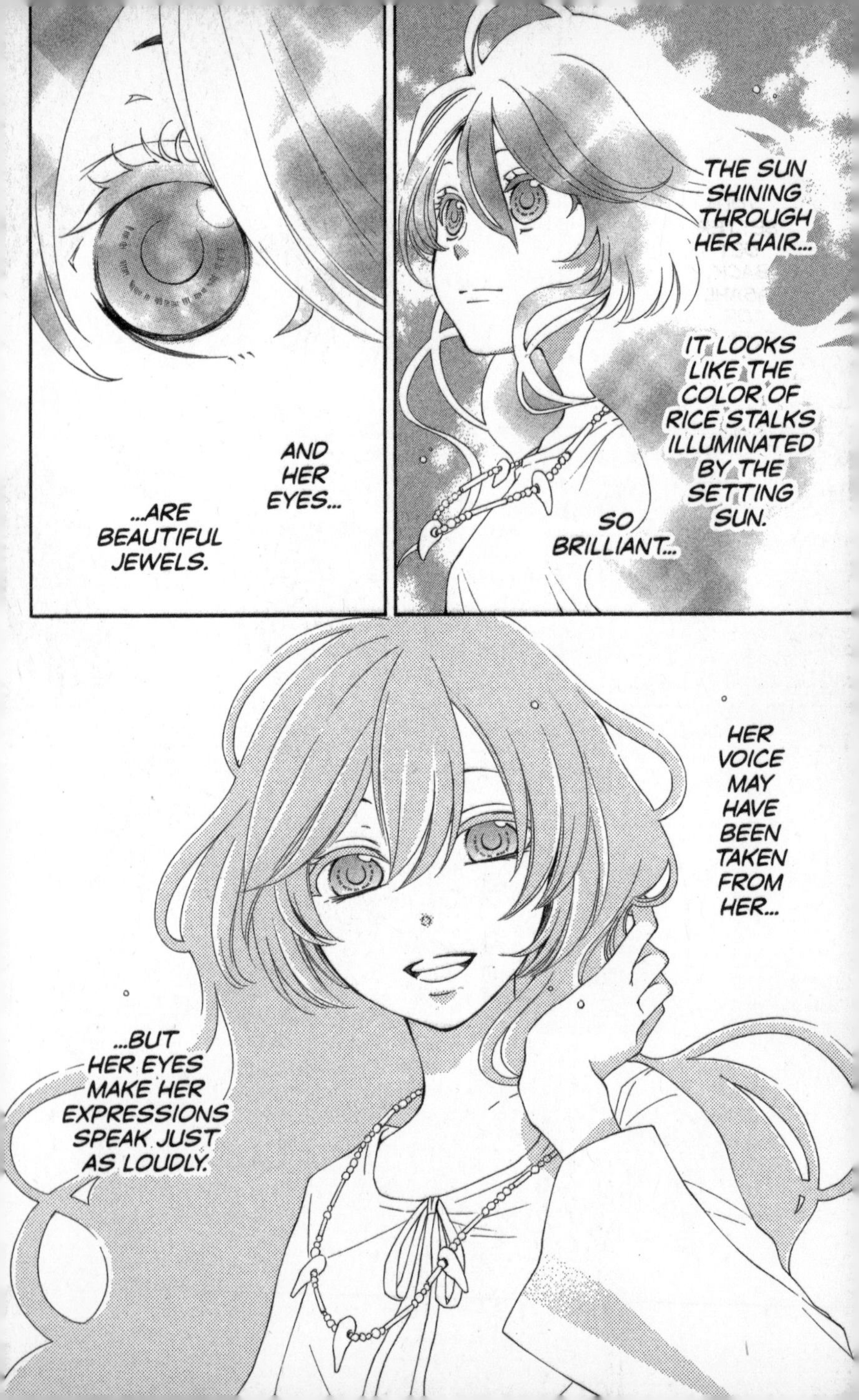
THE SUN SHINING THROUGH HER HAIR...
IT LOOKS LIKE THE COLOR OF RICE STALKS ILLUMINATED BY THE SETTING SUN.
SO BRILLIANT...
AND HER EYES...
...ARE BEAUTIFUL JEWELS.
HER VOICE MAY HAVE BEEN TAKEN FROM HER...
...BUT HER EYES MAKE HER EXPRESSIONS SPEAK JUST AS LOUDLY.

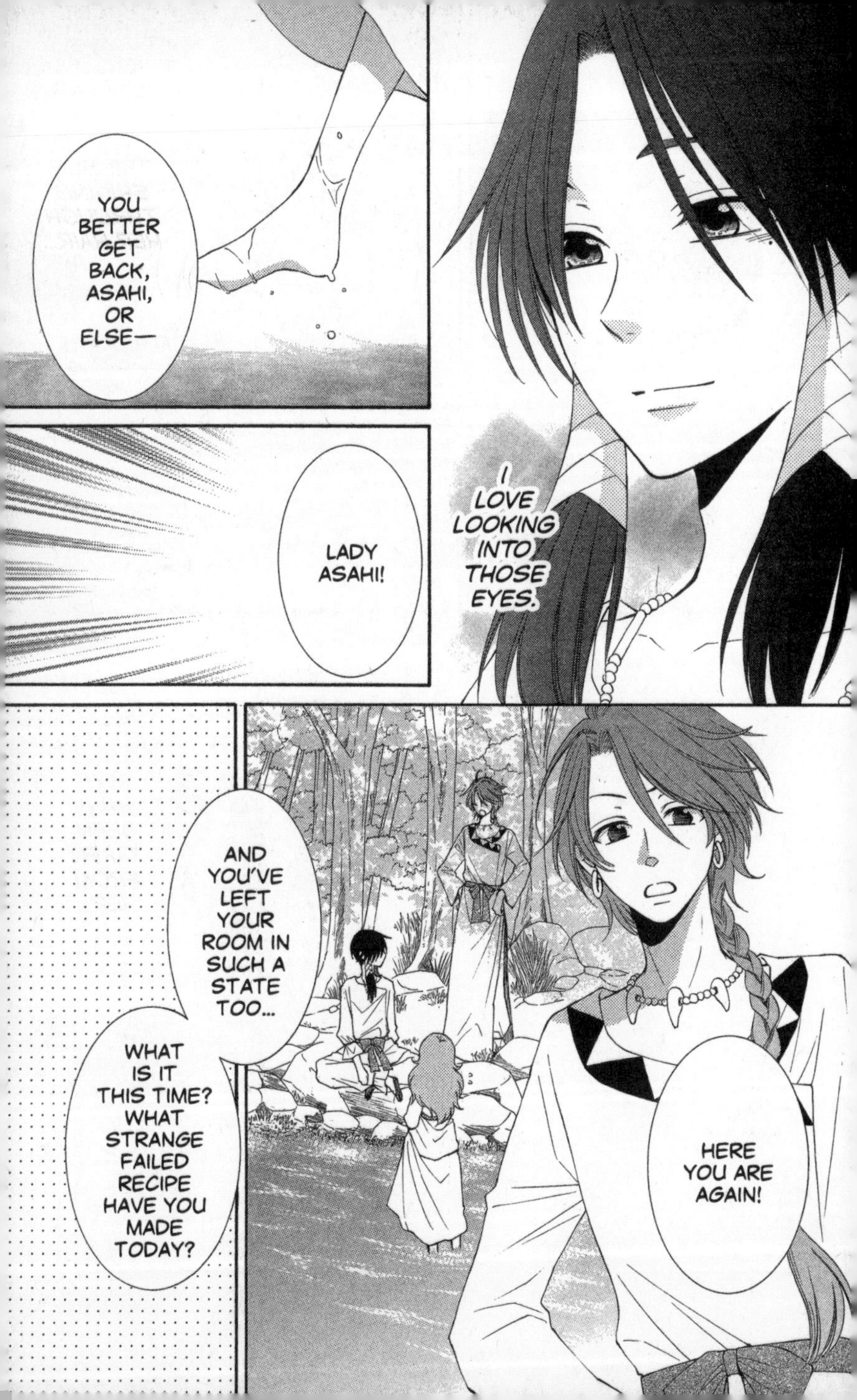
I LOVE LOOKING INTO THOSE EYES.
YOU BETTER GET BACK, ASAHI, OR ELSE—
LADY ASAHI!
HERE YOU ARE AGAIN!
AND YOU'VE LEFT YOUR ROOM IN SUCH A STATE TOO...
WHAT IS IT THIS TIME? WHAT STRANGE FAILED RECIPE HAVE YOU MADE TODAY?

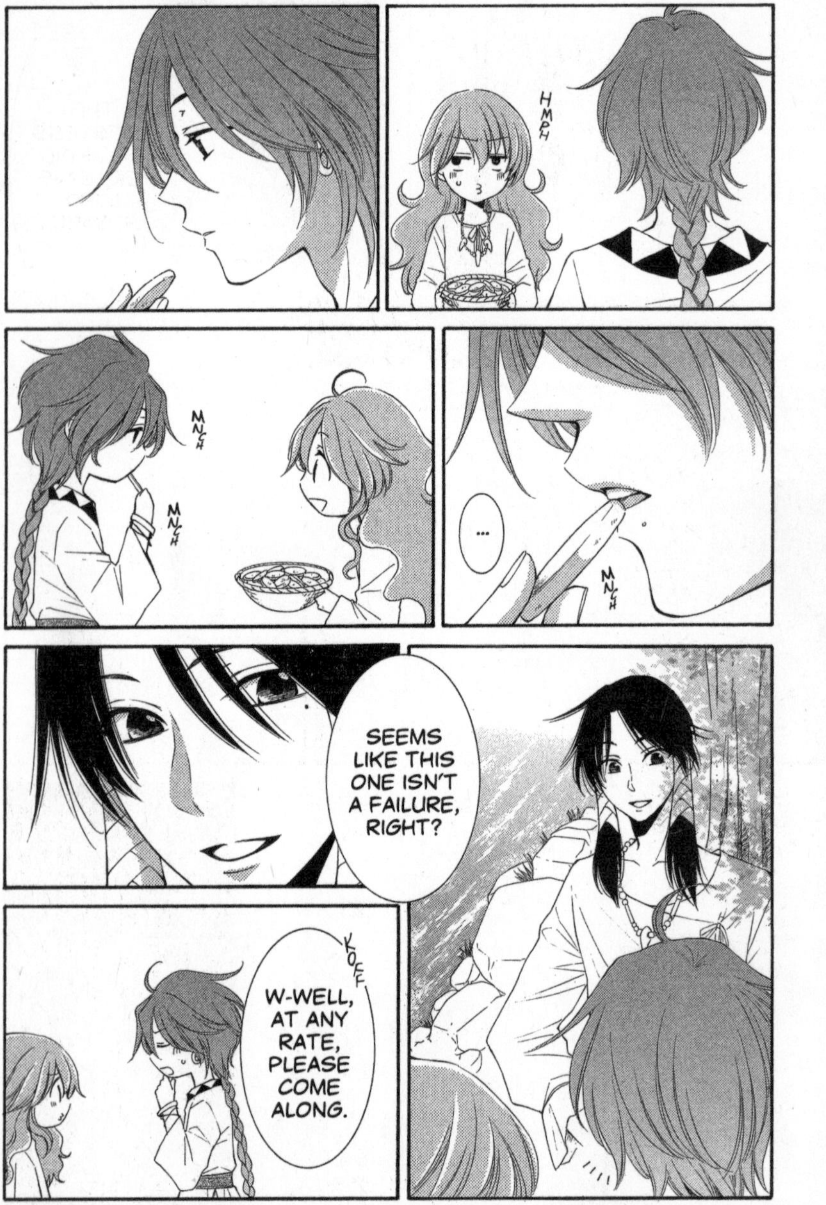
HMPH
...
MNCH
MNCH
MNCH
SEEMS LIKE THIS ONE ISN'T A FAILURE, RIGHT?
KOFF
W-WELL, AT ANY RATE, PLEASE COME ALONG.

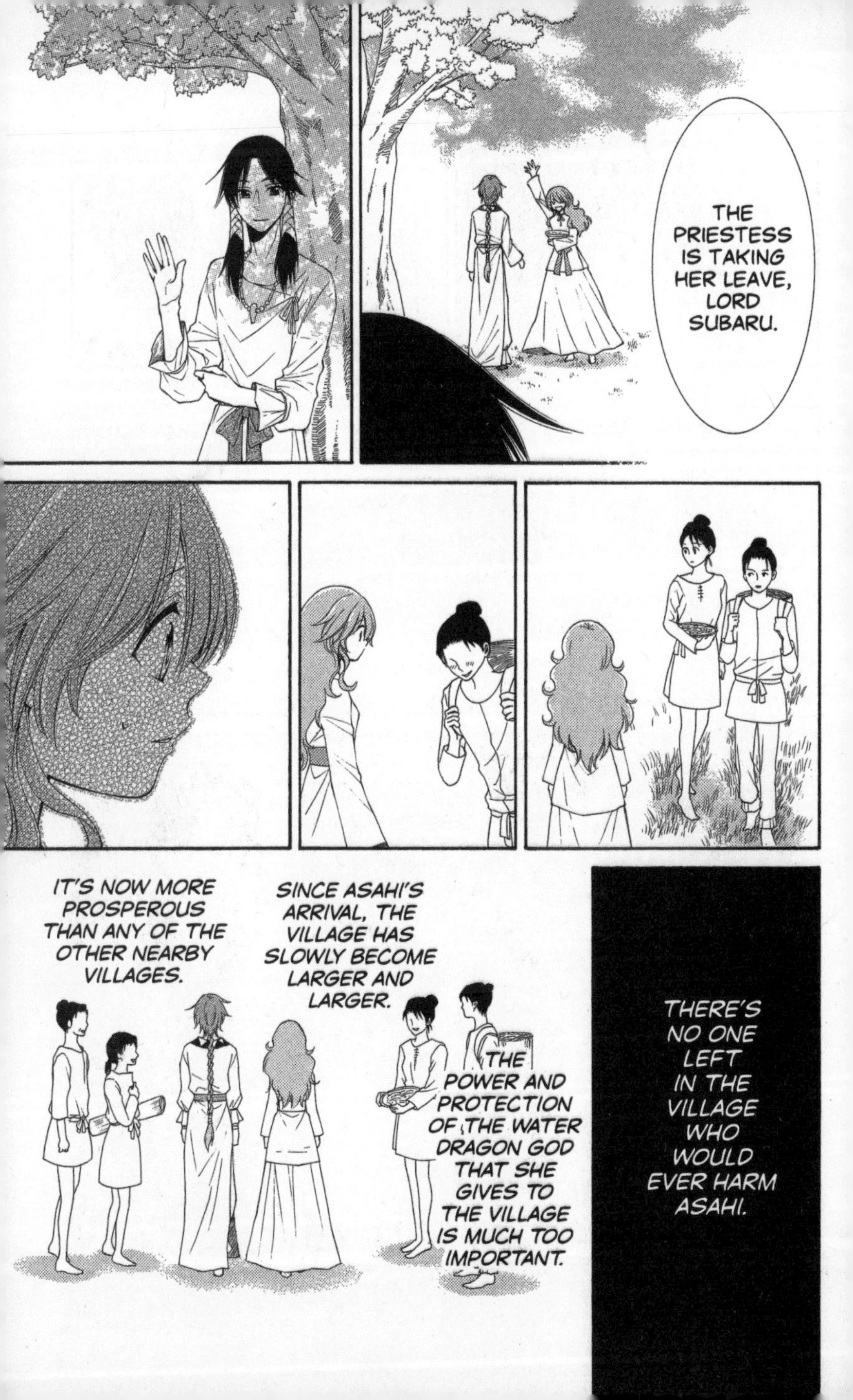
THE PRIESTESS IS TAKING HER LEAVE, LORD SUBARU.
THERE'S NO ONE LEFT IN THE VILLAGE WHO WOULD EVER HARM ASAHI.
SINCE ASAHI'S ARRIVAL, THE VILLAGE HAS SLOWLY BECOME LARGER AND LARGER.
IT'S NOW MORE PROSPEROUS THAN ANY OF THE OTHER NEARBY VILLAGES.
THE POWER AND PROTECTION OF THE WATER DRAGON GOD THAT SHE GIVES TO THE VILLAGE IS MUCH TOO IMPORTANT.

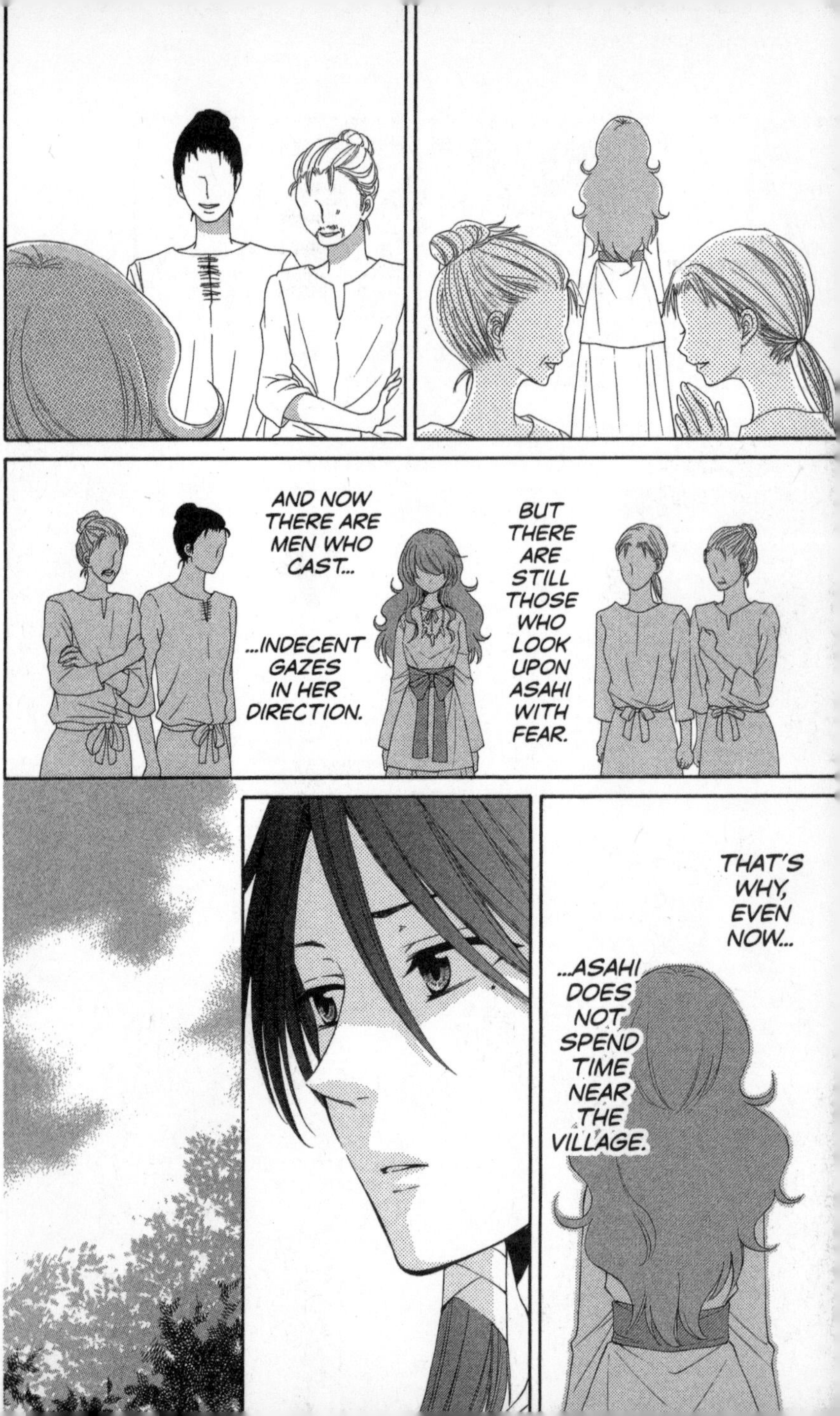
BUT THERE ARE STILL THOSE WHO LOOK UPON ASAHI WITH FEAR.
AND NOW THERE ARE MEN WHO CAST...
...INDECENT GAZES IN HER DIRECTION.
THAT'S WHY, EVEN NOW...
...ASAHI DOES NOT SPEND TIME NEAR THE VILLAGE.

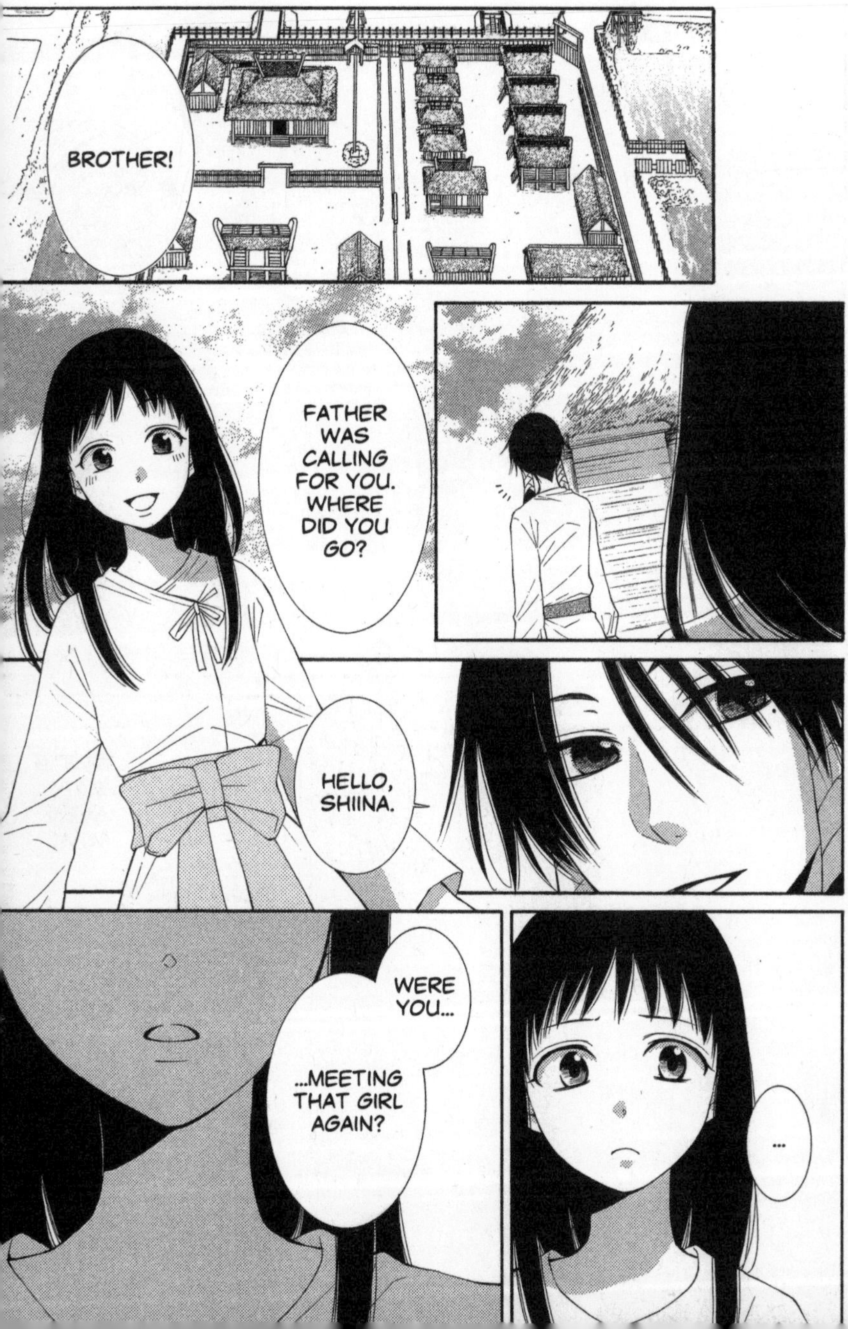
BROTHER!
FATHER WAS CALLING FOR YOU. WHERE DID YOU GO?
HELLO, SHIINA.
...
WERE YOU...
...MEETING THAT GIRL AGAIN?

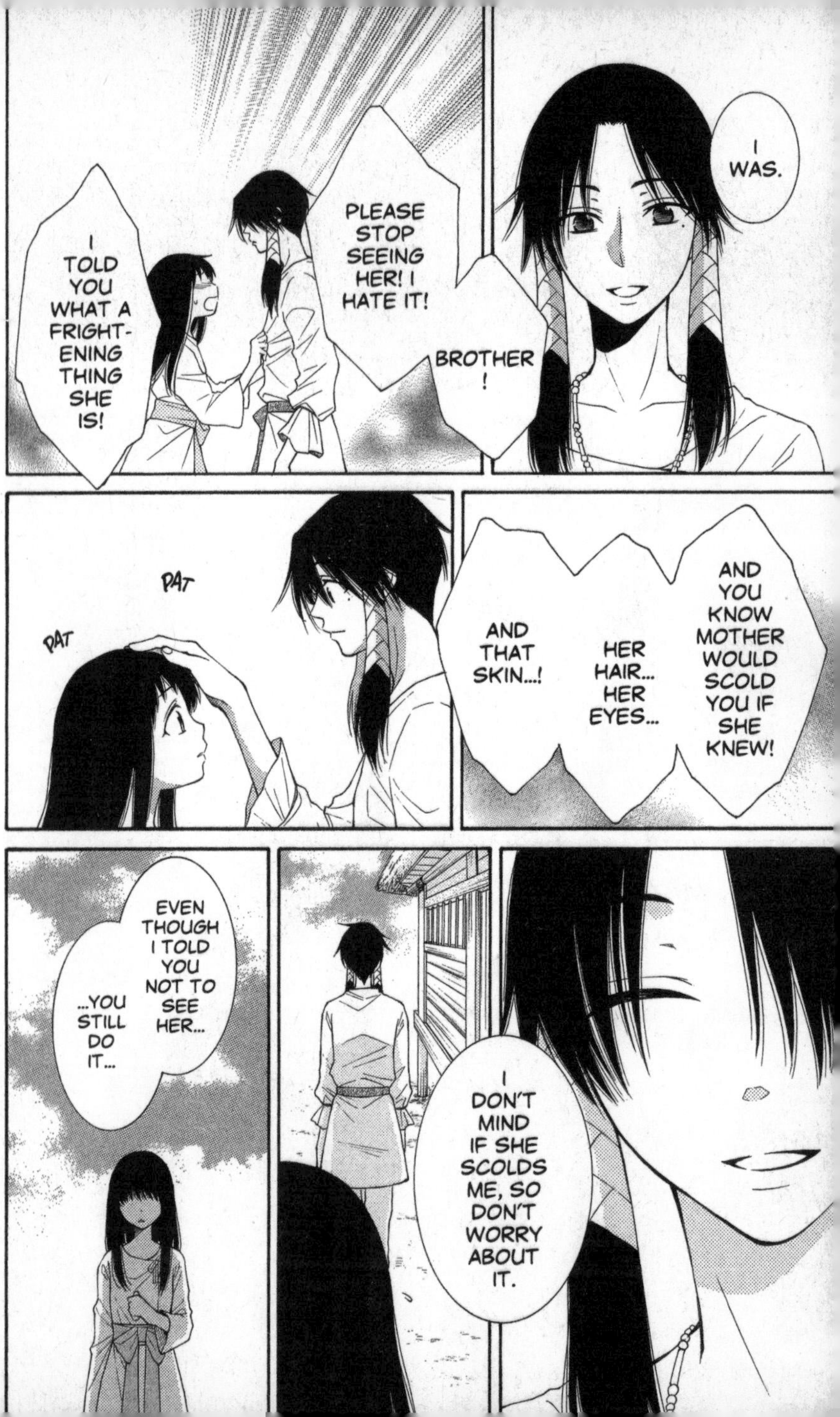
I WAS.
BROTHER!
PLEASE STOP SEEING HER! I HATE IT!
I TOLD YOU WHAT A FRIGHT-ENING THING SHE IS!
AND YOU KNOW MOTHER WOULD SCOLD YOU IF SHE KNEW!
HER HAIR... HER EYES...
AND THAT SKIN...!
PAT
PAT
I DON'T MIND IF SHE SCOLDS ME, SO DON'T WORRY ABOUT IT.
EVEN THOUGH I TOLD YOU NOT TO SEE HER...
...YOU STILL DO IT...

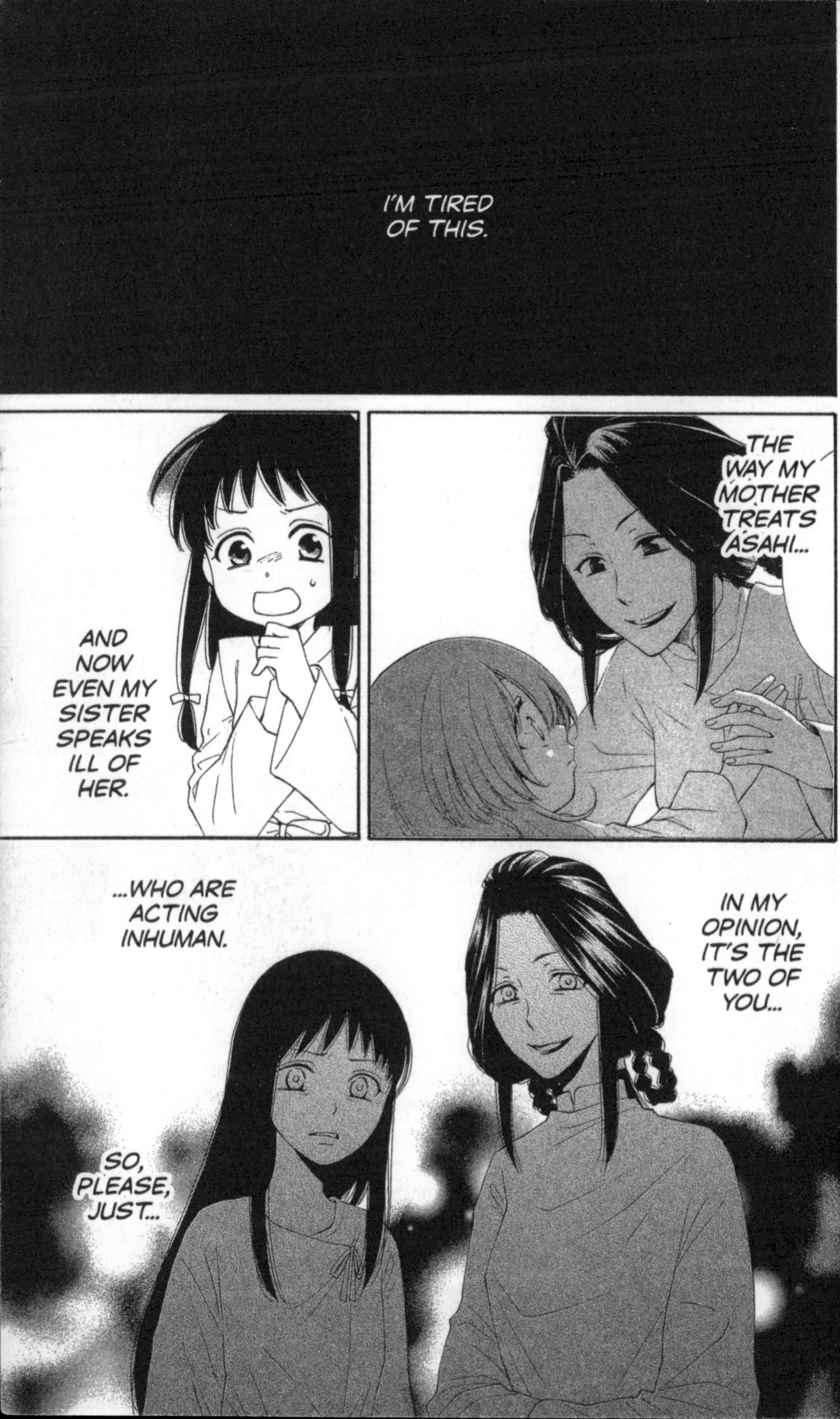
I'M TIRED OF THIS.
THE WAY MY MOTHER TREATS ASAHI...
AND NOW EVEN MY SISTER SPEAKS ILL OF HER.
IN MY OPINION, IT'S THE TWO OF YOU...
...WHO ARE ACTING INHUMAN.
SO, PLEASE, JUST...

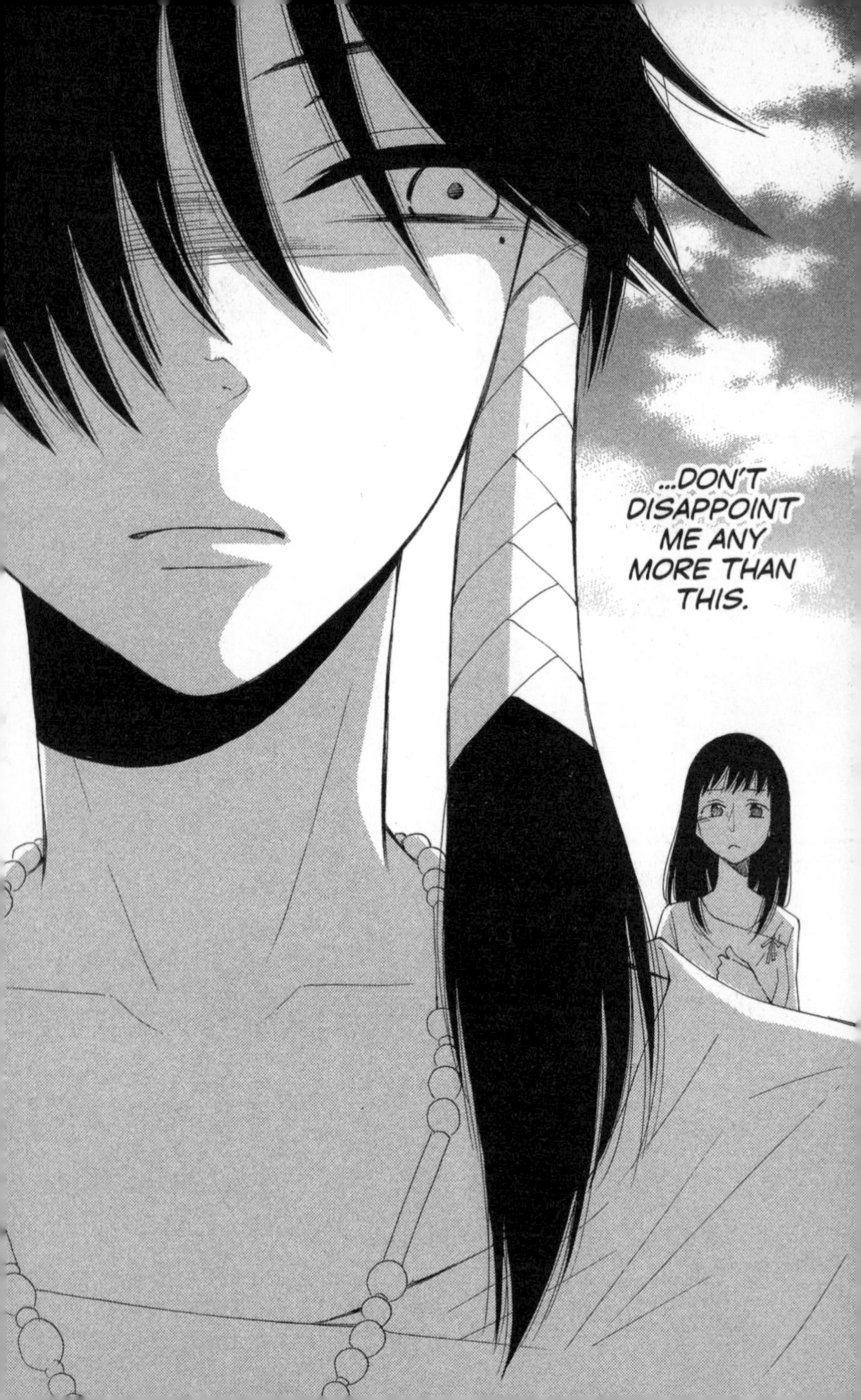
...DON'T DISAPPOINT ME ANY MORE THAN THIS.

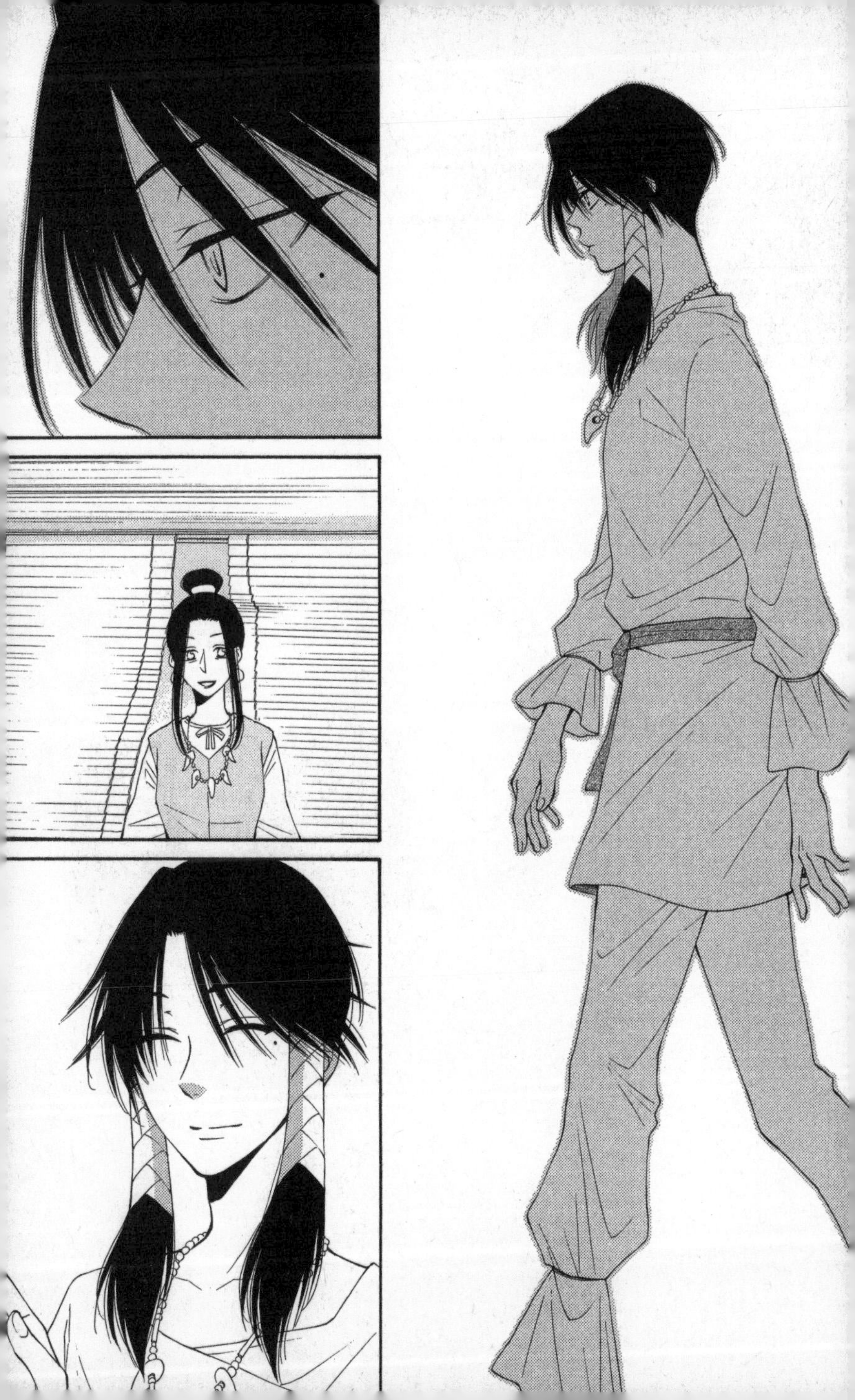

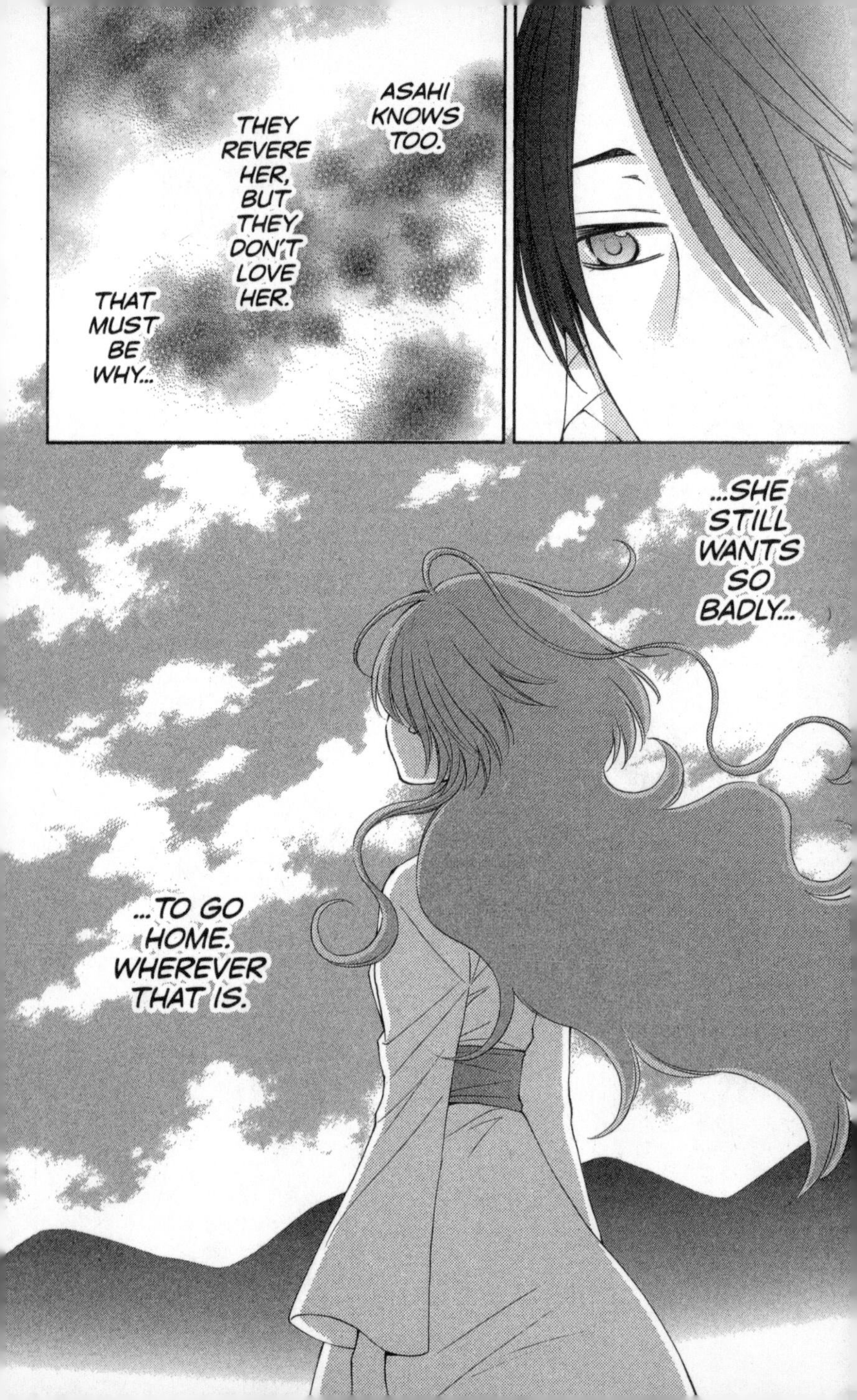
ASAHI KNOWS TOO.
THEY REVERE HER, BUT THEY DON'T LOVE HER.
THAT MUST BE WHY...
...SHE STILL WANTS SO BADLY...
...TO GO HOME. WHEREVER THAT IS.

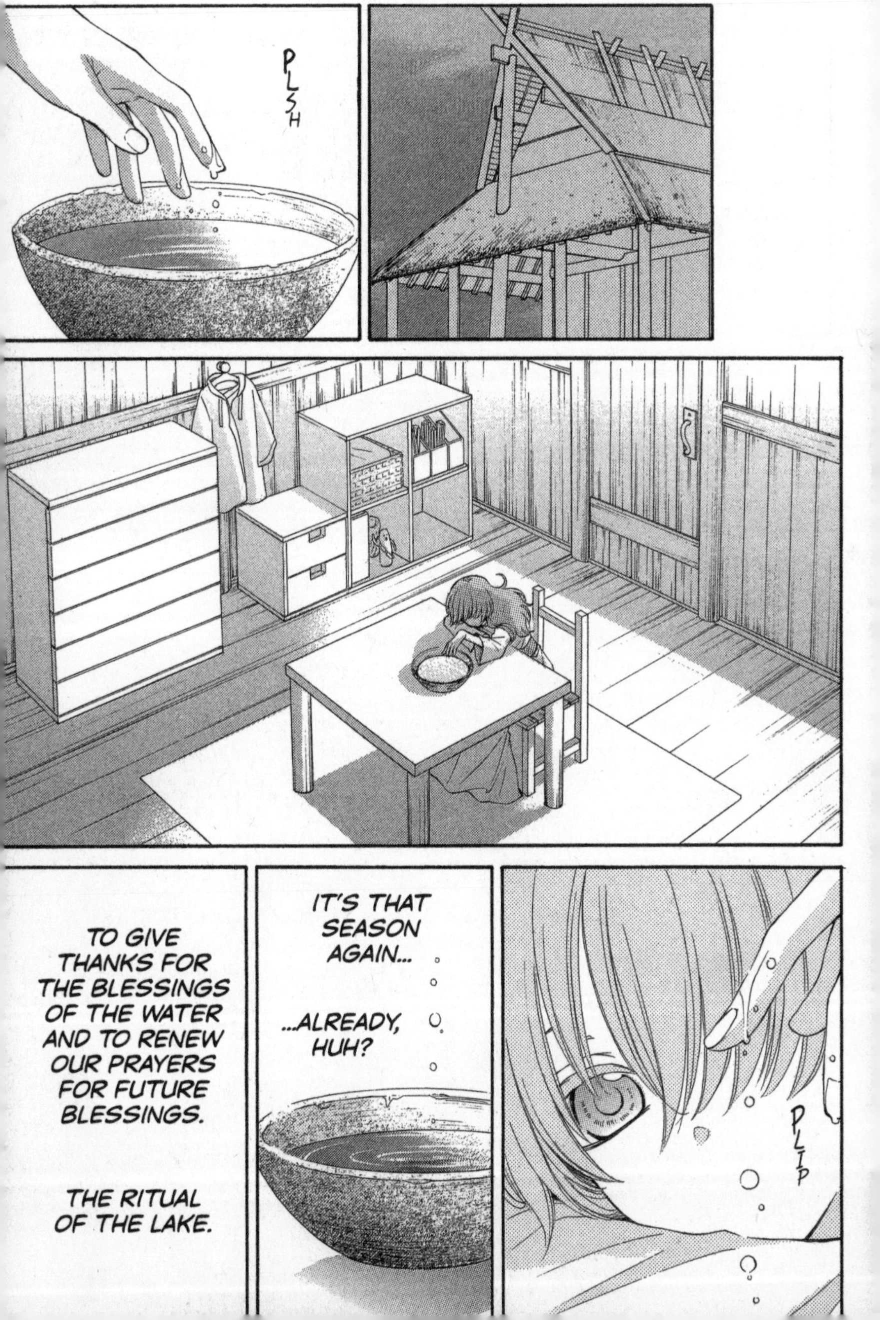
PLSH
PLIP
IT'S THAT SEASON AGAIN...
...ALREADY, HUH?
TO GIVE THANKS FOR THE BLESSINGS OF THE WATER AND TO RENEW OUR PRAYERS FOR FUTURE BLESSINGS.
THE RITUAL OF THE LAKE.

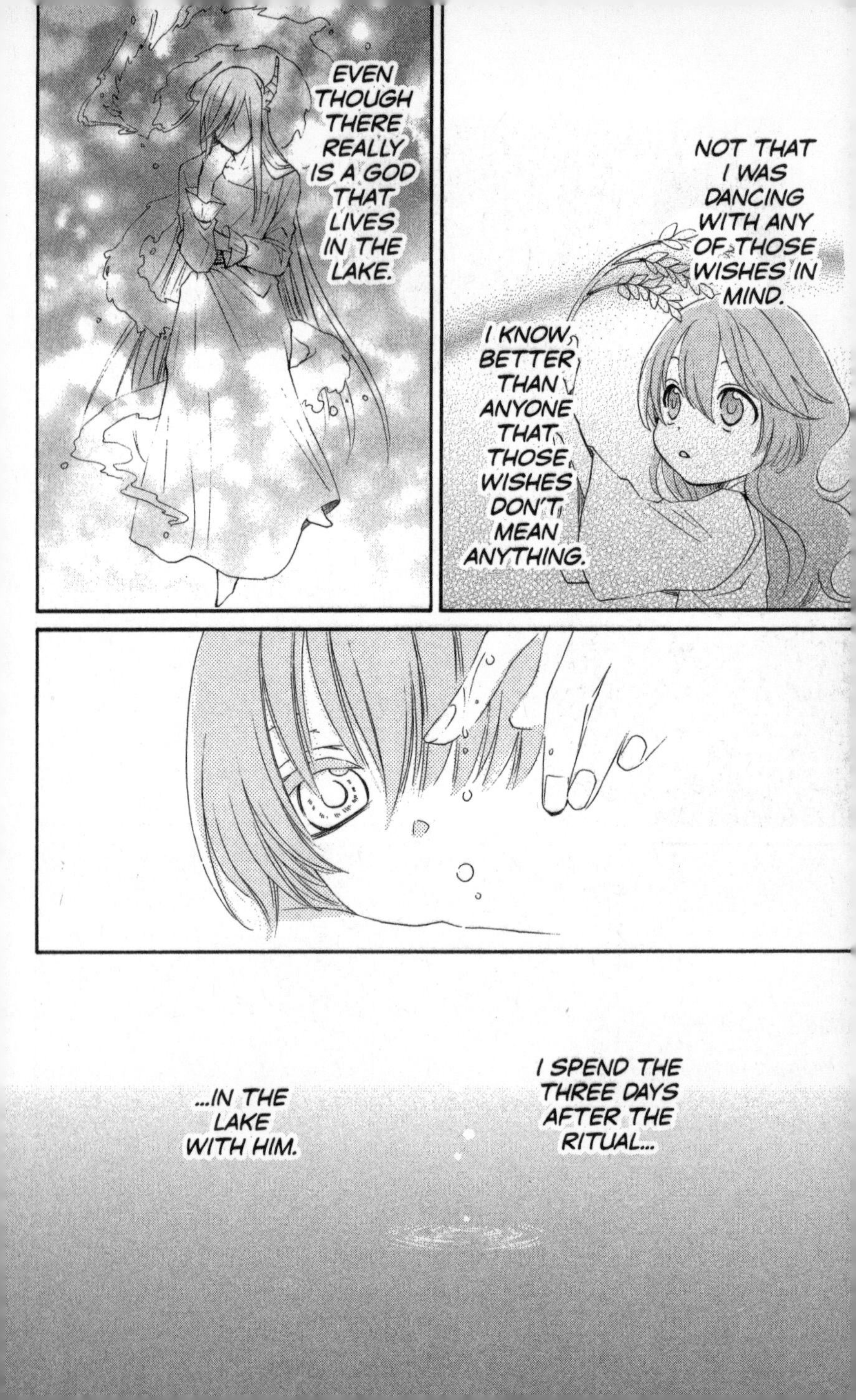
NOT THAT I WAS DANCING WITH ANY OF THOSE WISHES IN MIND.
I KNOW BETTER THAN ANYONE THAT THOSE WISHES DON'T MEAN ANYTHING.
EVEN THOUGH THERE REALLY IS A GOD THAT LIVES IN THE LAKE.
I SPEND THE THREE DAYS AFTER THE RITUAL...
...IN THE LAKE WITH HIM.

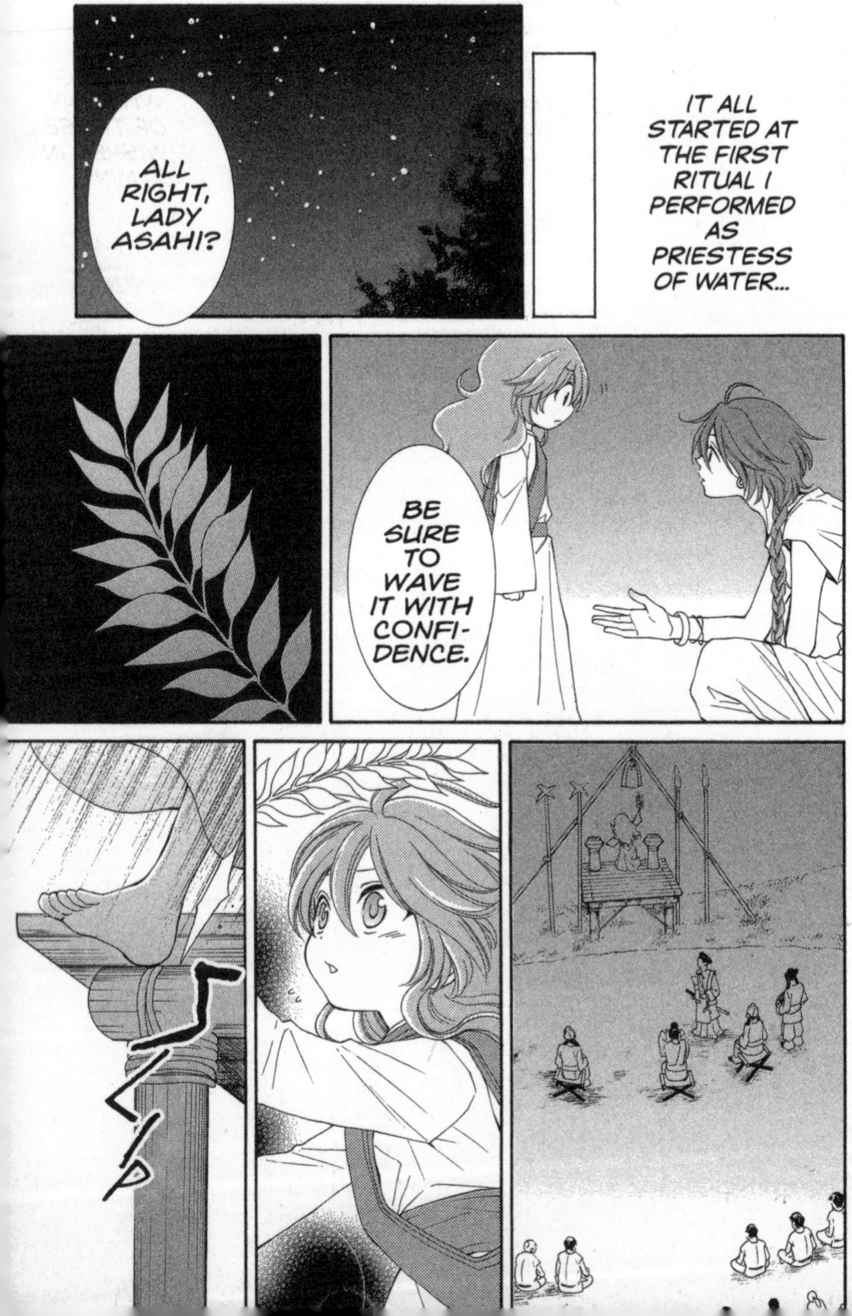
IT ALL STARTED AT THE FIRST RITUAL I PERFORMED AS PRIESTESS OF WATER...
ALL RIGHT, LADY ASAHI?
BE SURE TO WAVE IT WITH CONFIDENCE.

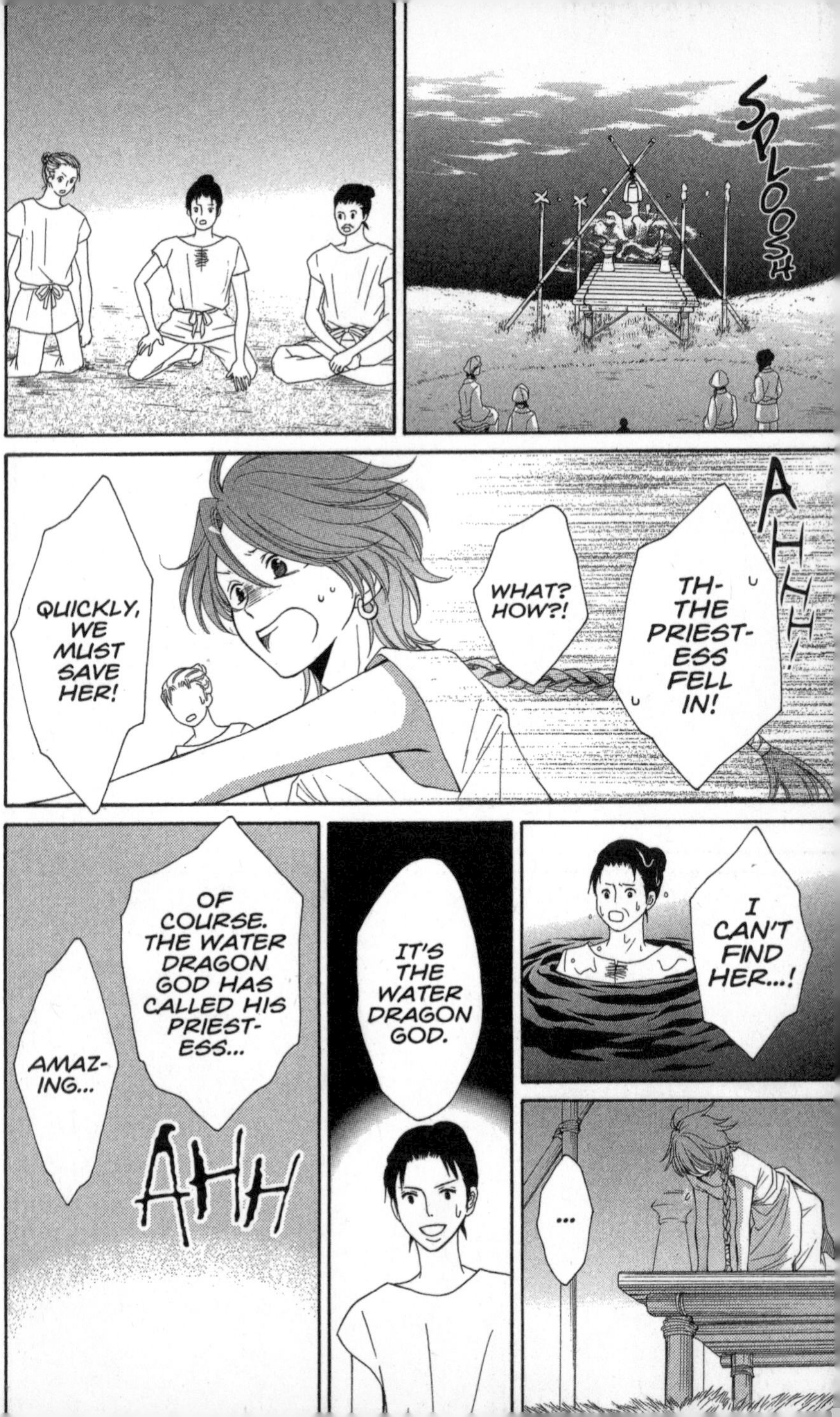
SPLOOSH
AHHH!
TH-THE PRIEST-ESS FELL IN!
WHAT? HOW?!
QUICKLY, WE MUST SAVE HER!
I CAN'T FIND HER...!
...
IT'S THE WATER DRAGON GOD.
OF COURSE. THE WATER DRAGON GOD HAS CALLED HIS PRIEST-ESS...
AMAZ-ING...
AHH

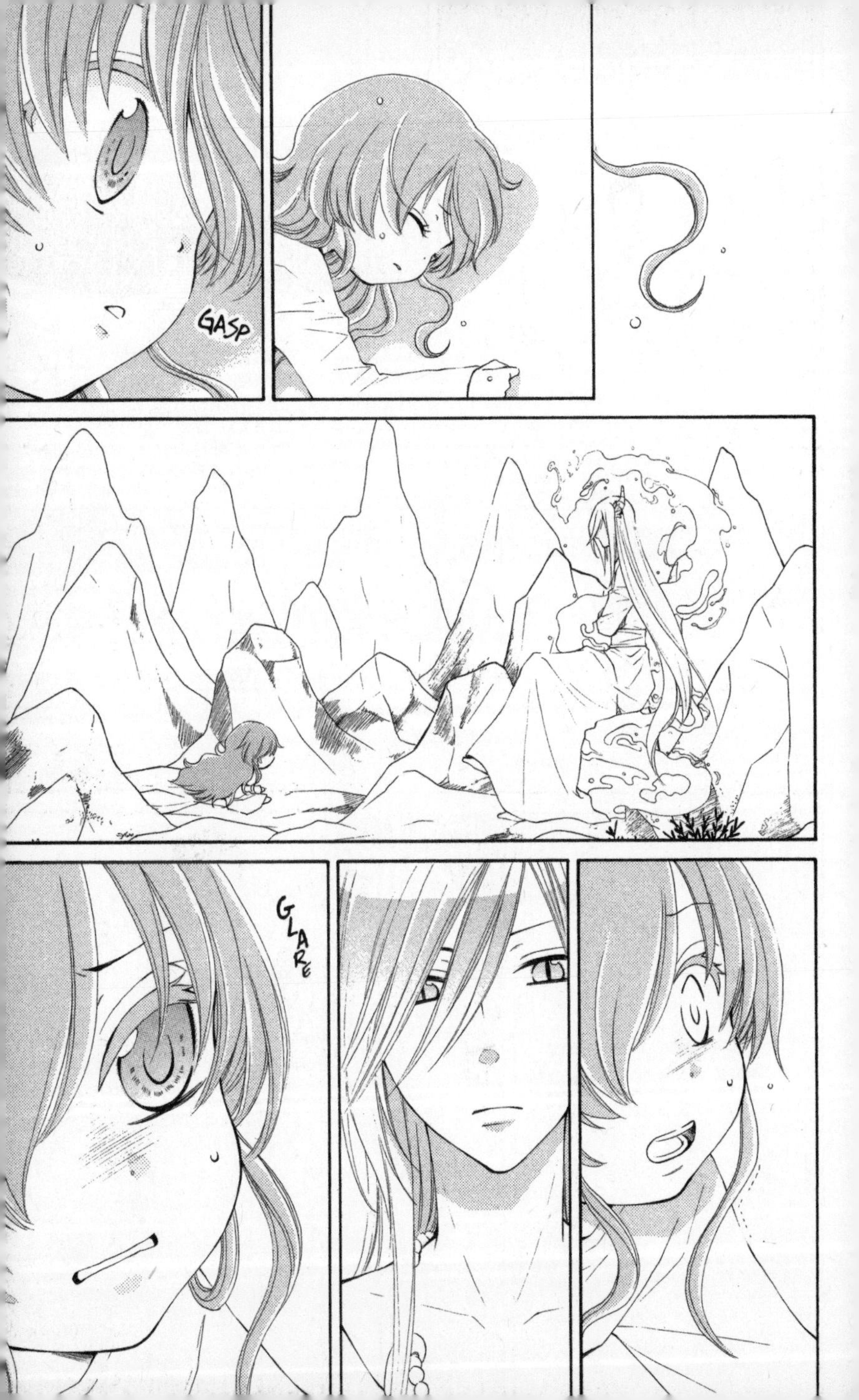
GASP
GLARE

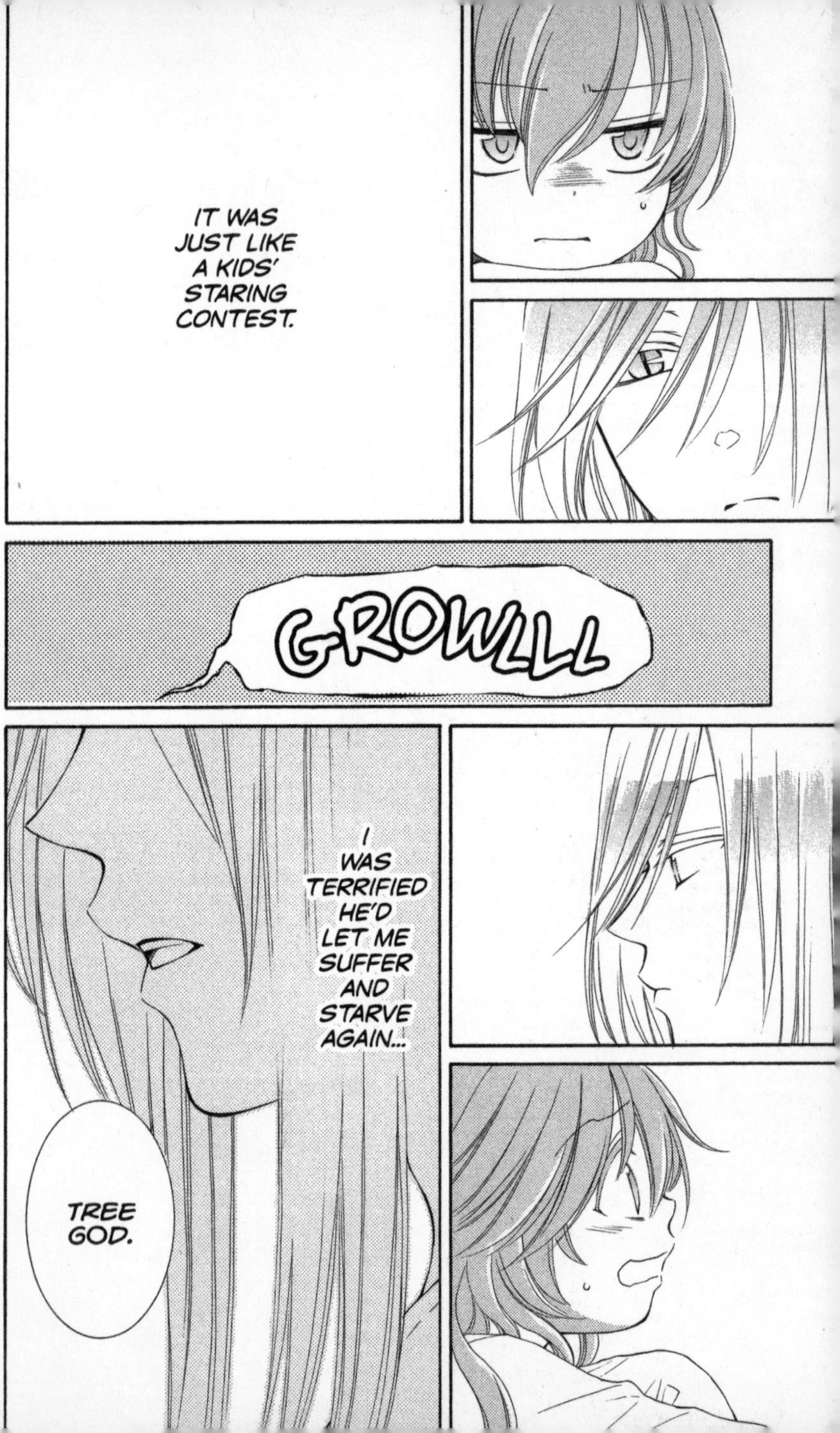
IT WAS JUST LIKE A KIDS' STARING CONTEST.
GROWLLL
I WAS TERRIFIED HE'D LET ME SUFFER AND STARVE AGAIN...
TREE GOD.

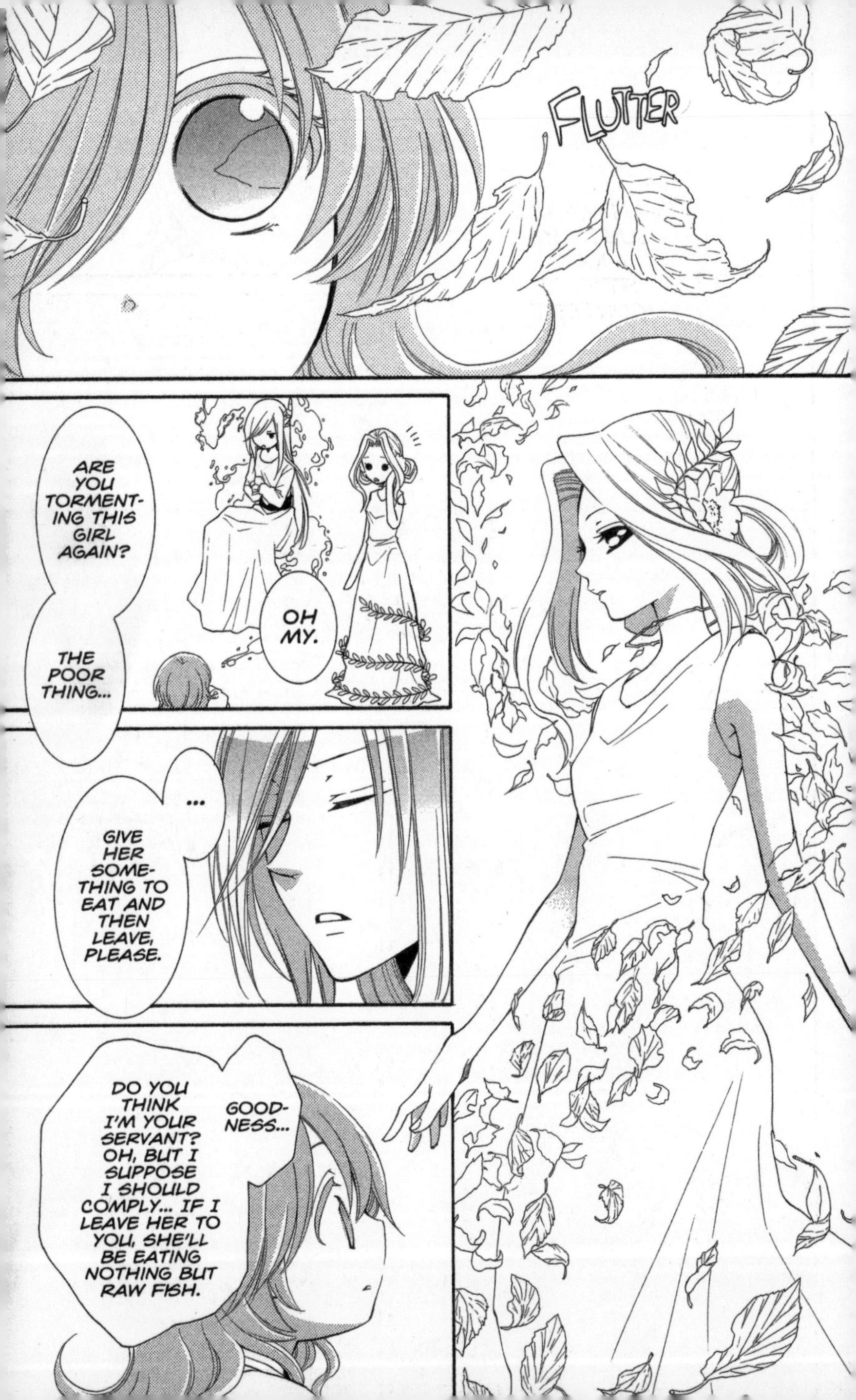
FLUTTER
ARE YOU TORMENTING THIS GIRL AGAIN?
THE POOR THING...
OH MY.
...
GIVE HER SOMETHING TO EAT AND THEN LEAVE, PLEASE.
GOODNESS...
DO YOU THINK I'M YOUR SERVANT? OH, BUT I SUPPOSE I SHOULD COMPLY... IF I LEAVE HER TO YOU, SHE'LL BE EATING NOTHING BUT RAW FISH.

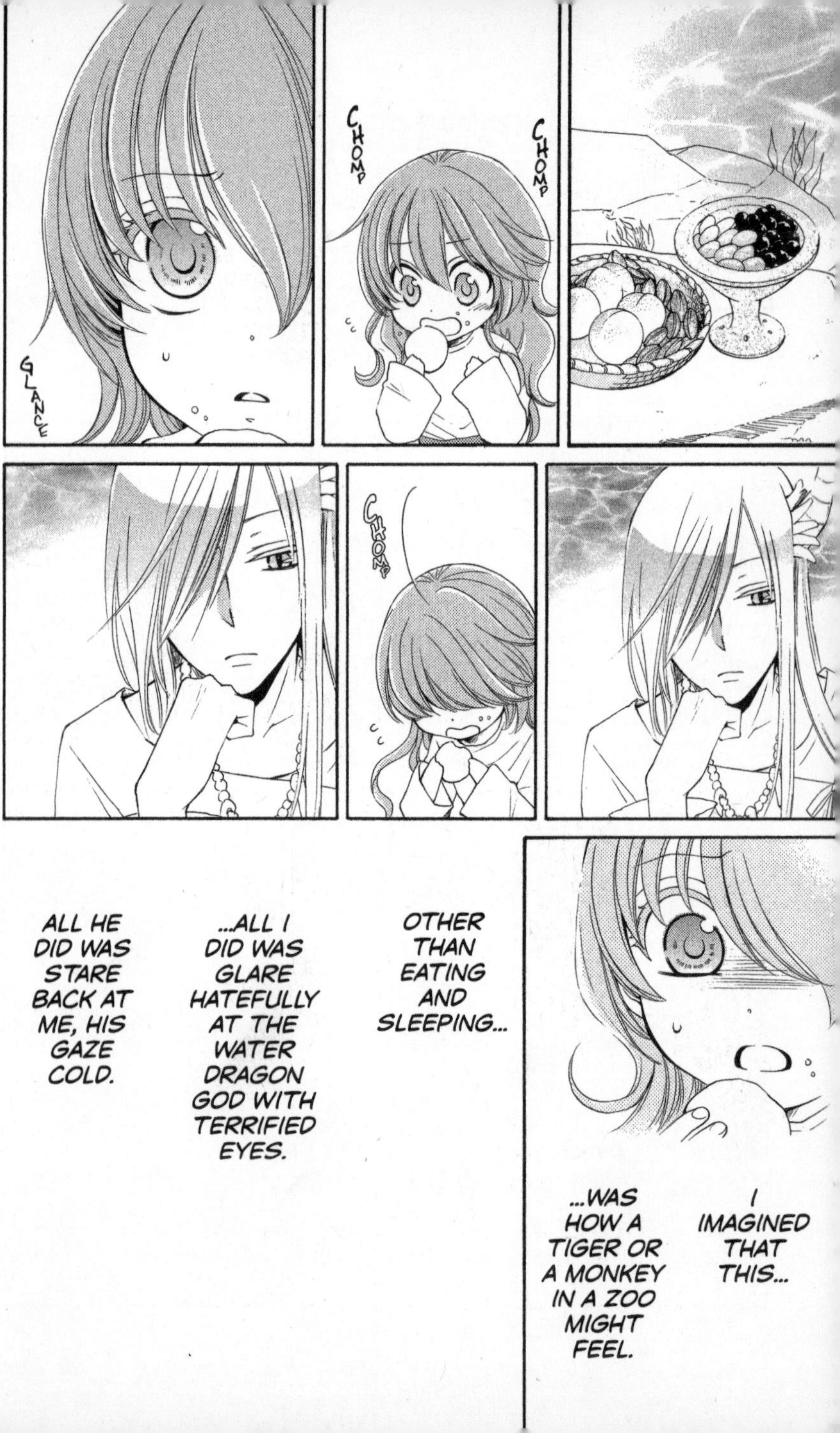
CHOMP
CHOMP
GLANCE
CHOMP
I IMAGINED THAT THIS...
...WAS HOW A TIGER OR A MONKEY IN A ZOO MIGHT FEEL.
OTHER THAN EATING AND SLEEPING...
...ALL I DID WAS GLARE HATEFULLY AT THE WATER DRAGON GOD WITH TERRIFIED EYES.
ALL HE DID WAS STARE BACK AT ME, HIS GAZE COLD.

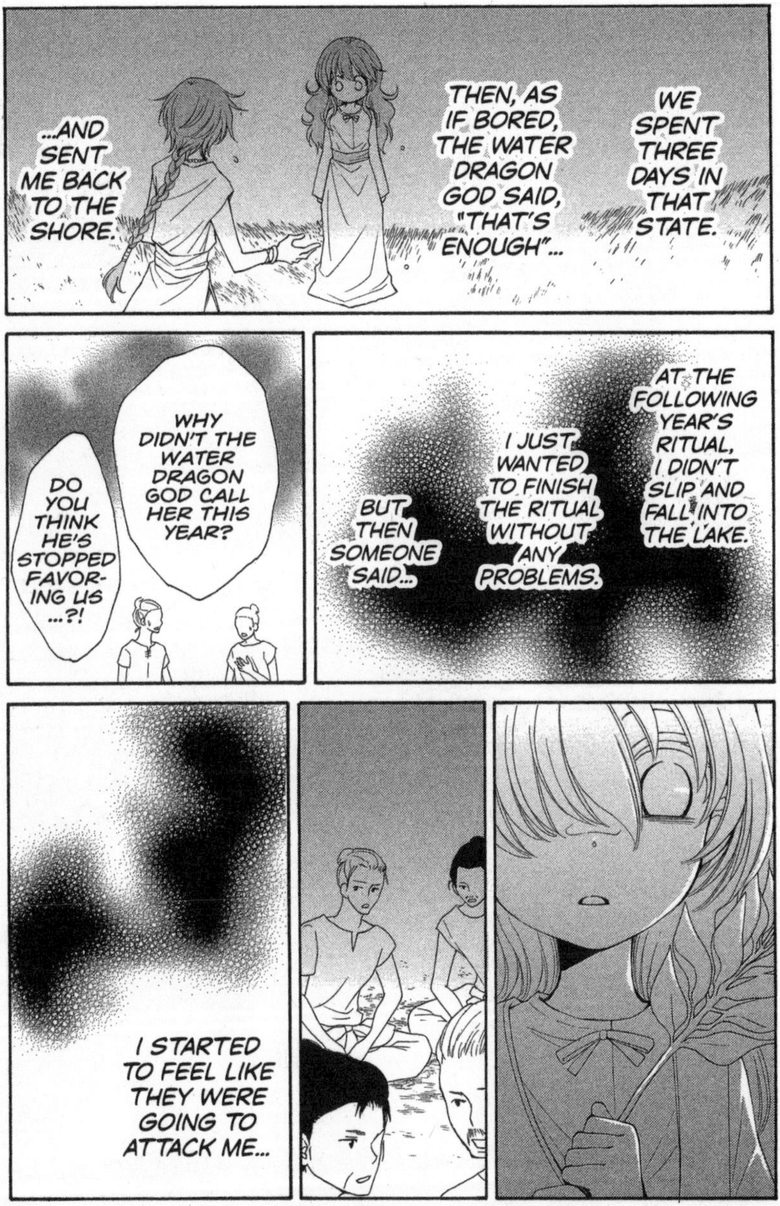
WE SPENT THREE DAYS IN THAT STATE.
THEN, AS IF BORED, THE WATER DRAGON GOD SAID, "THAT'S ENOUGH"...
...AND SENT ME BACK TO THE SHORE.
AT THE FOLLOWING YEAR'S RITUAL, I DIDN'T SLIP AND FALL INTO THE LAKE.
I JUST WANTED TO FINISH THE RITUAL WITHOUT ANY PROBLEMS.
BUT THEN SOMEONE SAID...
WHY DIDN'T THE WATER DRAGON GOD CALL HER THIS YEAR?
DO YOU THINK HE'S STOPPED FAVORING US ...?!
I STARTED TO FEEL LIKE THEY WERE GOING TO ATTACK ME...

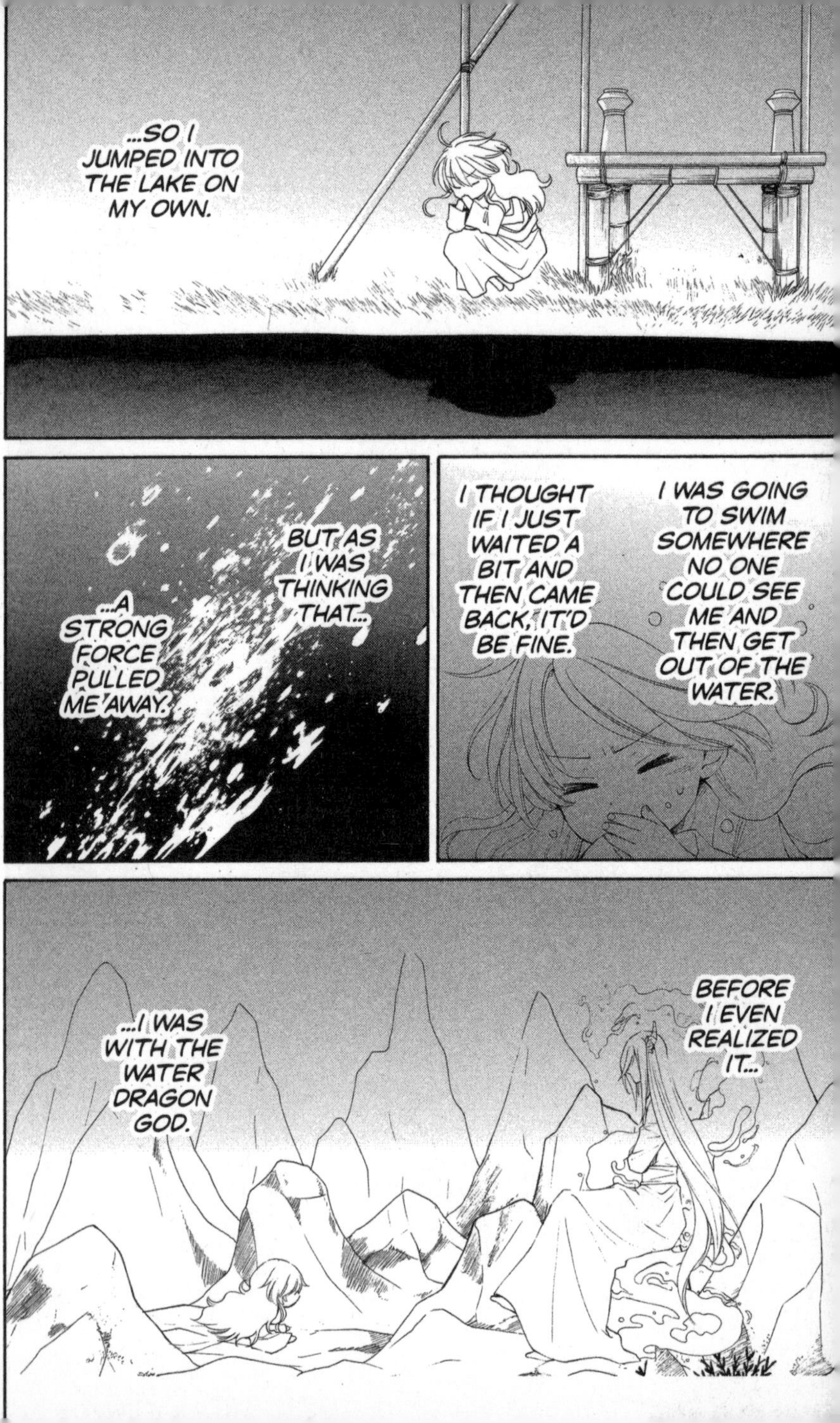
...SO I JUMPED INTO THE LAKE ON MY OWN.
I WAS GOING TO SWIM SOMEWHERE NO ONE COULD SEE ME AND THEN GET OUT OF THE WATER.
I THOUGHT IF I JUST WAITED A BIT AND THEN CAME BACK, IT'D BE FINE.
BUT AS I WAS THINKING THAT...
...A STRONG FORCE PULLED ME AWAY.
BEFORE I EVEN REALIZED IT...
...I WAS WITH THE WATER DRAGON GOD.

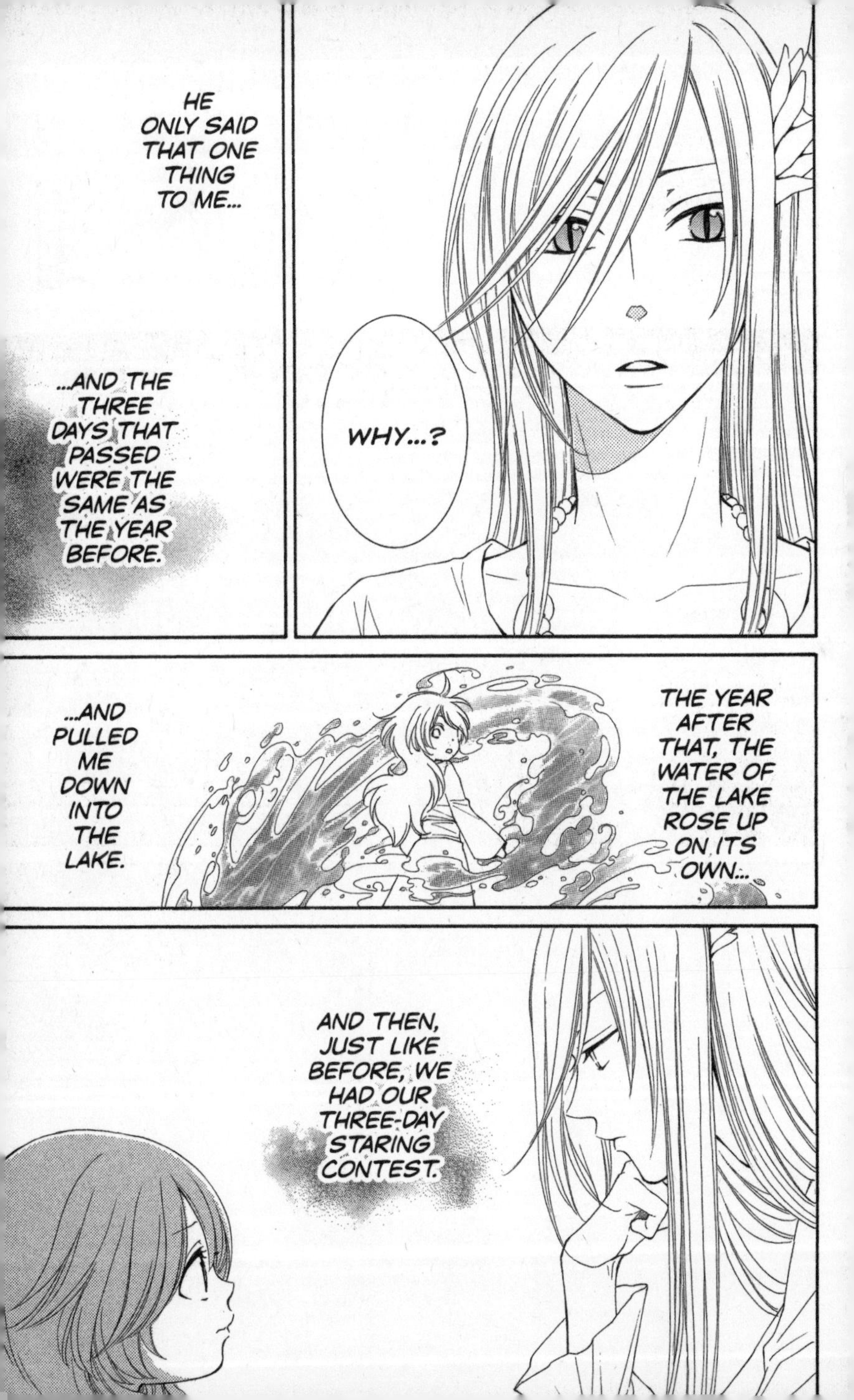
WHY...?
HE ONLY SAID THAT ONE THING TO ME...
...AND THE THREE DAYS THAT PASSED WERE THE SAME AS THE YEAR BEFORE.
THE YEAR AFTER THAT, THE WATER OF THE LAKE ROSE UP ON ITS OWN...
...AND PULLED ME DOWN INTO THE LAKE.
AND THEN, JUST LIKE BEFORE, WE HAD OUR THREE-DAY STARING CONTEST.

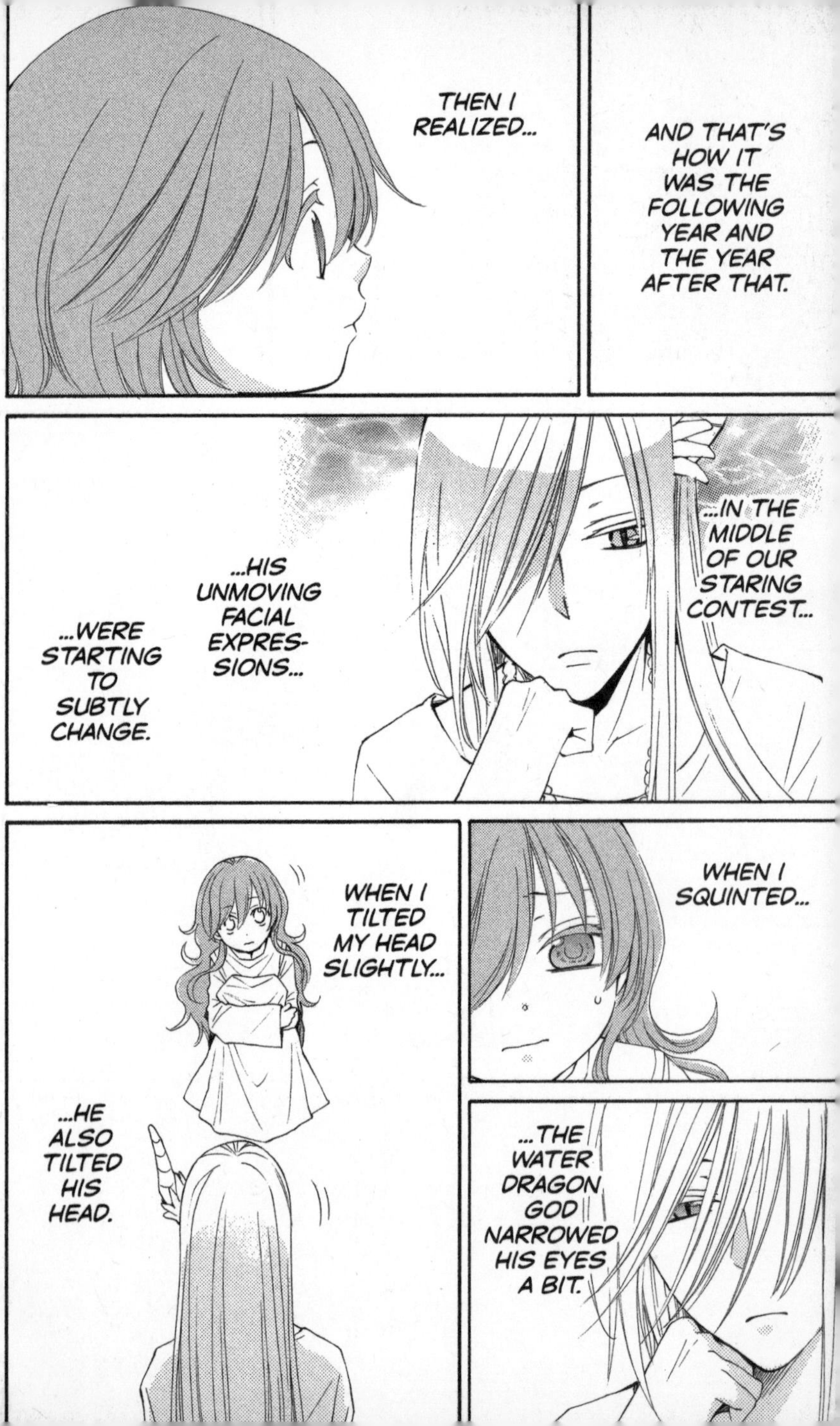
AND THAT'S HOW IT WAS THE FOLLOWING YEAR AND THE YEAR AFTER THAT.
THEN I REALIZED...
...IN THE MIDDLE OF OUR STARING CONTEST...
...HIS UNMOVING FACIAL EXPRES-SIONS...
...WERE STARTING TO SUBTLY CHANGE.
WHEN I SQUINTED...
...THE WATER DRAGON GOD NARROWED HIS EYES A BIT.
WHEN I TILTED MY HEAD SLIGHTLY...
...HE ALSO TILTED HIS HEAD.

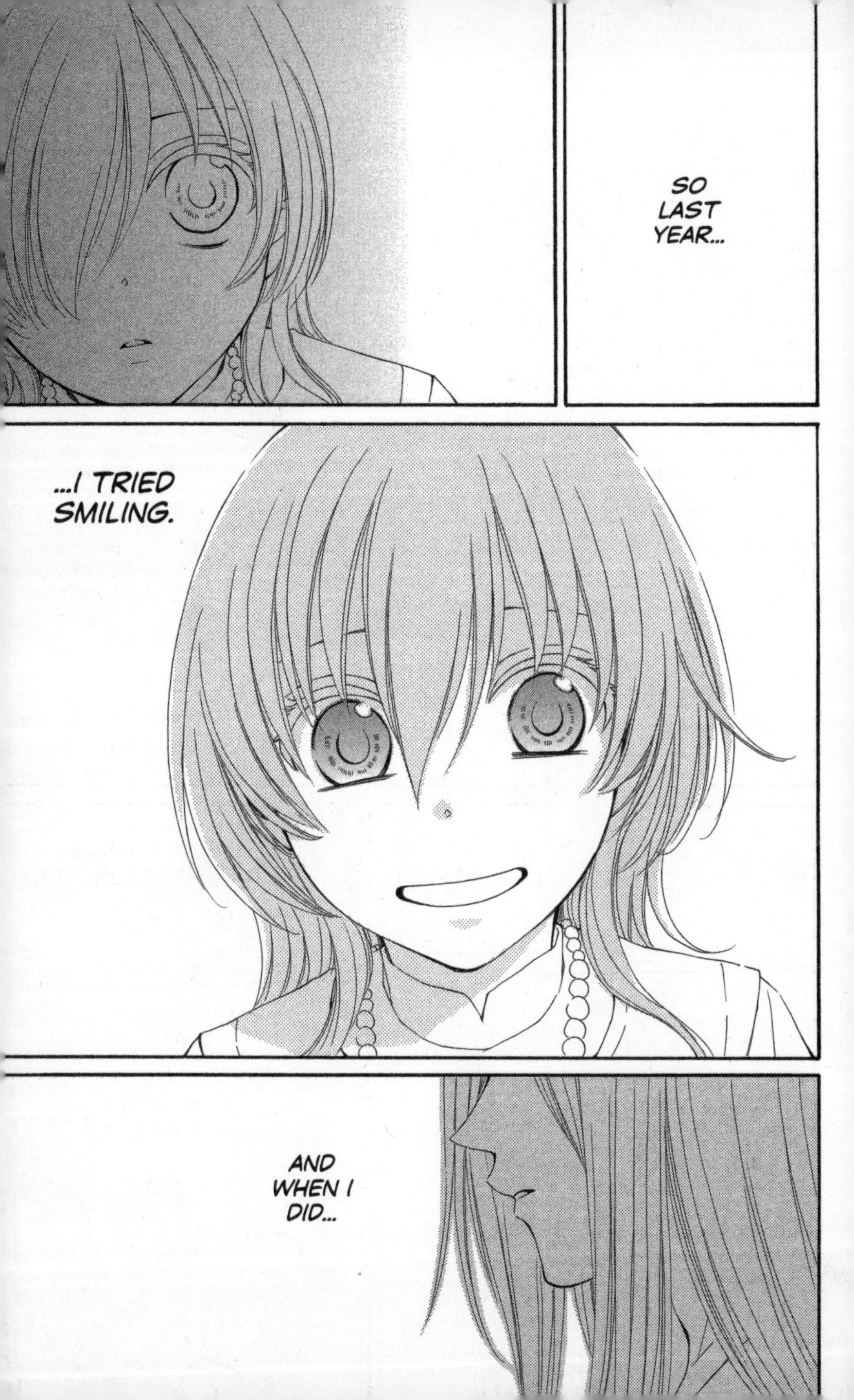
SO LAST YEAR...
...I TRIED SMILING.
AND WHEN I DID...

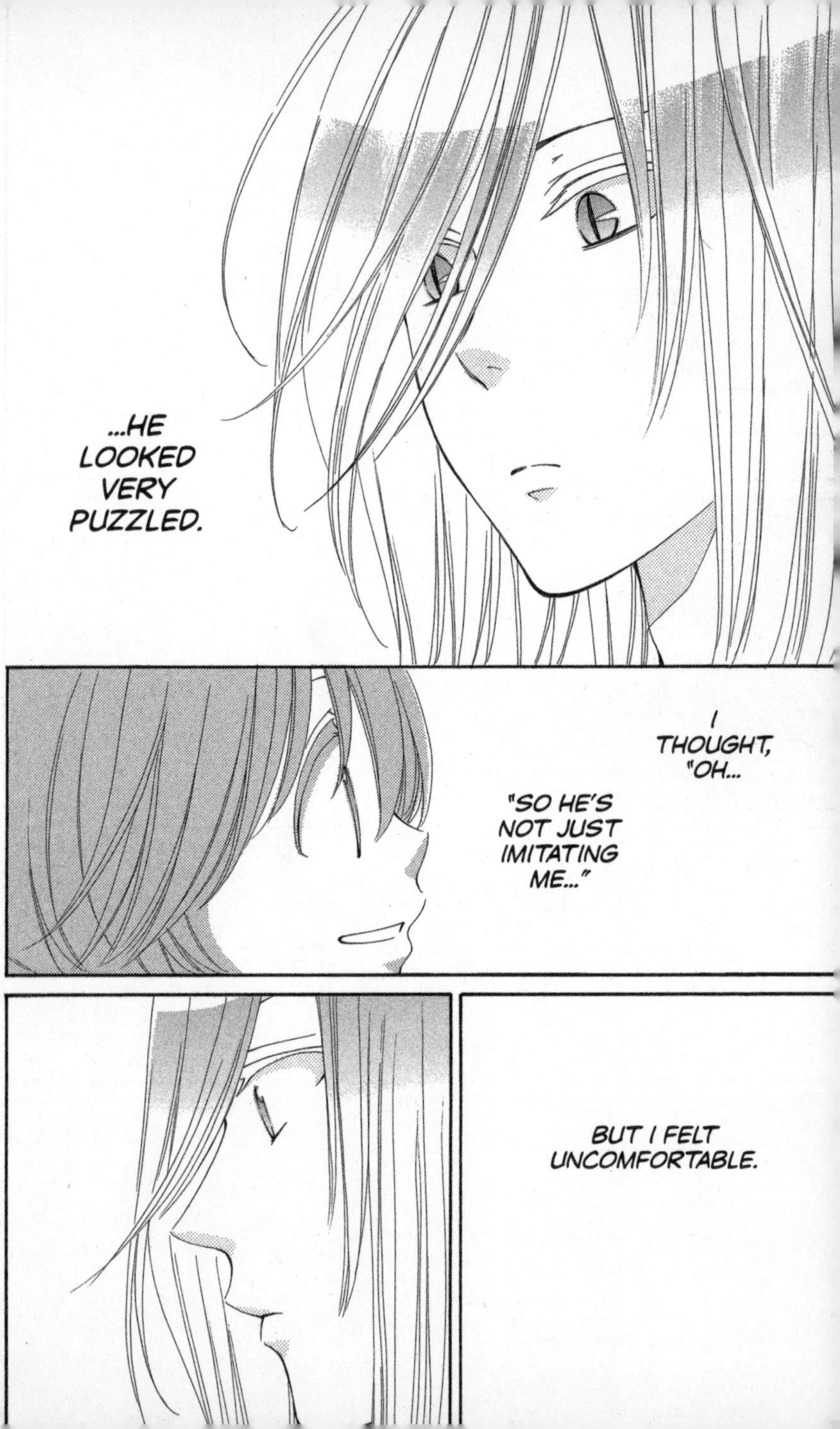
...HE LOOKED VERY PUZZLED.
I THOUGHT, "OH...
"SO HE'S NOT JUST IMITATING ME..."
BUT I FELT UNCOMFORTABLE.

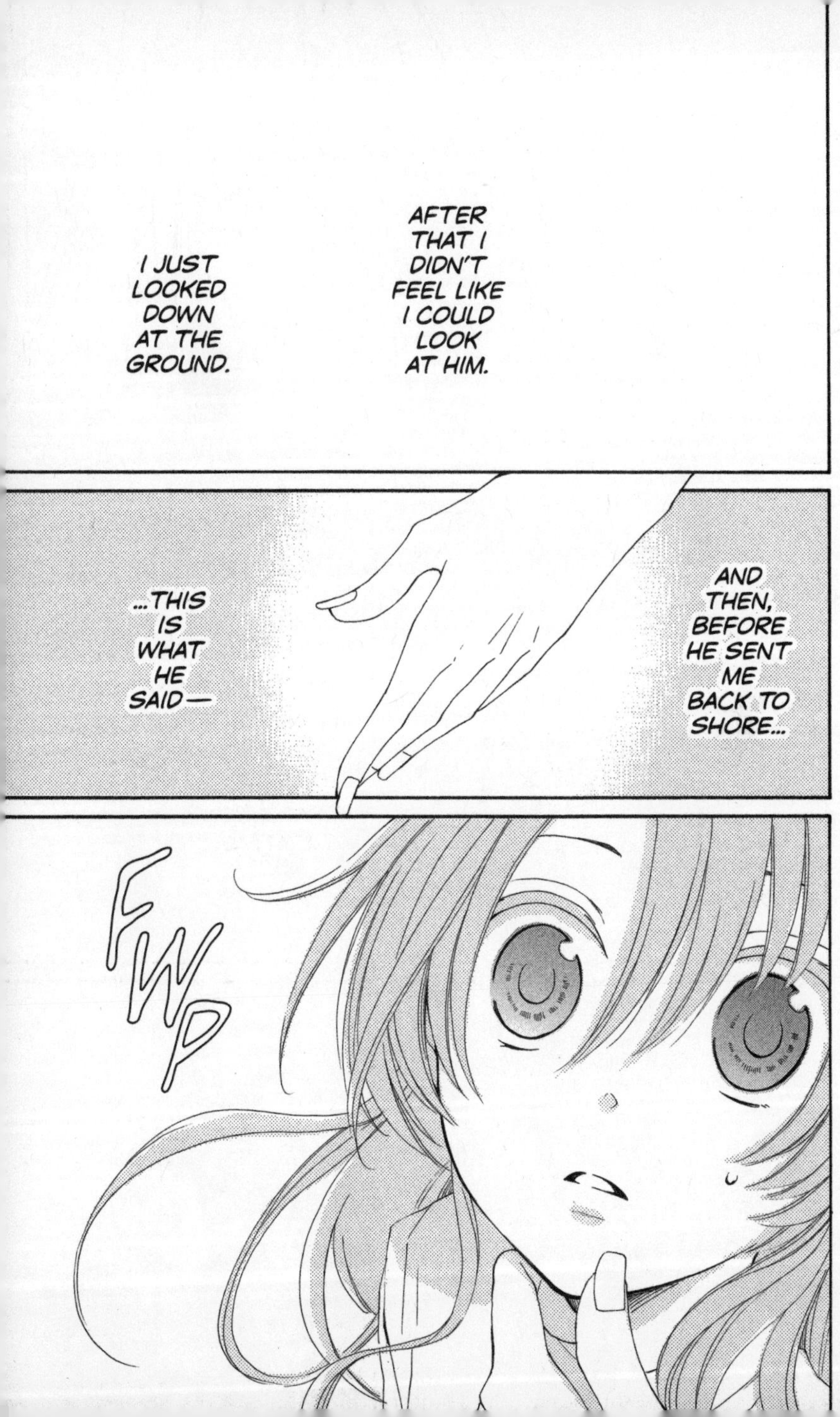
AFTER THAT I DIDN'T FEEL LIKE I COULD LOOK AT HIM.
I JUST LOOKED DOWN AT THE GROUND.
AND THEN, BEFORE HE SENT ME BACK TO SHORE...
...THIS IS WHAT HE SAID—
FWP

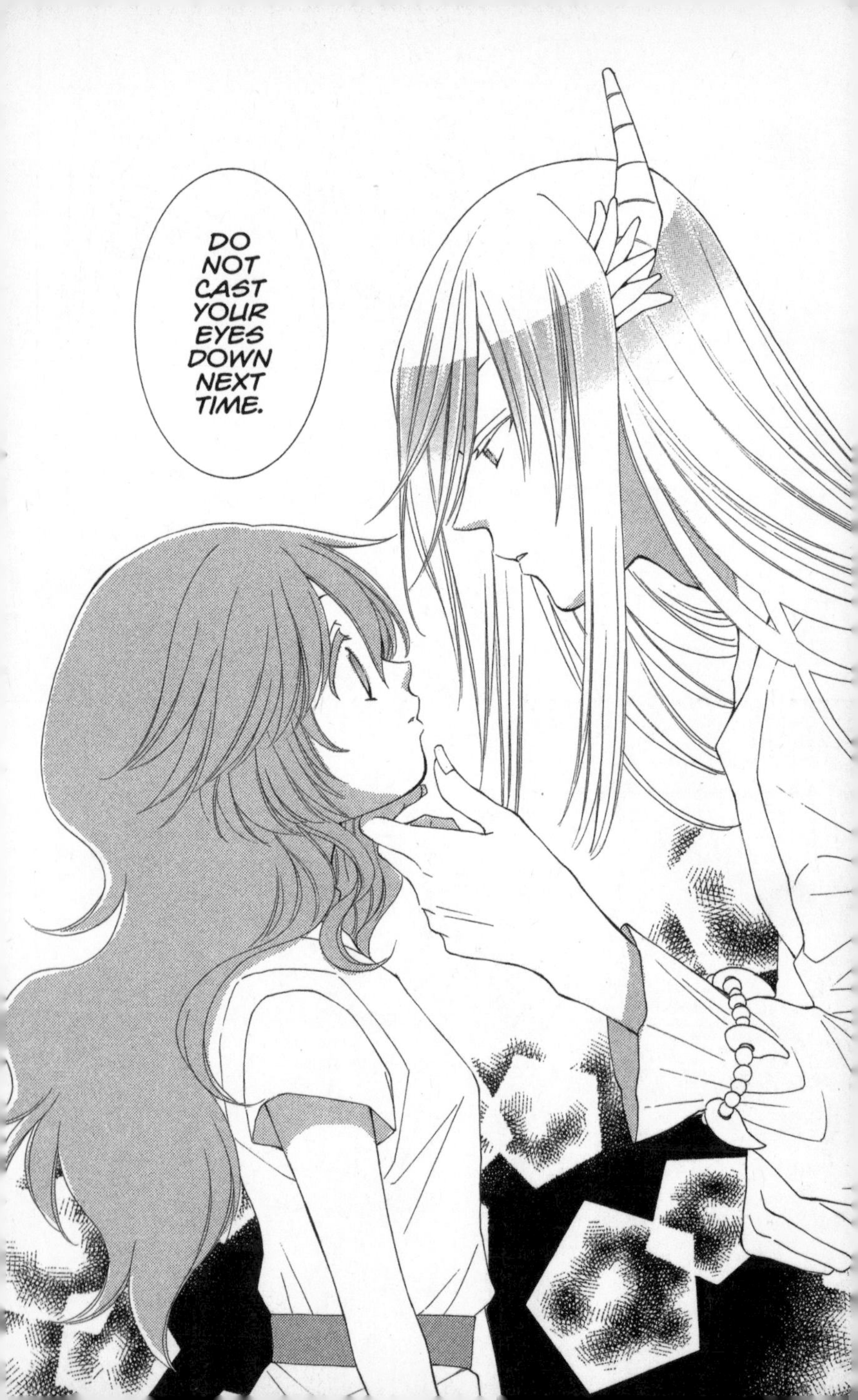
DO NOT CAST YOUR EYES DOWN NEXT TIME.

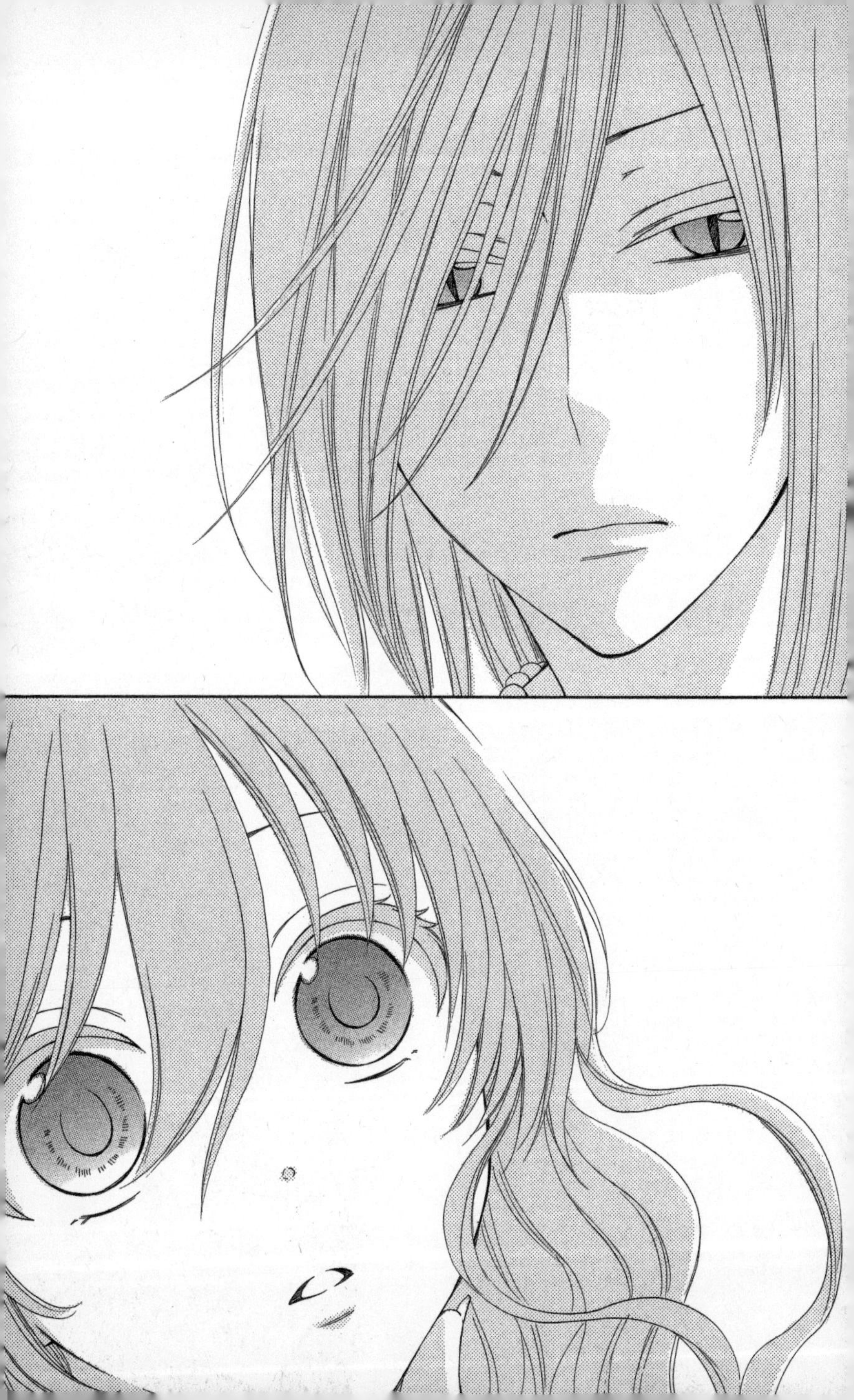

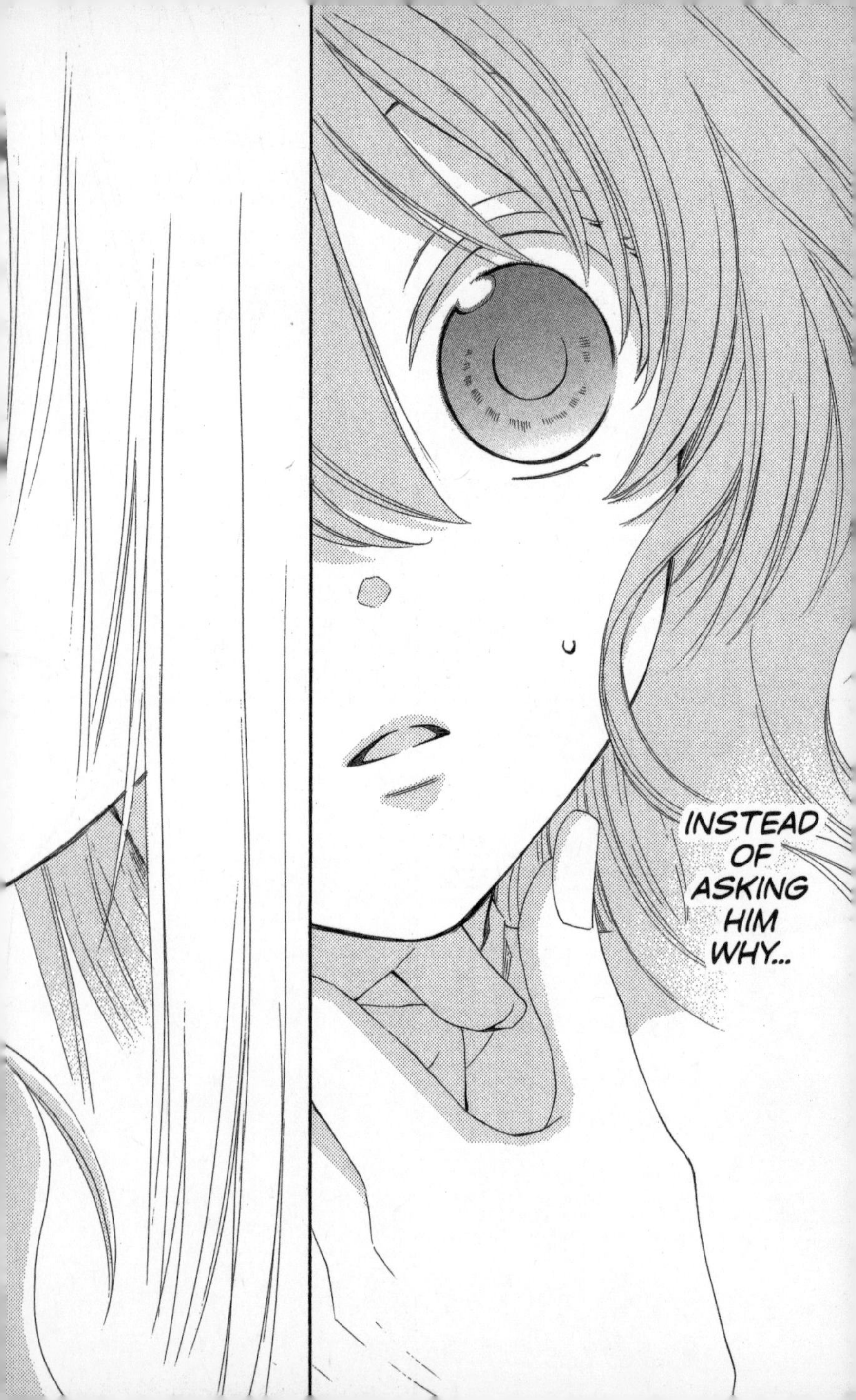
INSTEAD OF ASKING HIM WHY...

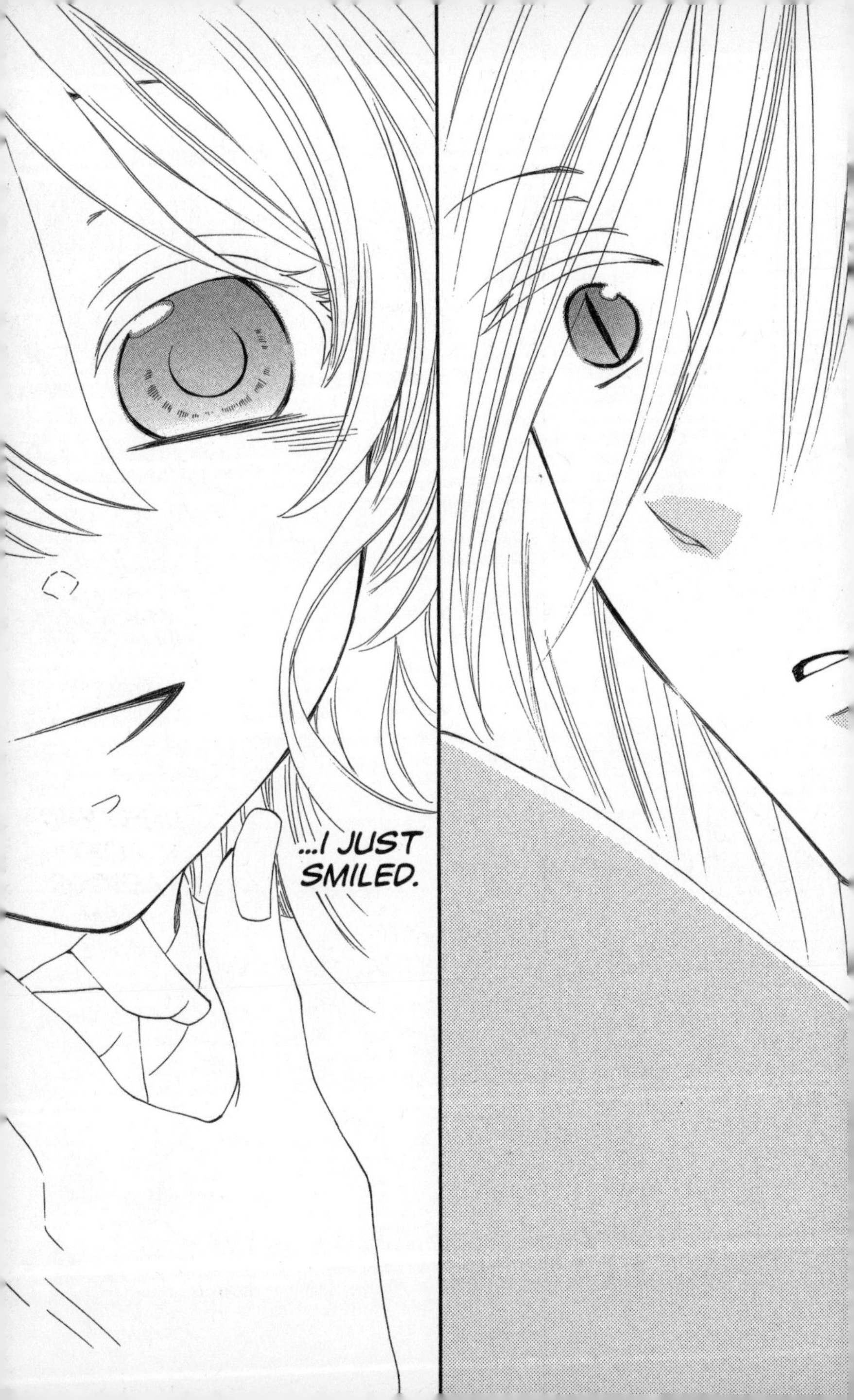
...I JUST SMILED.

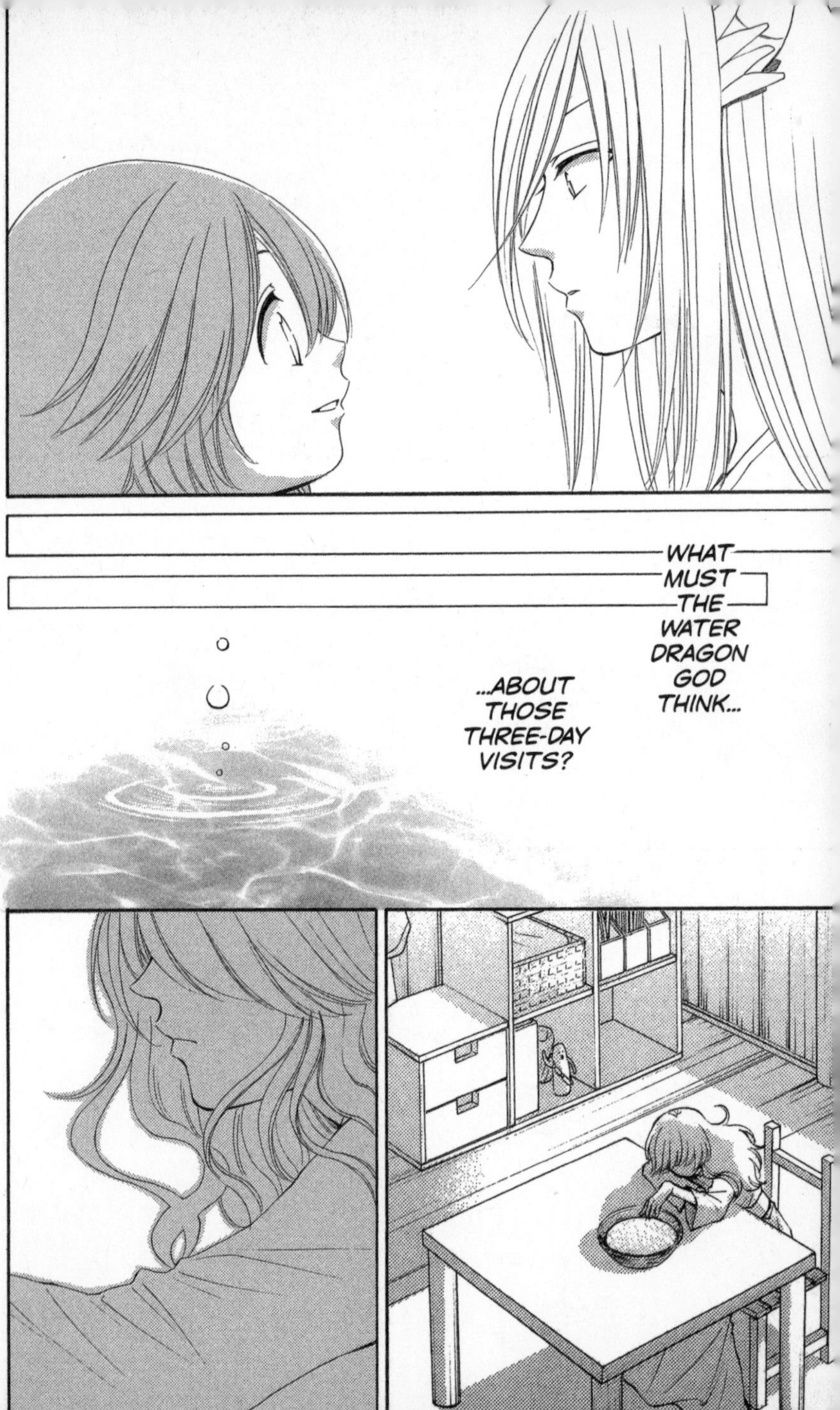
WHAT MUST THE WATER DRAGON GOD THINK...
...ABOUT THOSE THREE-DAY VISITS?

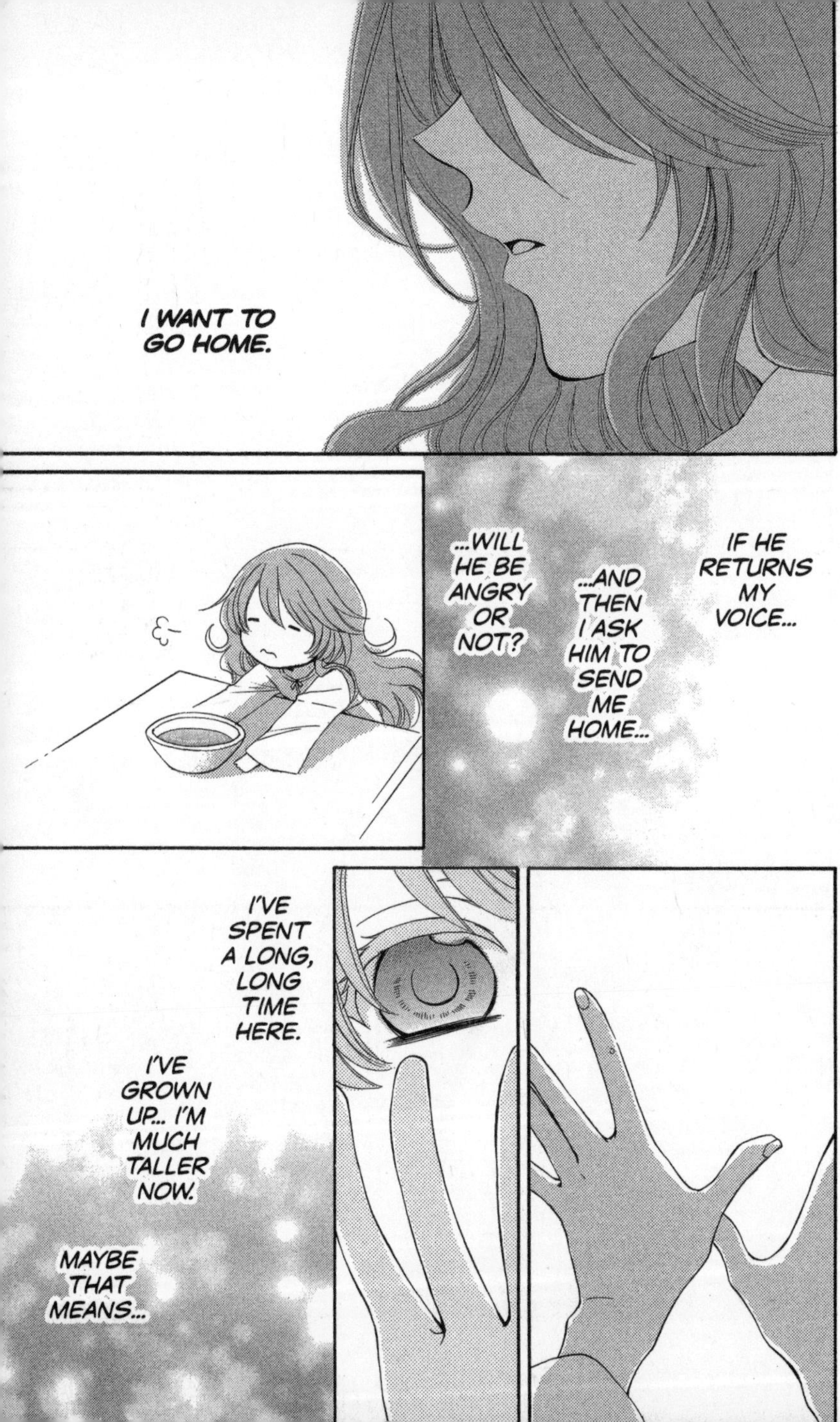
I WANT TO GO HOME.
IF HE RETURNS MY VOICE...
...AND THEN I ASK HIM TO SEND ME HOME...
...WILL HE BE ANGRY OR NOT?
I'VE SPENT A LONG, LONG TIME HERE.
I'VE GROWN UP... I'M MUCH TALLER NOW.
MAYBE THAT MEANS...

...I'M OLD ENOUGH TO MARRY.

COULD THIS BE THE YEAR?

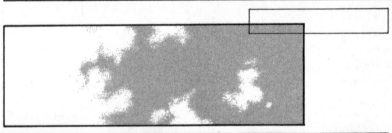

LET US GO TO PERFORM THE PURIFICATION CEREMONY, LADY ASAHI.

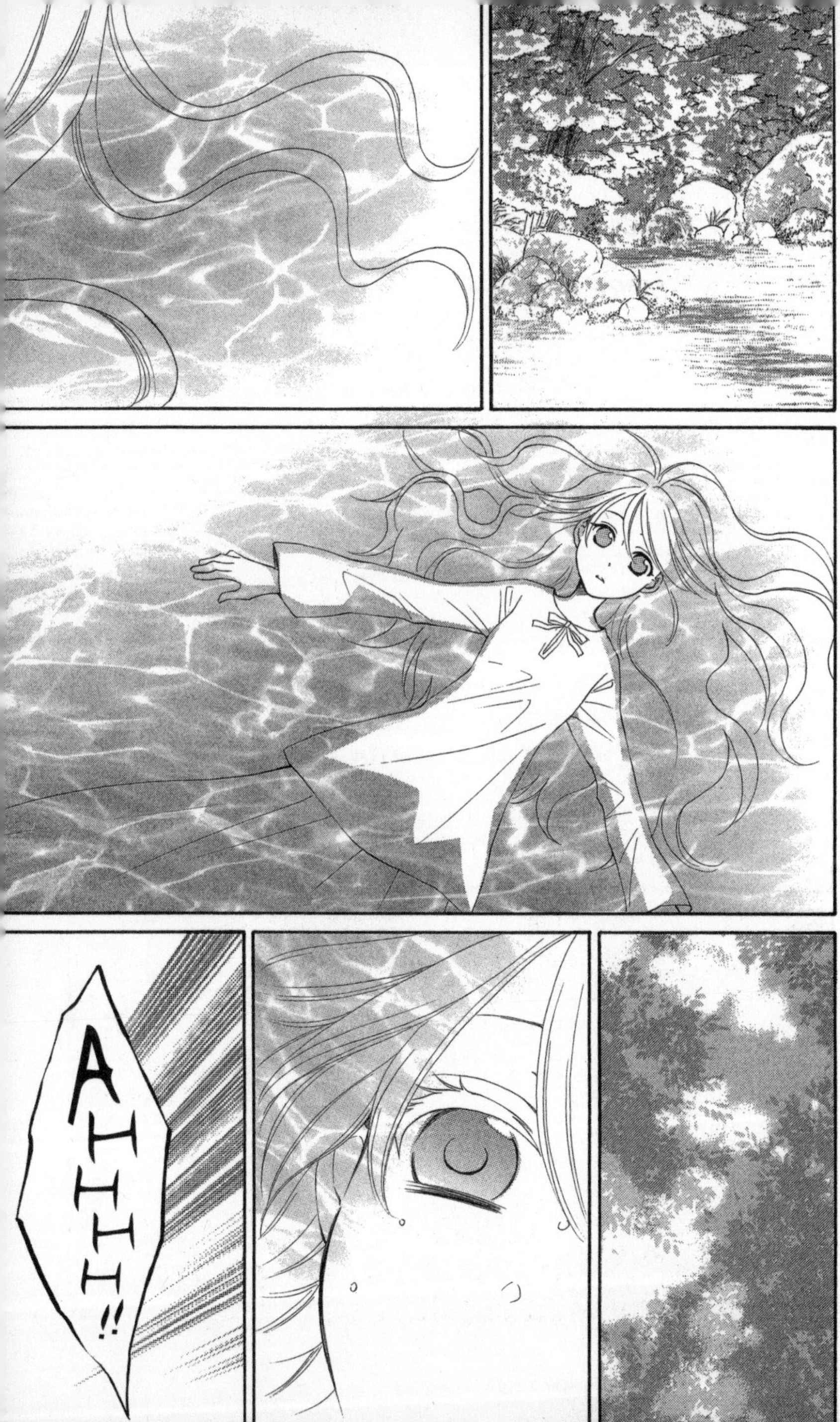
AHHH!!

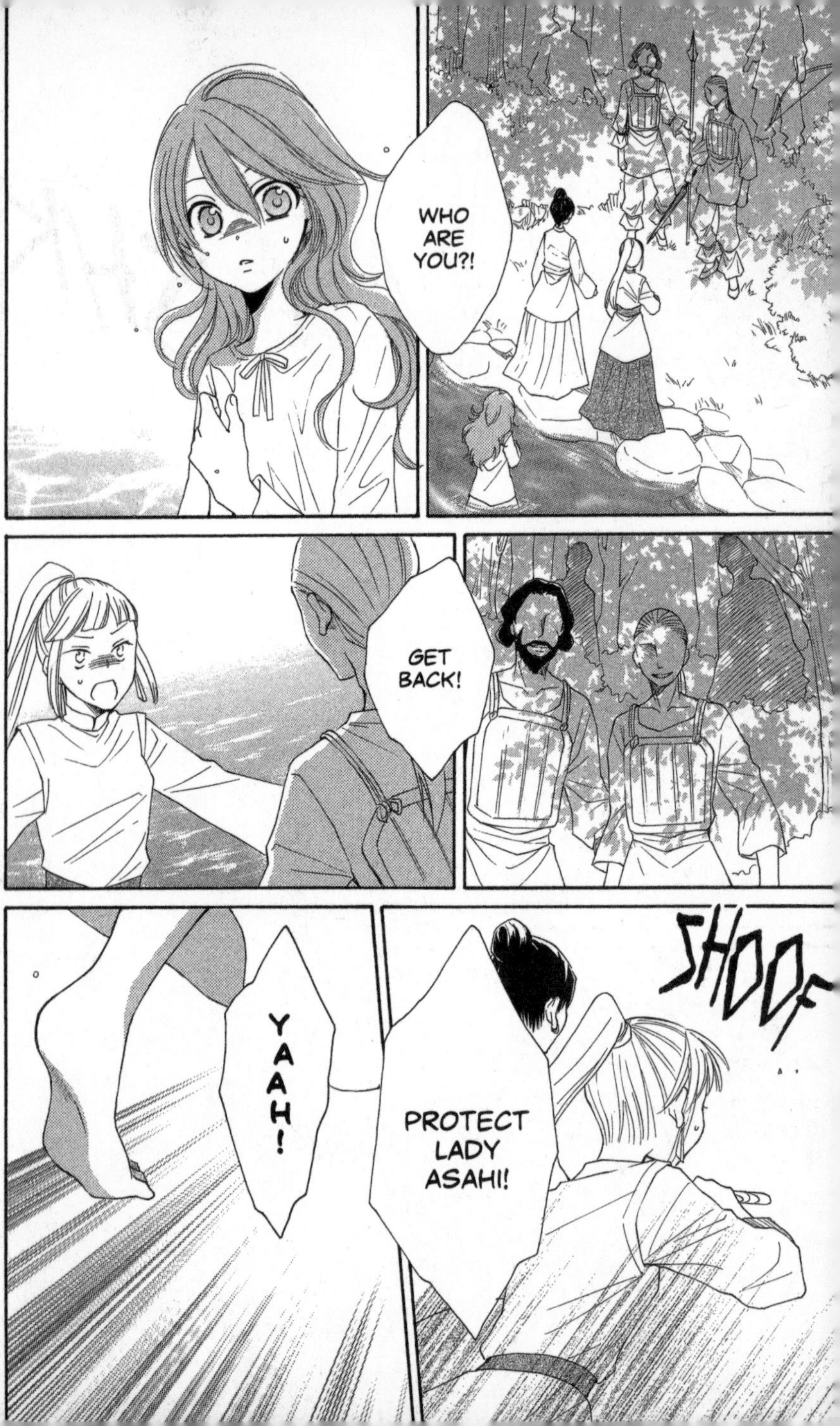
WHO ARE YOU?!
GET BACK!
SHOOF
PROTECT LADY ASAHI!
YAAH!

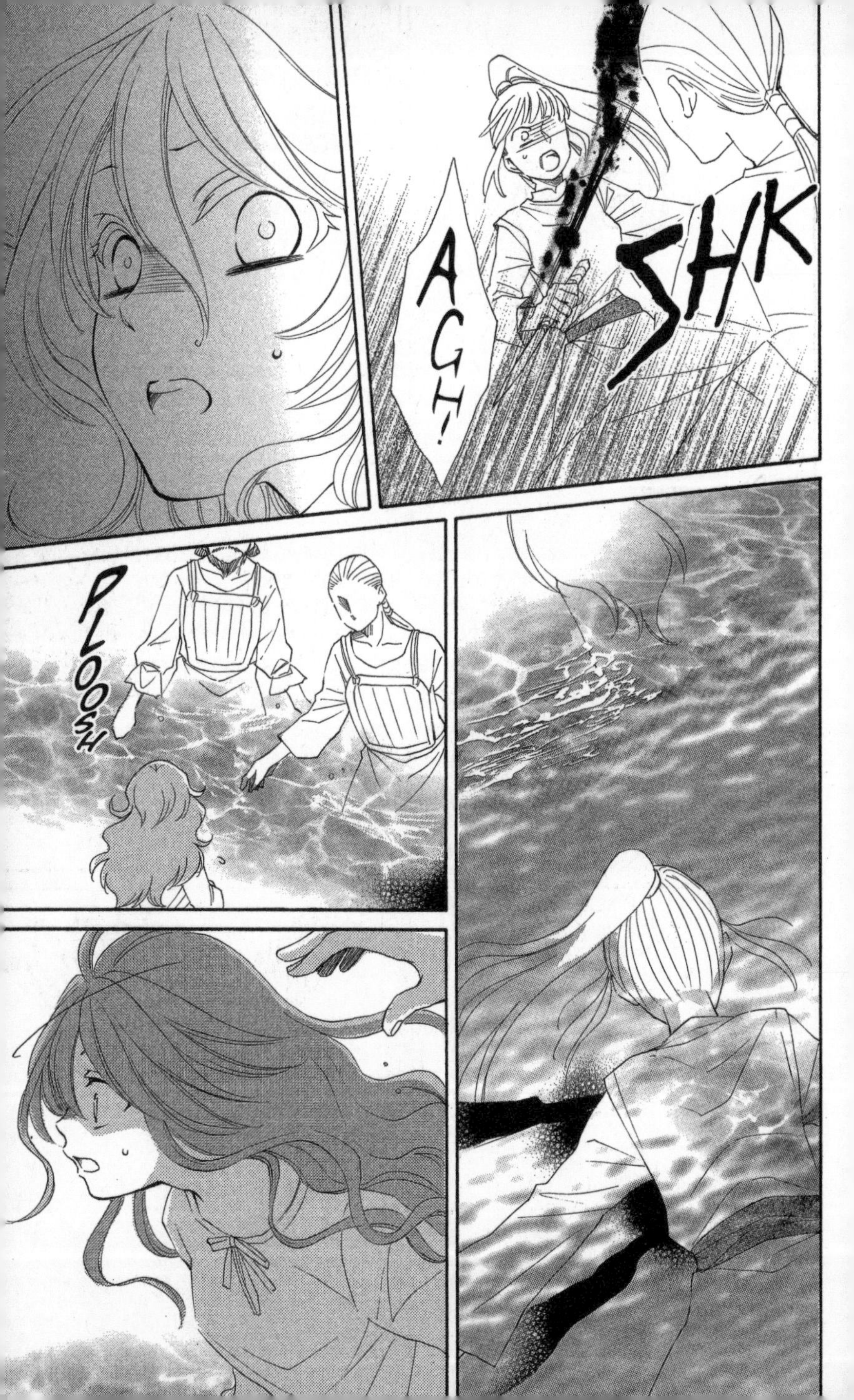
SHK
AGH!
PLOOSH

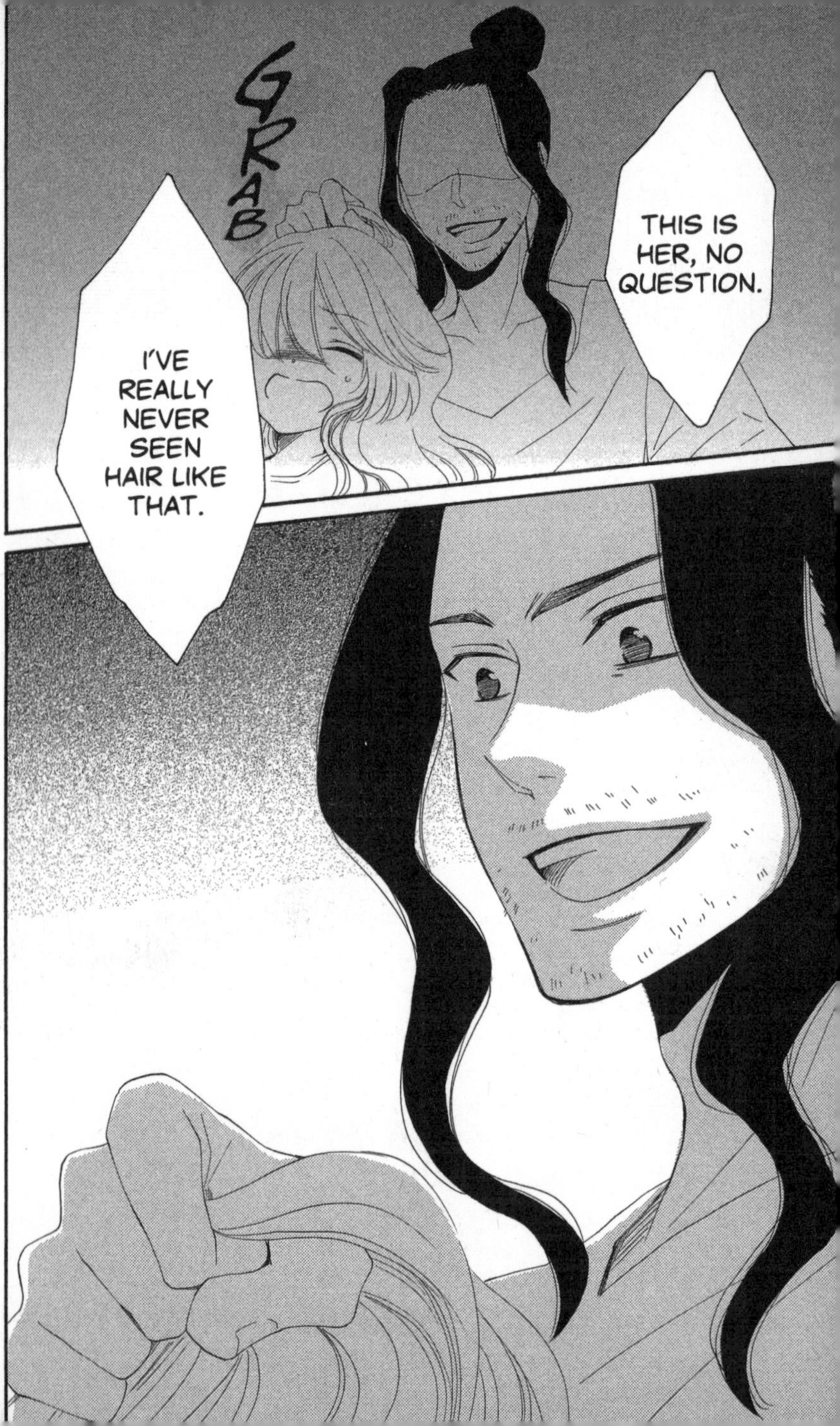
THIS IS HER, NO QUESTION.
GRAB
I'VE REALLY NEVER SEEN HAIR LIKE THAT.

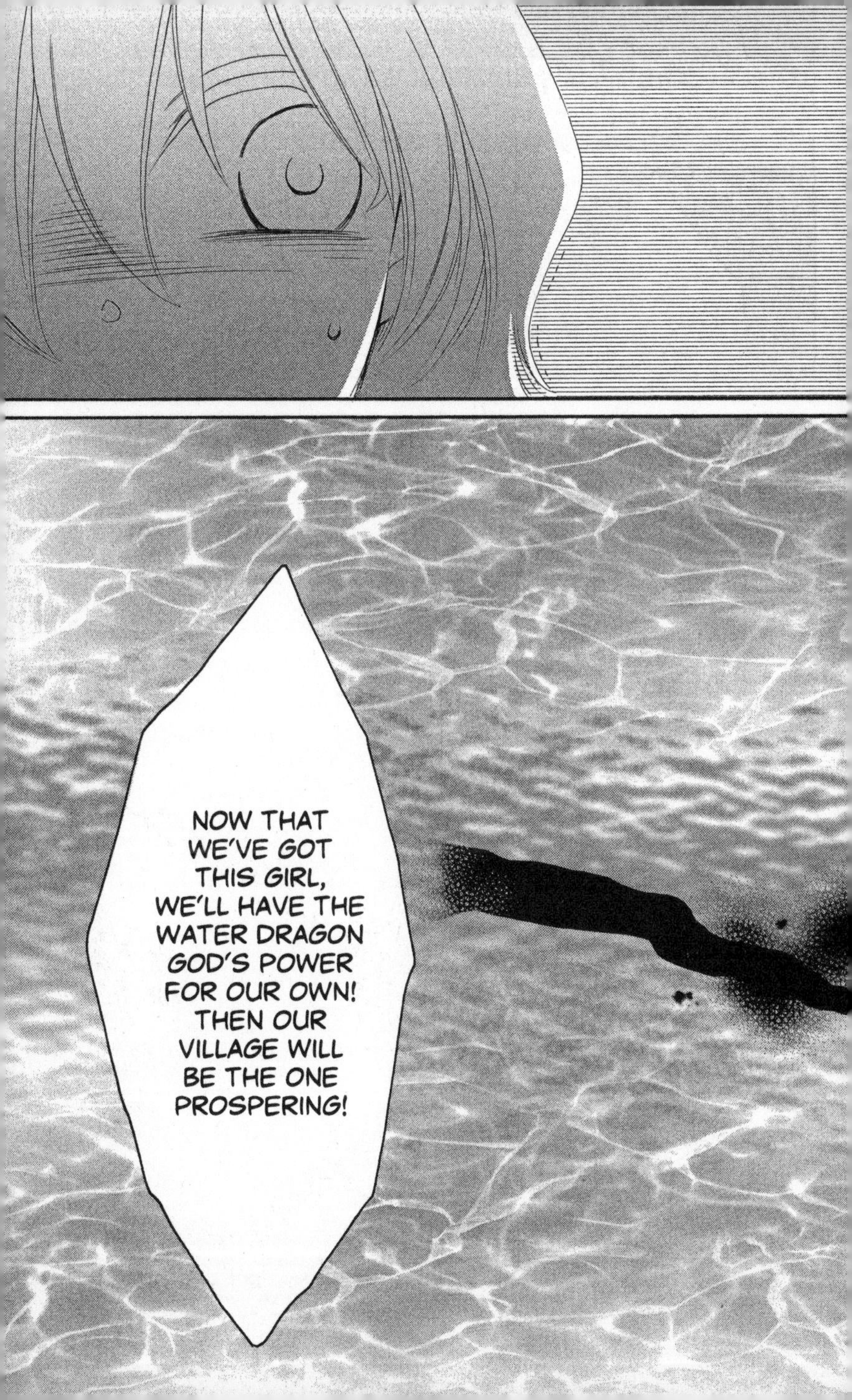
NOW THAT WE'VE GOT THIS GIRL, WE'LL HAVE THE WATER DRAGON GOD'S POWER FOR OUR OWN! THEN OUR VILLAGE WILL BE THE ONE PROSPERING!

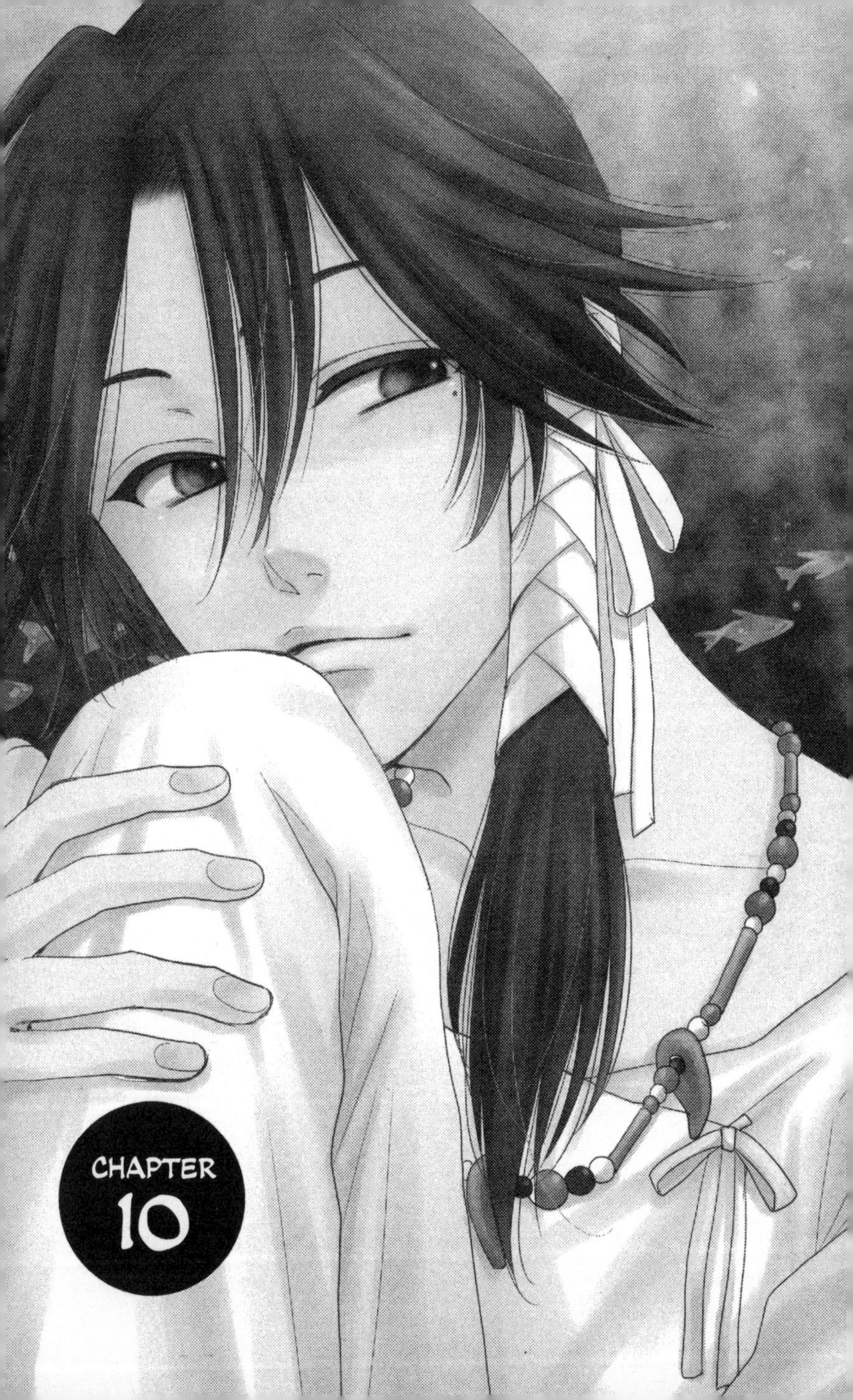
CHAPTER
10

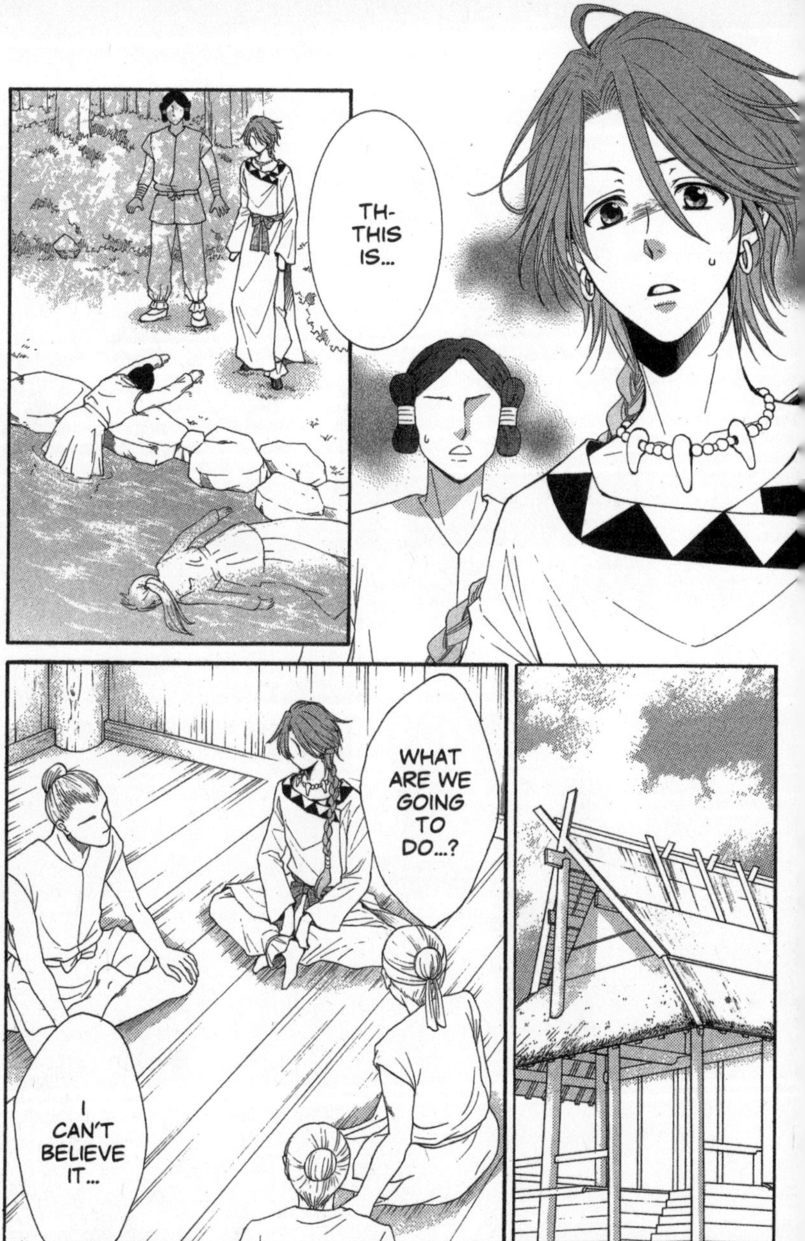
TH- THIS IS...
WHAT ARE WE GOING TO DO...?
I CAN'T BELIEVE IT...

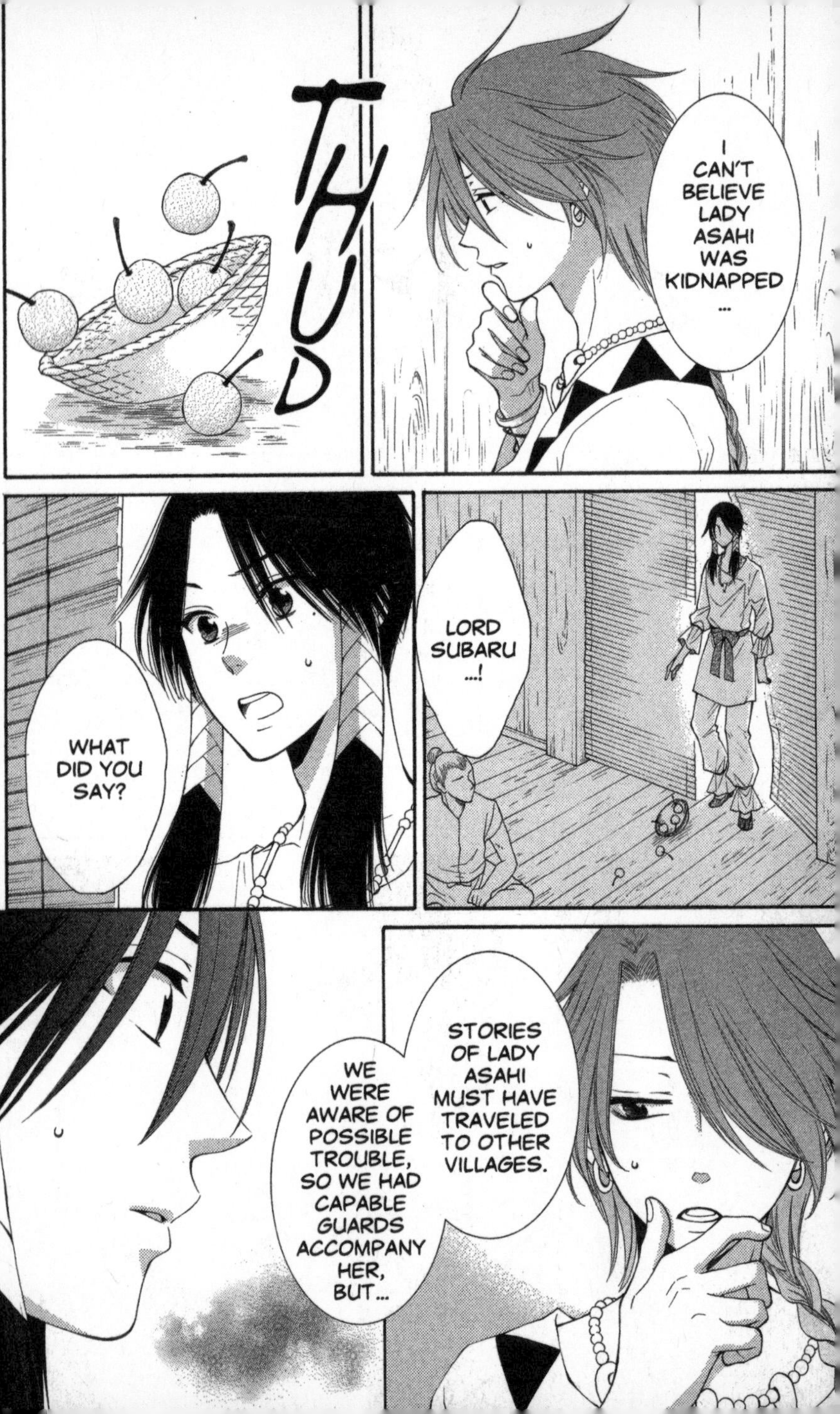
I CAN'T BELIEVE LADY ASAHI WAS KIDNAPPED...
THUD
LORD SUBARU...!
WHAT DID YOU SAY?
STORIES OF LADY ASAHI MUST HAVE TRAVELED TO OTHER VILLAGES.
WE WERE AWARE OF POSSIBLE TROUBLE, SO WE HAD CAPABLE GUARDS ACCOMPANY HER, BUT...

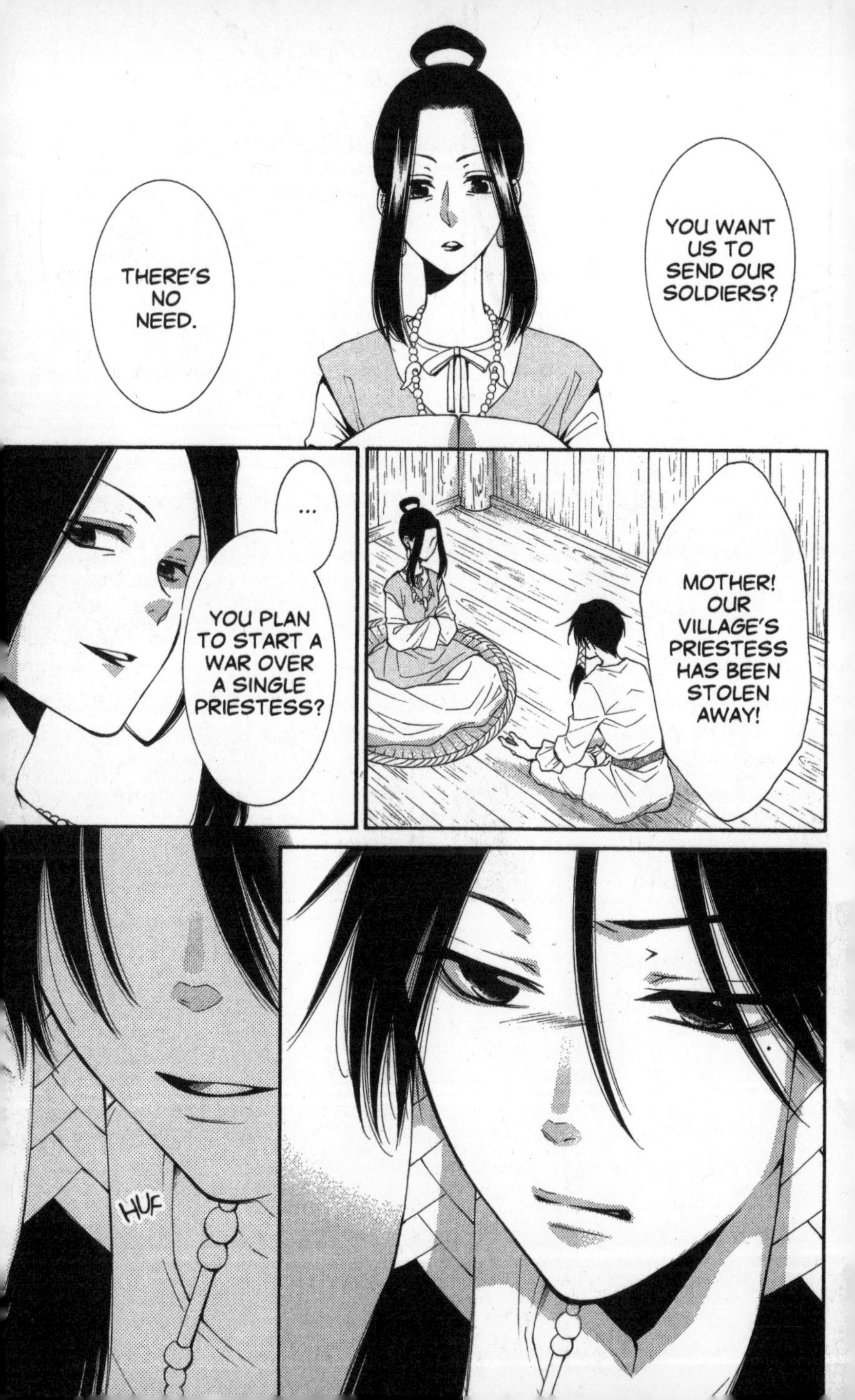
YOU WANT US TO SEND OUR SOLDIERS?
THERE'S NO NEED.
MOTHER! OUR VILLAGE'S PRIESTESS HAS BEEN STOLEN AWAY!
...
YOU PLAN TO START A WAR OVER A SINGLE PRIESTESS?
HUF

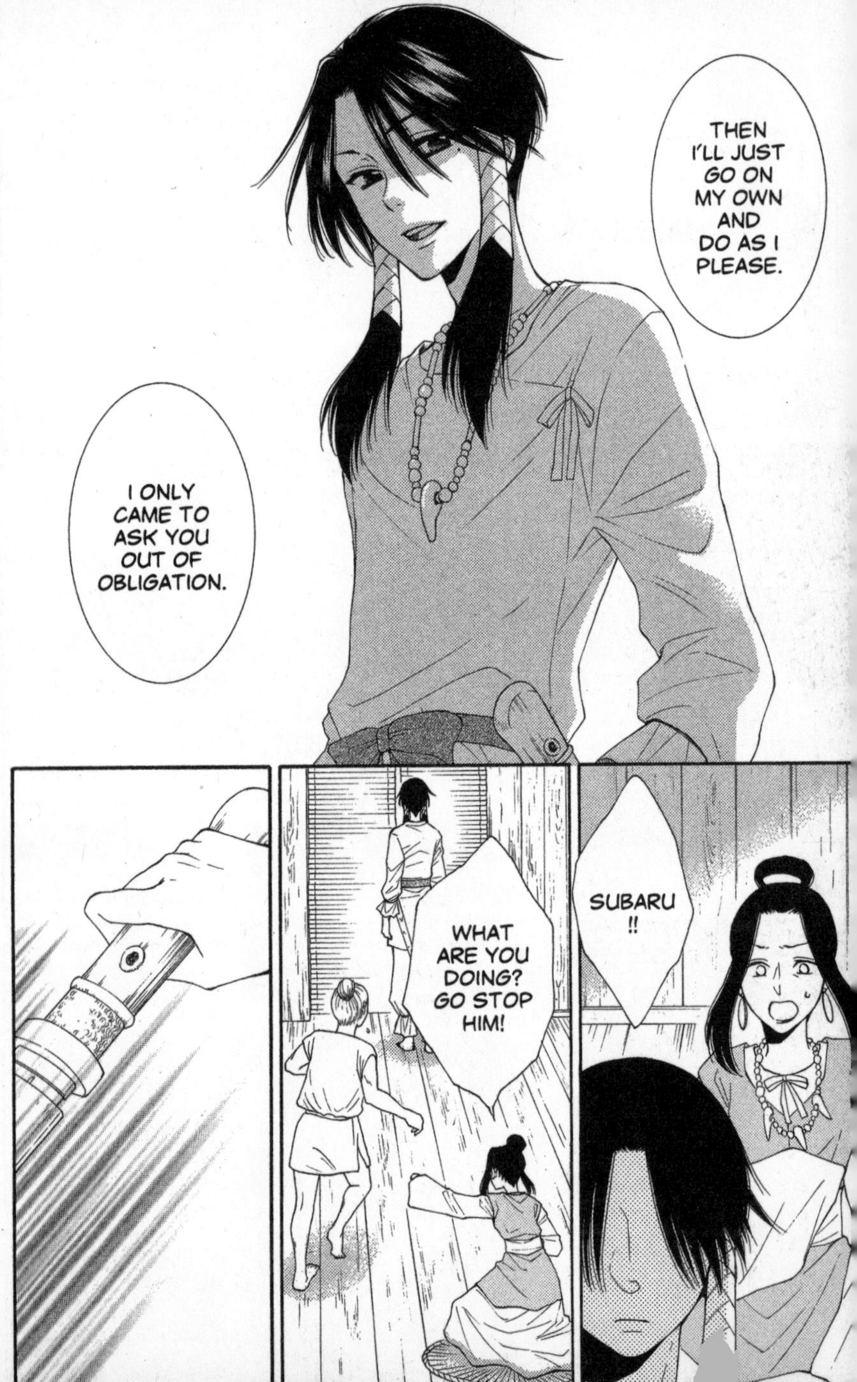
THEN I'LL JUST GO ON MY OWN AND DO AS I PLEASE.
I ONLY CAME TO ASK YOU OUT OF OBLIGATION.
SUBARU !!
WHAT ARE YOU DOING? GO STOP HIM!

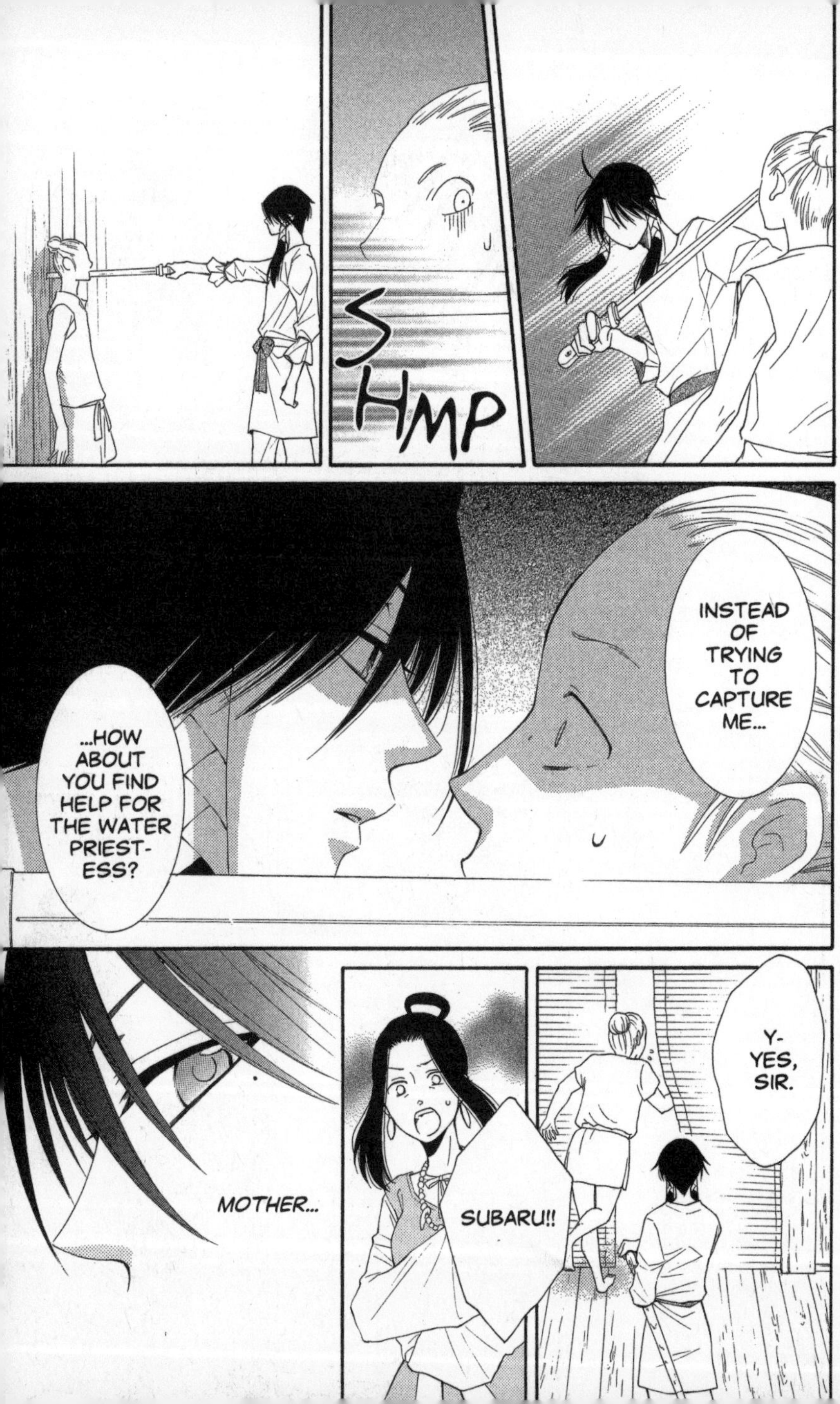
SHMP
INSTEAD OF TRYING TO CAPTURE ME...
...HOW ABOUT YOU FIND HELP FOR THE WATER PRIEST-ESS?
Y-YES, SIR.
SUBARU!!
MOTHER...

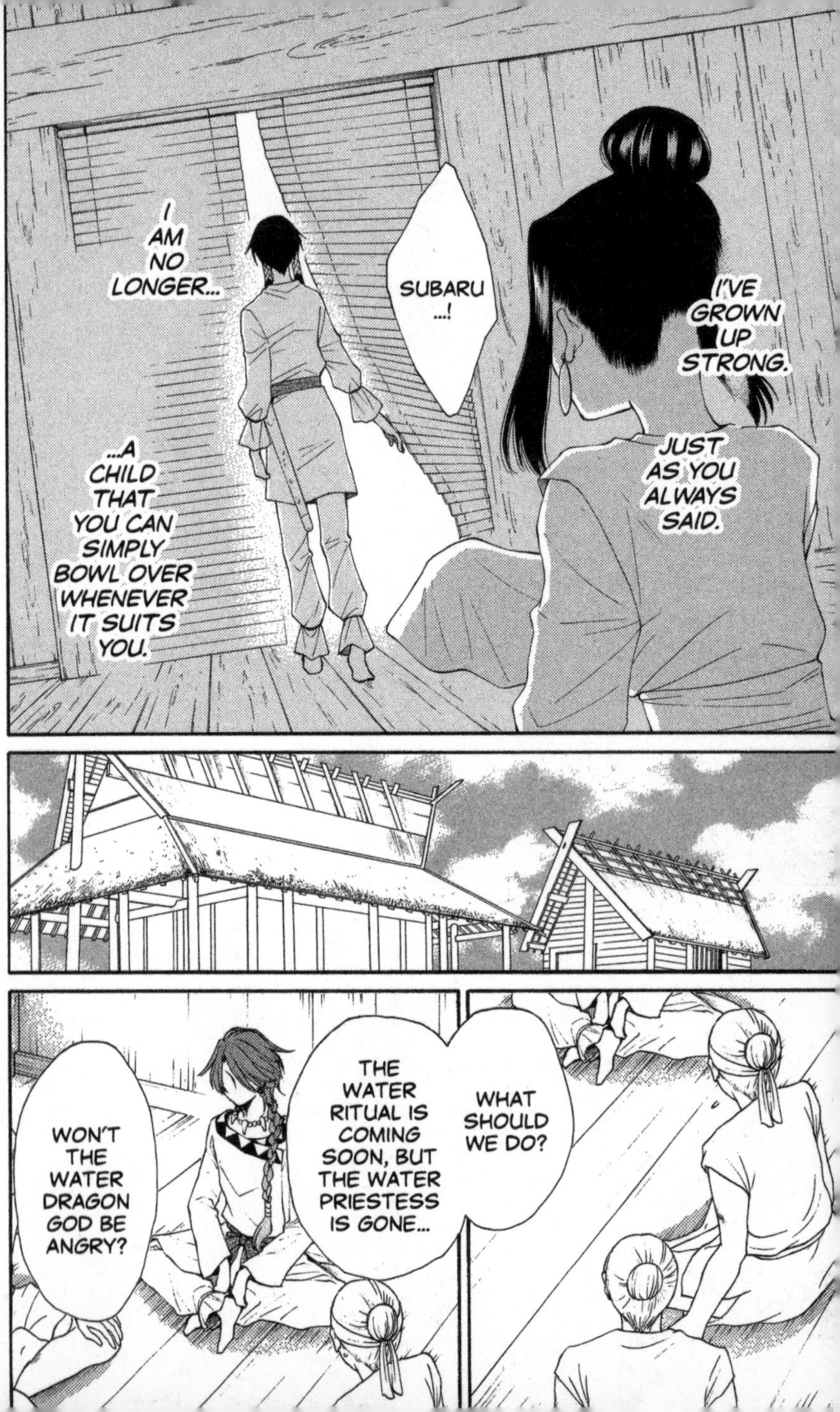
I'VE GROWN UP STRONG.
JUST AS YOU ALWAYS SAID.
SUBARU ...!
I AM NO LONGER...
...A CHILD THAT YOU CAN SIMPLY BOWL OVER WHENEVER IT SUITS YOU.
WHAT SHOULD WE DO?
THE WATER RITUAL IS COMING SOON, BUT THE WATER PRIESTESS IS GONE...
WON'T THE WATER DRAGON GOD BE ANGRY?

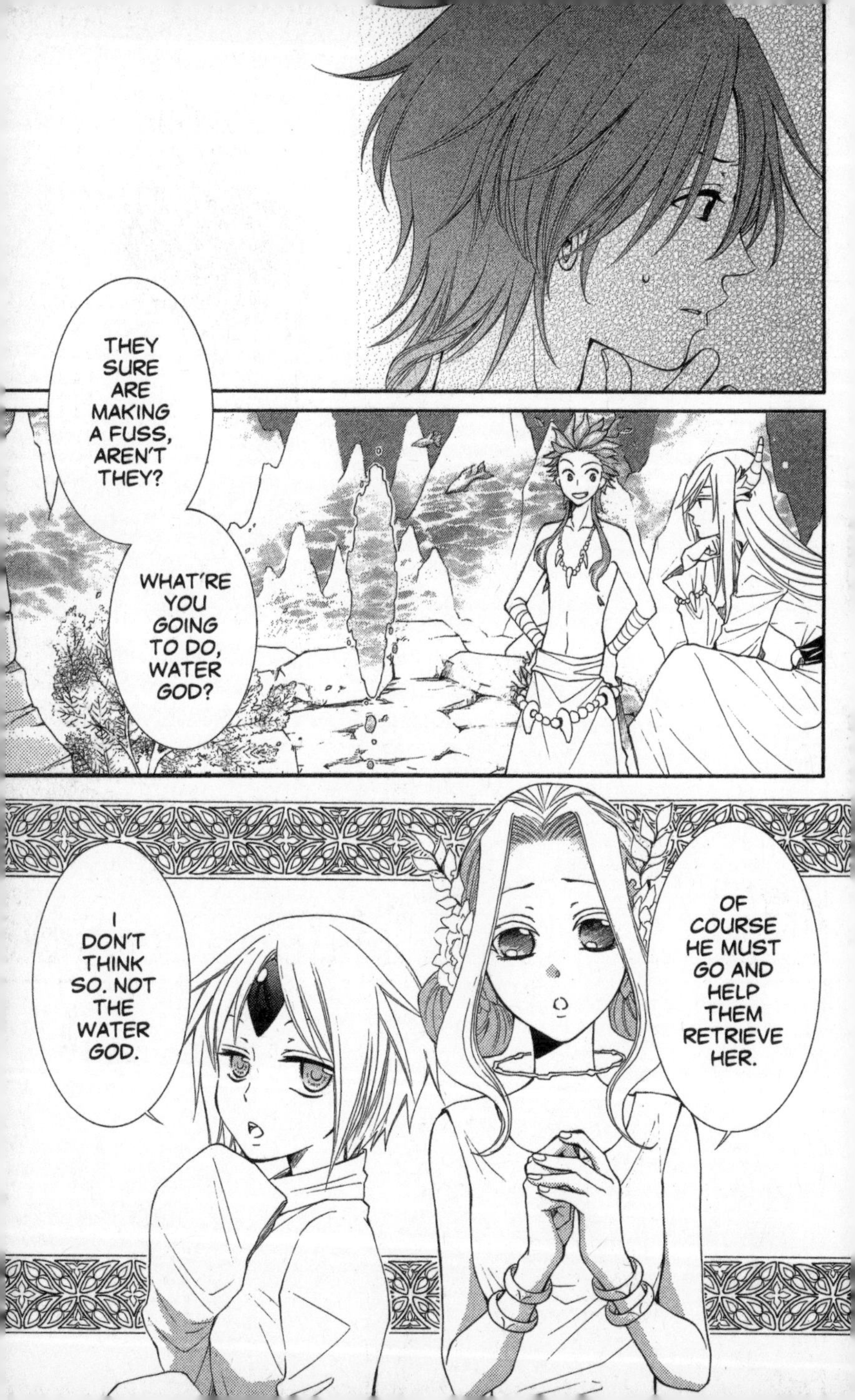
THEY SURE ARE MAKING A FUSS, AREN'T THEY?
WHAT'RE YOU GOING TO DO, WATER GOD?
OF COURSE HE MUST GO AND HELP THEM RETRIEVE HER.
I DON'T THINK SO. NOT THE WATER GOD.

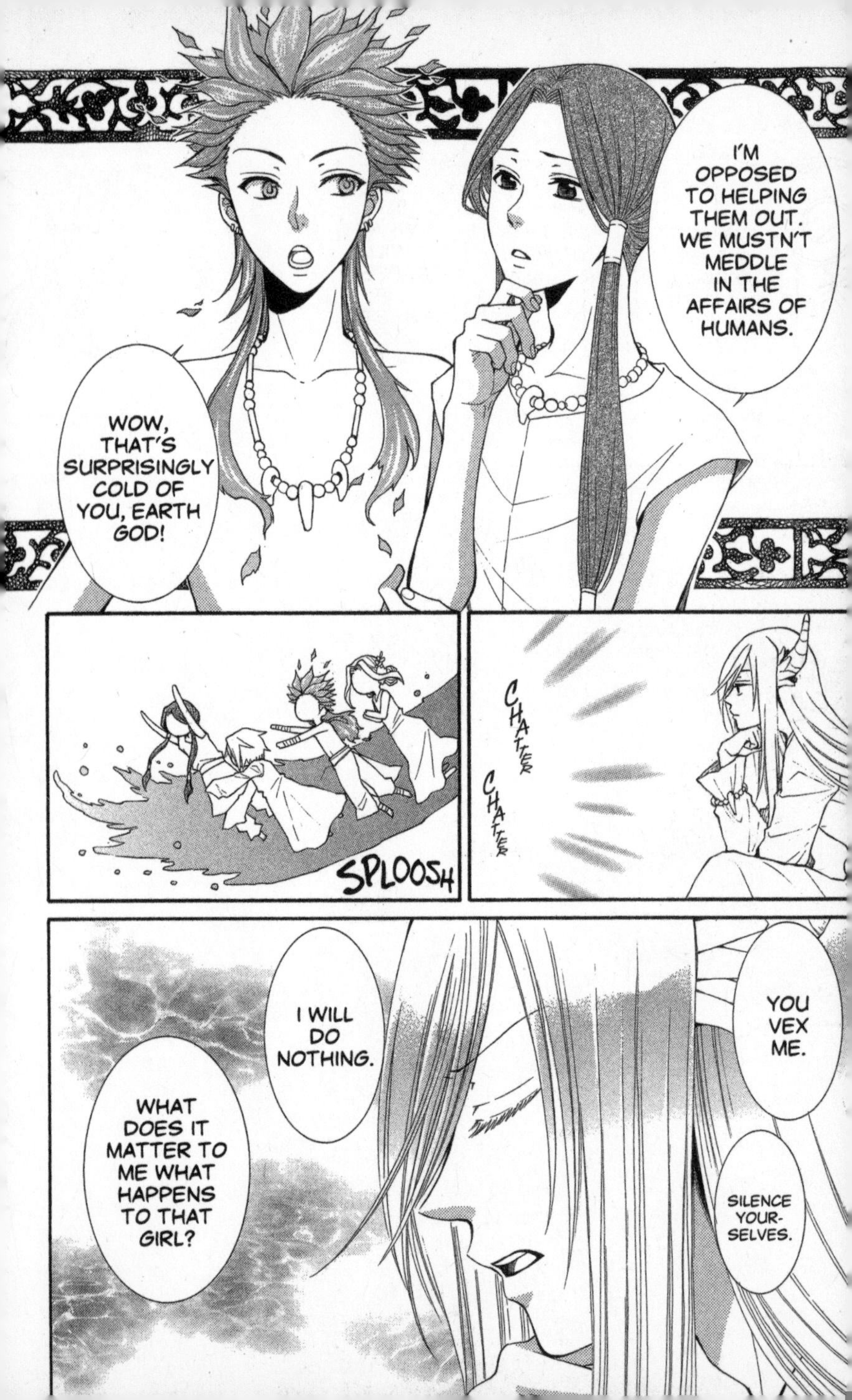
I'M OPPOSED TO HELPING THEM OUT. WE MUSTN'T MEDDLE IN THE AFFAIRS OF HUMANS.
WOW, THAT'S SURPRISINGLY COLD OF YOU, EARTH GOD!
CHATTER
CHATTER
SPLOOSH
YOU VEX ME.
SILENCE YOUR-SELVES.
I WILL DO NOTHING.
WHAT DOES IT MATTER TO ME WHAT HAPPENS TO THAT GIRL?

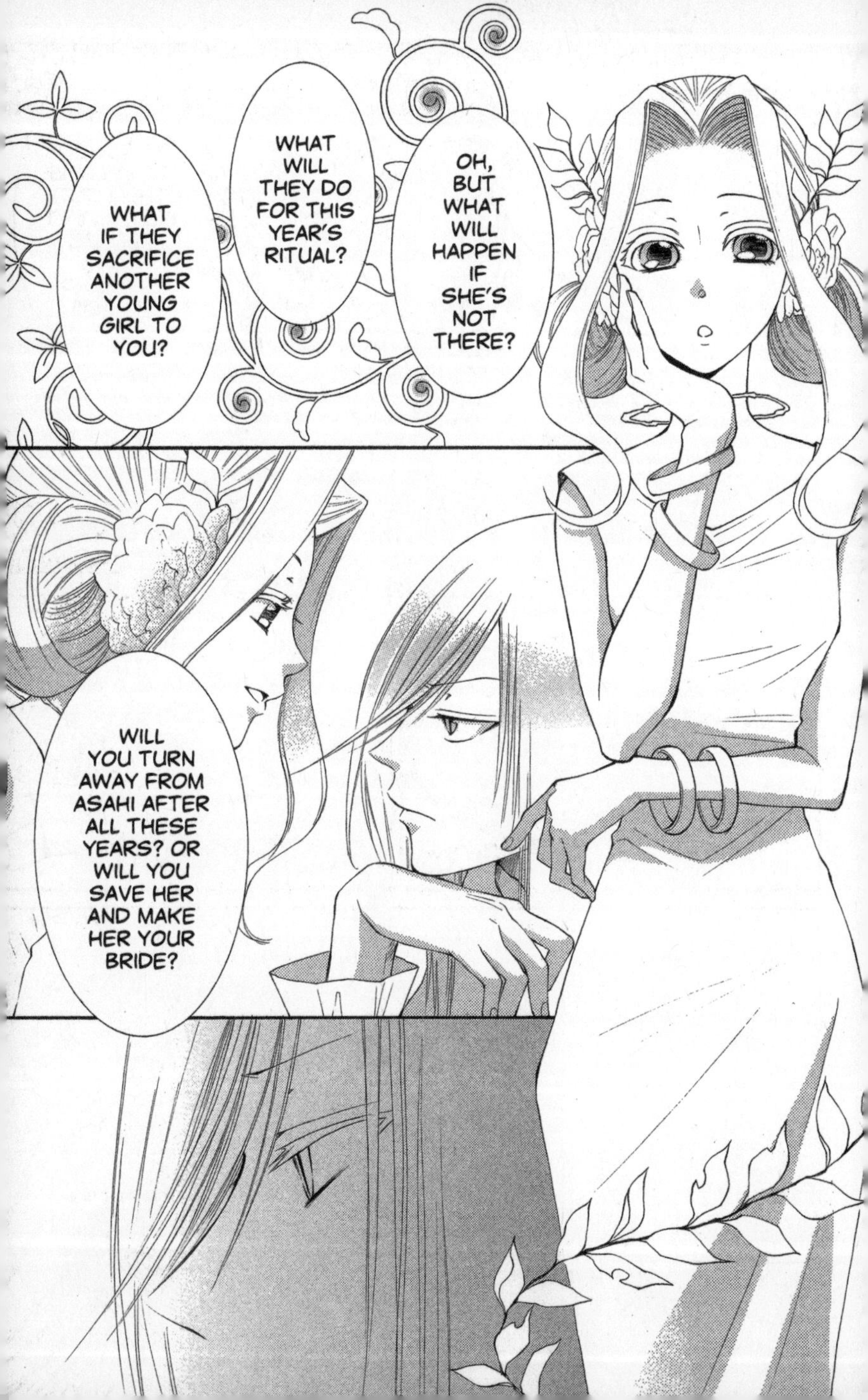
OH, BUT WHAT WILL HAPPEN IF SHE'S NOT THERE?
WHAT WILL THEY DO FOR THIS YEAR'S RITUAL?
WHAT IF THEY SACRIFICE ANOTHER YOUNG GIRL TO YOU?
WILL YOU TURN AWAY FROM ASAHI AFTER ALL THESE YEARS? OR WILL YOU SAVE HER AND MAKE HER YOUR BRIDE?

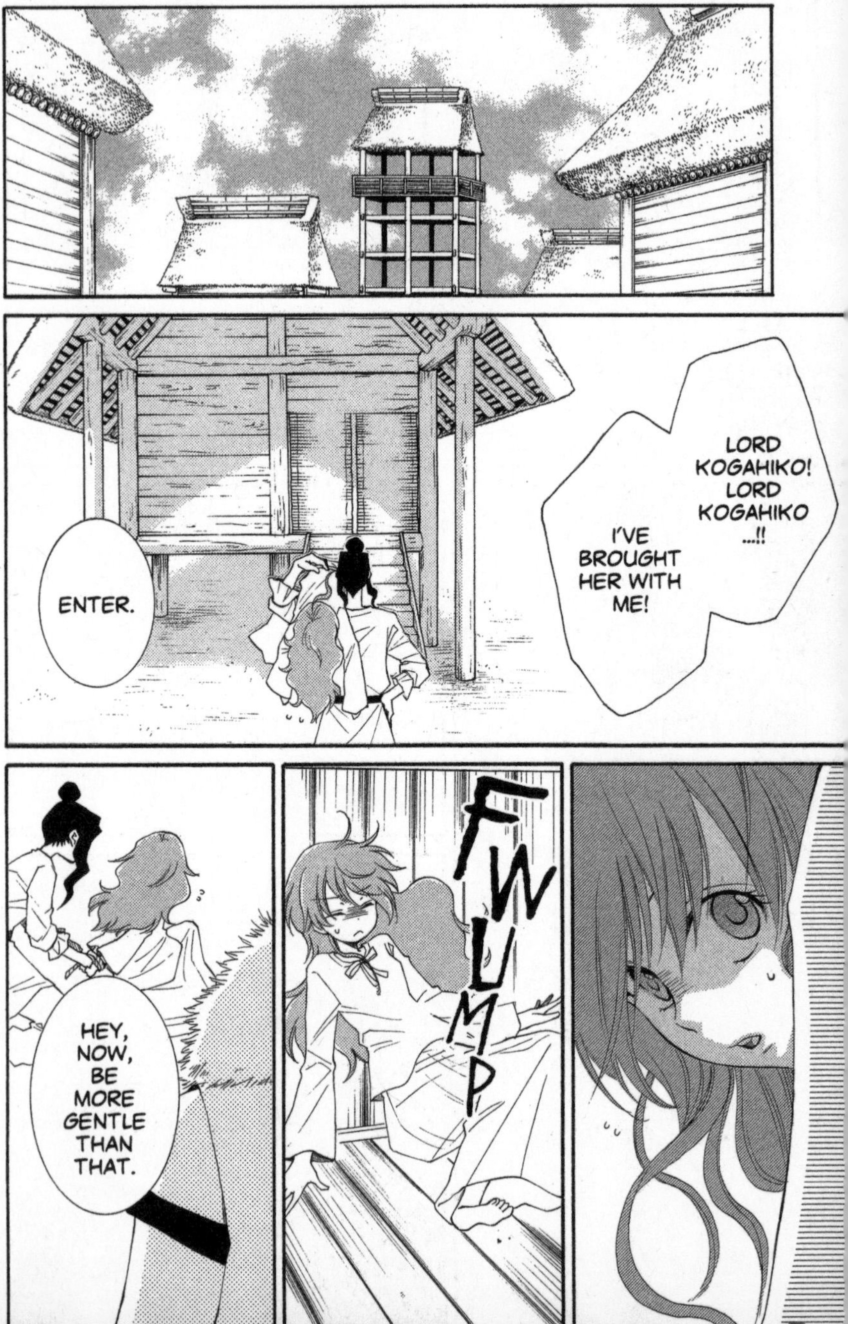
LORD KOGAHIKO! LORD KOGAHIKO ...!!
I'VE BROUGHT HER WITH ME!
ENTER.
FWUMP
HEY, NOW, BE MORE GENTLE THAN THAT.

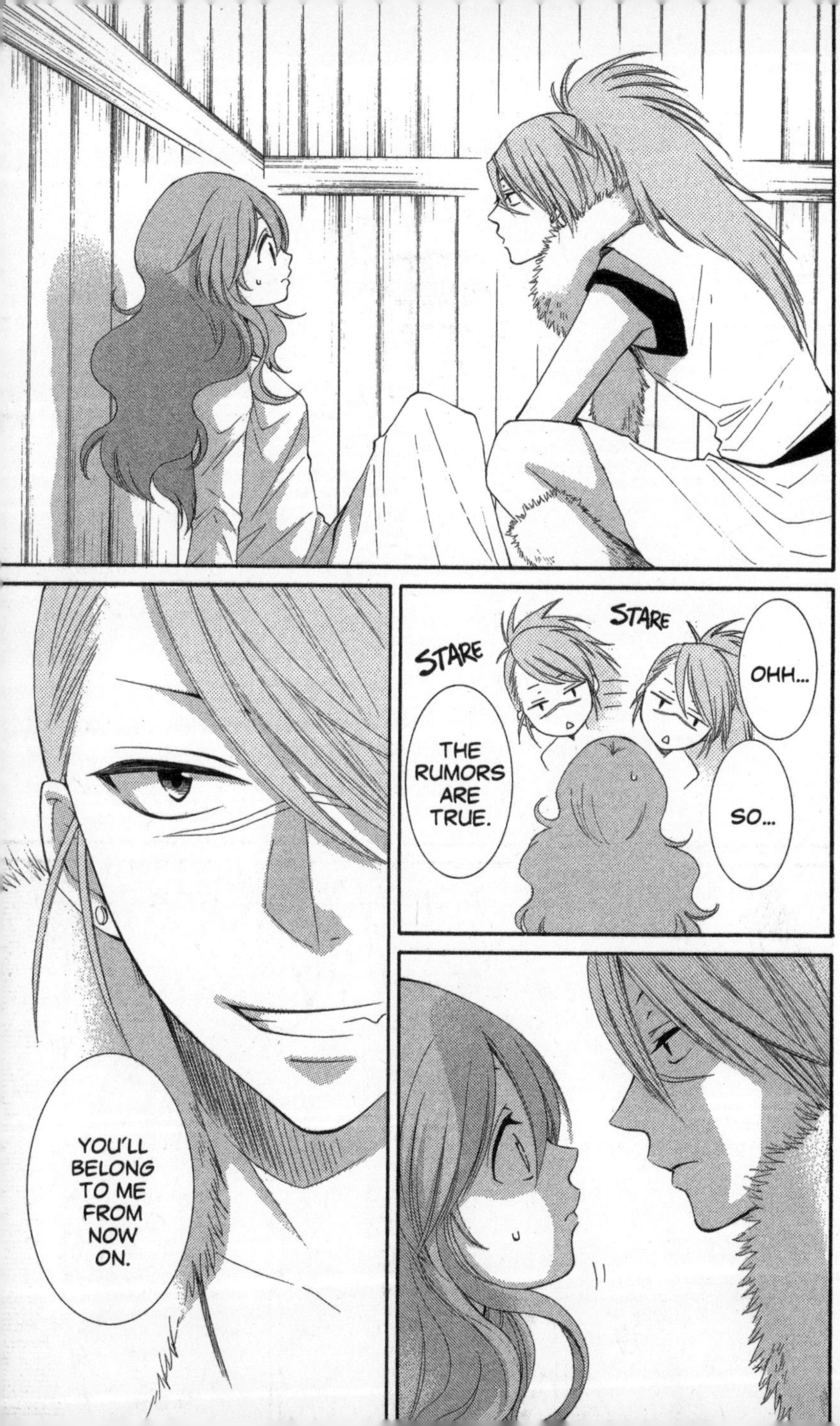
OHH...
STARE
SO...
STARE
THE RUMORS ARE TRUE.
YOU'LL BELONG TO ME FROM NOW ON.

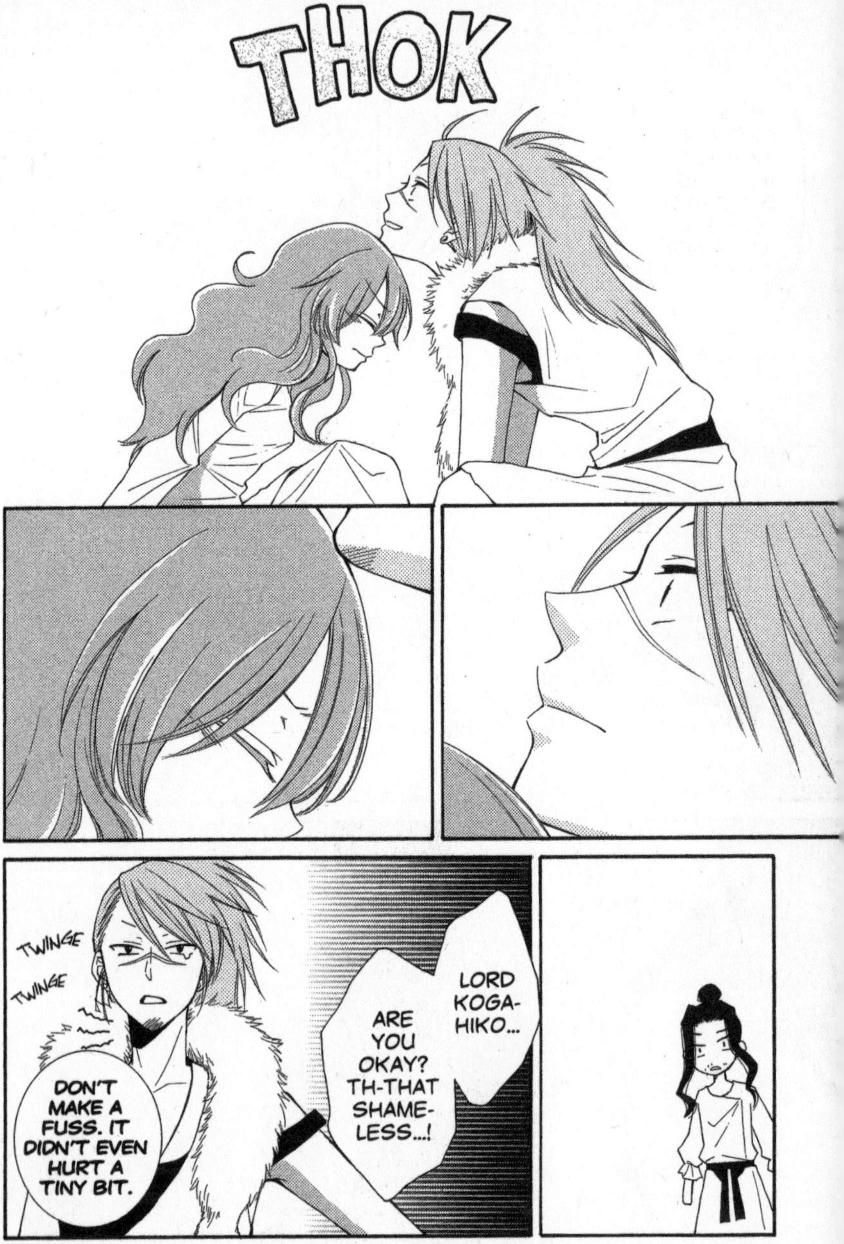
THOK
LORD KOGAHIKO...
ARE YOU OKAY? TH-THAT SHAMELESS...!
TWINGE
TWINGE
DON'T MAKE A FUSS. IT DIDN'T EVEN HURT A TINY BIT.

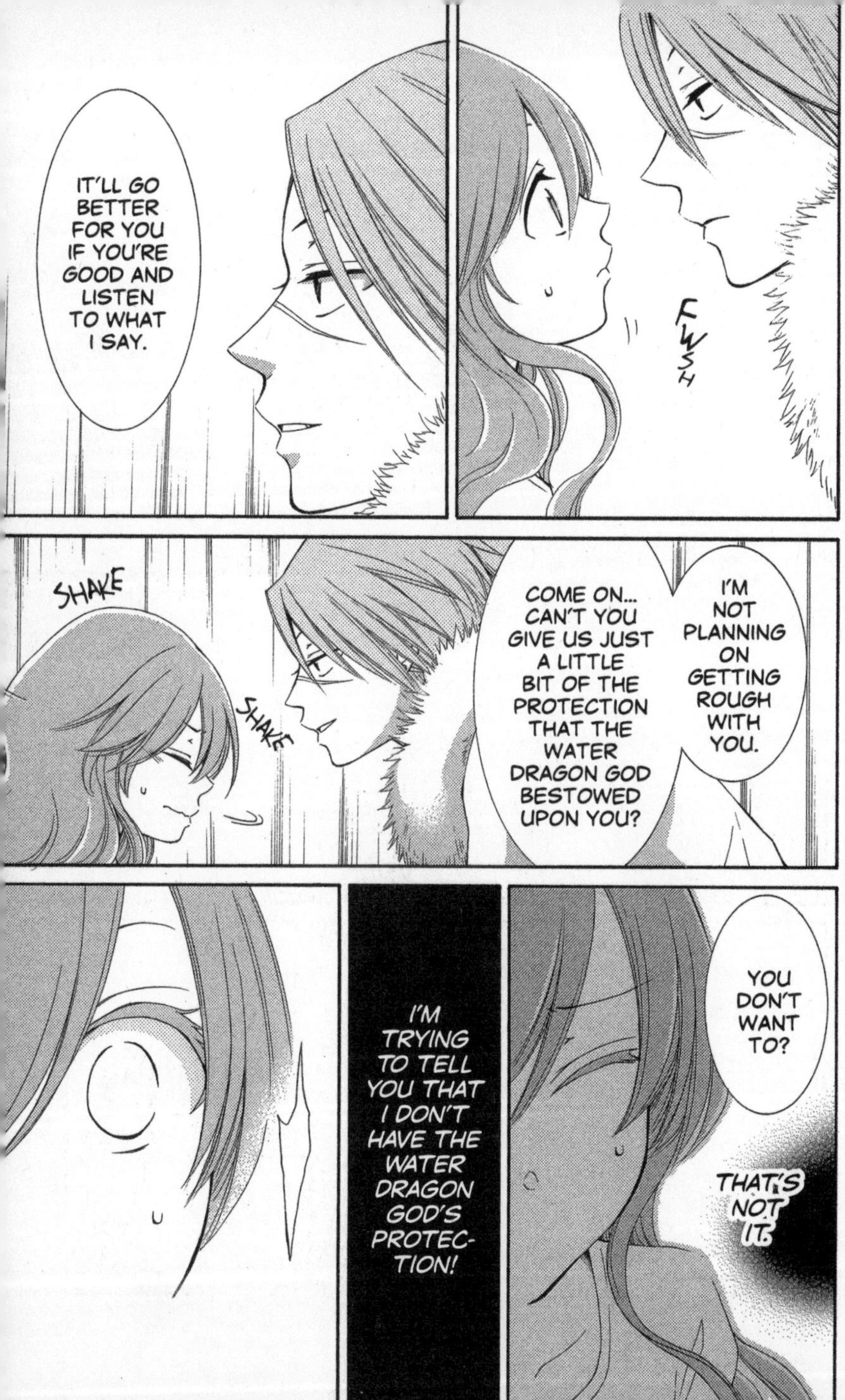
FWSH
IT'LL GO BETTER FOR YOU IF YOU'RE GOOD AND LISTEN TO WHAT I SAY.
I'M NOT PLANNING ON GETTING ROUGH WITH YOU.
COME ON... CAN'T YOU GIVE US JUST A LITTLE BIT OF THE PROTECTION THAT THE WATER DRAGON GOD BESTOWED UPON YOU?
SHAKE
SHAKE
YOU DON'T WANT TO?
THAT'S NOT IT.
I'M TRYING TO TELL YOU THAT I DON'T HAVE THE WATER DRAGON GOD'S PROTECTION!

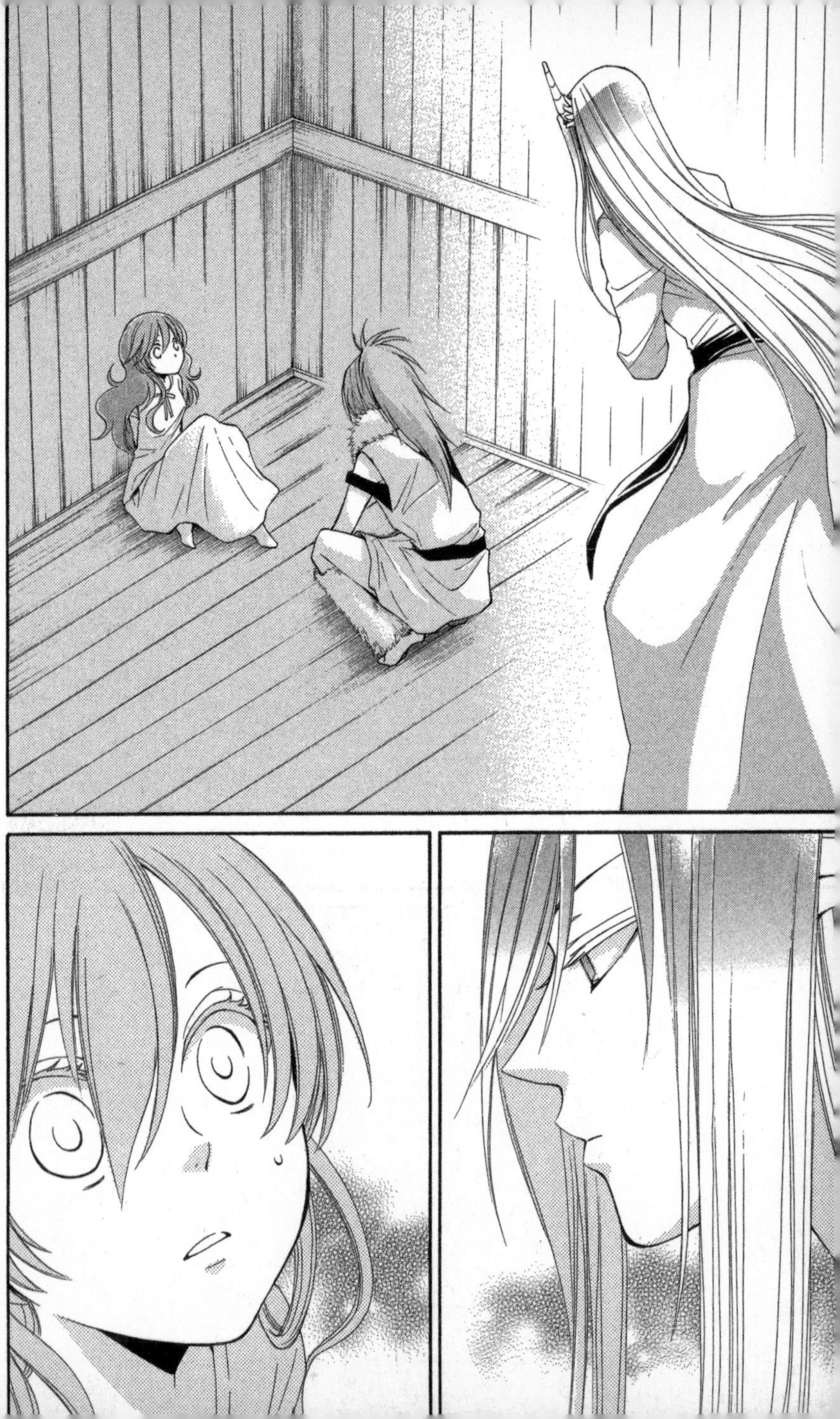

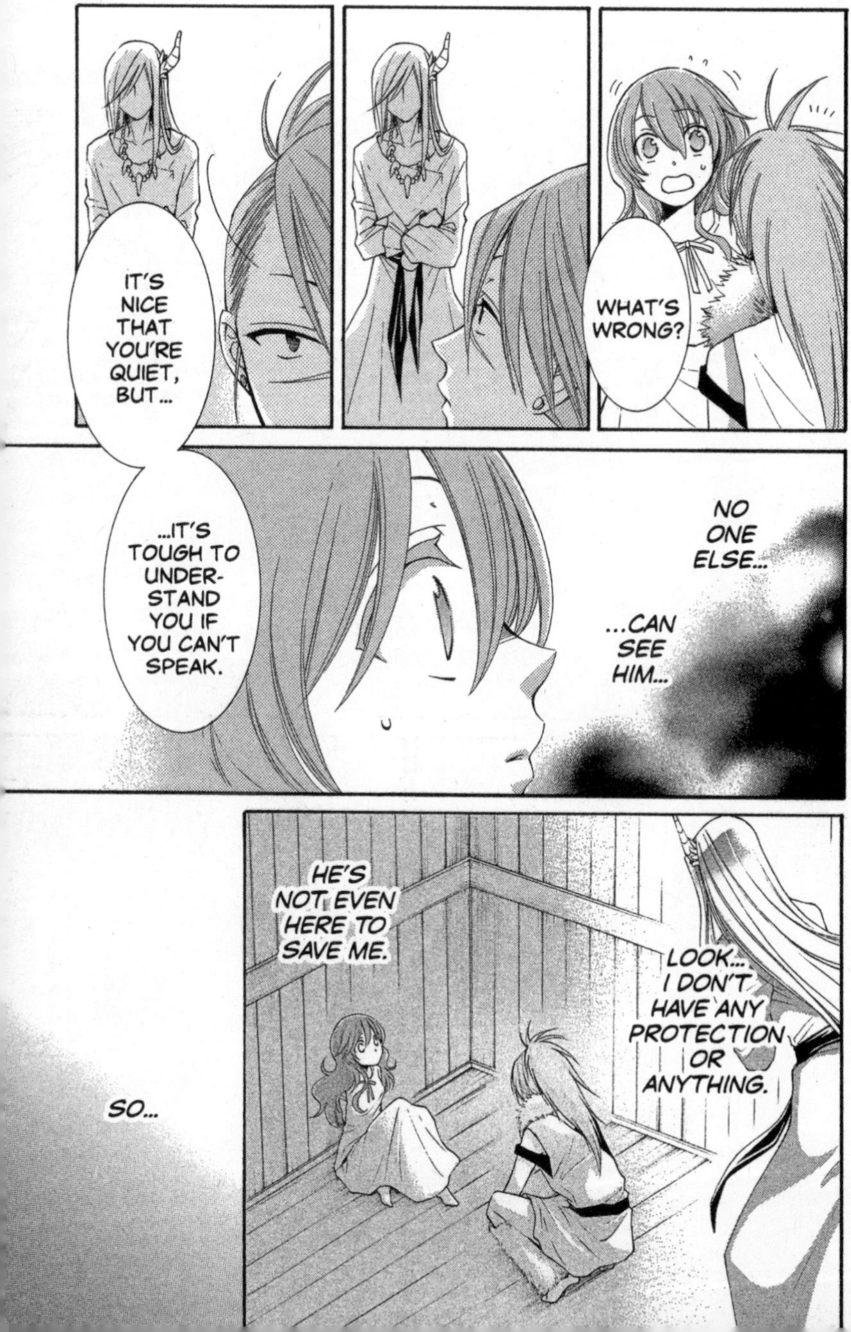
WHAT'S WRONG?
IT'S NICE THAT YOU'RE QUIET, BUT...
...IT'S TOUGH TO UNDERSTAND YOU IF YOU CAN'T SPEAK.
NO ONE ELSE...
...CAN SEE HIM...
LOOK... I DON'T HAVE ANY PROTECTION OR ANYTHING.
HE'S NOT EVEN HERE TO SAVE ME.
SO...

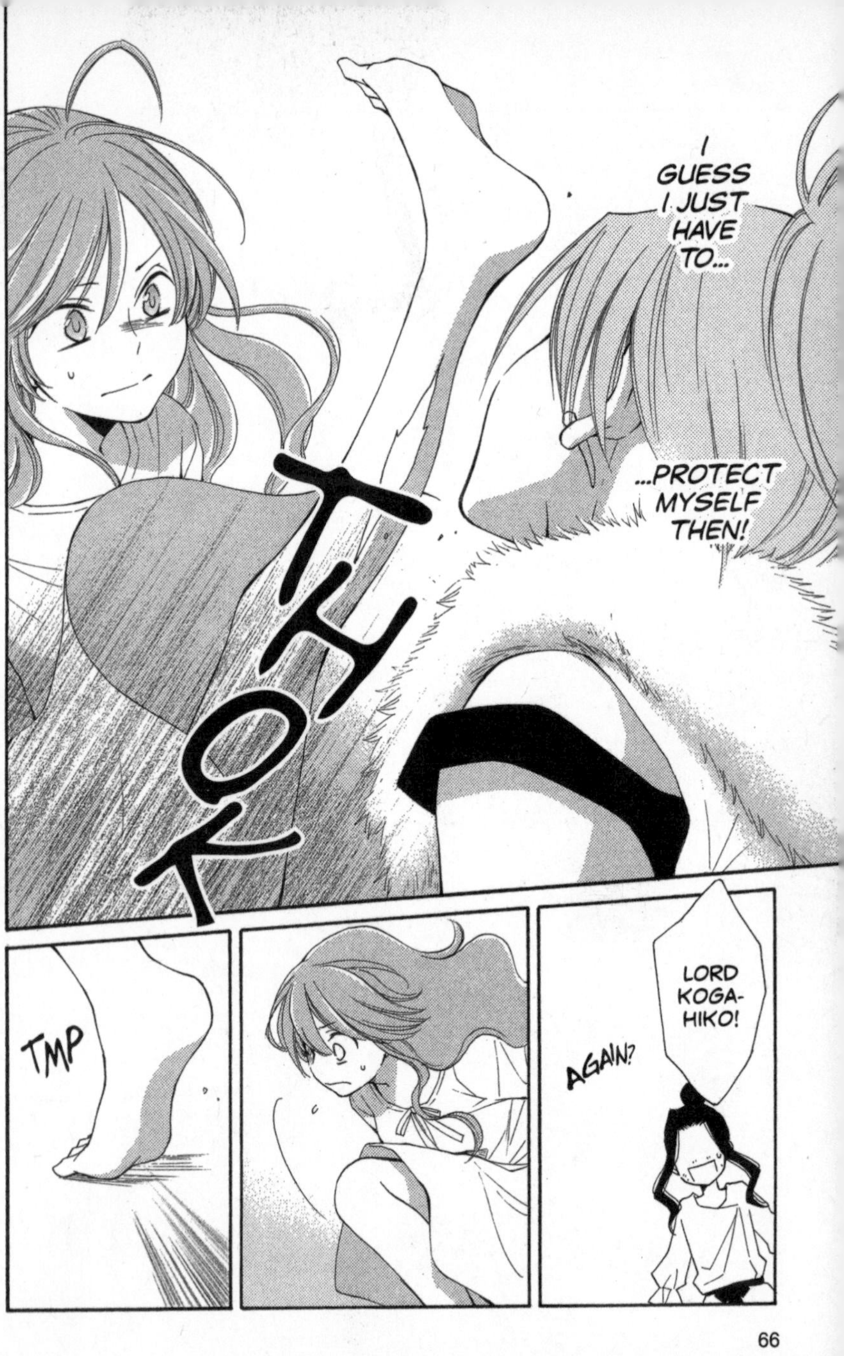
I GUESS I JUST HAVE TO...
...PROTECT MYSELF THEN!
THOK
LORD KOGA-HIKO!
AGAIN?
TMP

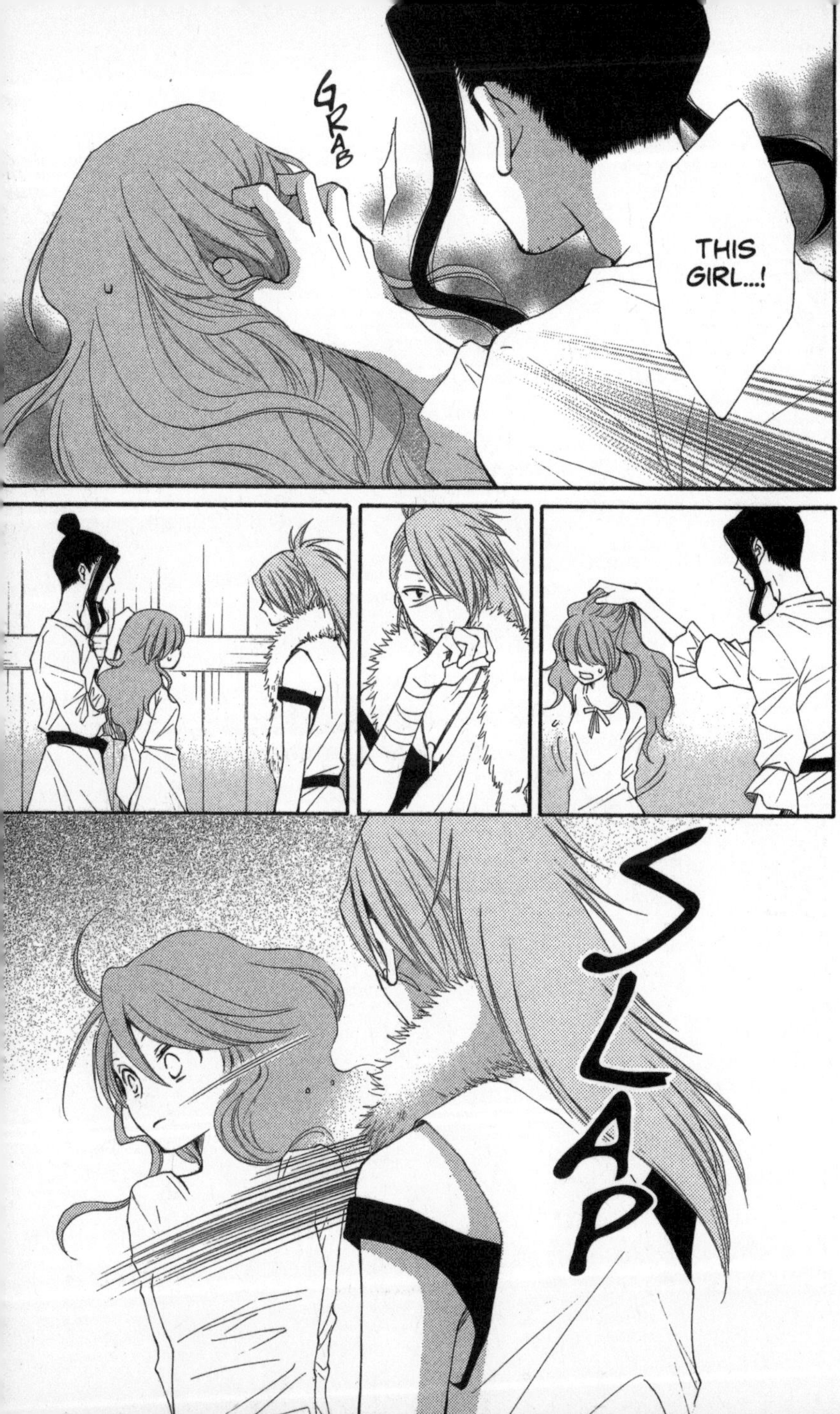
THIS GIRL...!
GRAB
SLAP

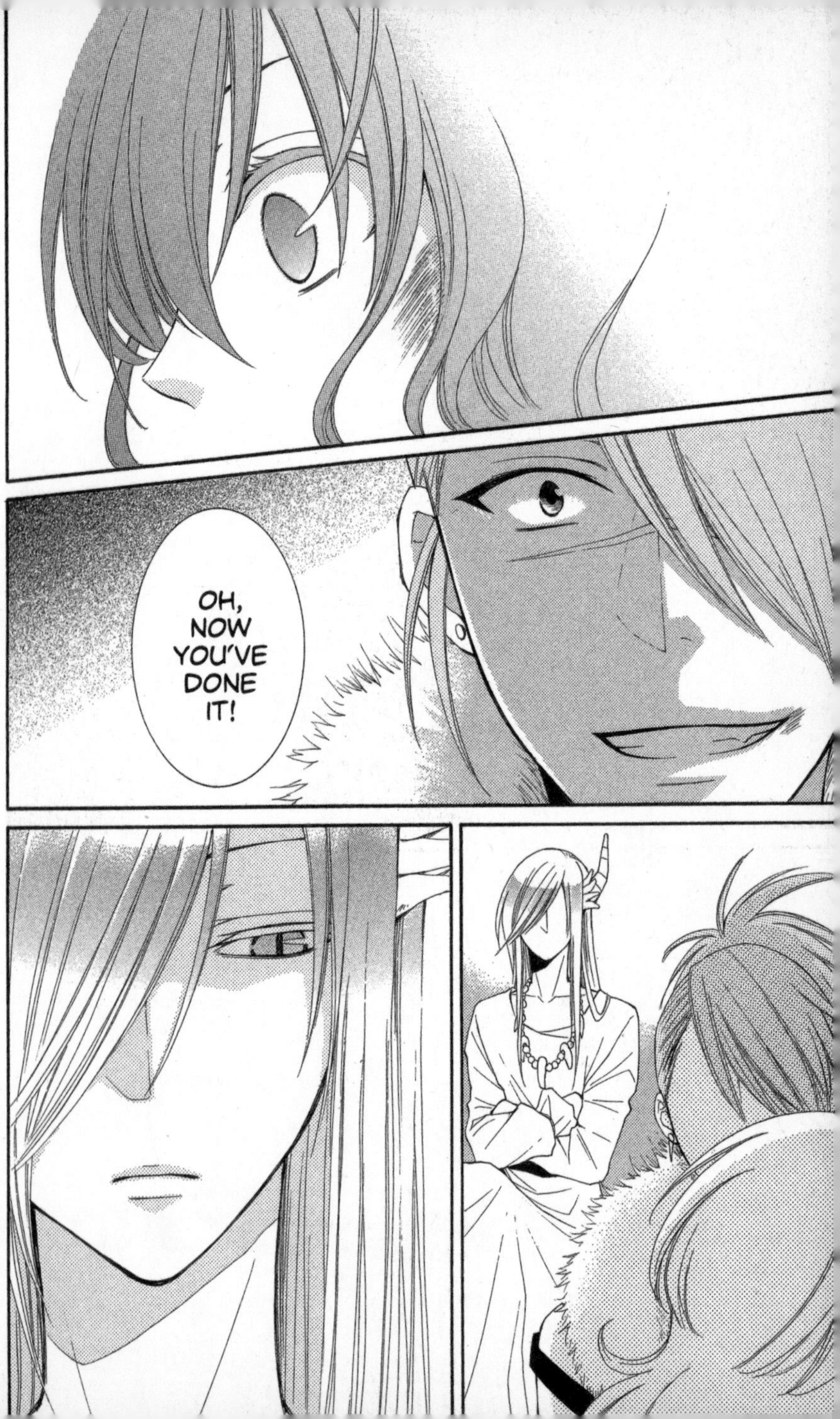
OH, NOW YOU'VE DONE IT!

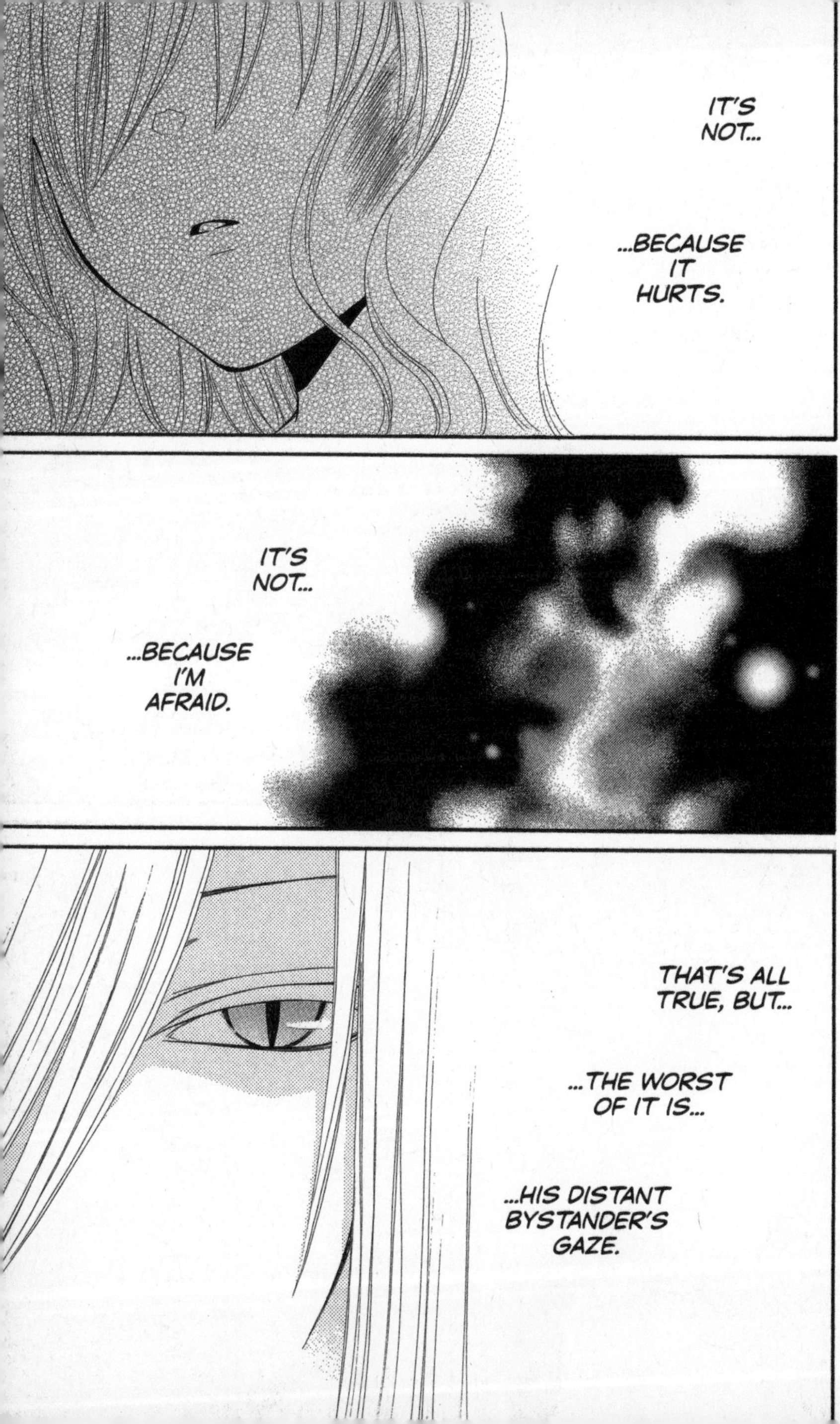
IT'S NOT...
...BECAUSE IT HURTS.
IT'S NOT...
...BECAUSE I'M AFRAID.
THAT'S ALL TRUE, BUT...
...THE WORST OF IT IS...
...HIS DISTANT BYSTANDER'S GAZE.

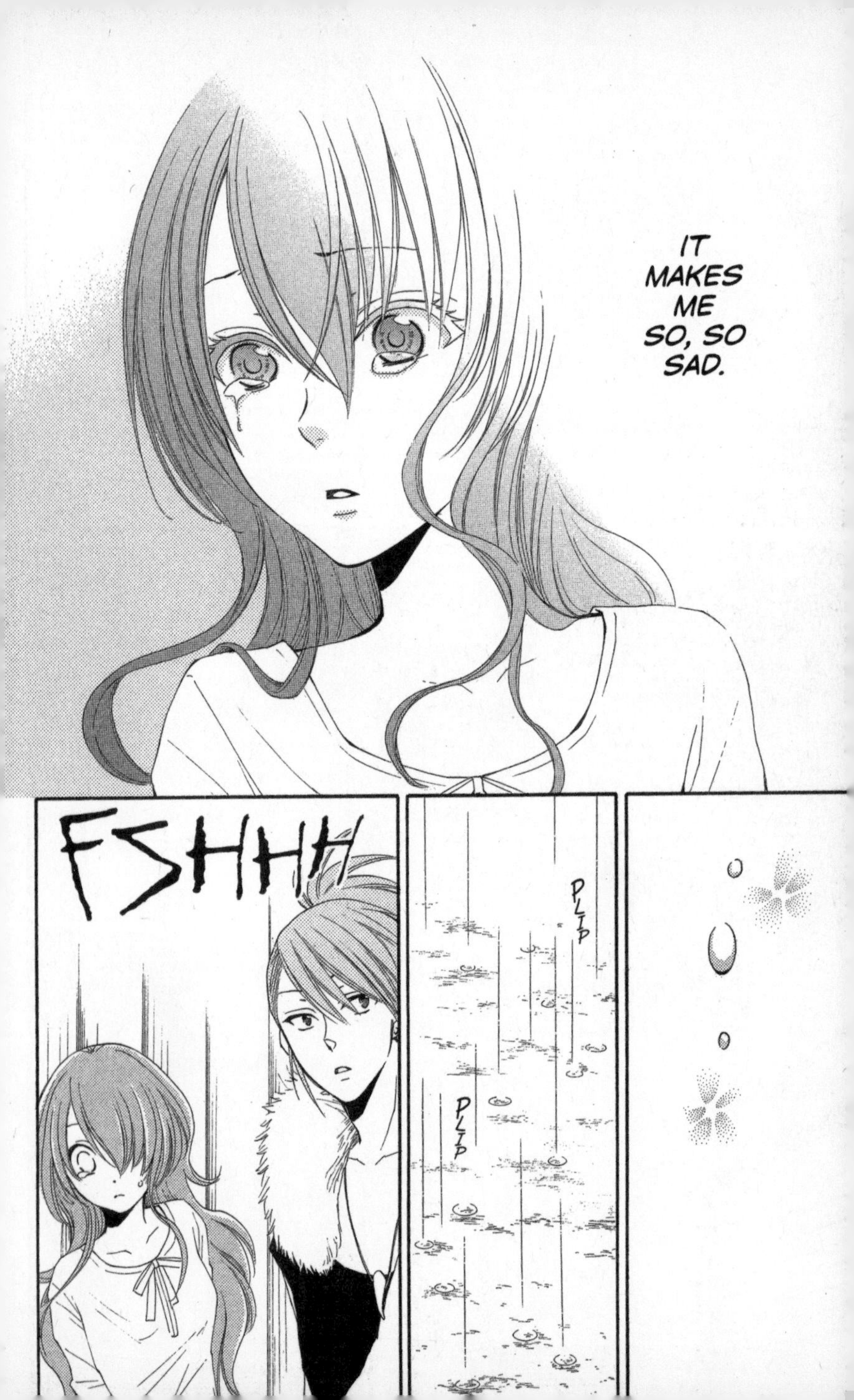
IT MAKES ME SO, SO SAD.
PLIP
PLIP
FSHH

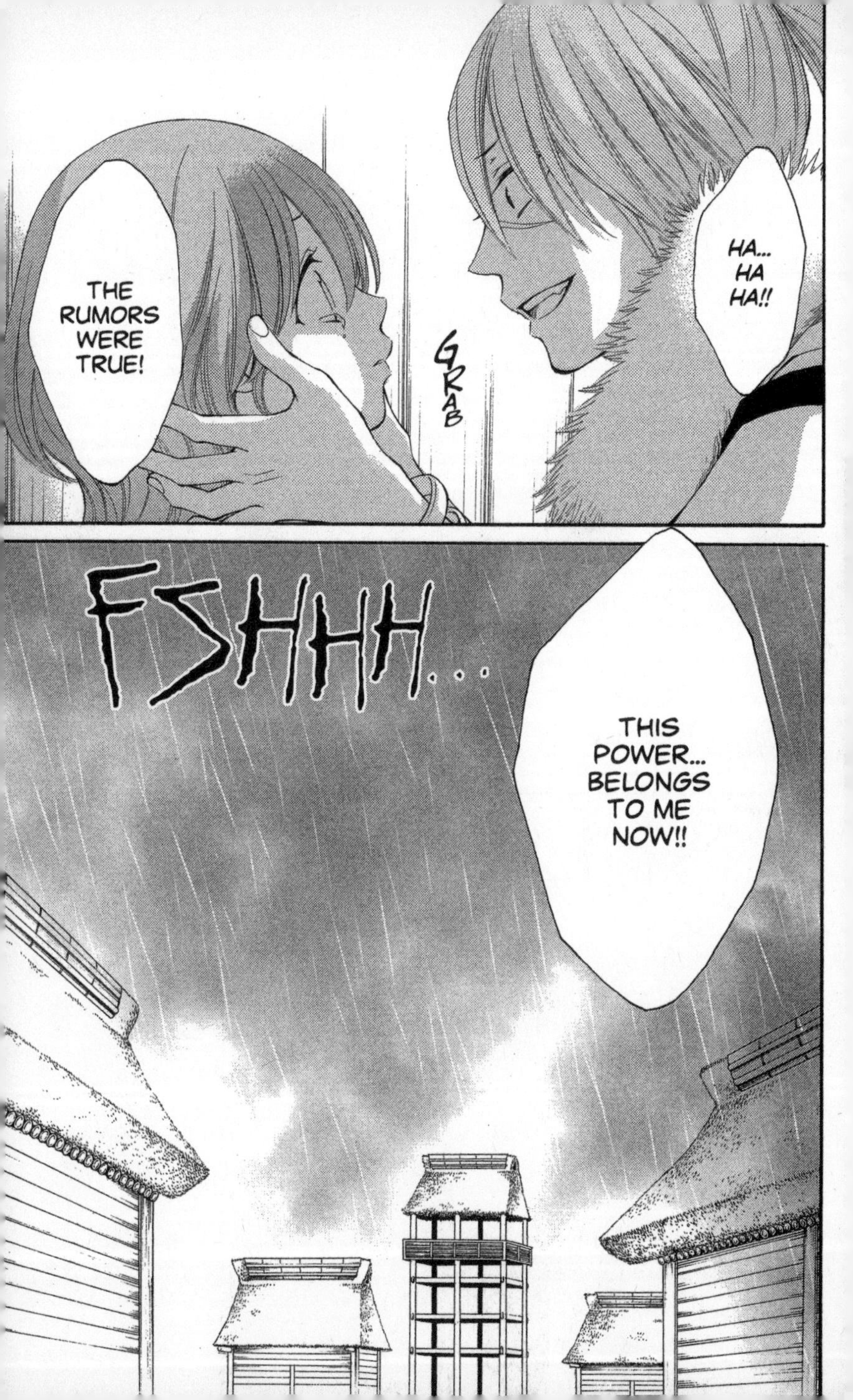
HA... HA HA!!
GRAB
THE RUMORS WERE TRUE!
THIS POWER... BELONGS TO ME NOW!!
FSHHH...

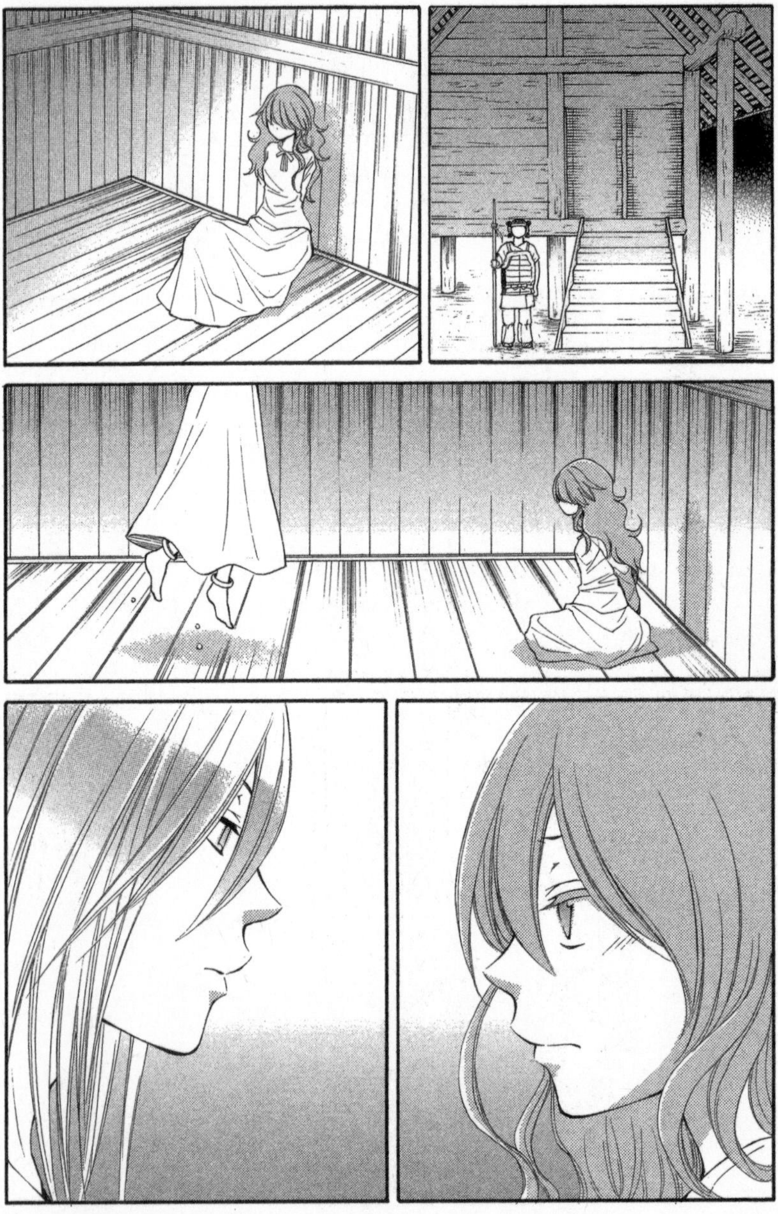

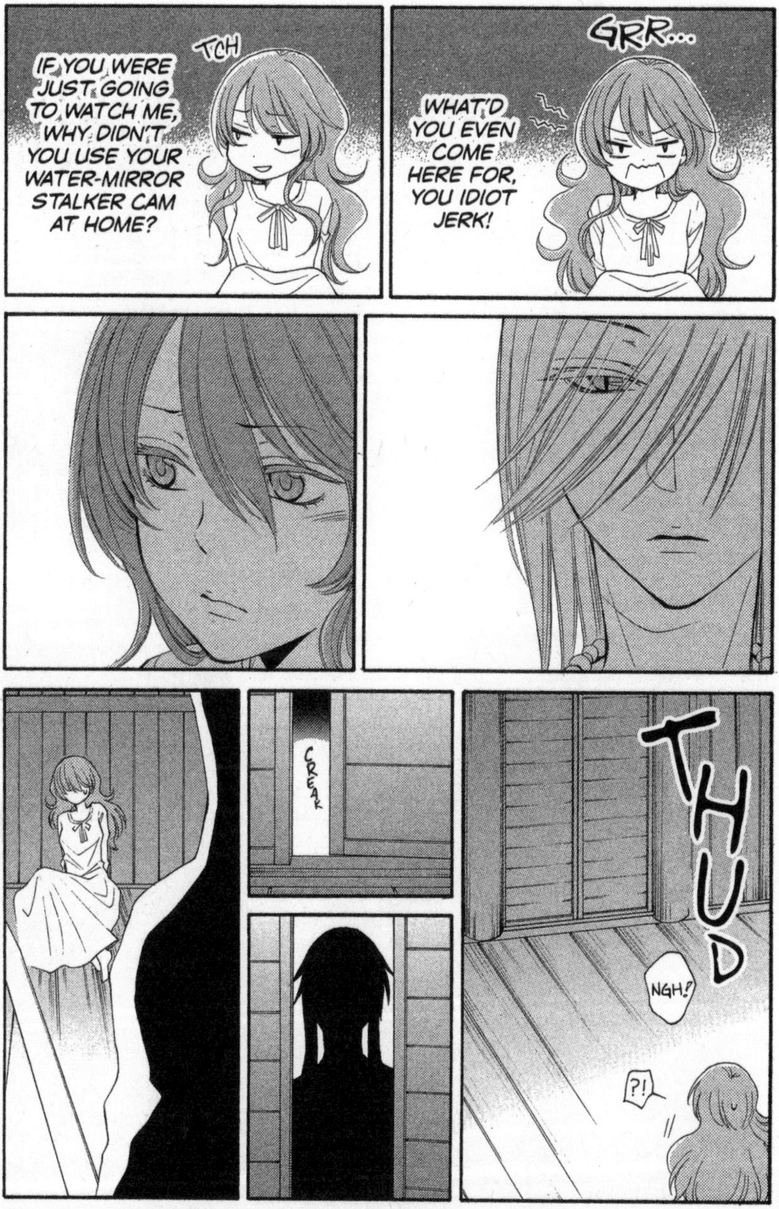
GRR...
WHAT'D YOU EVEN COME HERE FOR, YOU IDIOT JERK!
TCH
IF YOU WERE JUST GOING TO WATCH ME, WHY DIDN'T YOU USE YOUR WATER-MIRROR STALKER CAM AT HOME?
THUD
NGH!
?!
CREAK

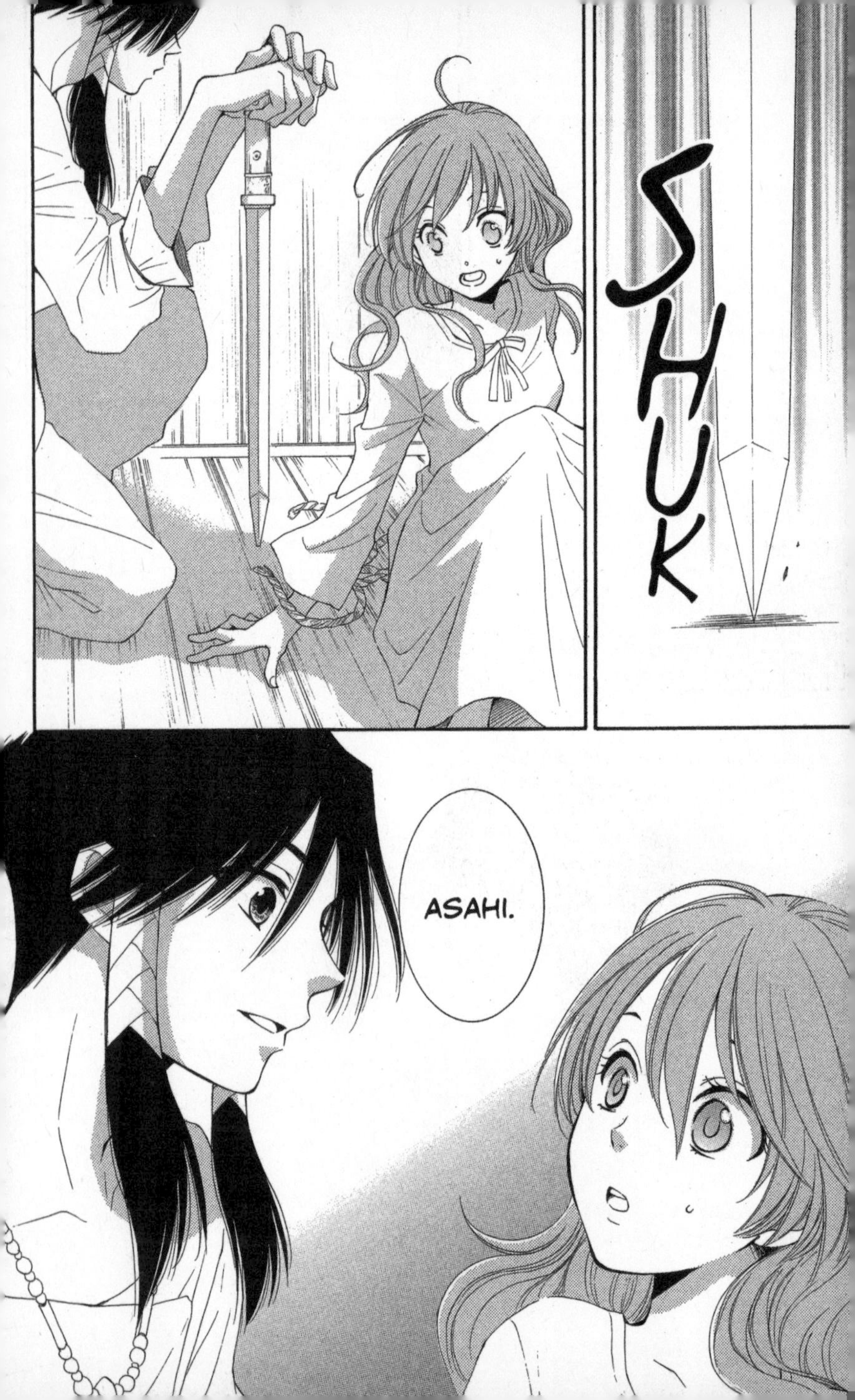
SHUK
ASAHI.

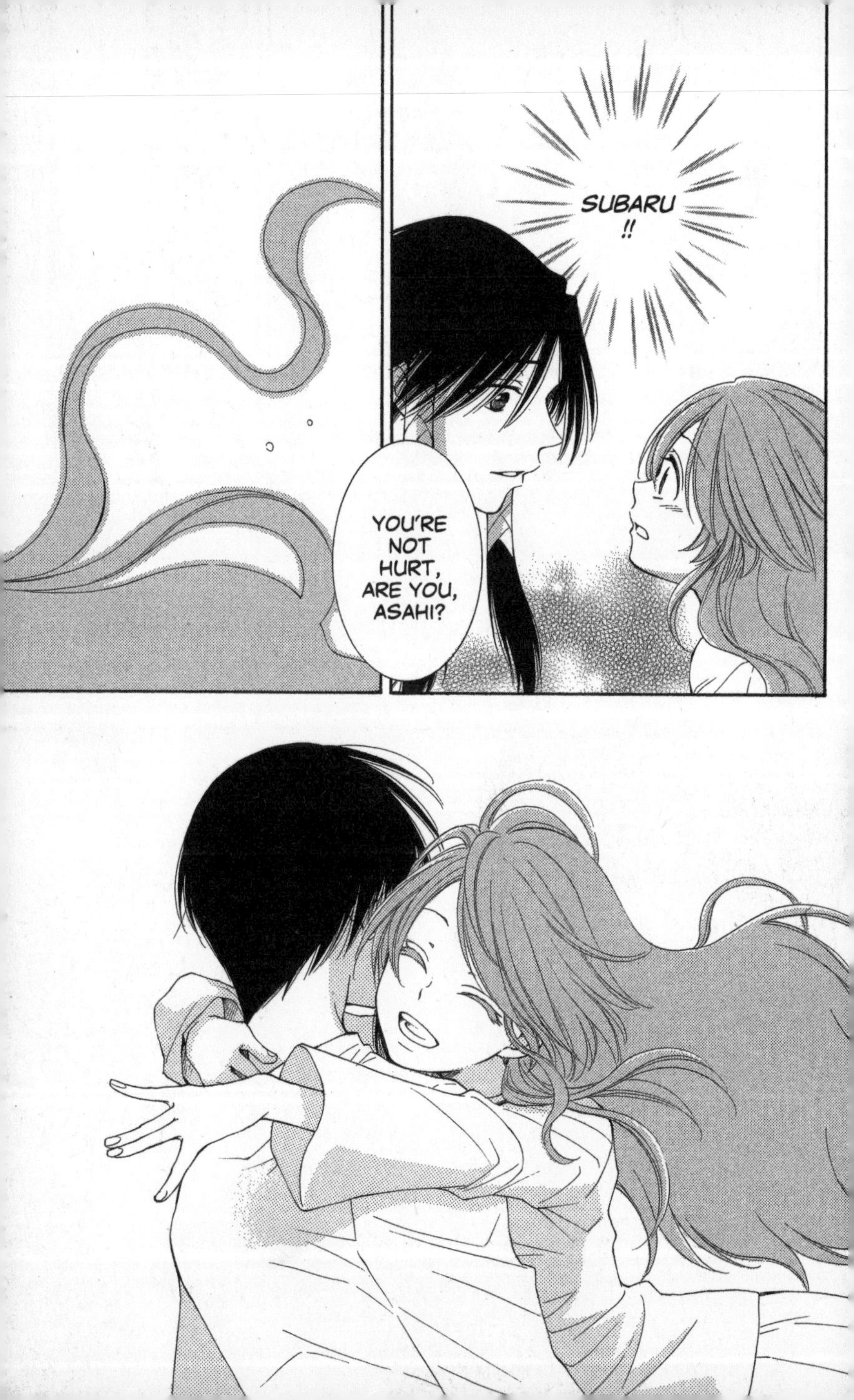
SUBARU !!
YOU'RE NOT HURT, ARE YOU, ASAHI?

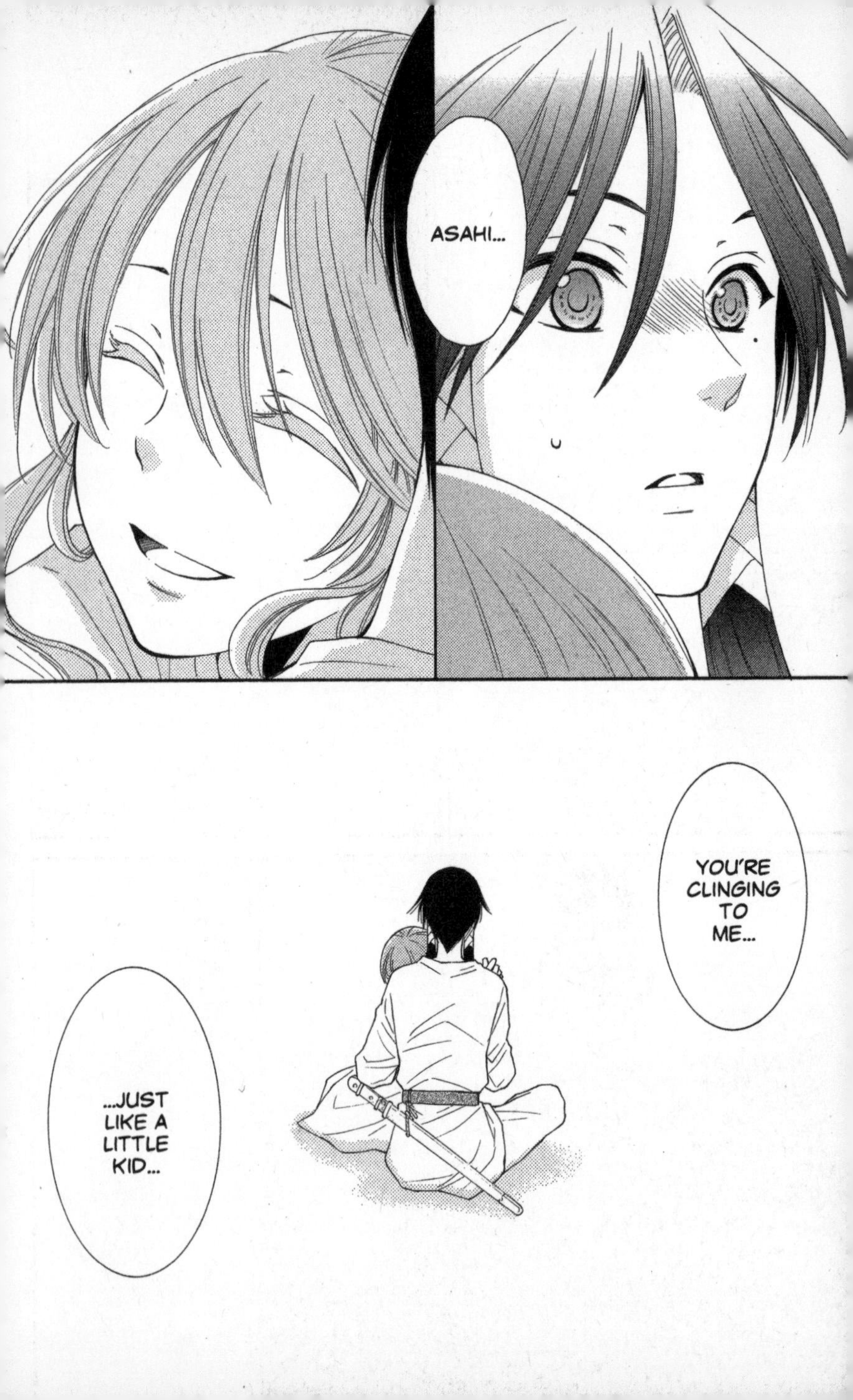
ASAHI...
YOU'RE CLINGING TO ME...
...JUST LIKE A LITTLE KID...

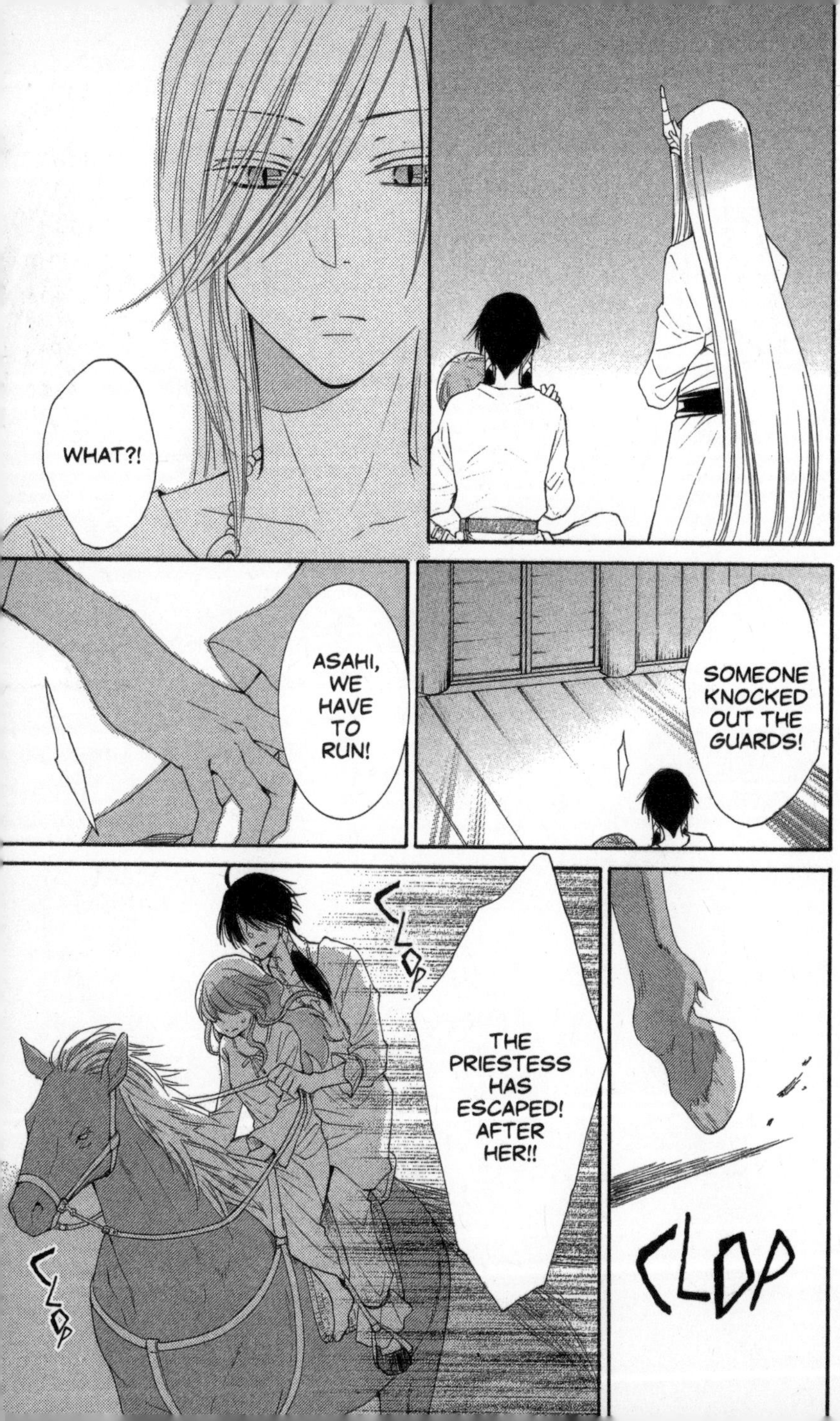
WHAT?!
SOMEONE KNOCKED OUT THE GUARDS!
ASAHI, WE HAVE TO RUN!
CLOP
THE PRIESTESS HAS ESCAPED! AFTER HER!!
CLOP
CLOP

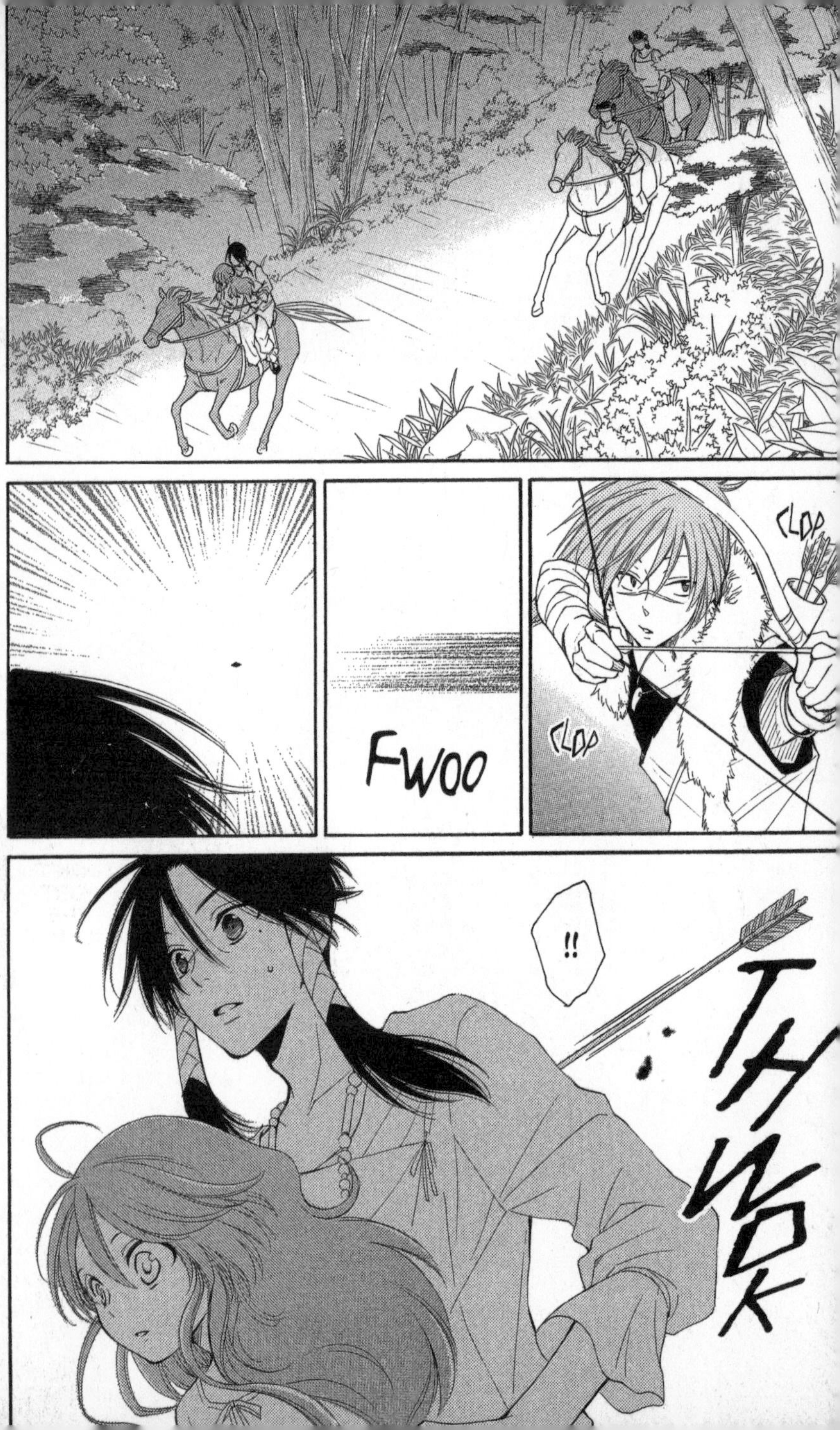
CLOP
CLOP
FWOO
!!
THWOK

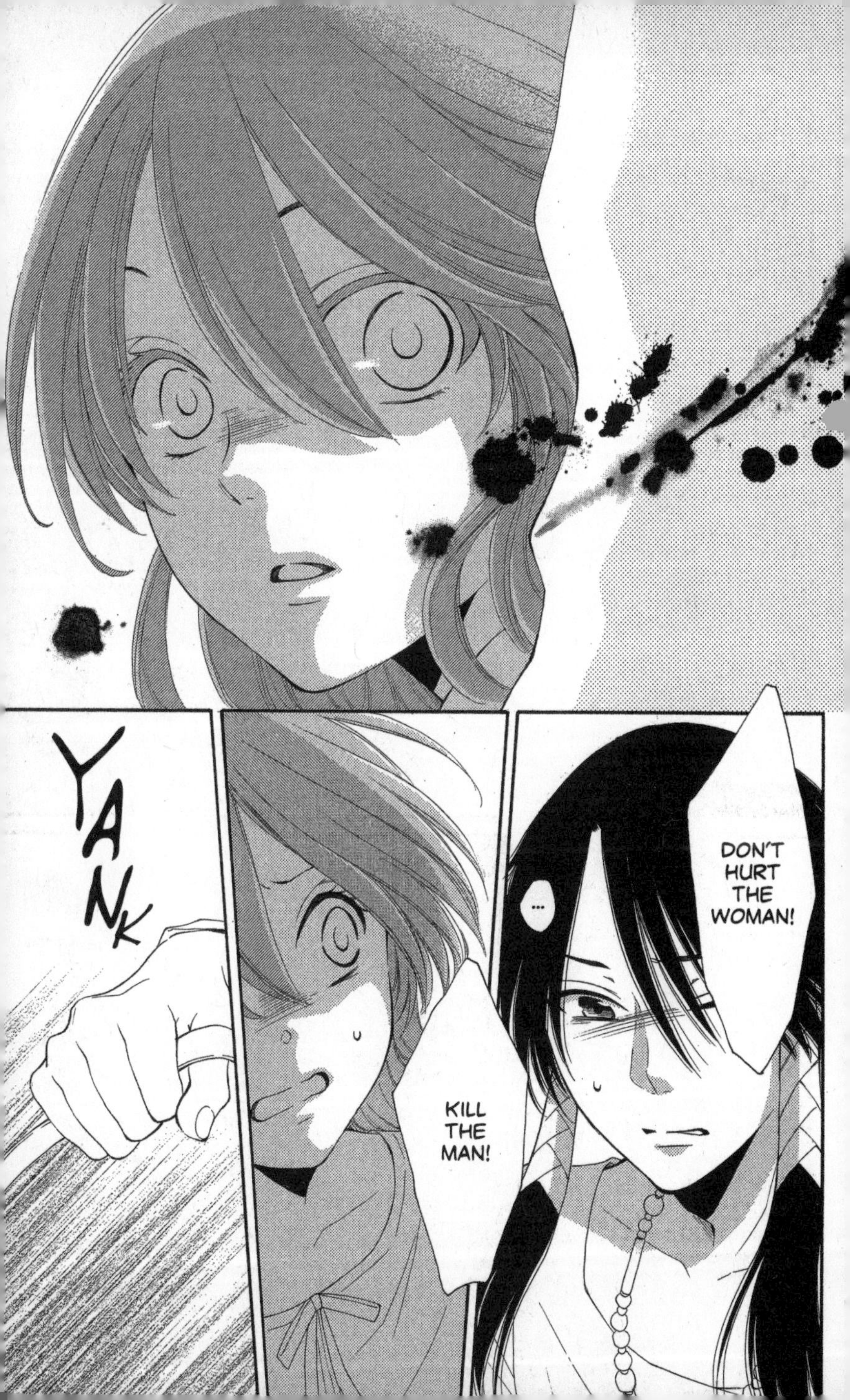

DON'T HURT THE WOMAN!
...
KILL THE MAN!
YANK

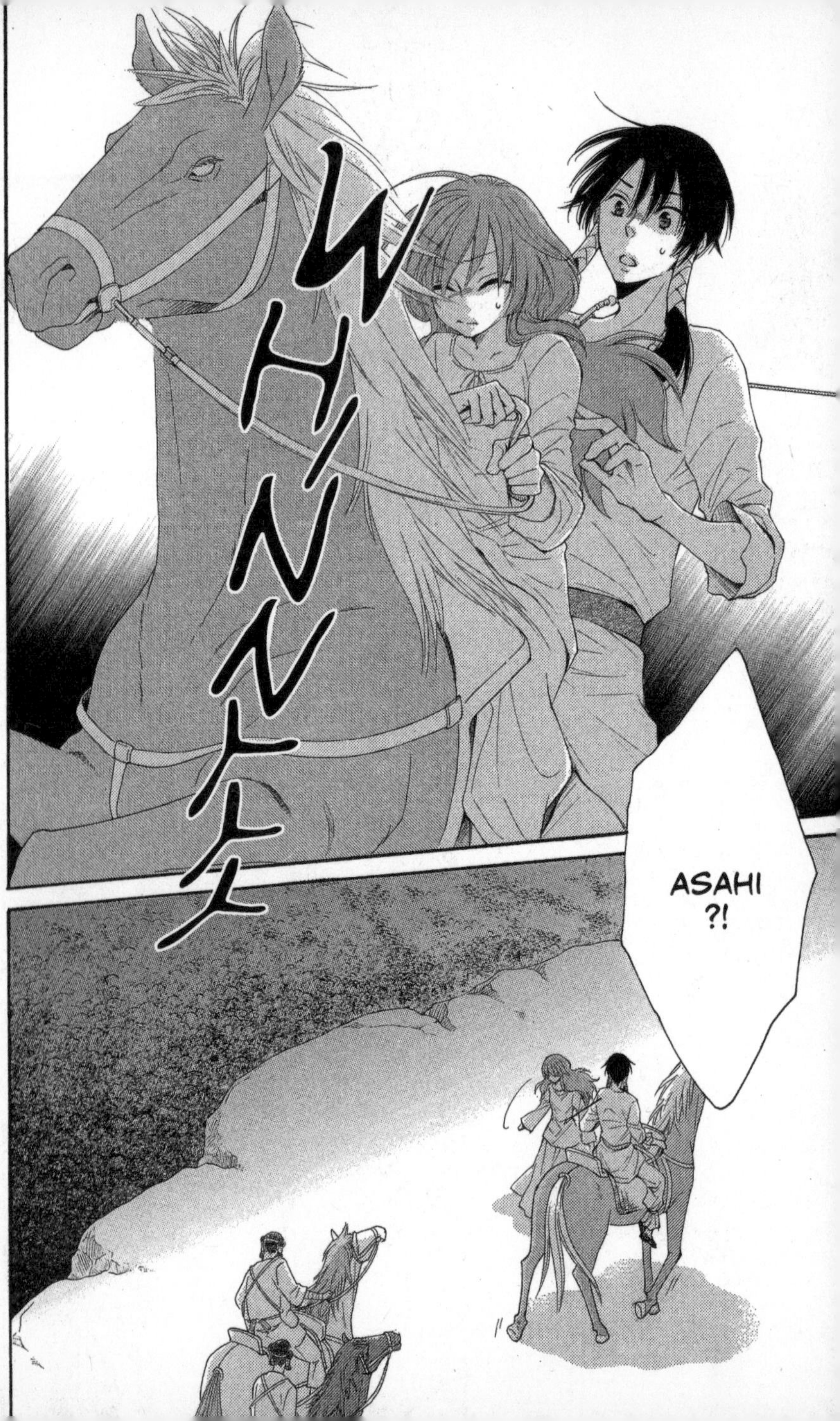
WHINNYYY
ASAHI ?!

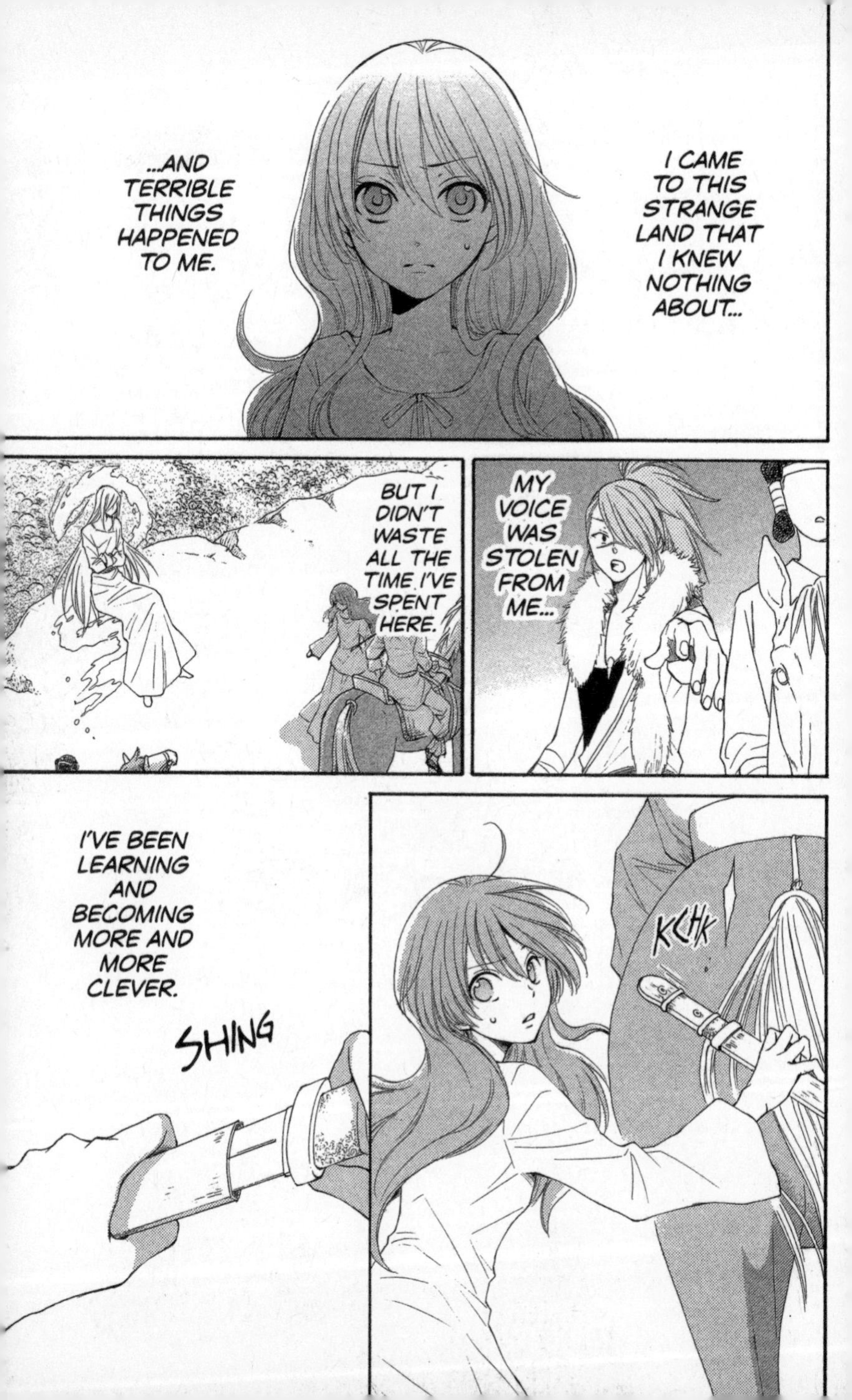
I CAME TO THIS STRANGE LAND THAT I KNEW NOTHING ABOUT...
...AND TERRIBLE THINGS HAPPENED TO ME.
MY VOICE WAS STOLEN FROM ME...
BUT I DIDN'T WASTE ALL THE TIME I'VE SPENT HERE.
KCHK
I'VE BEEN LEARNING AND BECOMING MORE AND MORE CLEVER.
SHING

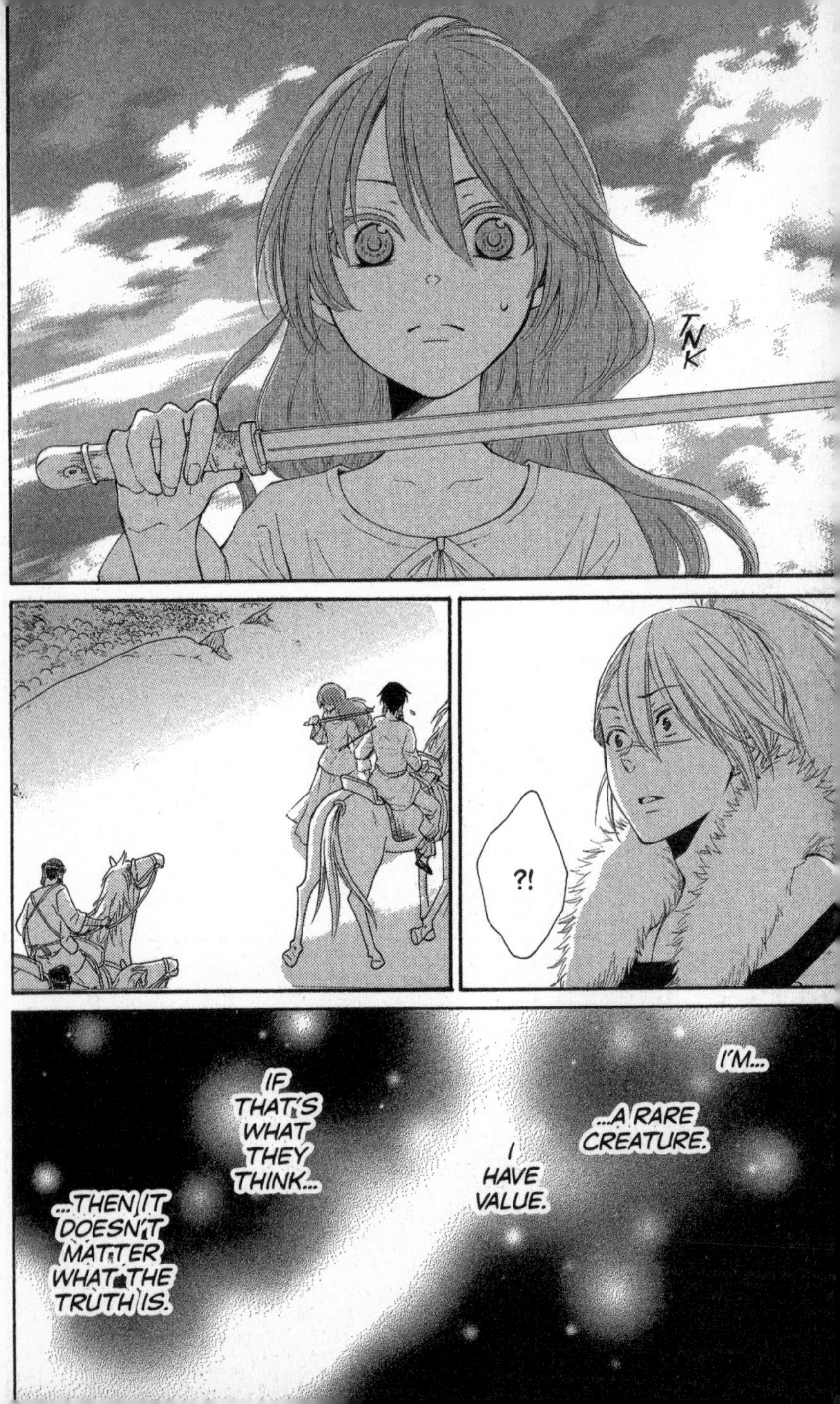
TNK
?!
I'M...
...A RARE CREATURE.
I HAVE VALUE.
IF THAT'S WHAT THEY THINK...
...THEN IT DOESN'T MATTER WHAT THE TRUTH IS.

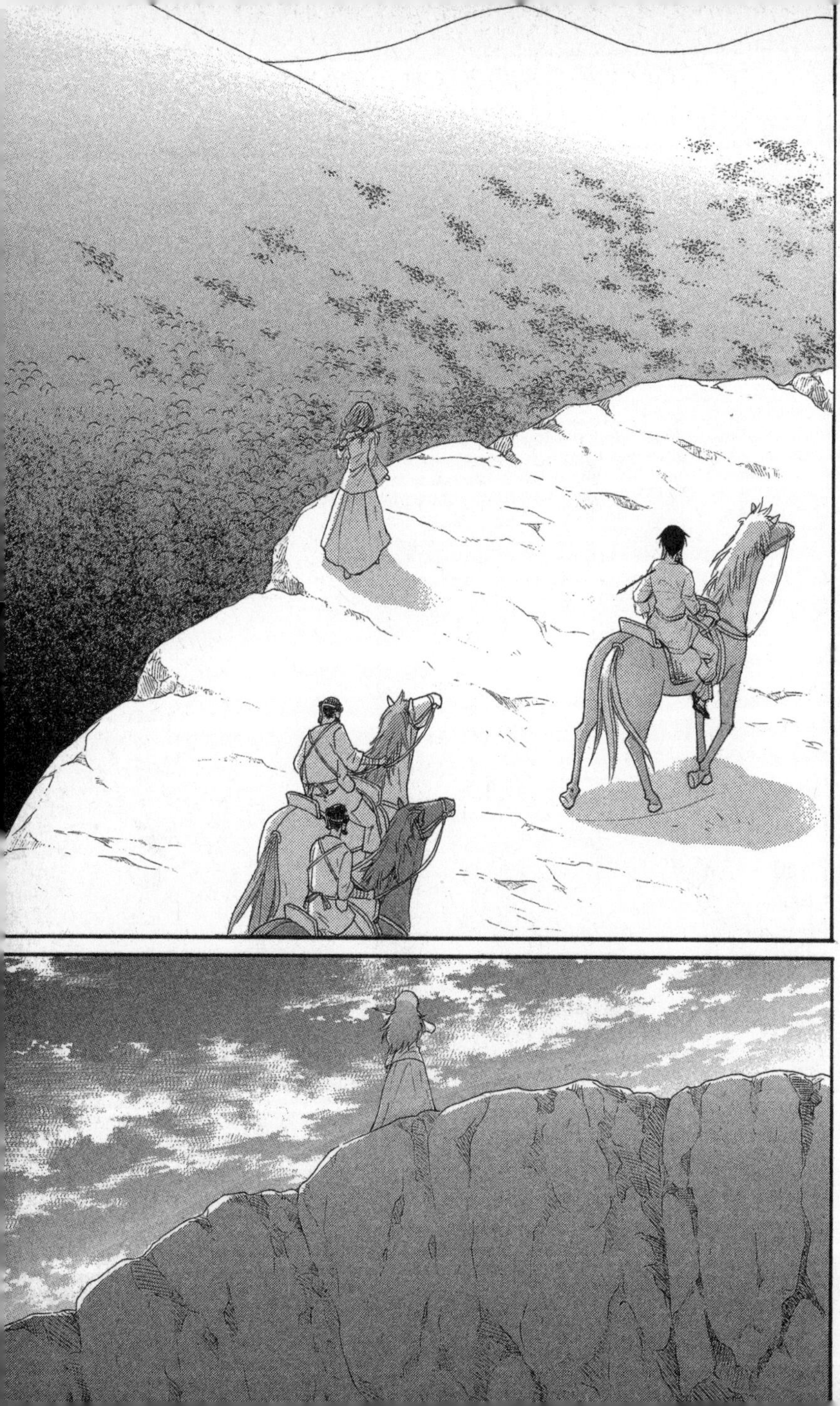

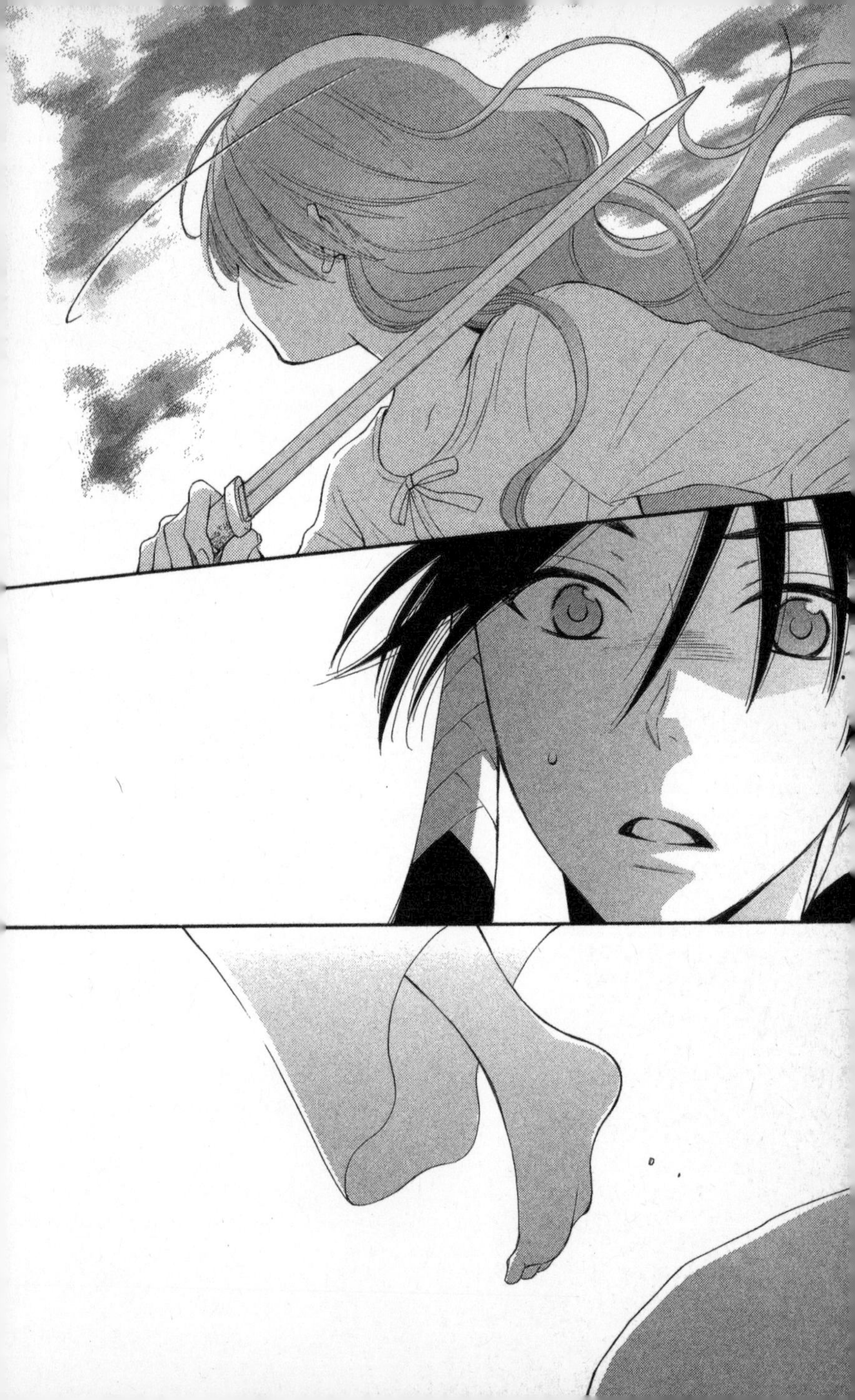

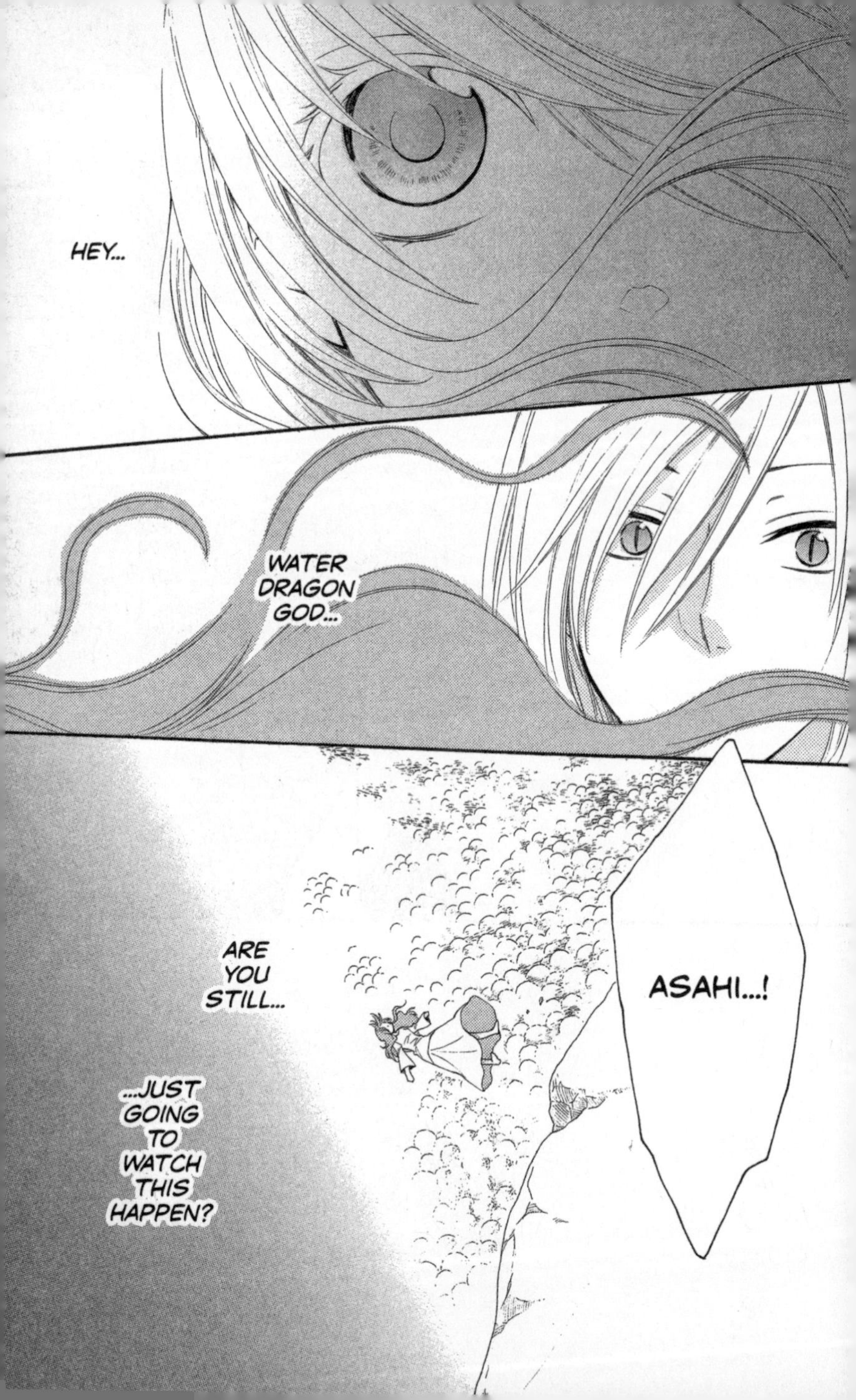
HEY...
WATER DRAGON GOD...
ASAHI...!
ARE YOU STILL...
...JUST GOING TO WATCH THIS HAPPEN?

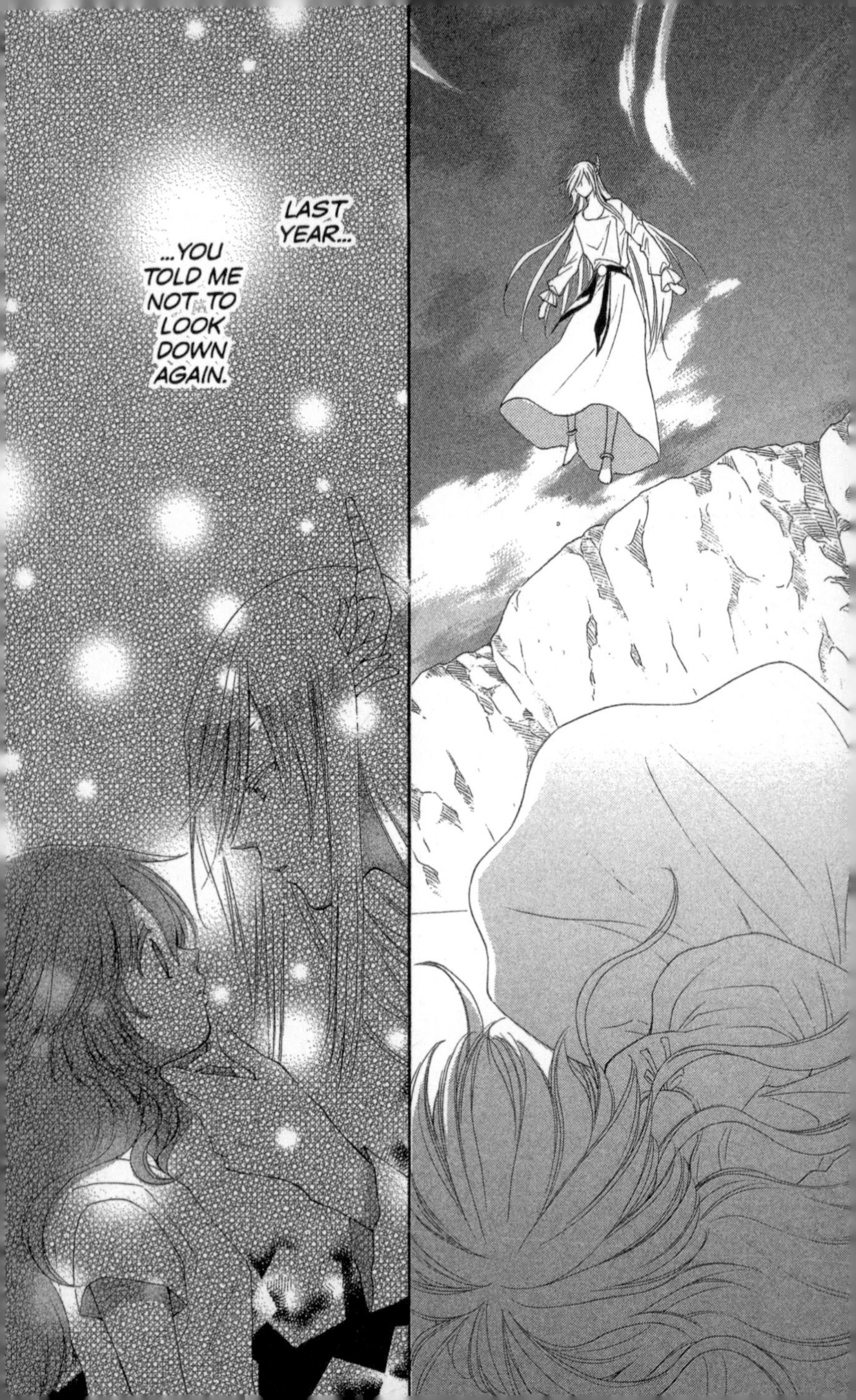
LAST YEAR...
...YOU TOLD ME NOT TO LOOK DOWN AGAIN.

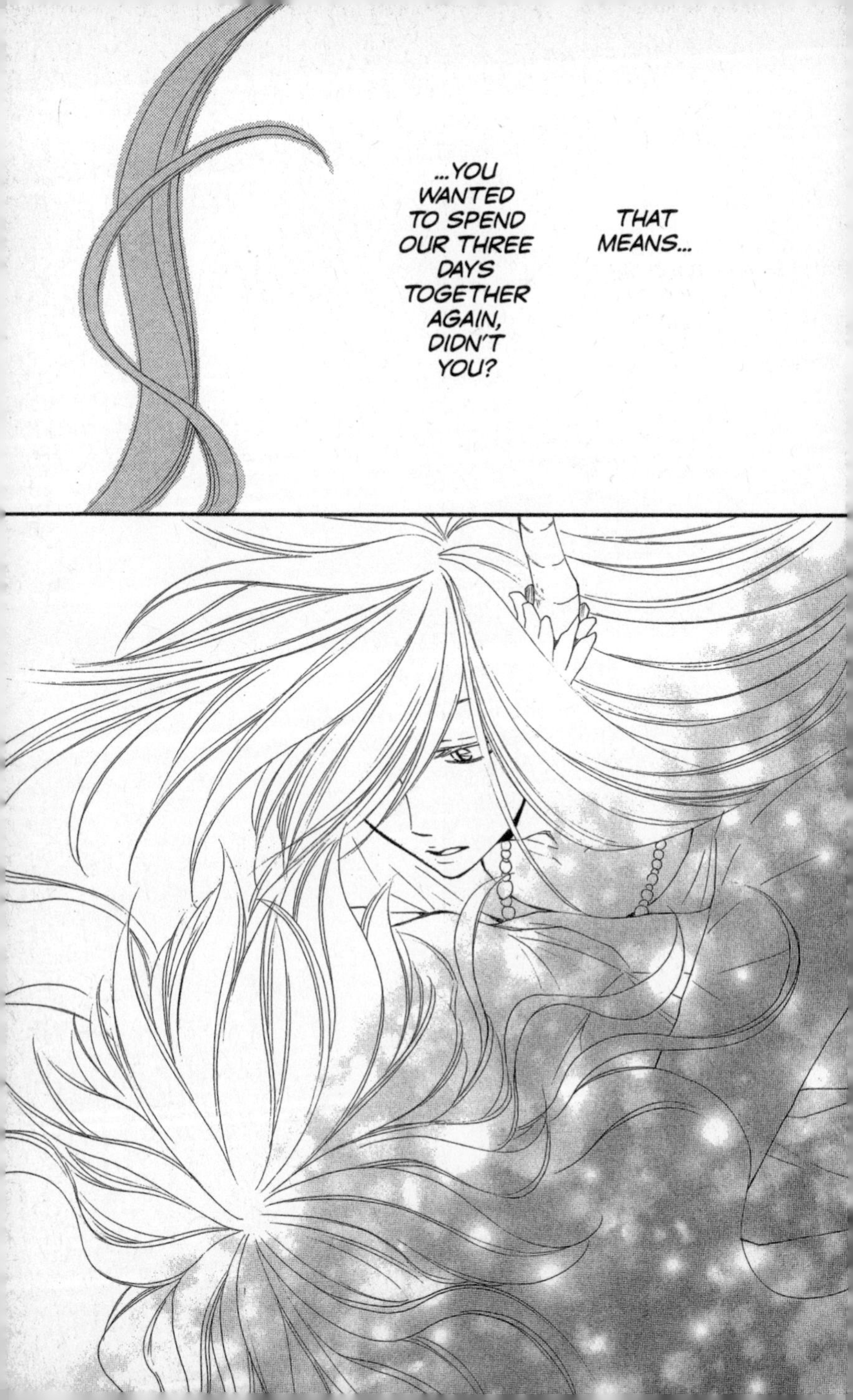
THAT MEANS...
...YOU WANTED TO SPEND OUR THREE DAYS TOGETHER AGAIN, DIDN'T YOU?

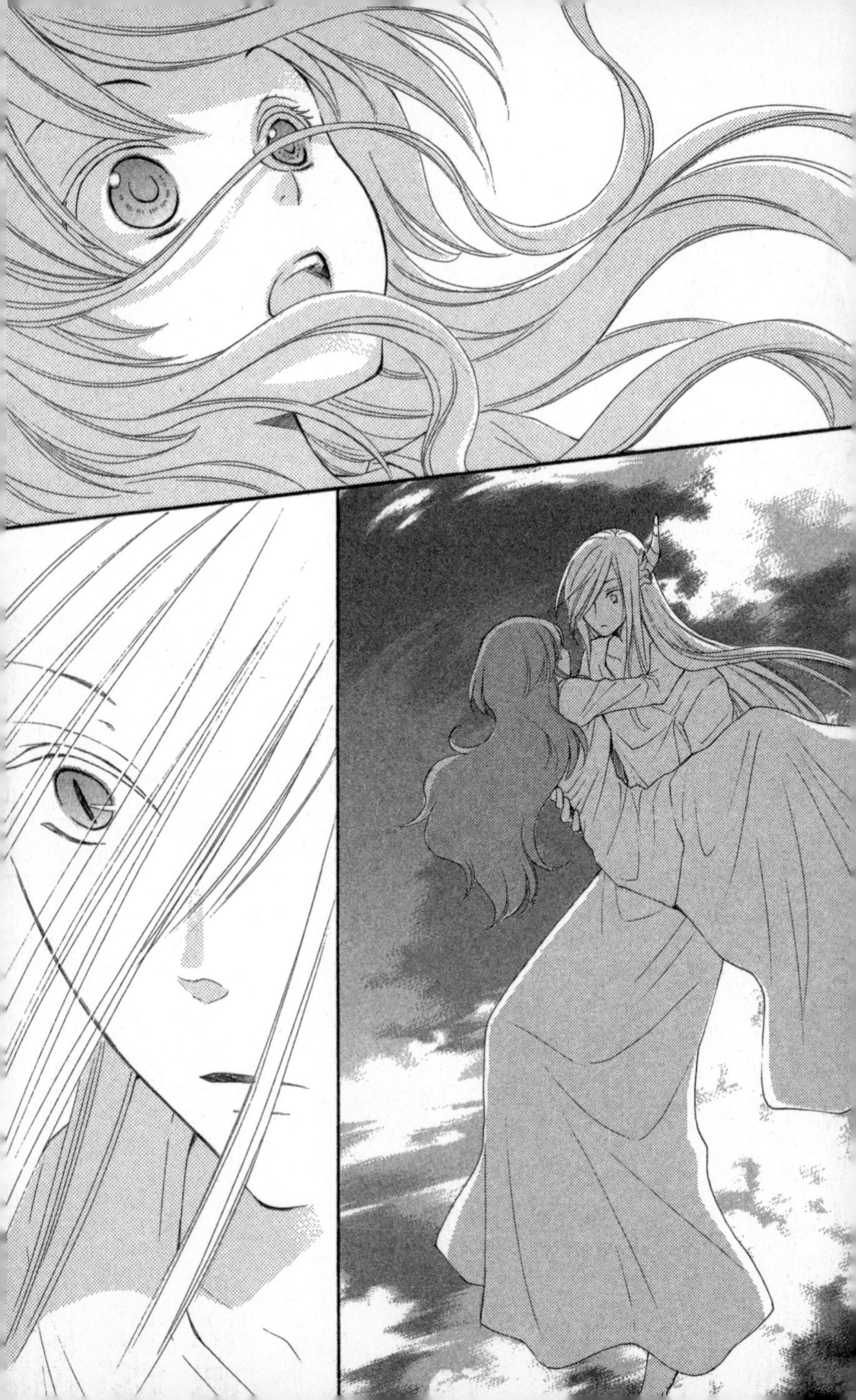

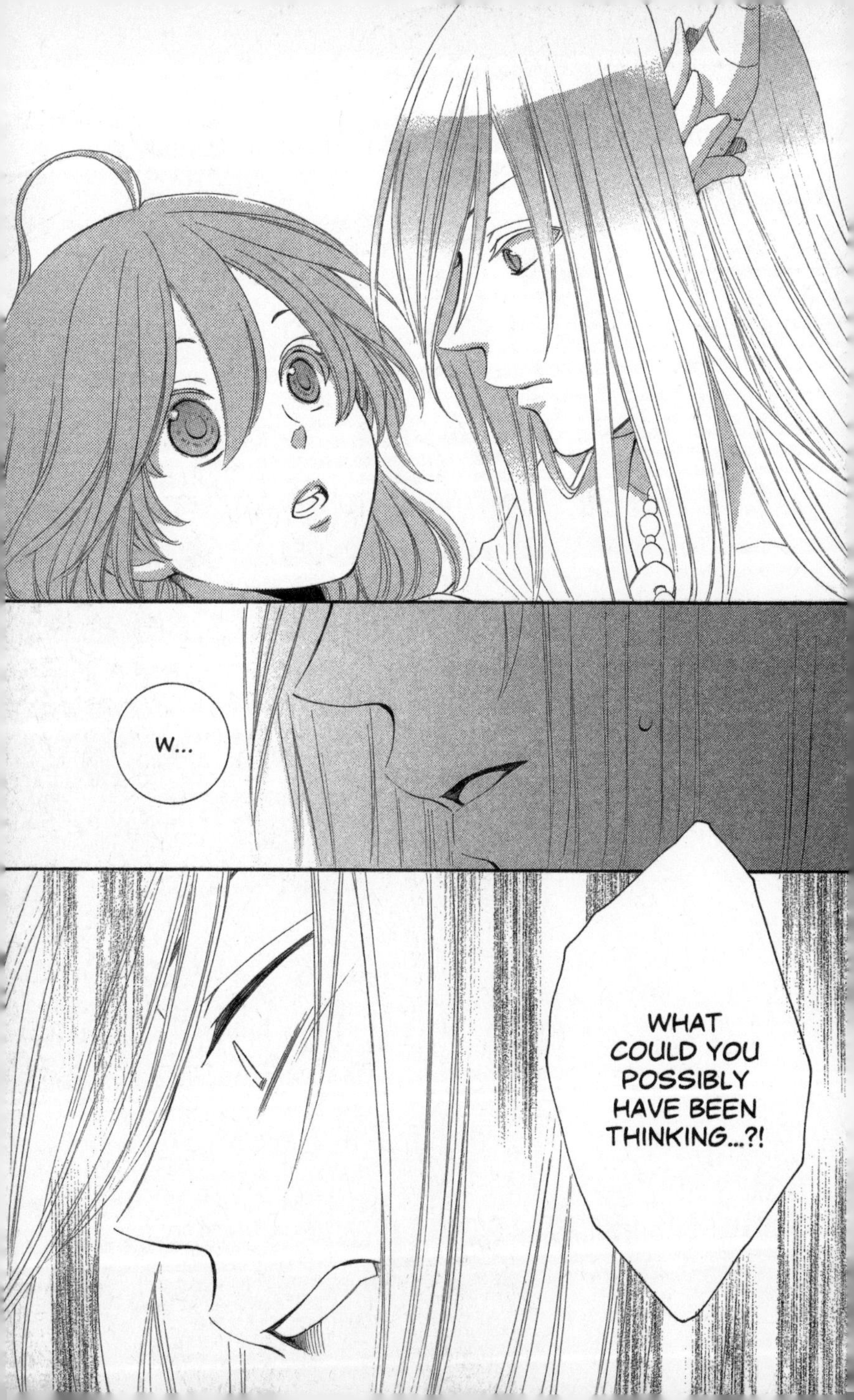
W...
WHAT COULD YOU POSSIBLY HAVE BEEN THINKING...?!

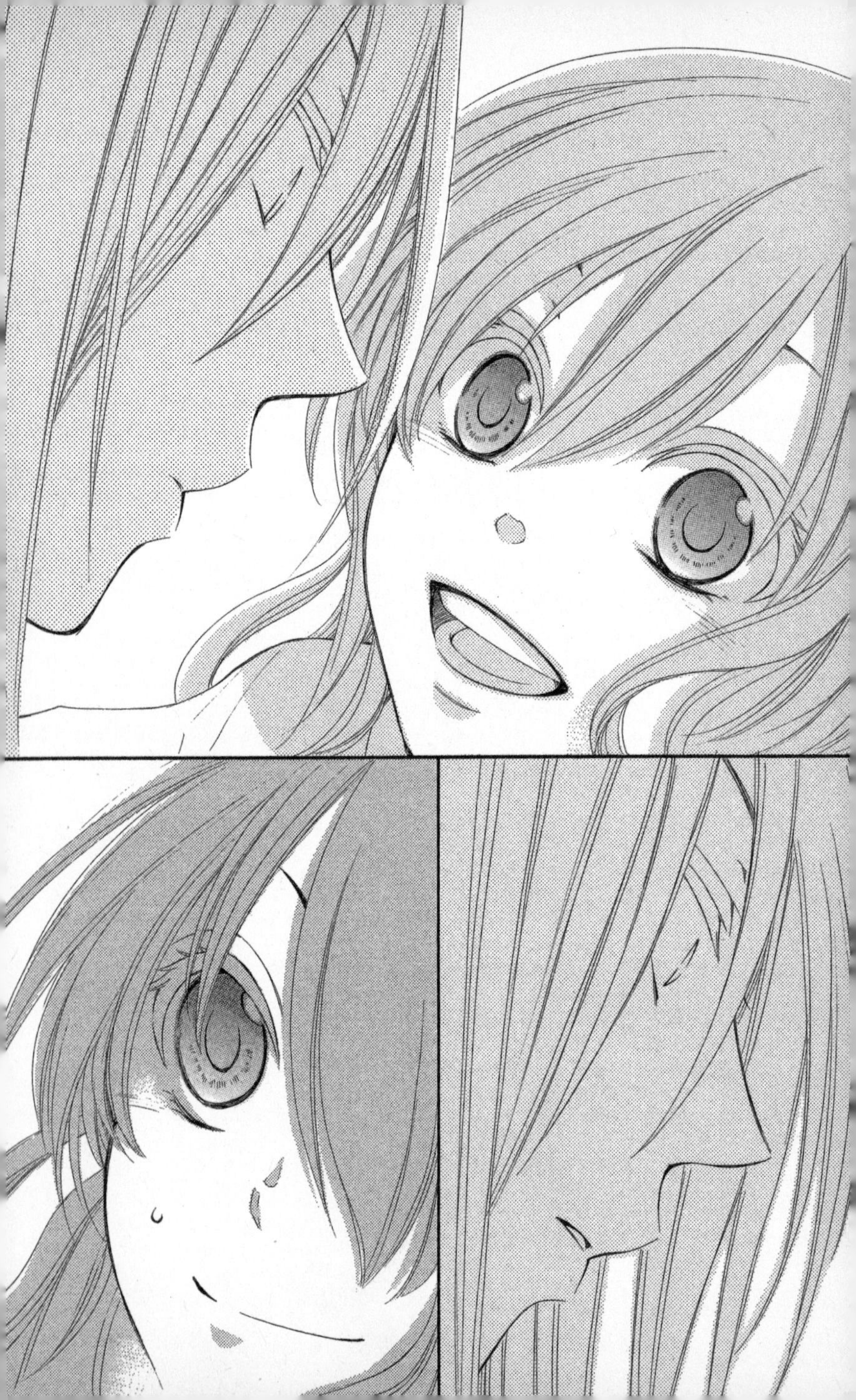

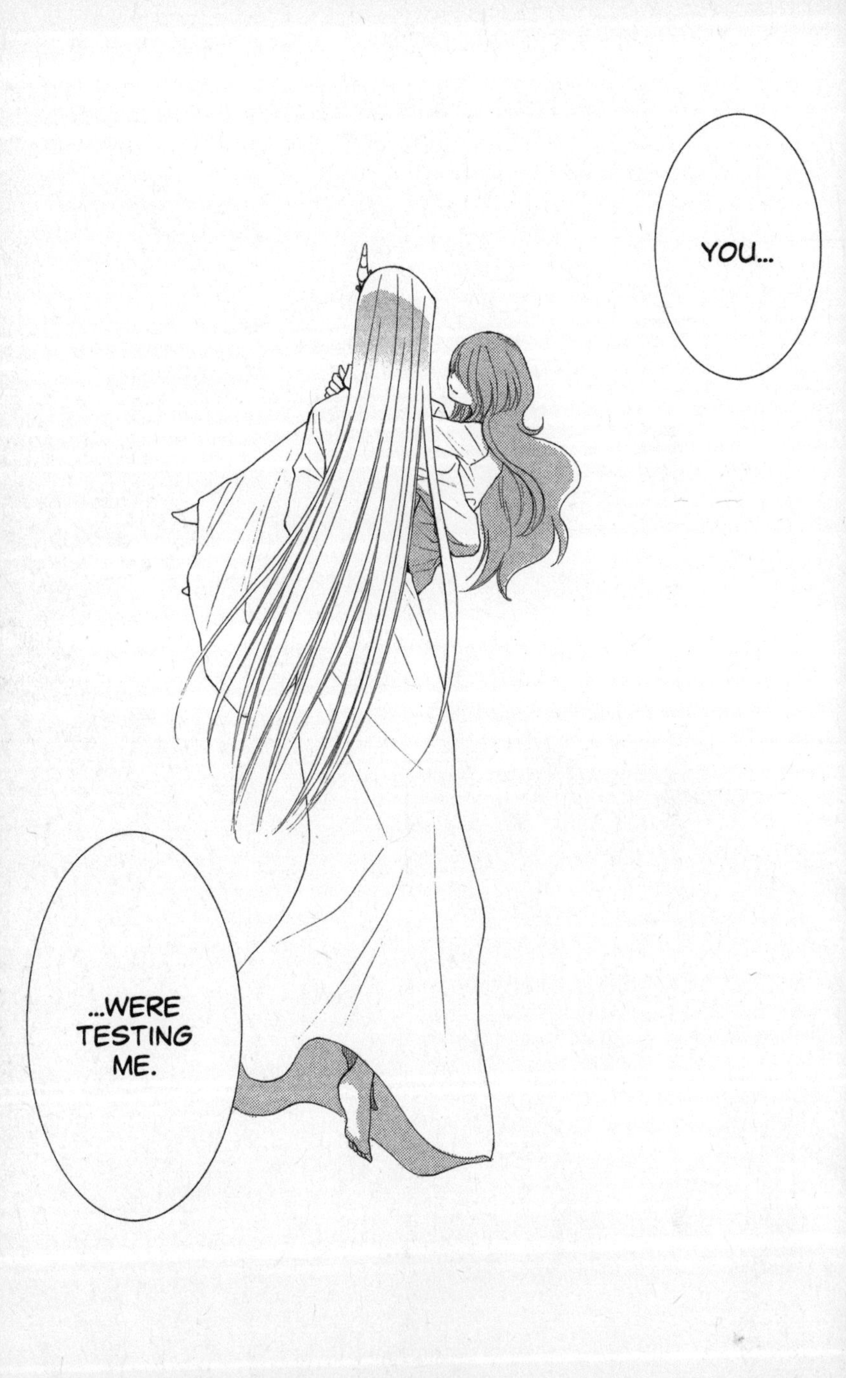
YOU...
...WERE TESTING ME.

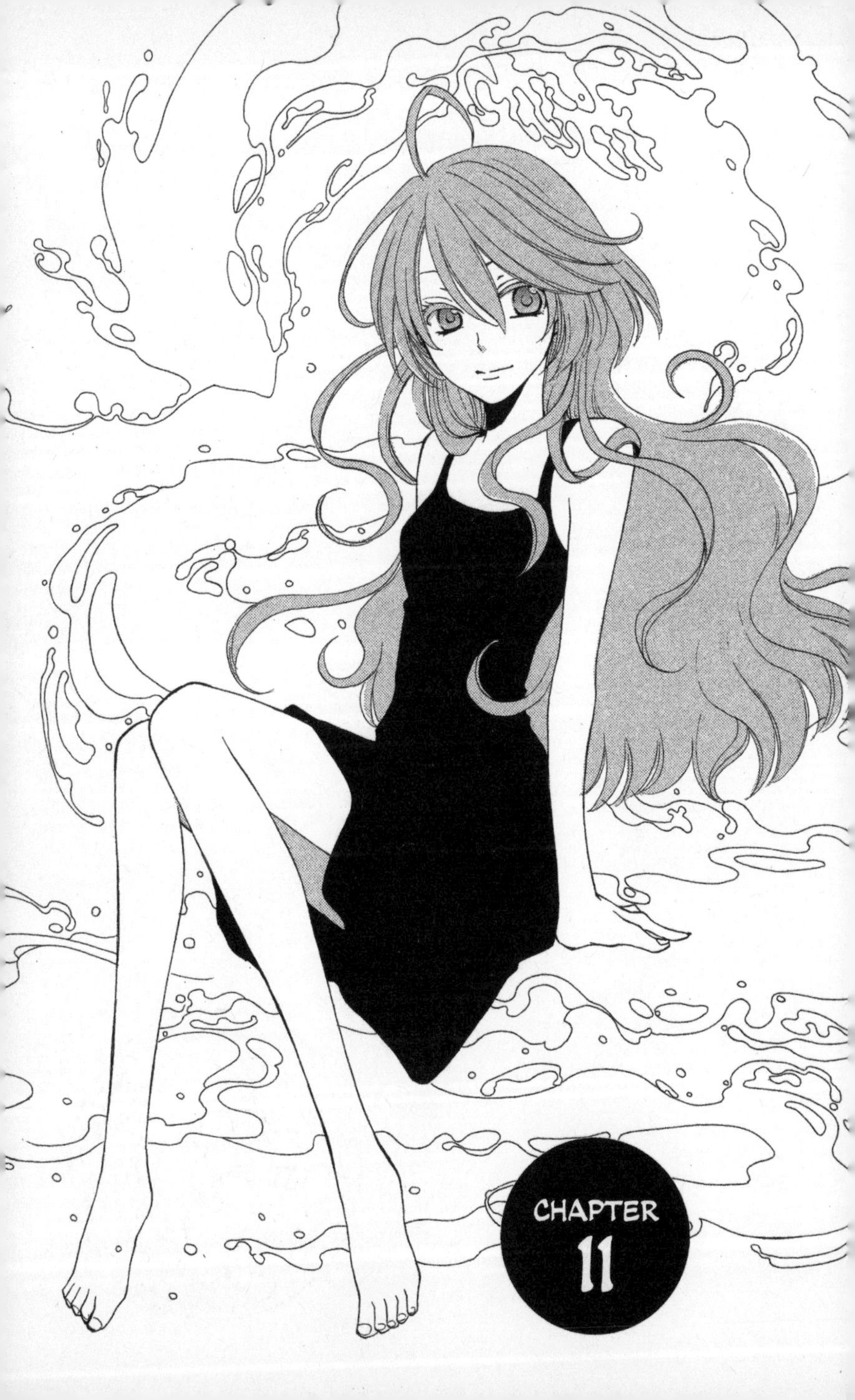
CHAPTER
11

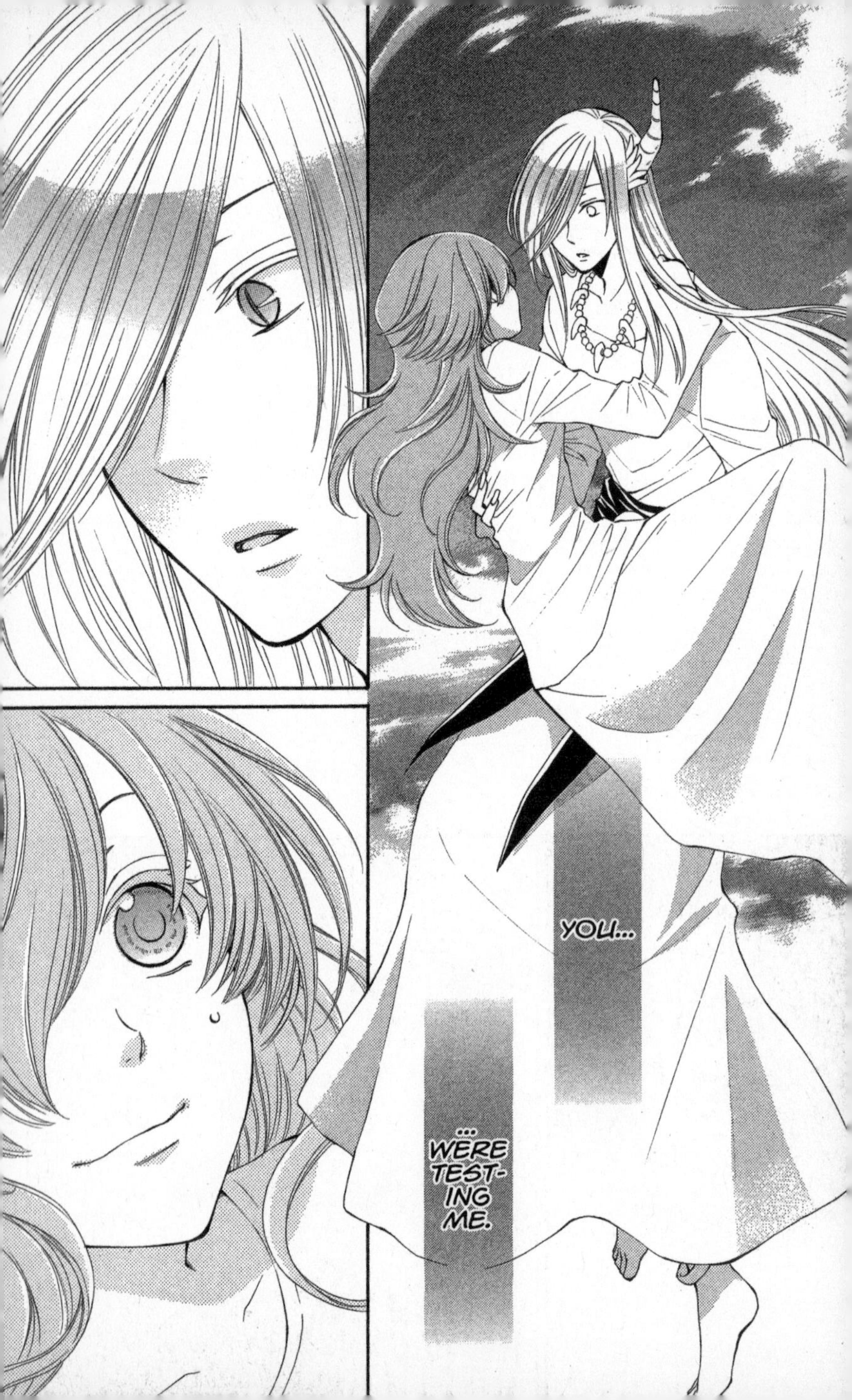
YOU...
...WERE TESTING ME.

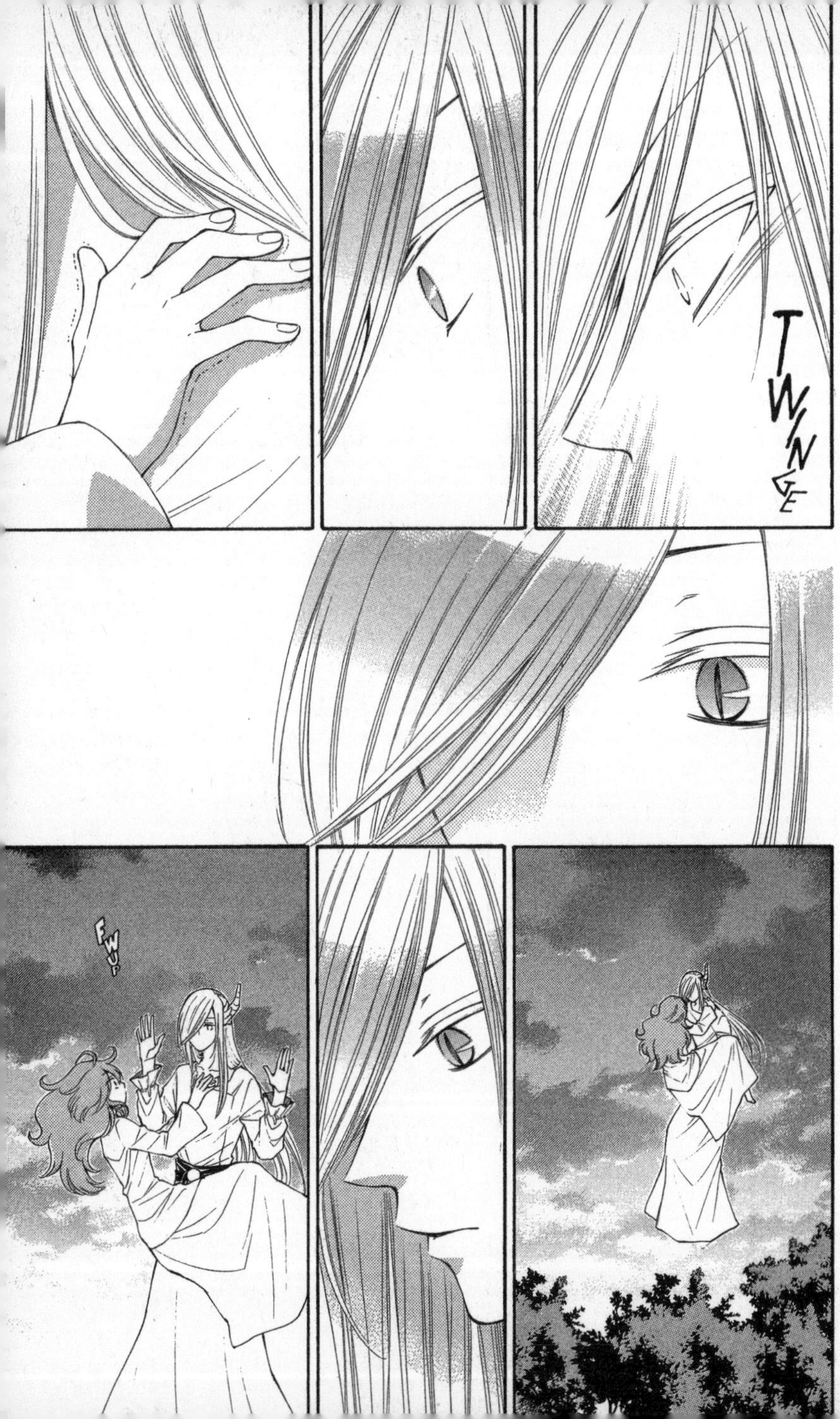
TWINGE
FWUP

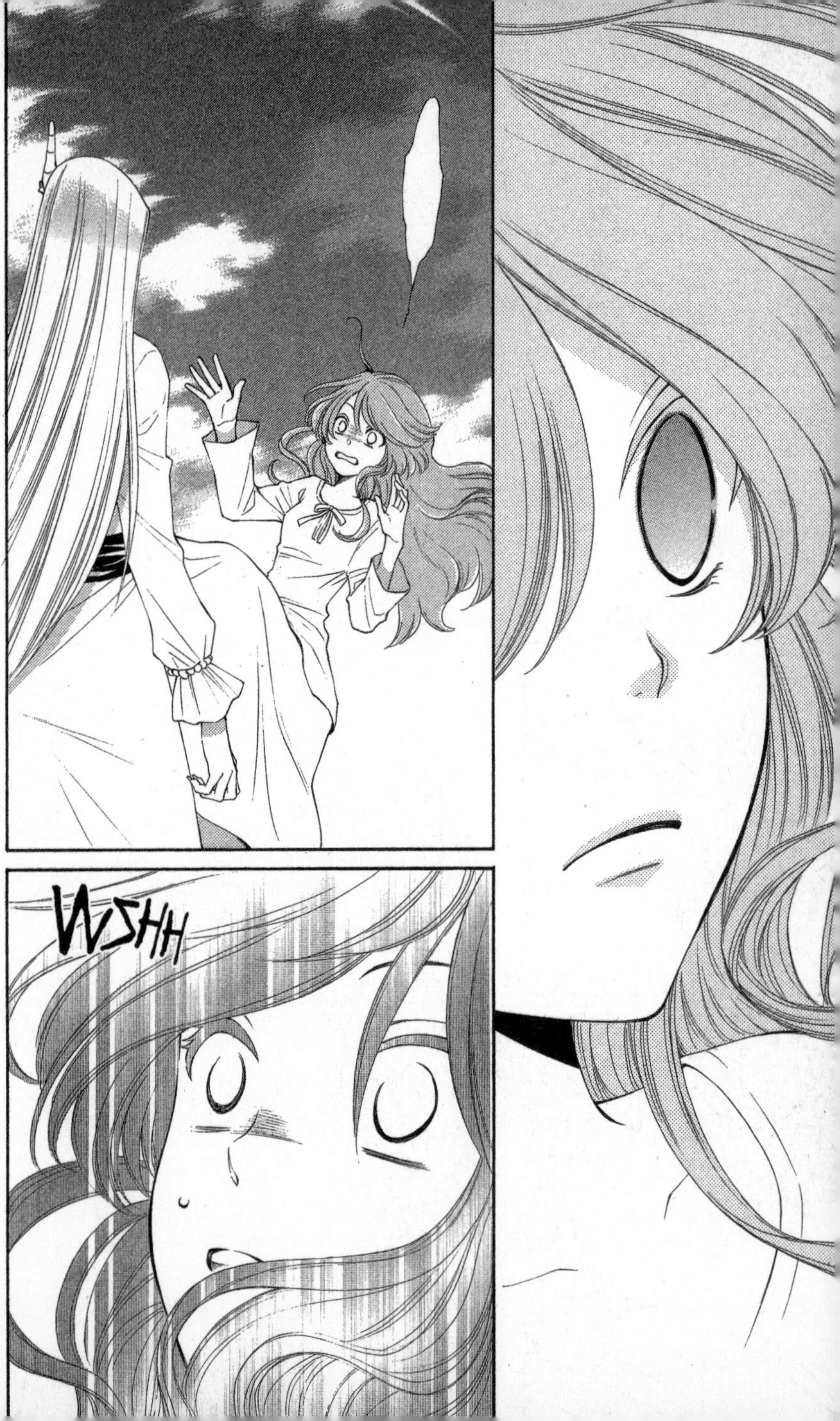
WSHH

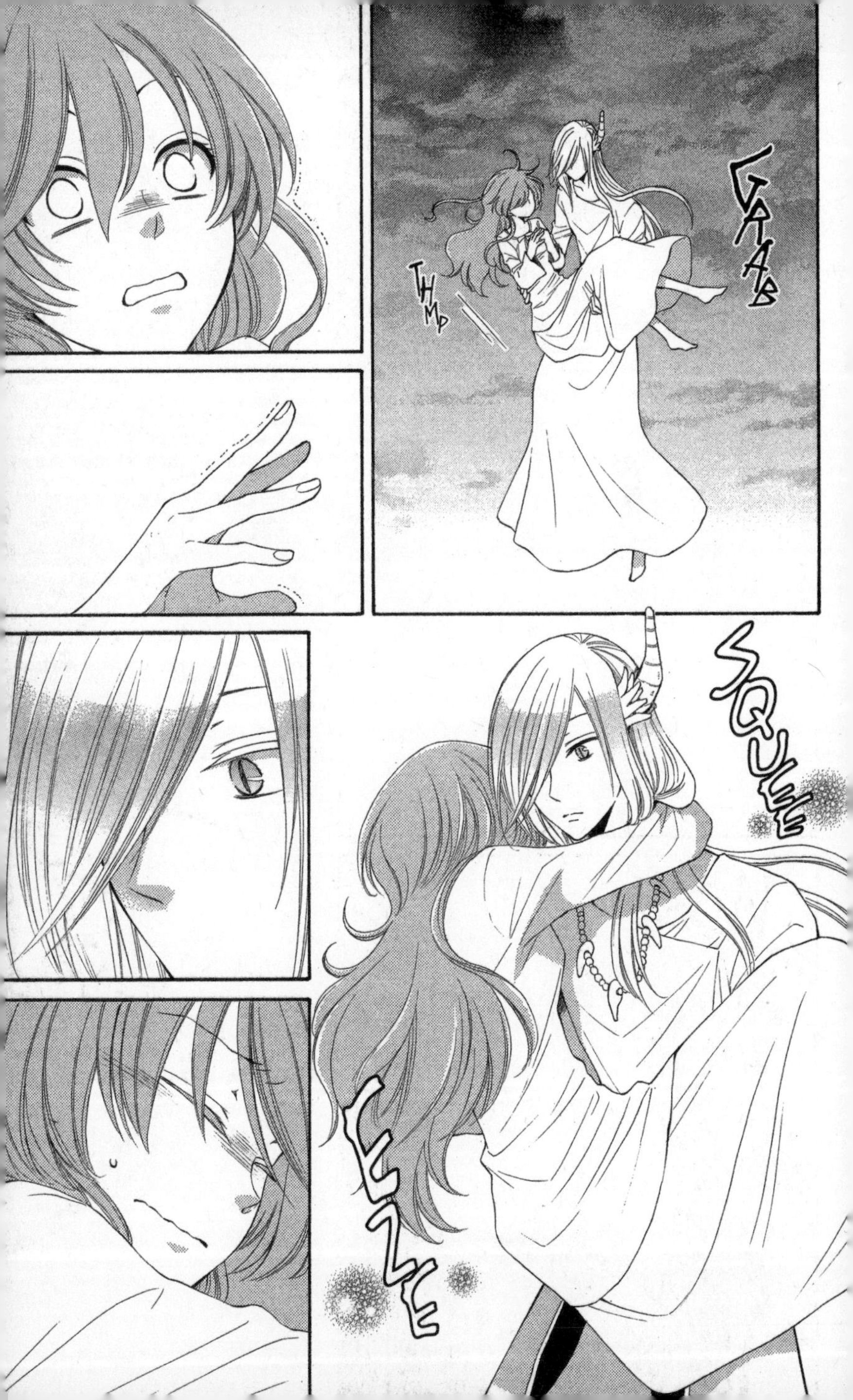
GRAB
THMP
SQUEE
EEZZE

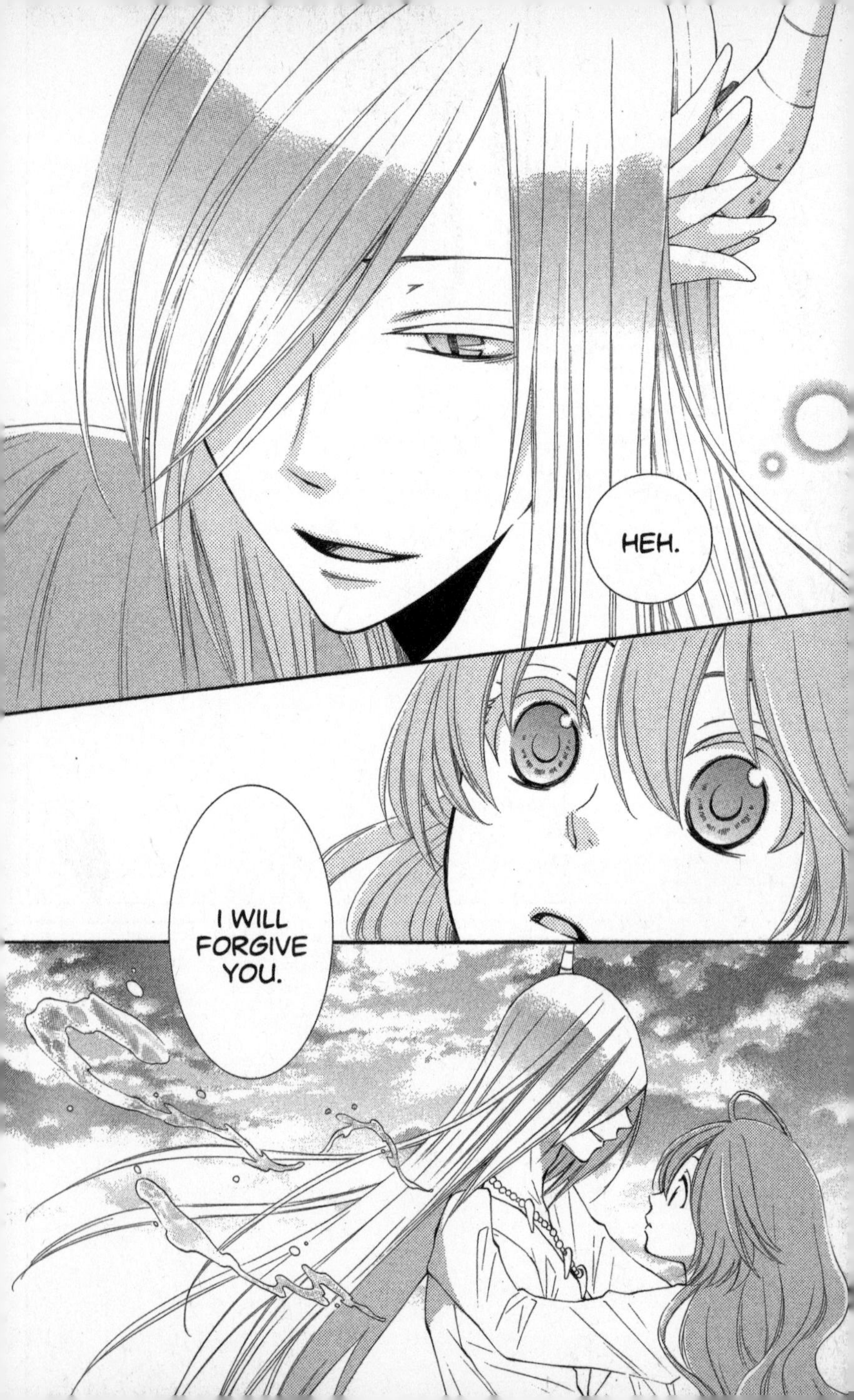
HEH.
I WILL FORGIVE YOU.

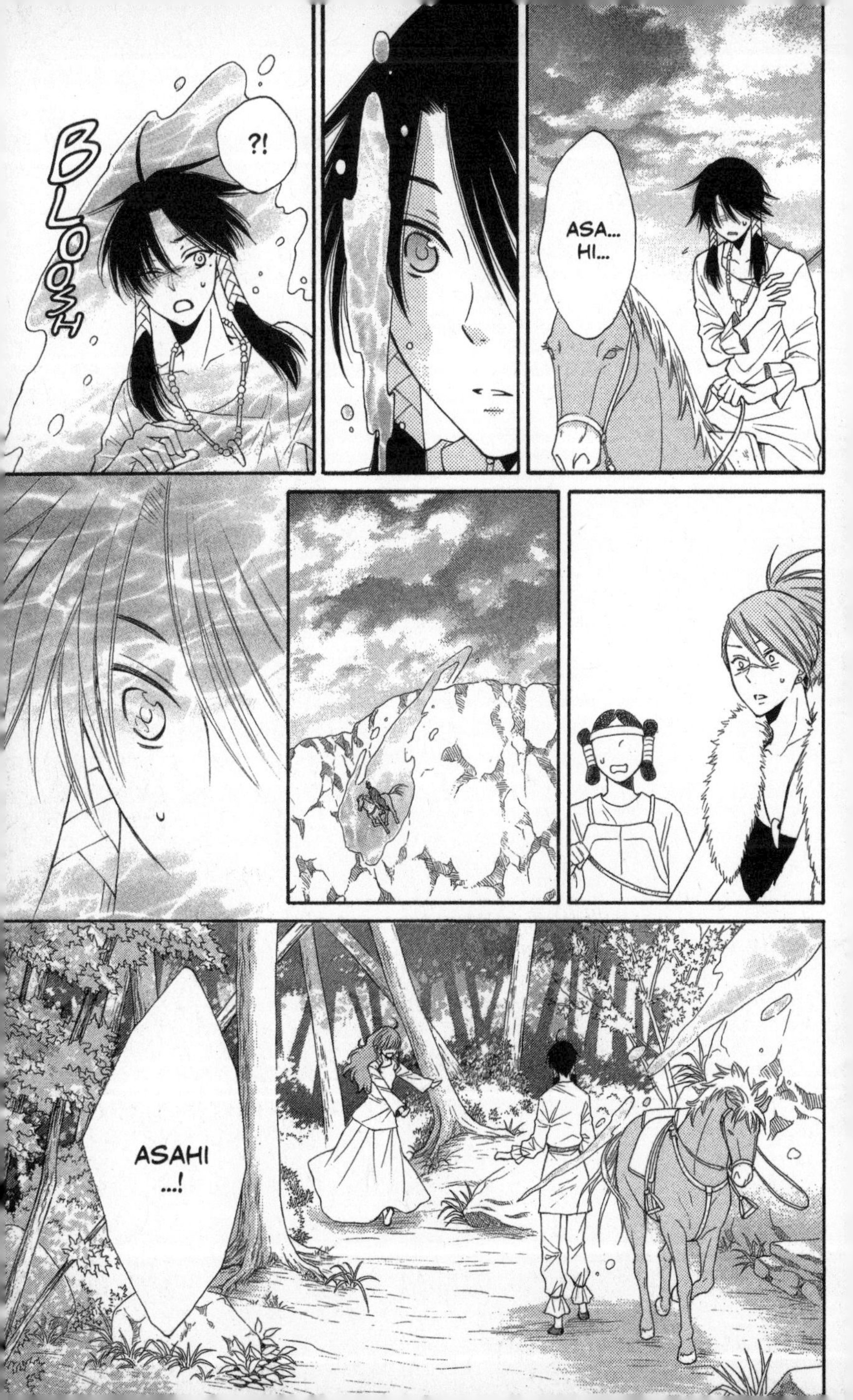
ASA... HI...
?!
BLOOSH
ASAHI ...!

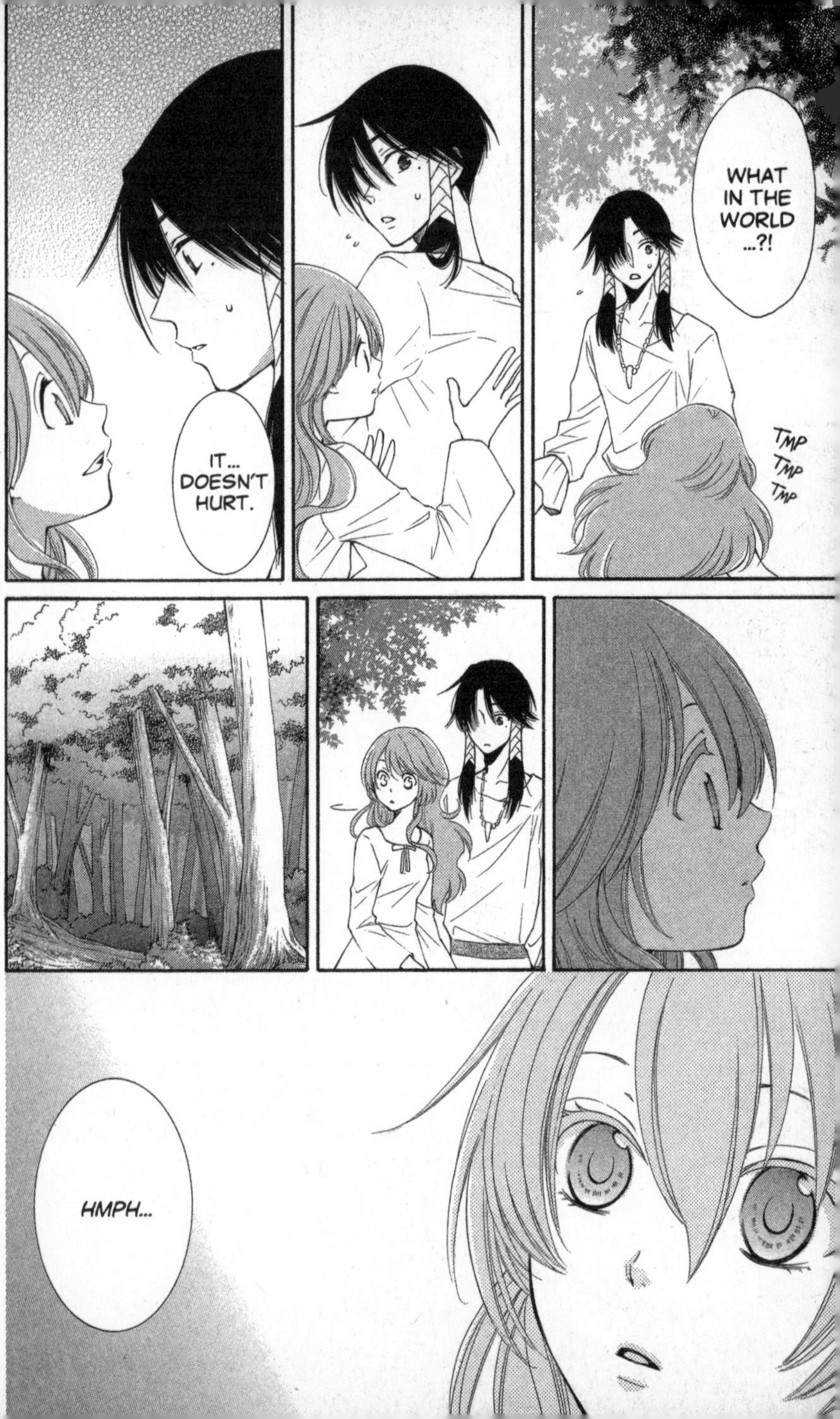
WHAT IN THE WORLD ...?!
TMP TMP TMP
IT... DOESN'T HURT.
HMPH...

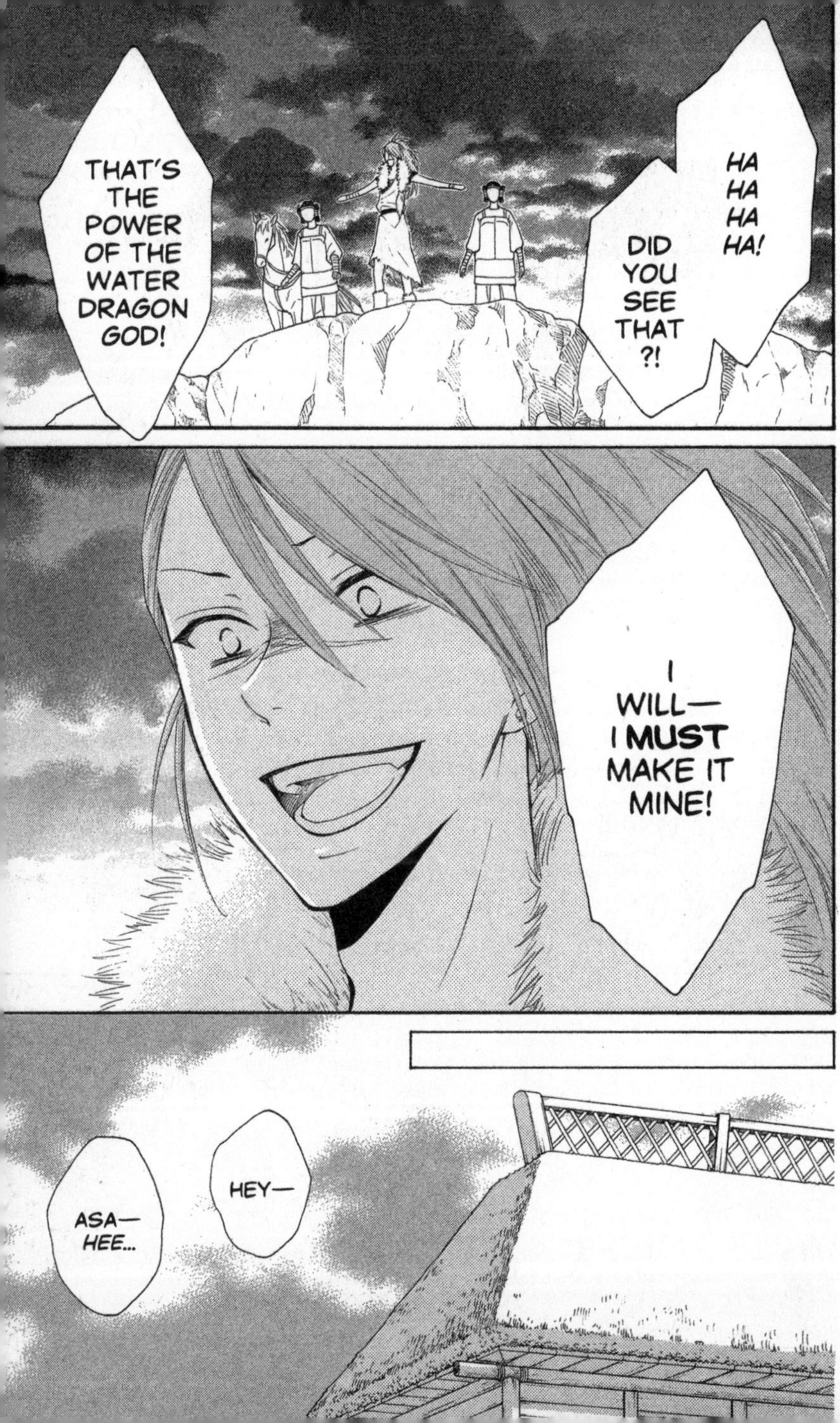
HA HA HA HA!
DID YOU SEE THAT?!
THAT'S THE POWER OF THE WATER DRAGON GOD!
I WILL— I MUST MAKE IT MINE!
HEY—
ASA— HEE...

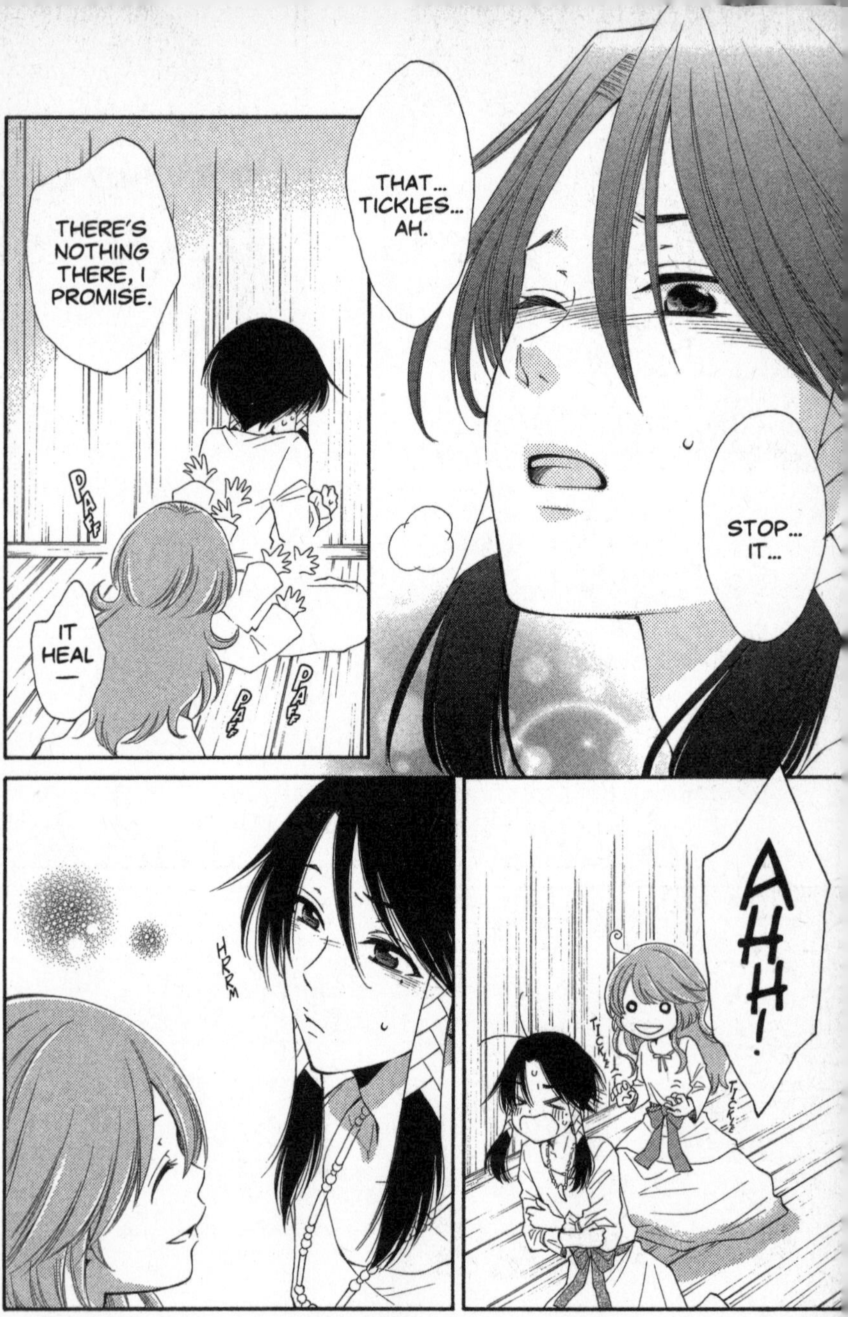
THAT... TICKLES... AH.
STOP... IT...
THERE'S NOTHING THERE, I PROMISE.
PAFF
IT HEAL—
PAFF
PAFF
AHH!
TICKLE
TICKLE
HRRM

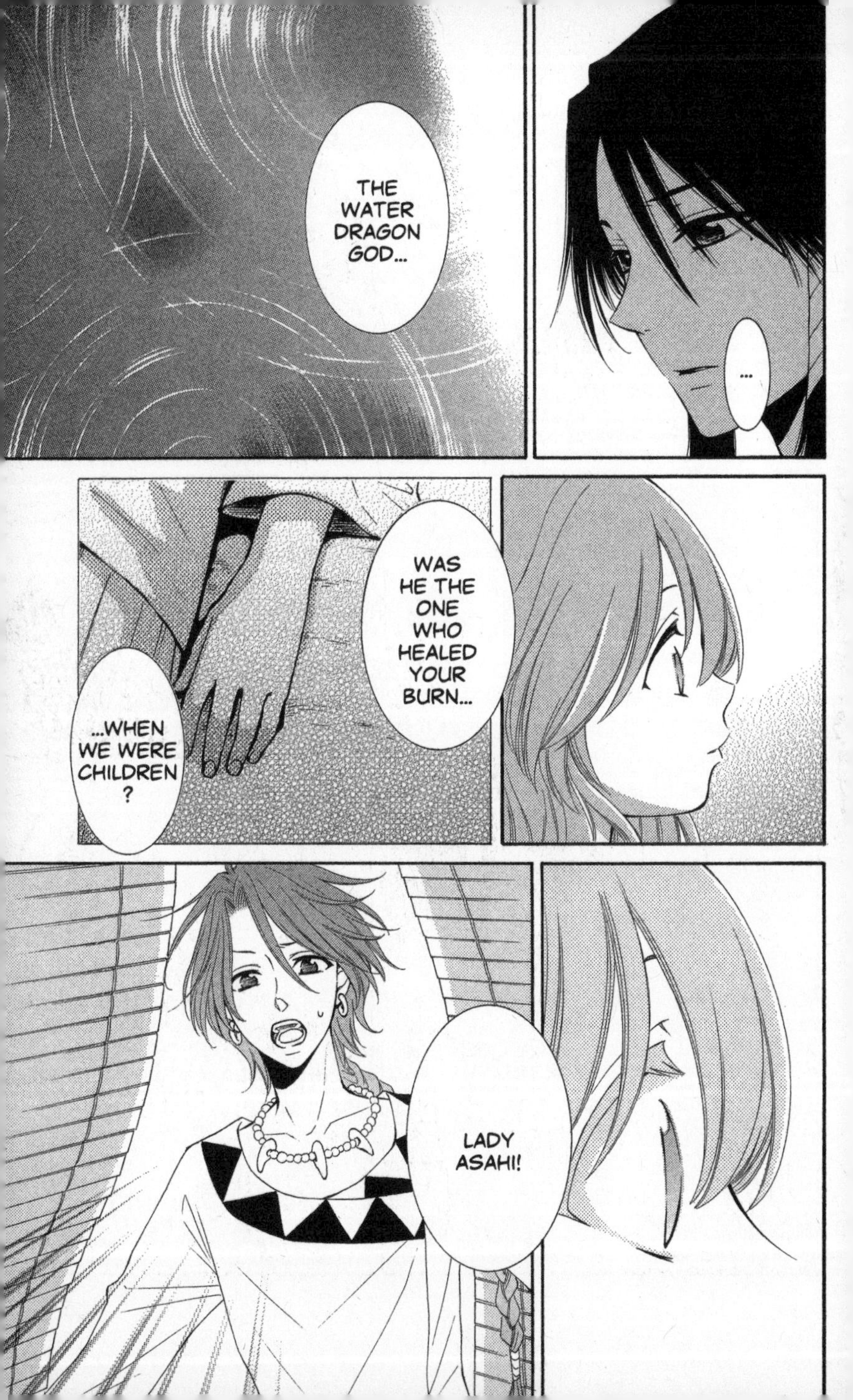
...
THE WATER DRAGON GOD...
WAS HE THE ONE WHO HEALED YOUR BURN...
...WHEN WE WERE CHILDREN?
LADY ASAHI!

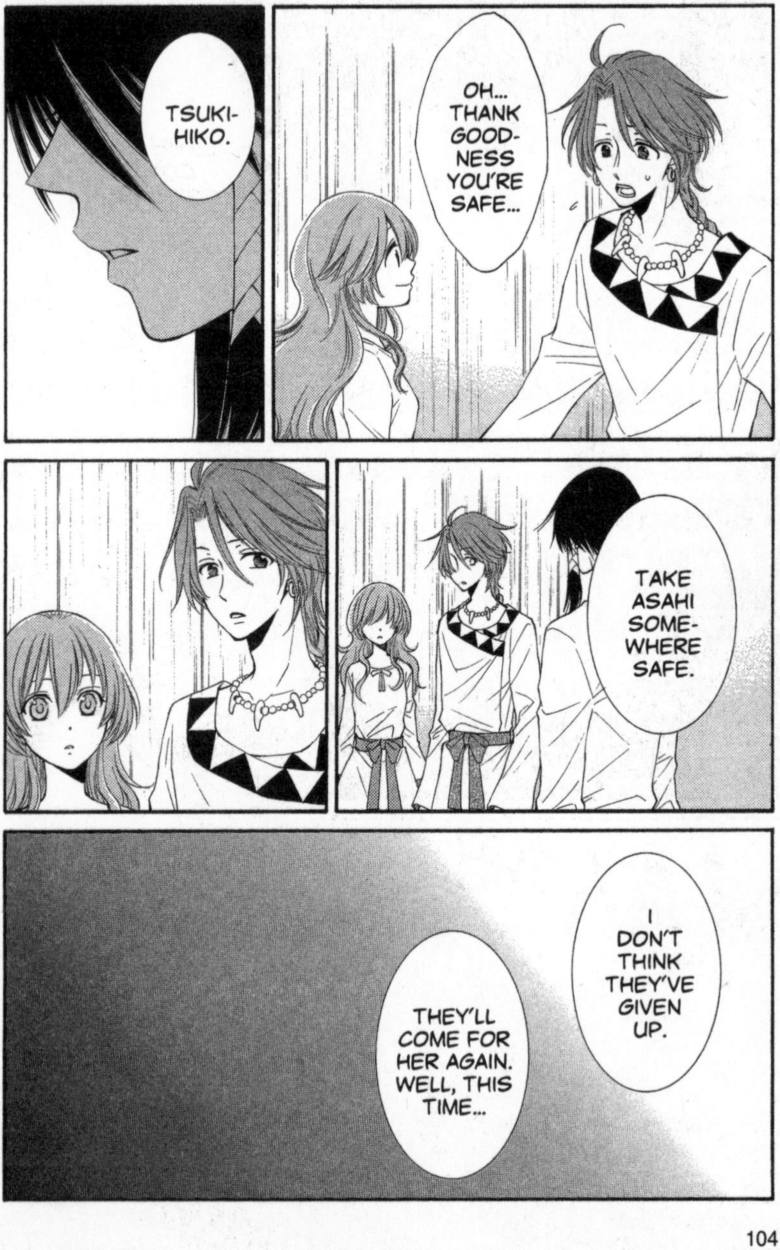
OH... THANK GOOD-NESS YOU'RE SAFE...
TSUKI-HIKO.
TAKE ASAHI SOME-WHERE SAFE.
I DON'T THINK THEY'VE GIVEN UP.
THEY'LL COME FOR HER AGAIN. WELL, THIS TIME...

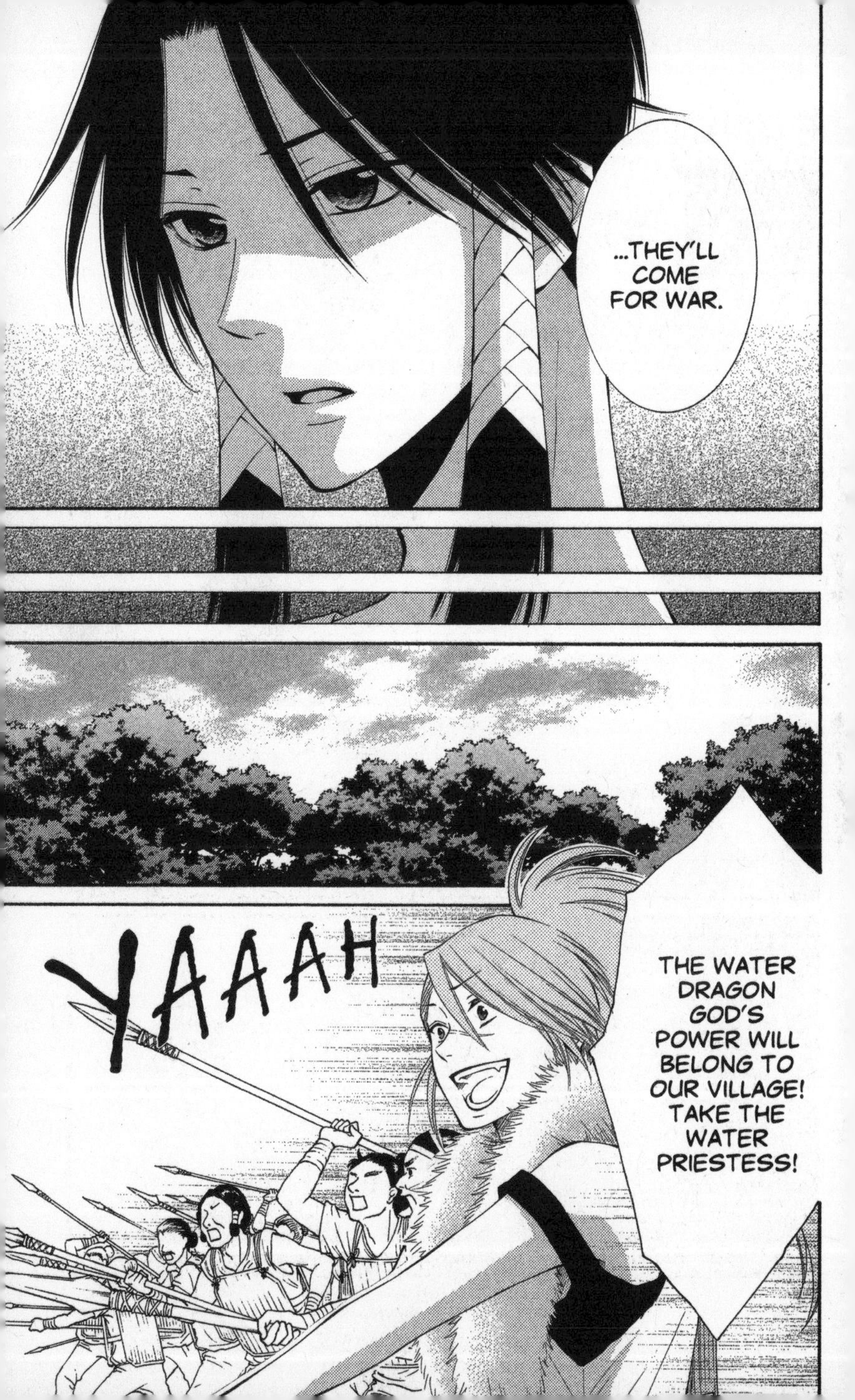
...THEY'LL COME FOR WAR.
THE WATER DRAGON GOD'S POWER WILL BELONG TO OUR VILLAGE! TAKE THE WATER PRIESTESS!
YAAAH

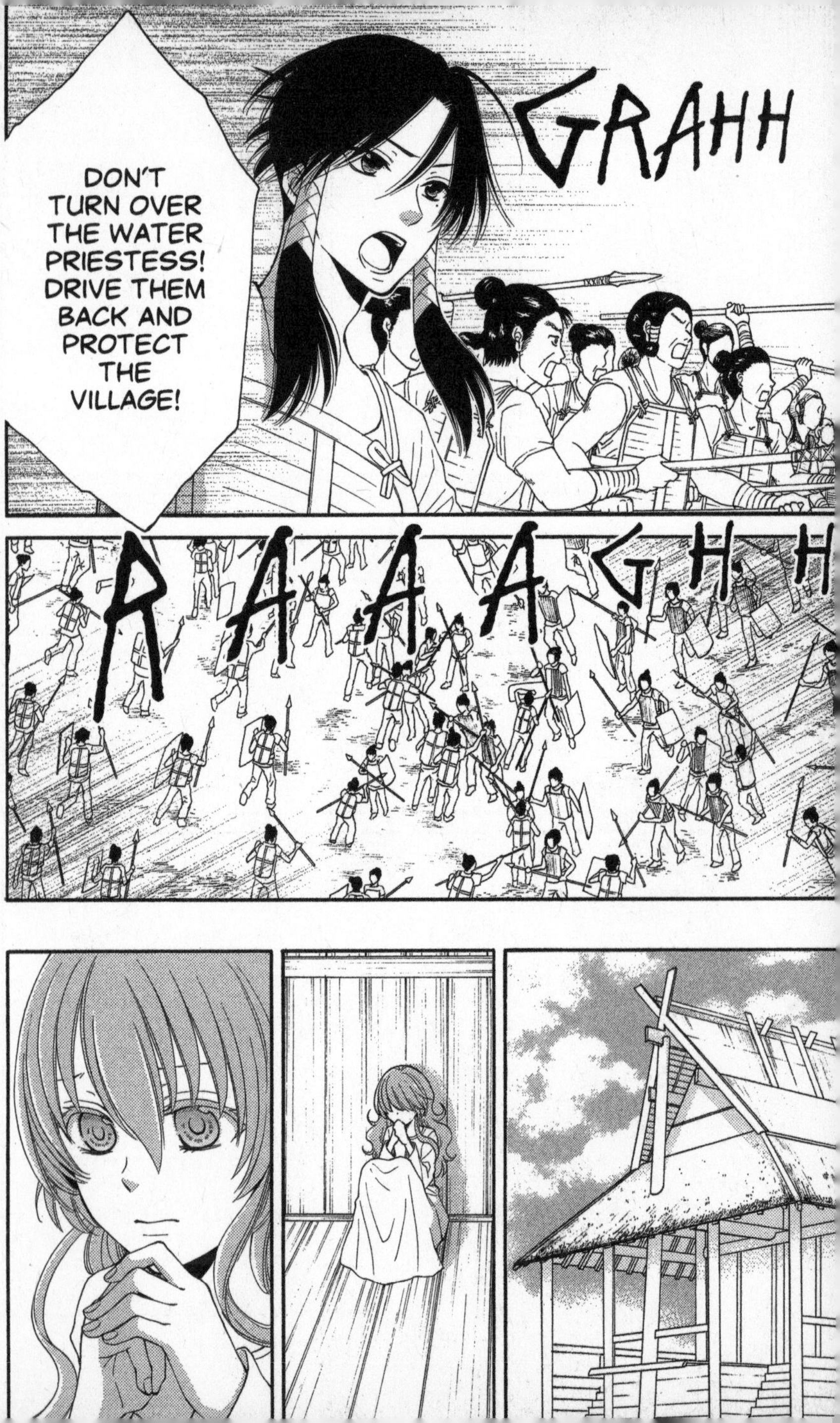
GRAHH
DON'T TURN OVER THE WATER PRIESTESS! DRIVE THEM BACK AND PROTECT THE VILLAGE!
RAAAGHH

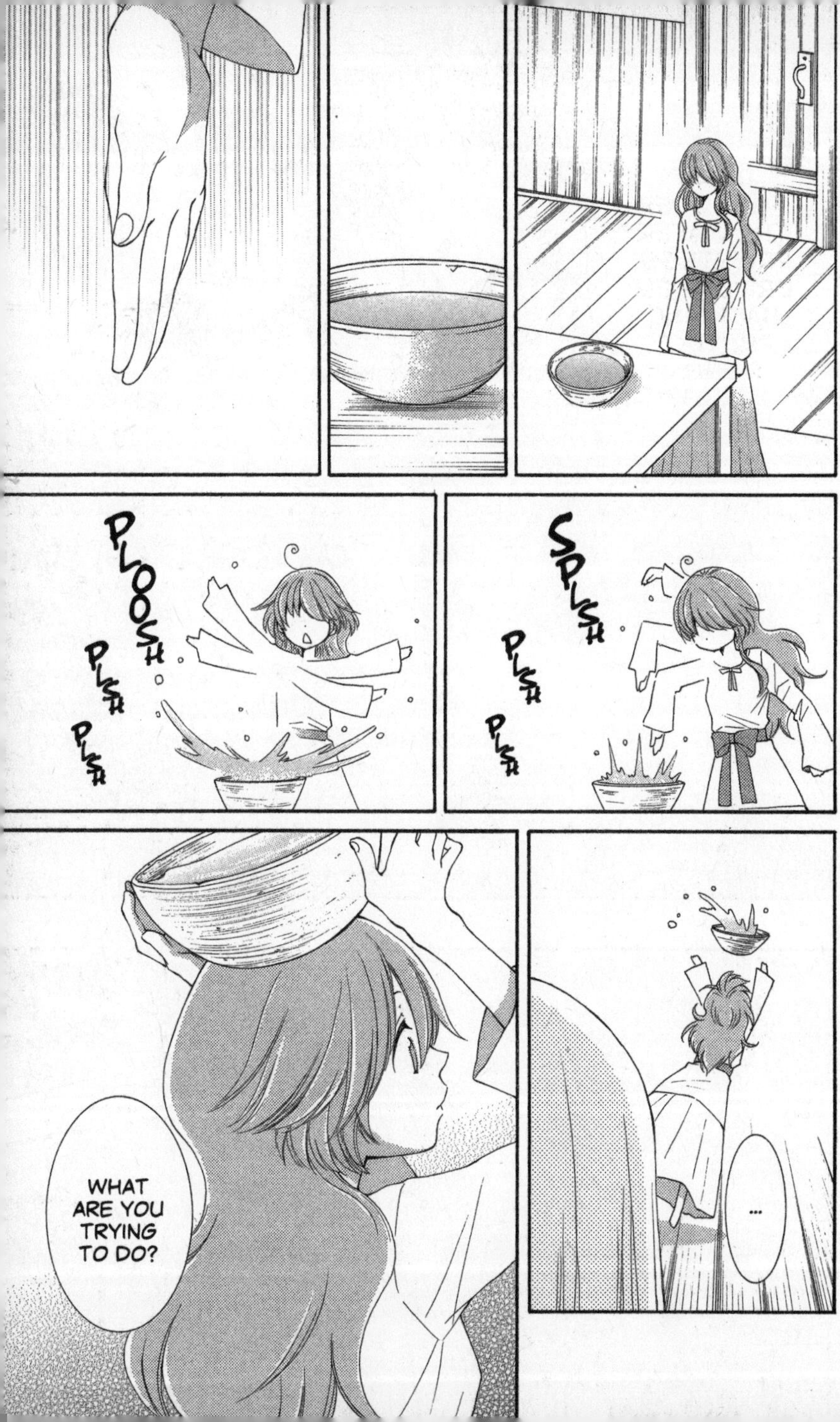
SPLSH
PLSH
PLSH
PLOOSH
PLSH
PLSH
...
WHAT ARE YOU TRYING TO DO?

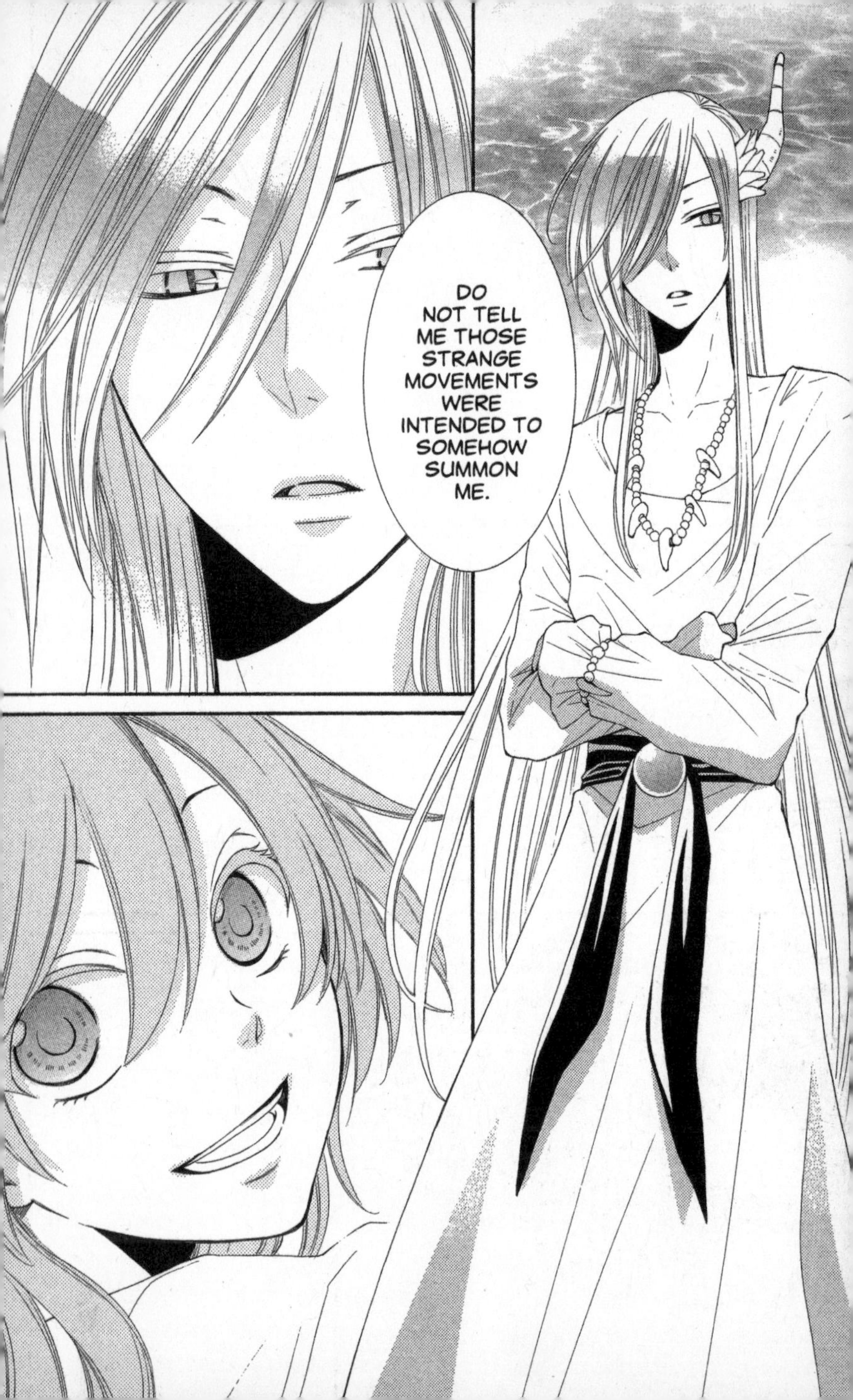
DO NOT TELL ME THOSE STRANGE MOVEMENTS WERE INTENDED TO SOMEHOW SUMMON ME.

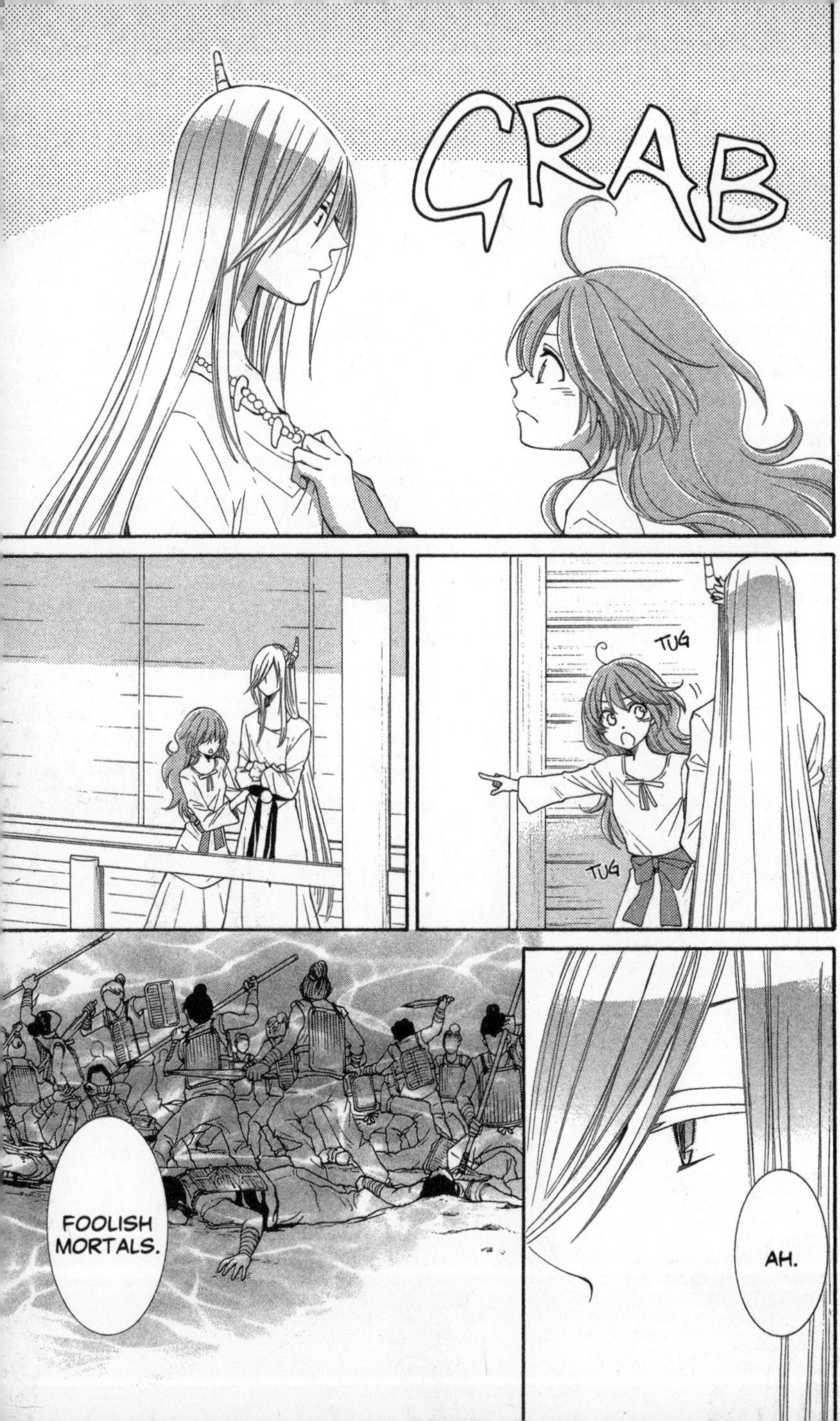
GRAB
TUG
TUG
AH.
FOOLISH MORTALS.

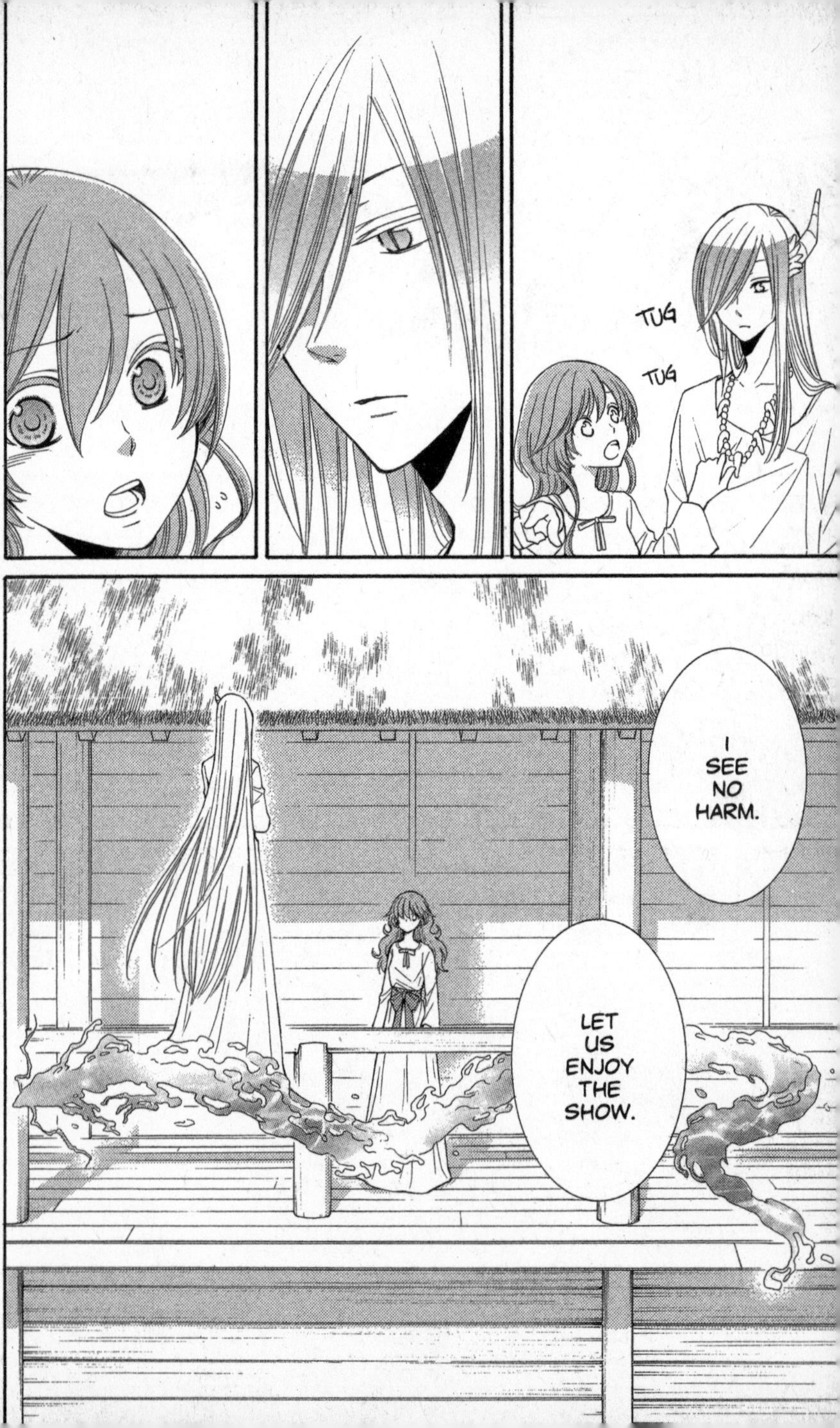
TUG
TUG
I SEE NO HARM.
LET US ENJOY THE SHOW.

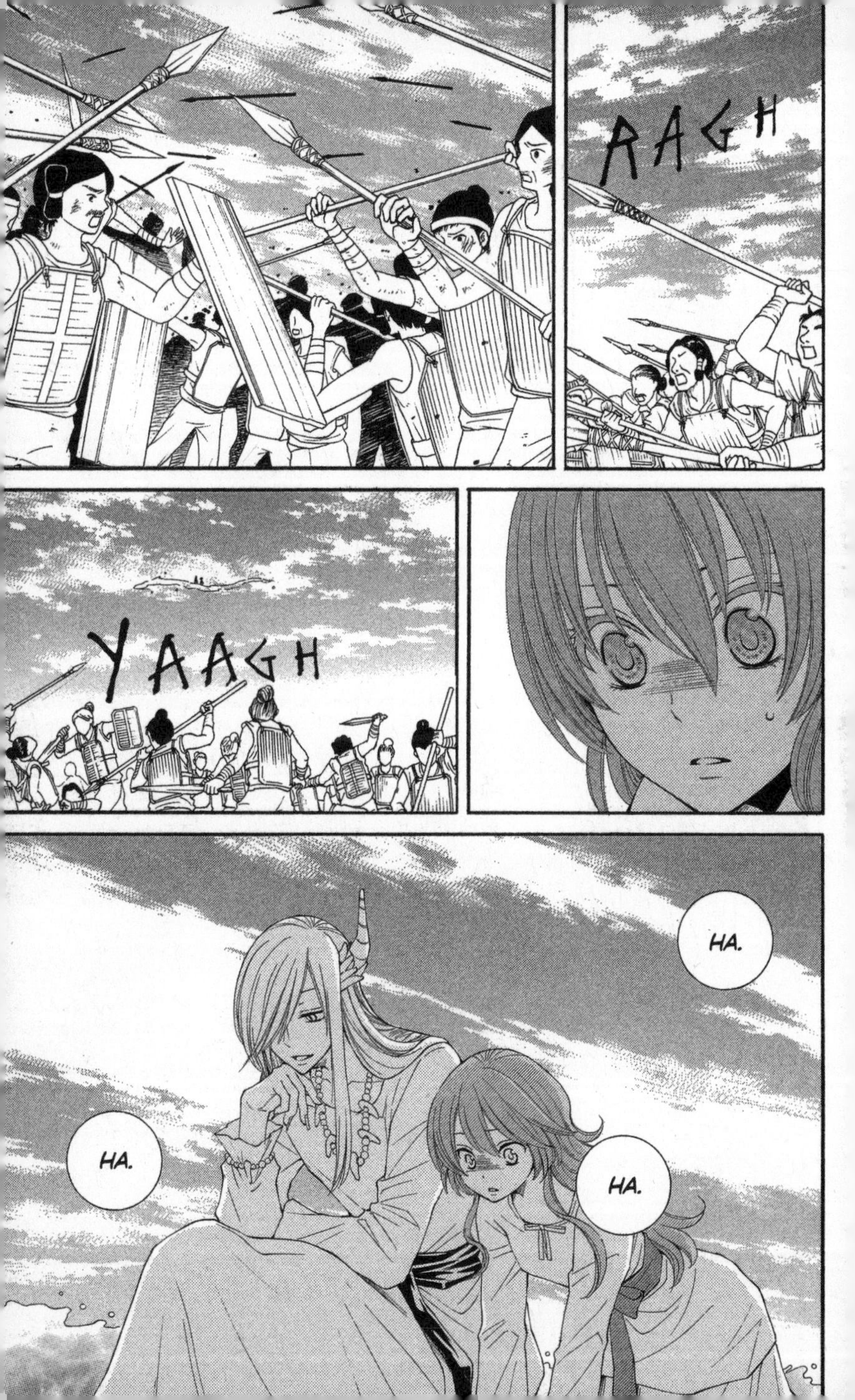
RAGH
YAAGH
HA.
HA.
HA.

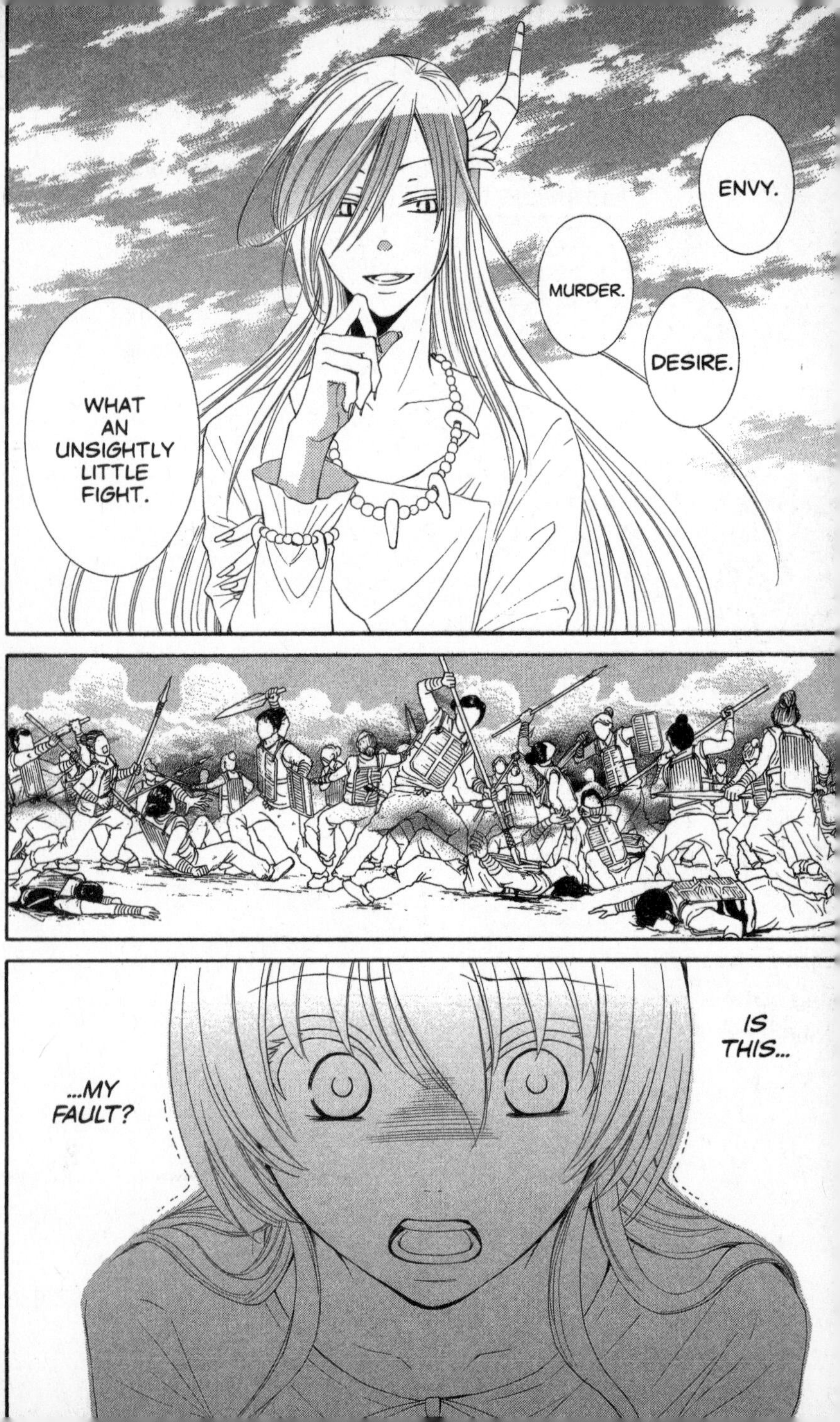
ENVY.
MURDER.
DESIRE.
WHAT AN UNSIGHTLY LITTLE FIGHT.
IS THIS...
...MY FAULT?

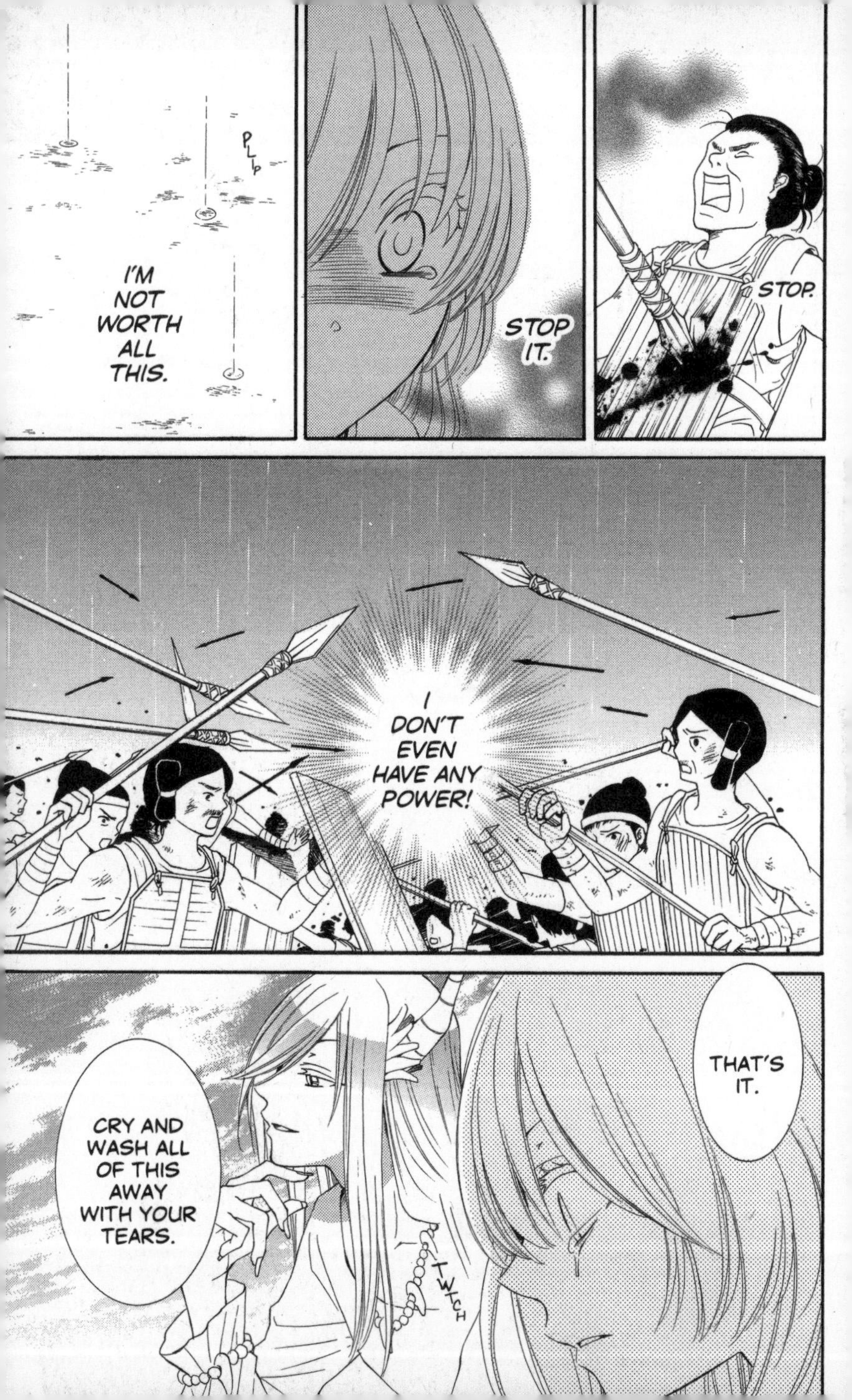
STOP.
STOP IT.
PLIP
I'M NOT WORTH ALL THIS.
I DON'T EVEN HAVE ANY POWER!
THAT'S IT.
TWITCH
CRY AND WASH ALL OF THIS AWAY WITH YOUR TEARS.

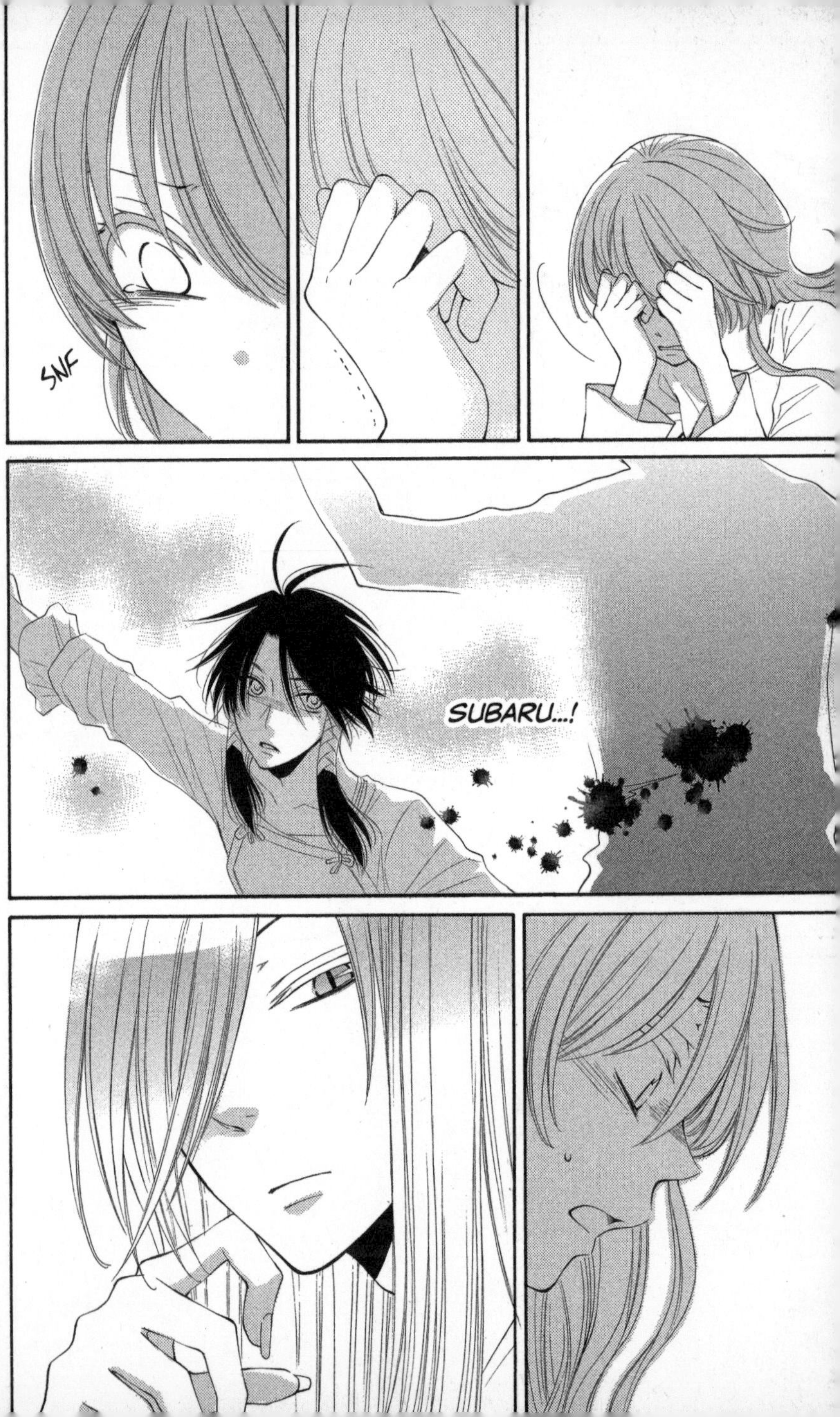
SNF
SUBARU...!

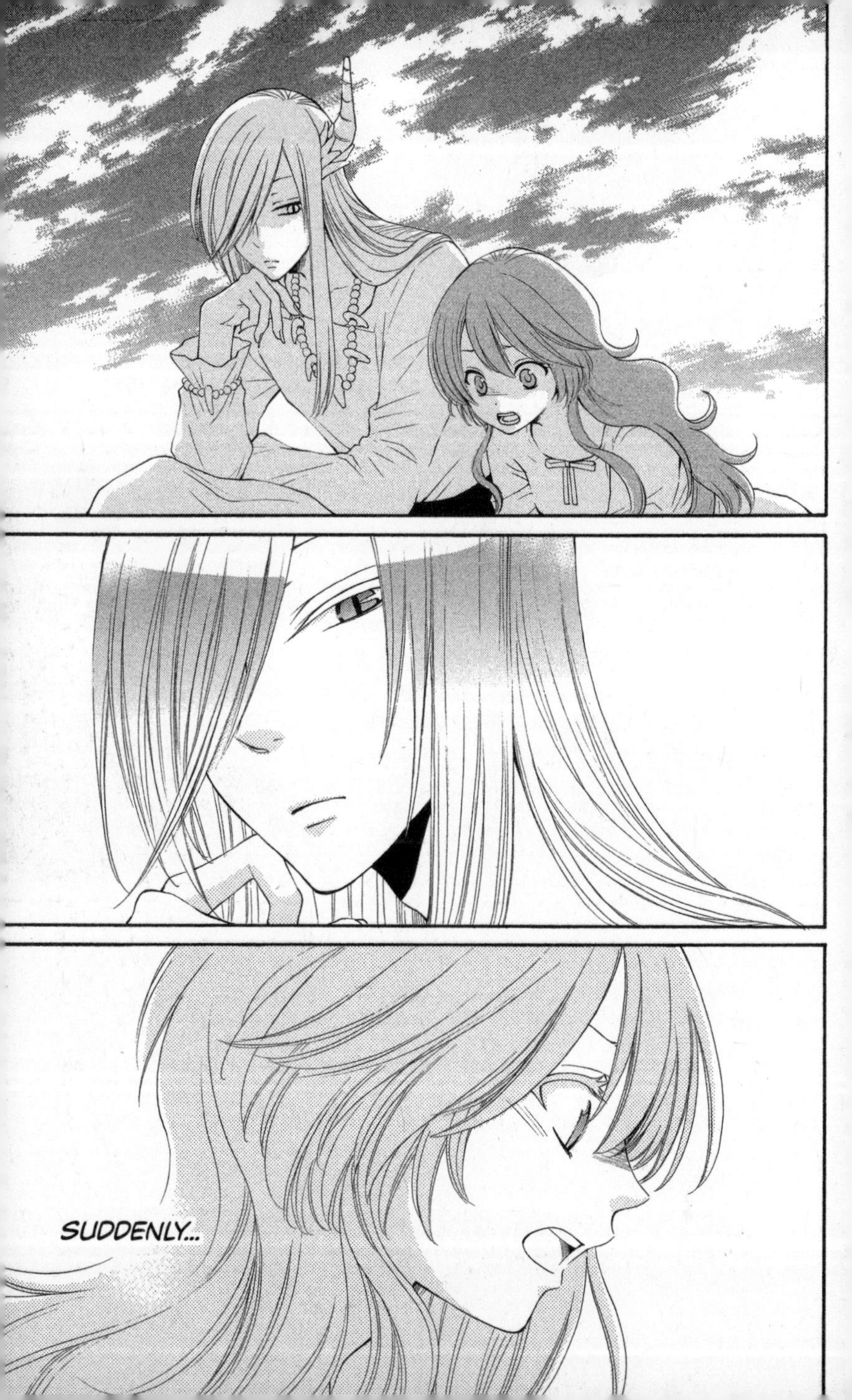
SUDDENLY...

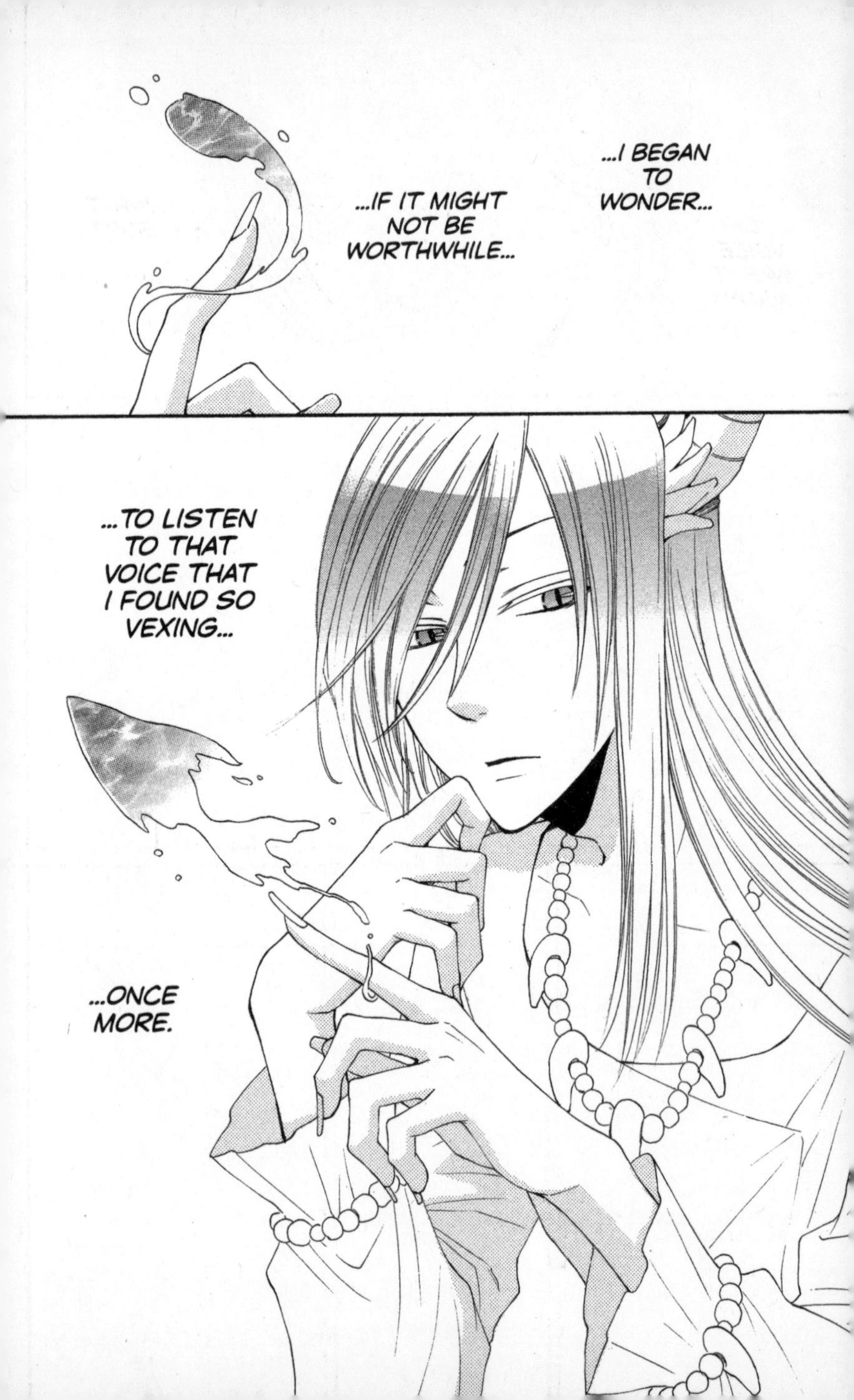
...I BEGAN TO WONDER...
...IF IT MIGHT NOT BE WORTHWHILE...
...TO LISTEN TO THAT VOICE THAT I FOUND SO VEXING...
...ONCE MORE.

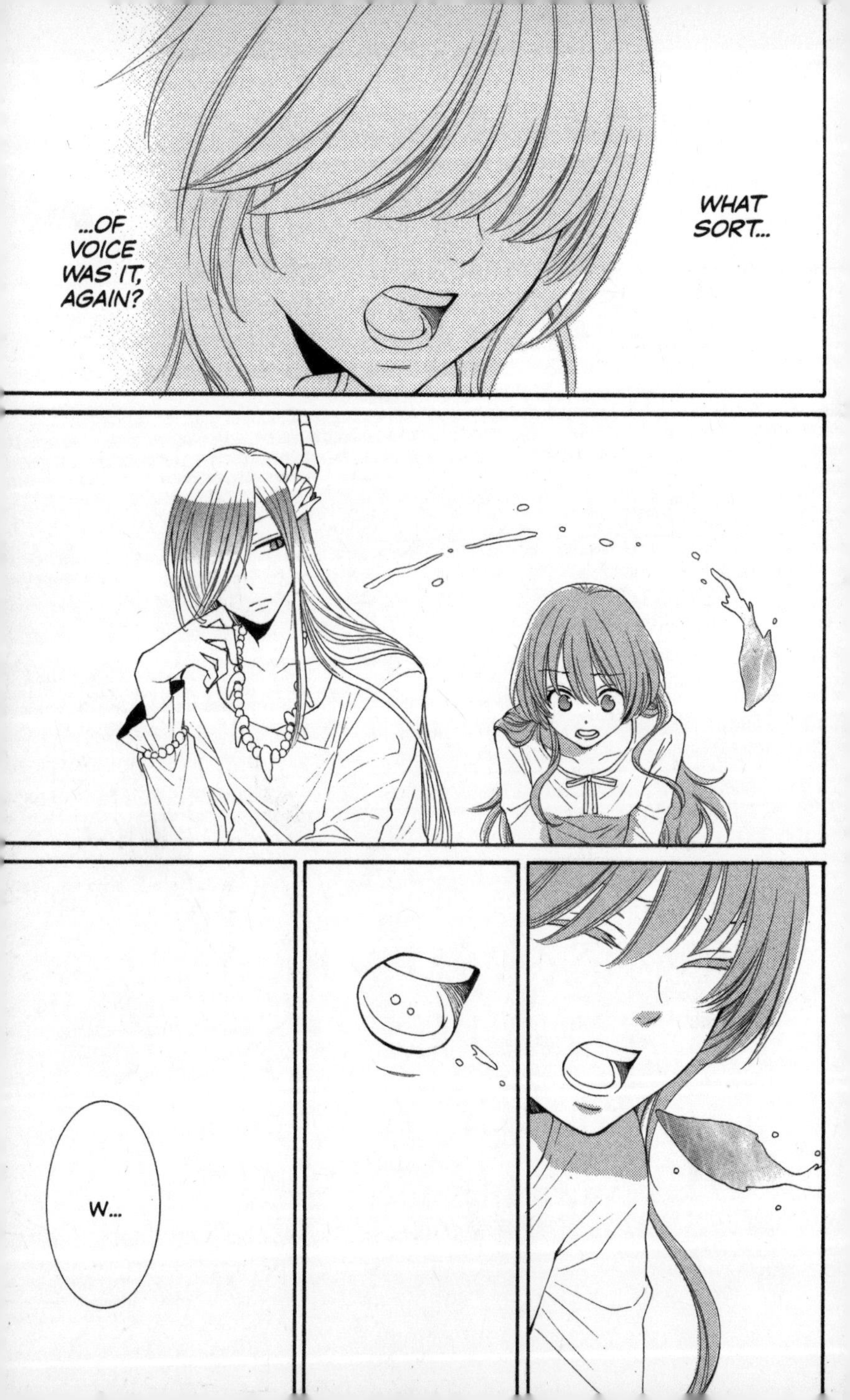
WHAT SORT...
...OF VOICE WAS IT, AGAIN?
W...

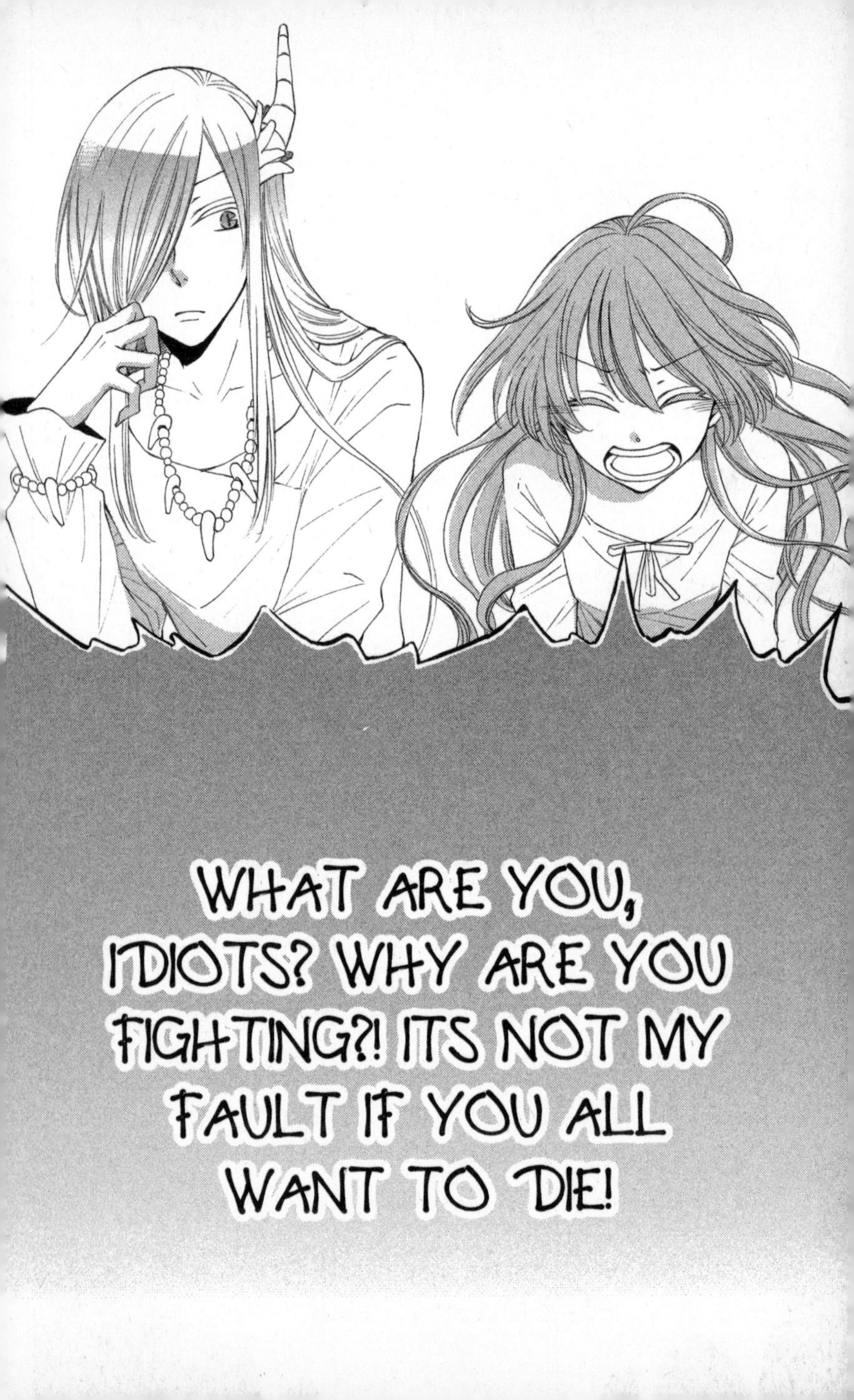
WHAT ARE YOU, IDIOTS? WHY ARE YOU FIGHTING?! ITS NOT MY FAULT IF YOU ALL WANT TO DIE!

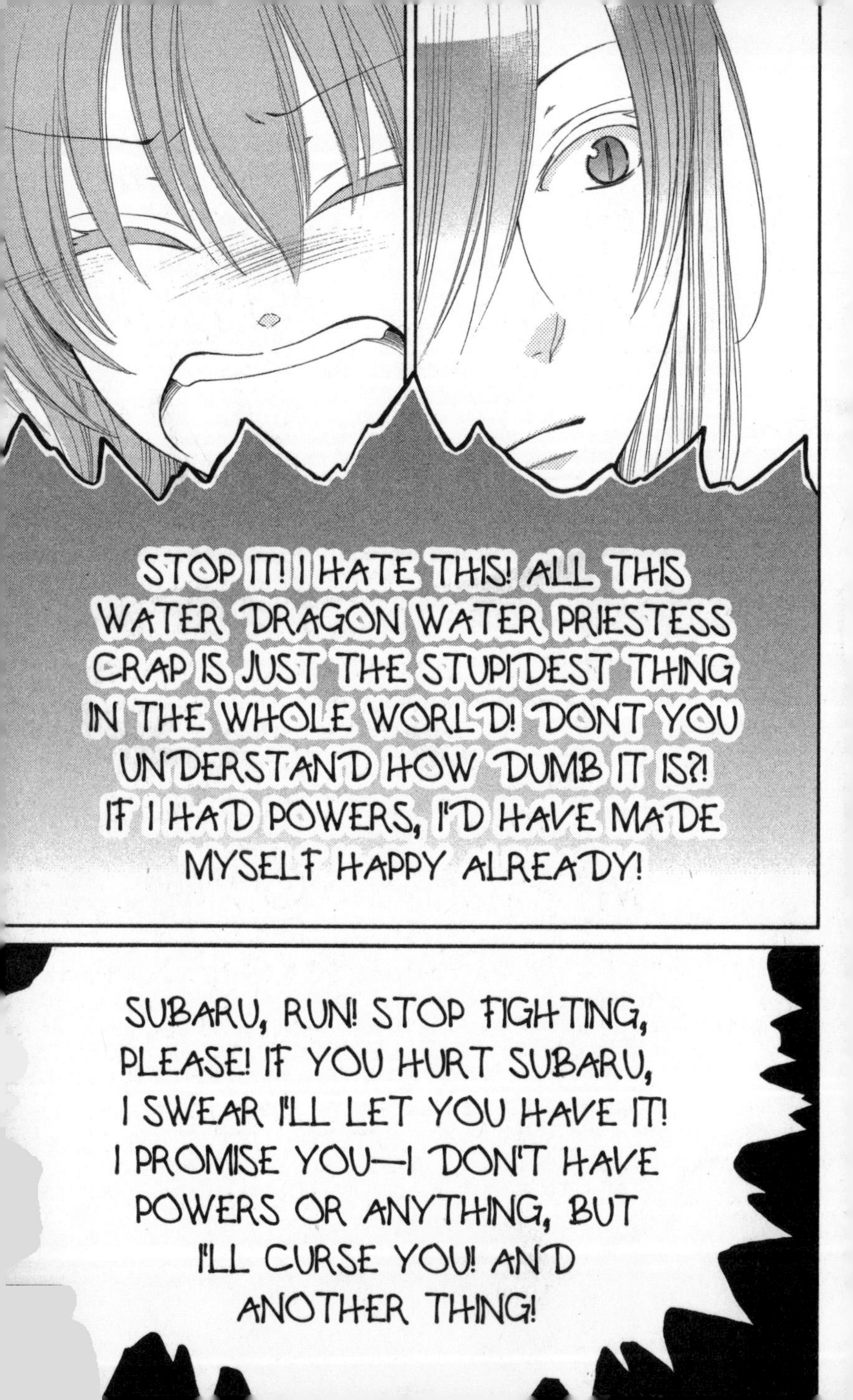
STOP IT! I HATE THIS! ALL THIS WATER DRAGON WATER PRIESTESS CRAP IS JUST THE STUPIDEST THING IN THE WHOLE WORLD! DONT YOU UNDERSTAND HOW DUMB IT IS?! IF I HAD POWERS, I'D HAVE MADE MYSELF HAPPY ALREADY!
SUBARU, RUN! STOP FIGHTING, PLEASE! IF YOU HURT SUBARU, I SWEAR I'LL LET YOU HAVE IT! I PROMISE YOU—I DON'T HAVE POWERS OR ANYTHING, BUT I'LL CURSE YOU! AND ANOTHER THING!

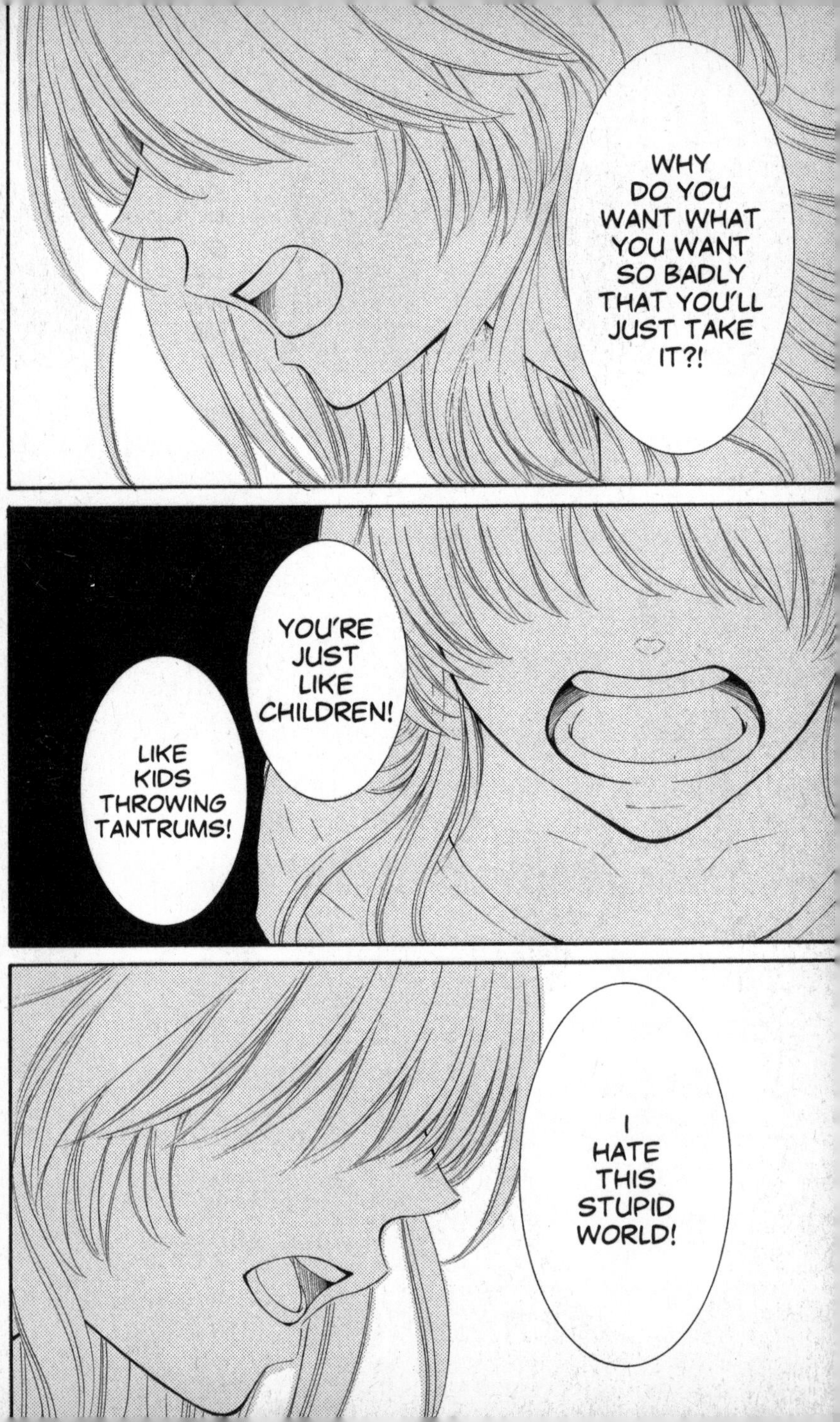
WHY DO YOU WANT WHAT YOU WANT SO BADLY THAT YOU'LL JUST TAKE IT?!
YOU'RE JUST LIKE CHILDREN!
LIKE KIDS THROWING TANTRUMS!
I HATE THIS STUPID WORLD!

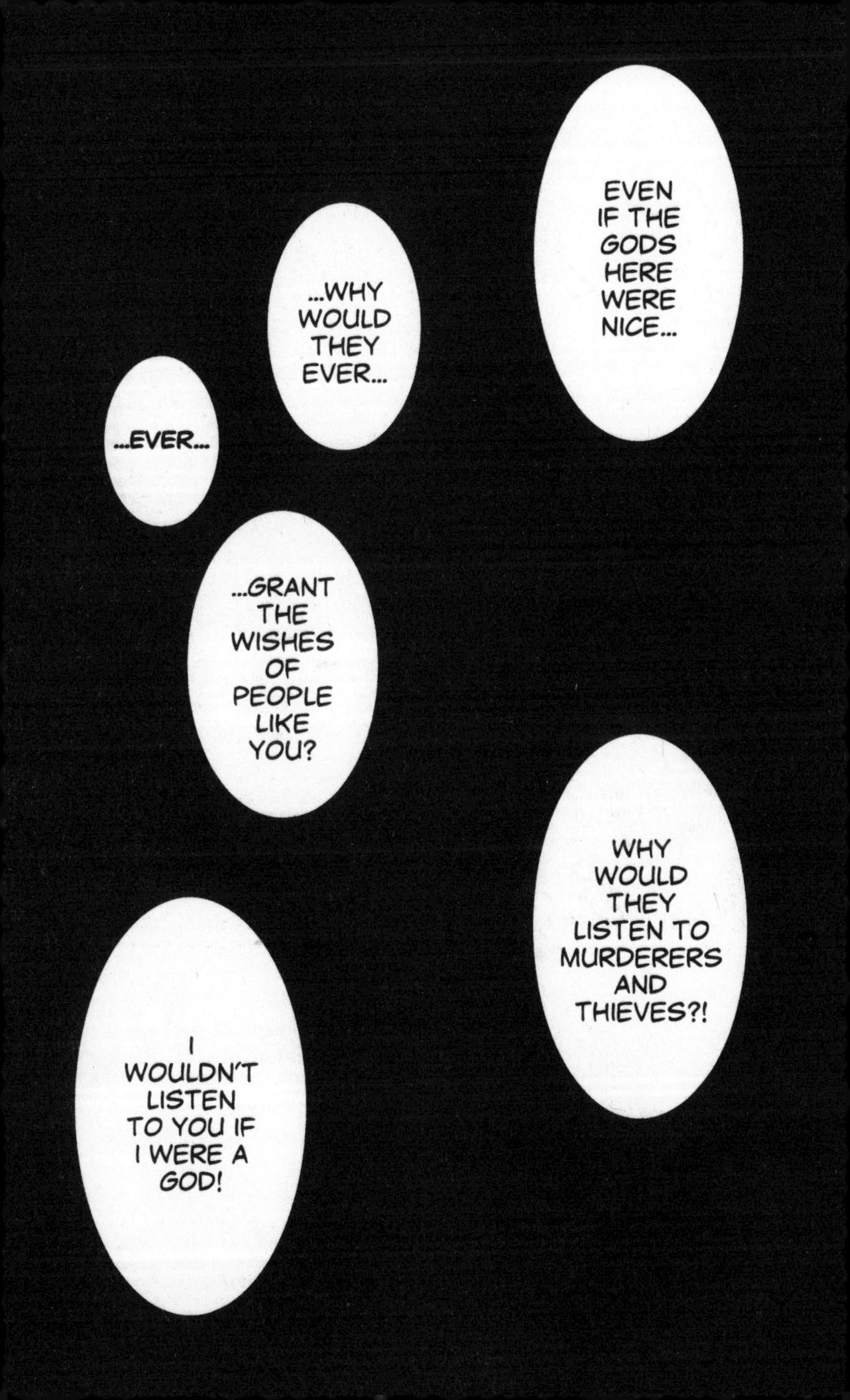
EVEN IF THE GODS HERE WERE NICE...
...WHY WOULD THEY EVER...
...EVER...
...GRANT THE WISHES OF PEOPLE LIKE YOU?
WHY WOULD THEY LISTEN TO MURDERERS AND THIEVES?!
I WOULDN'T LISTEN TO YOU IF I WERE A GOD!

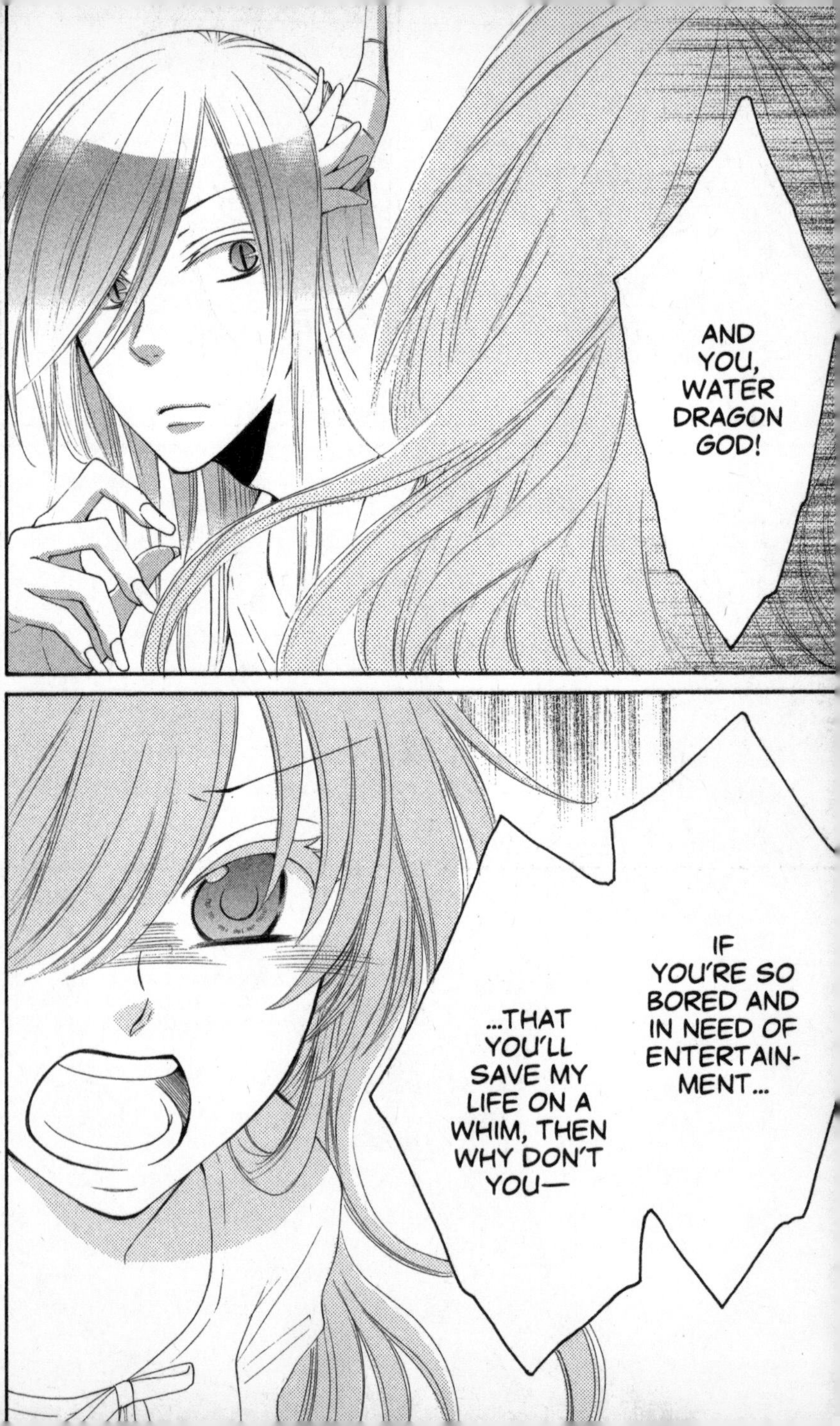
AND YOU, WATER DRAGON GOD!
IF YOU'RE SO BORED AND IN NEED OF ENTERTAIN-MENT...
...THAT YOU'LL SAVE MY LIFE ON A WHIM, THEN WHY DON'T YOU—

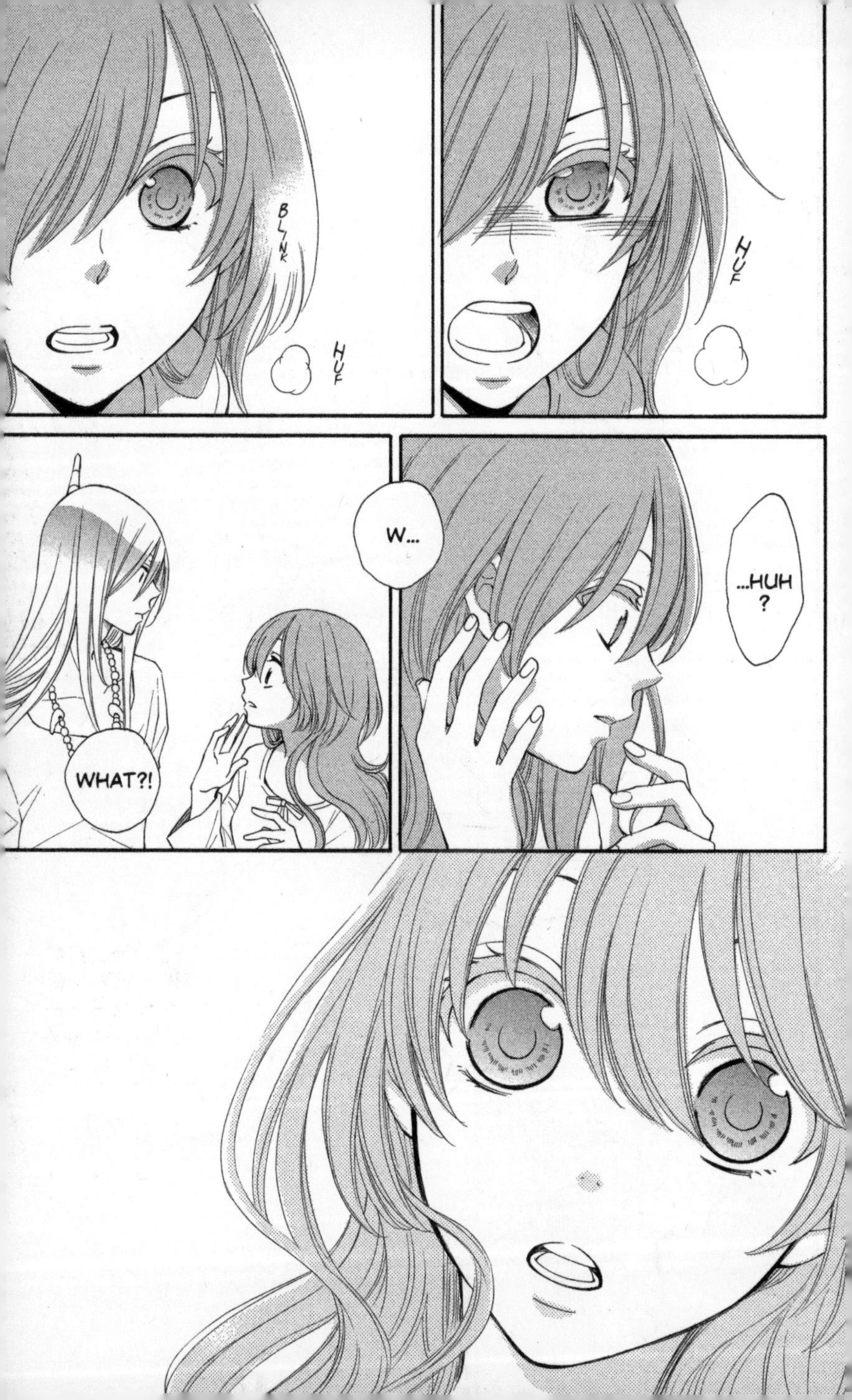
HUF
BLINK
HUF
...HUH?
W...
WHAT?!

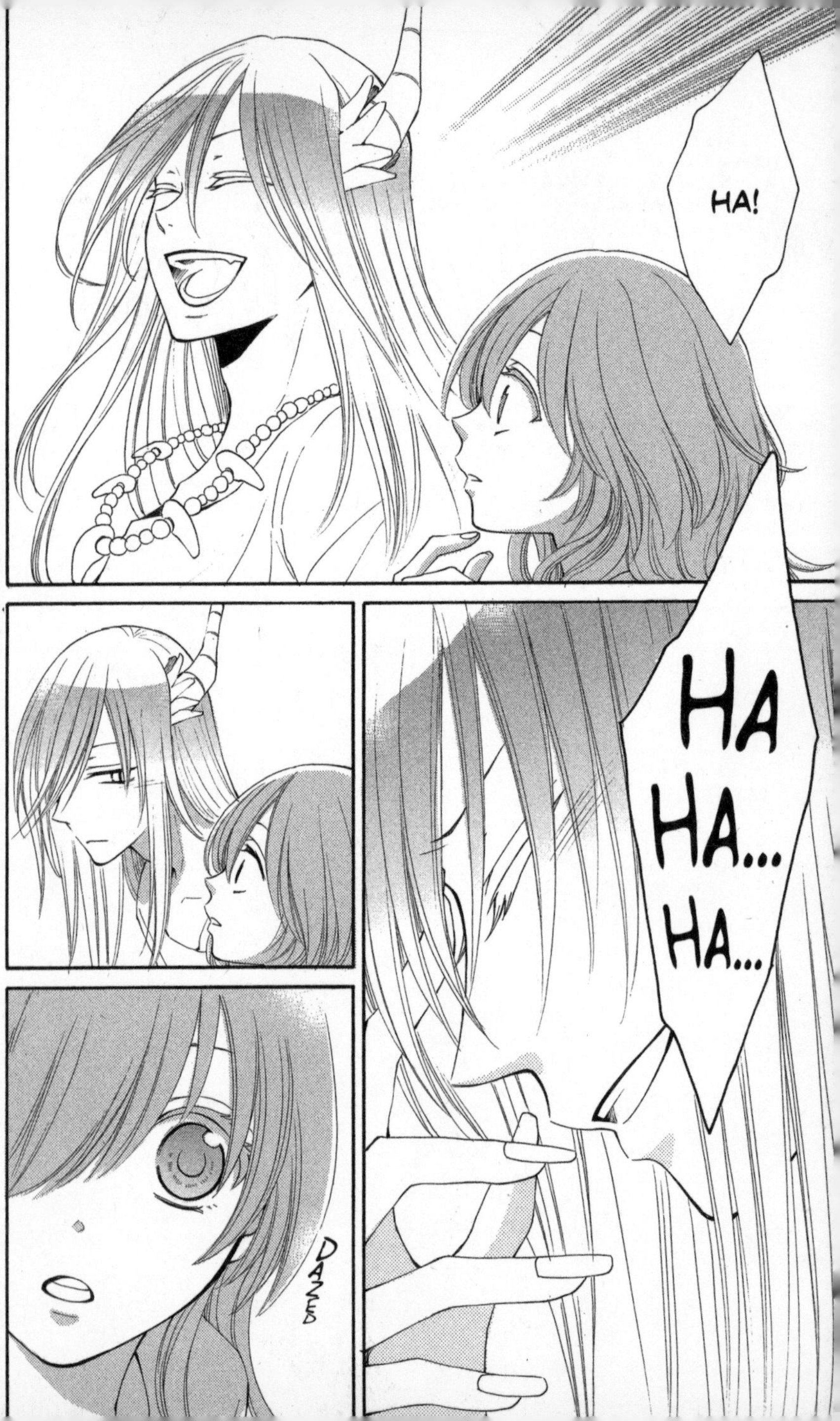
HA!
HA HA... HA...
DAZED

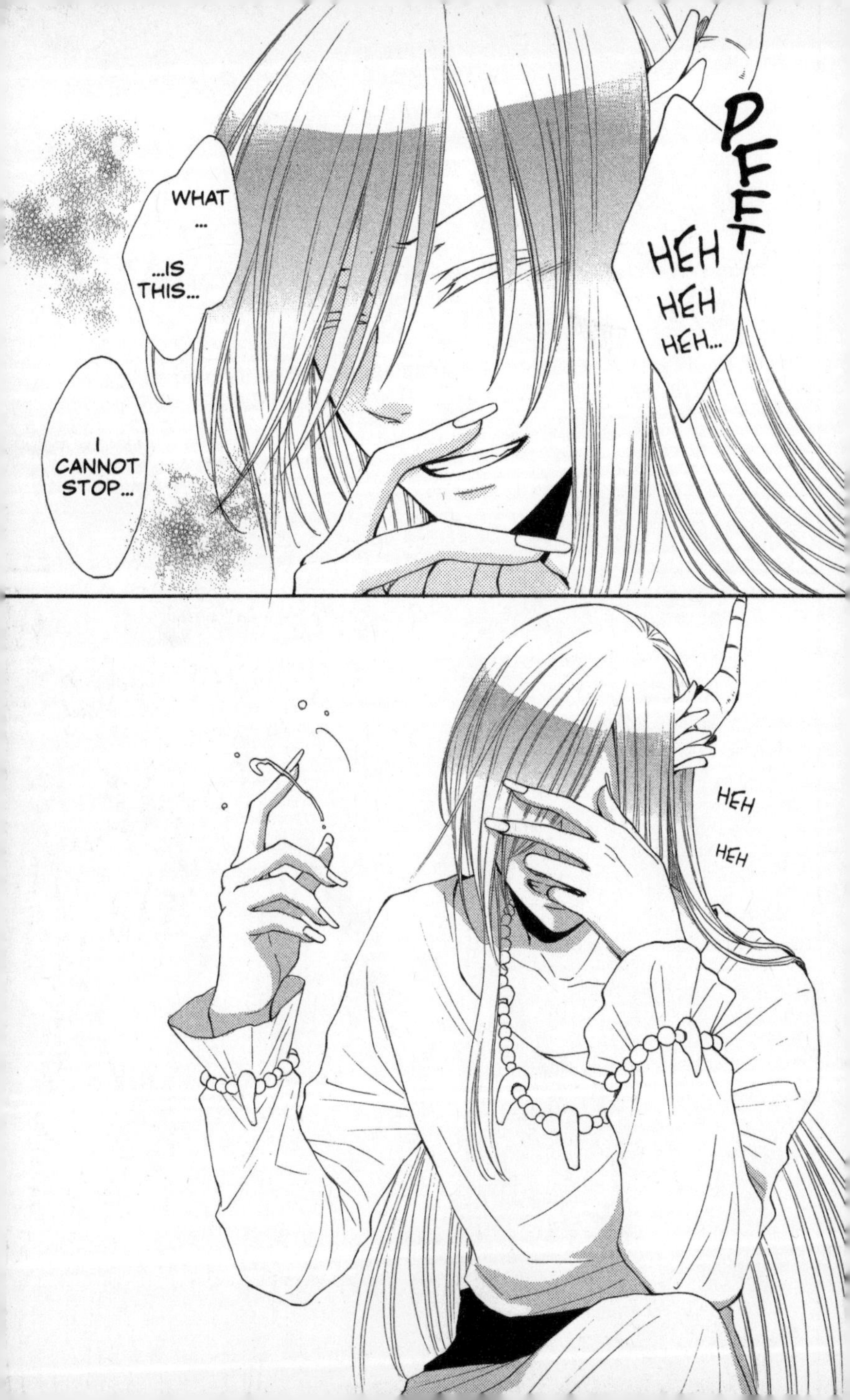
PFFT
HEH HEH HEH...
WHAT ... ...IS THIS...
I CANNOT STOP...
HEH HEH

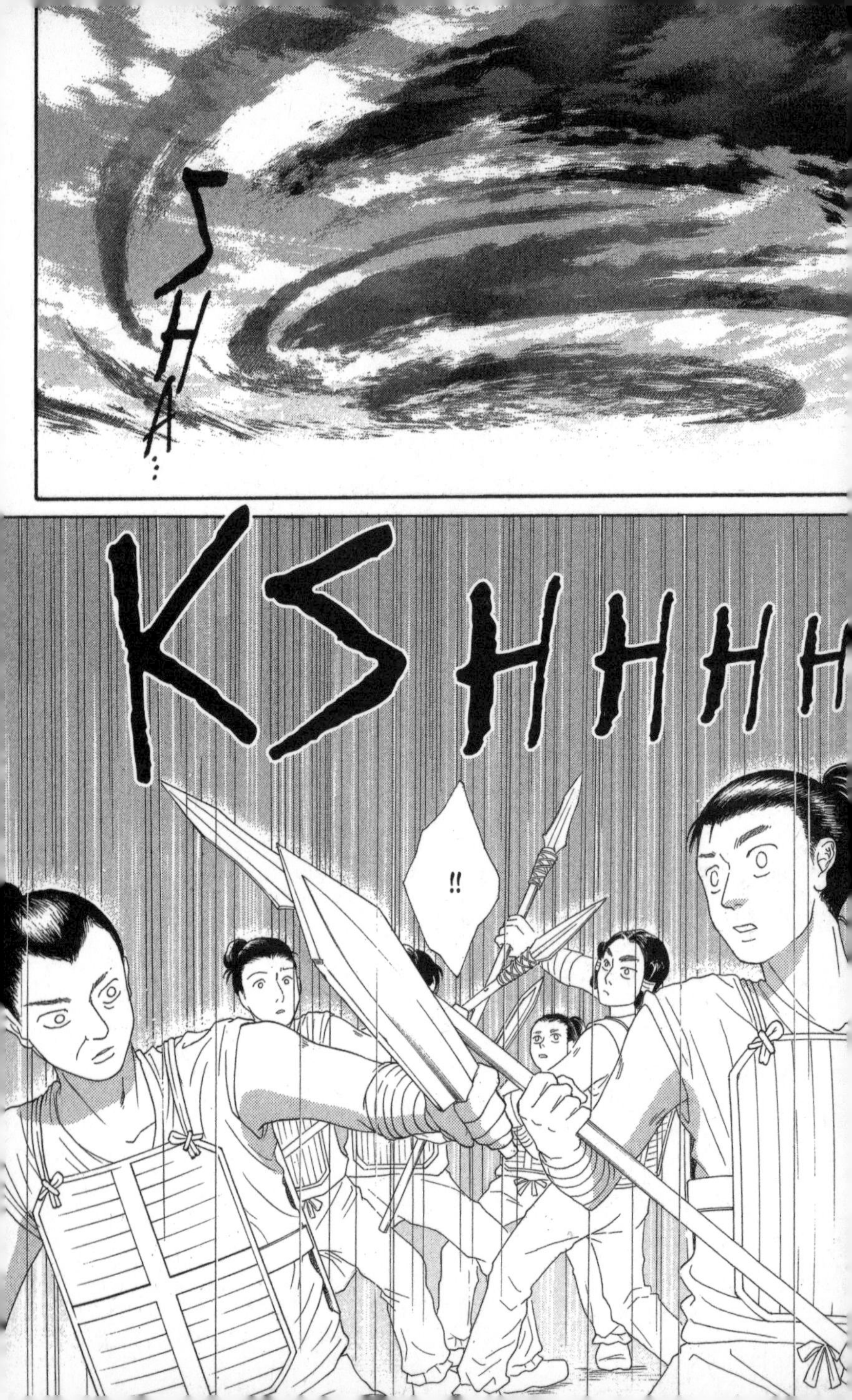

SHHA...
KSHHHHH
!!

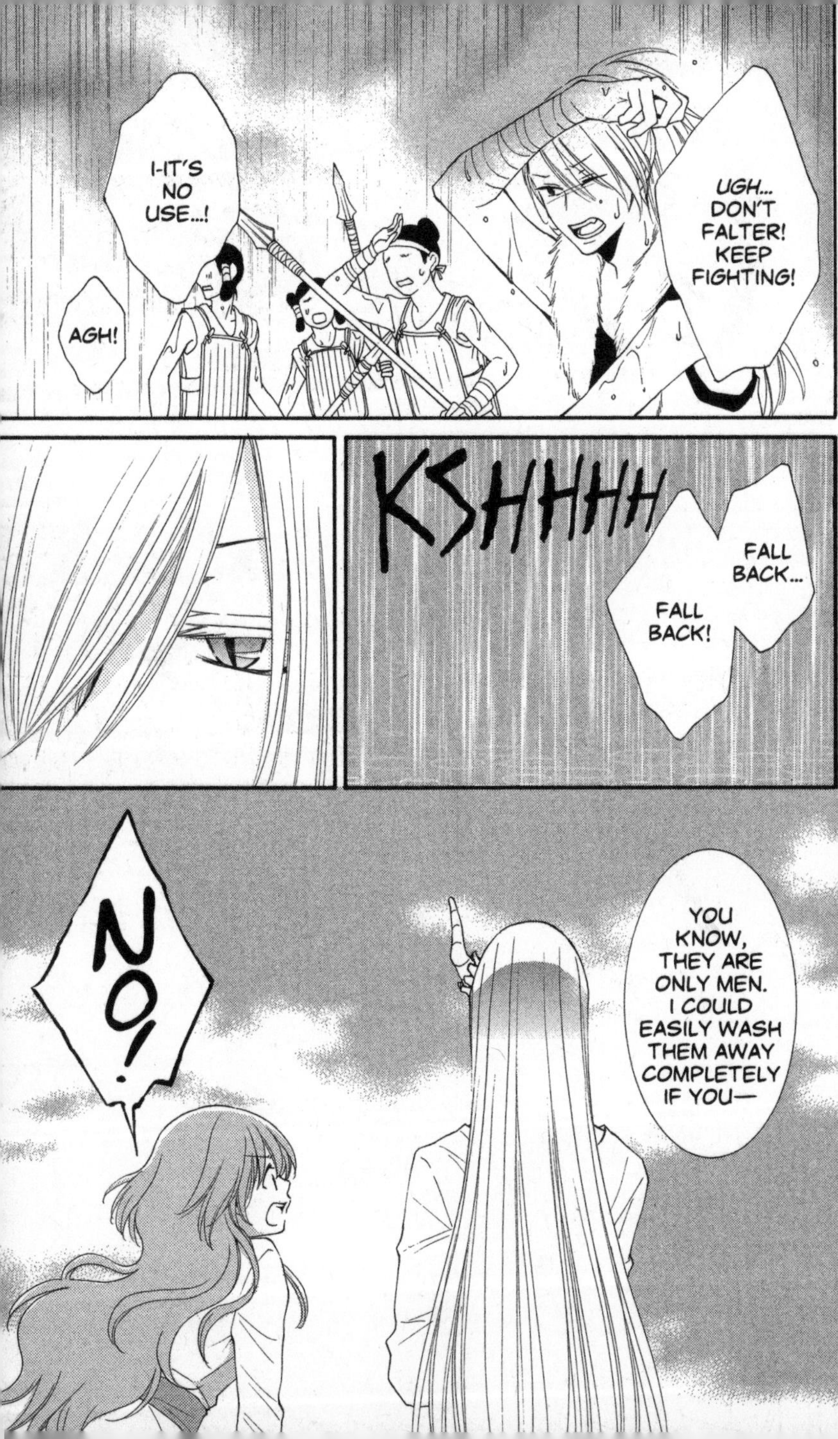
UGH... DON'T FALTER! KEEP FIGHTING!
I-IT'S NO USE...!
AGH!
KSHHHH
FALL BACK...
FALL BACK!
YOU KNOW, THEY ARE ONLY MEN. I COULD EASILY WASH THEM AWAY COMPLETELY IF YOU—
NO!

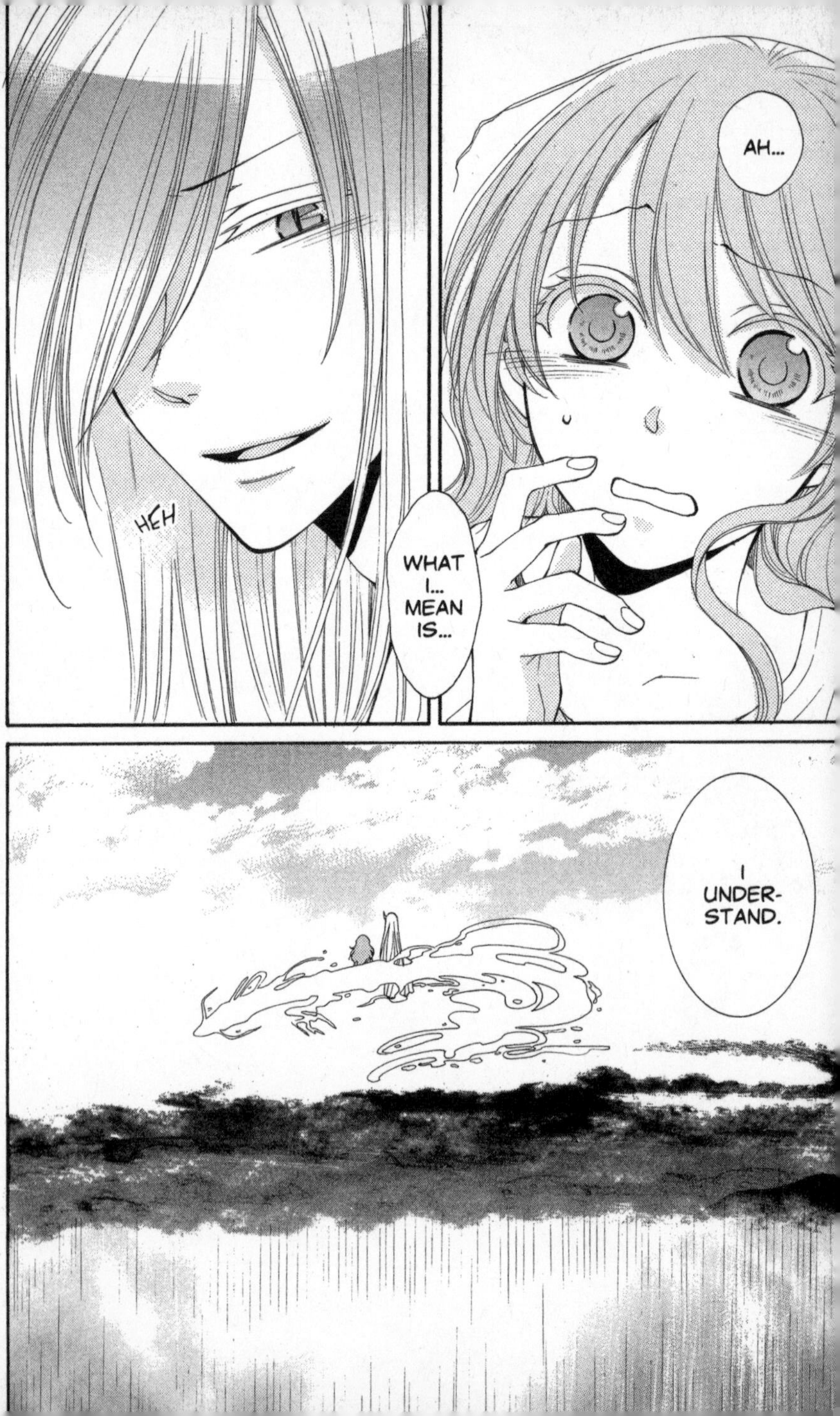
AH...
WHAT I... MEAN IS...
HEH
I UNDER-STAND.

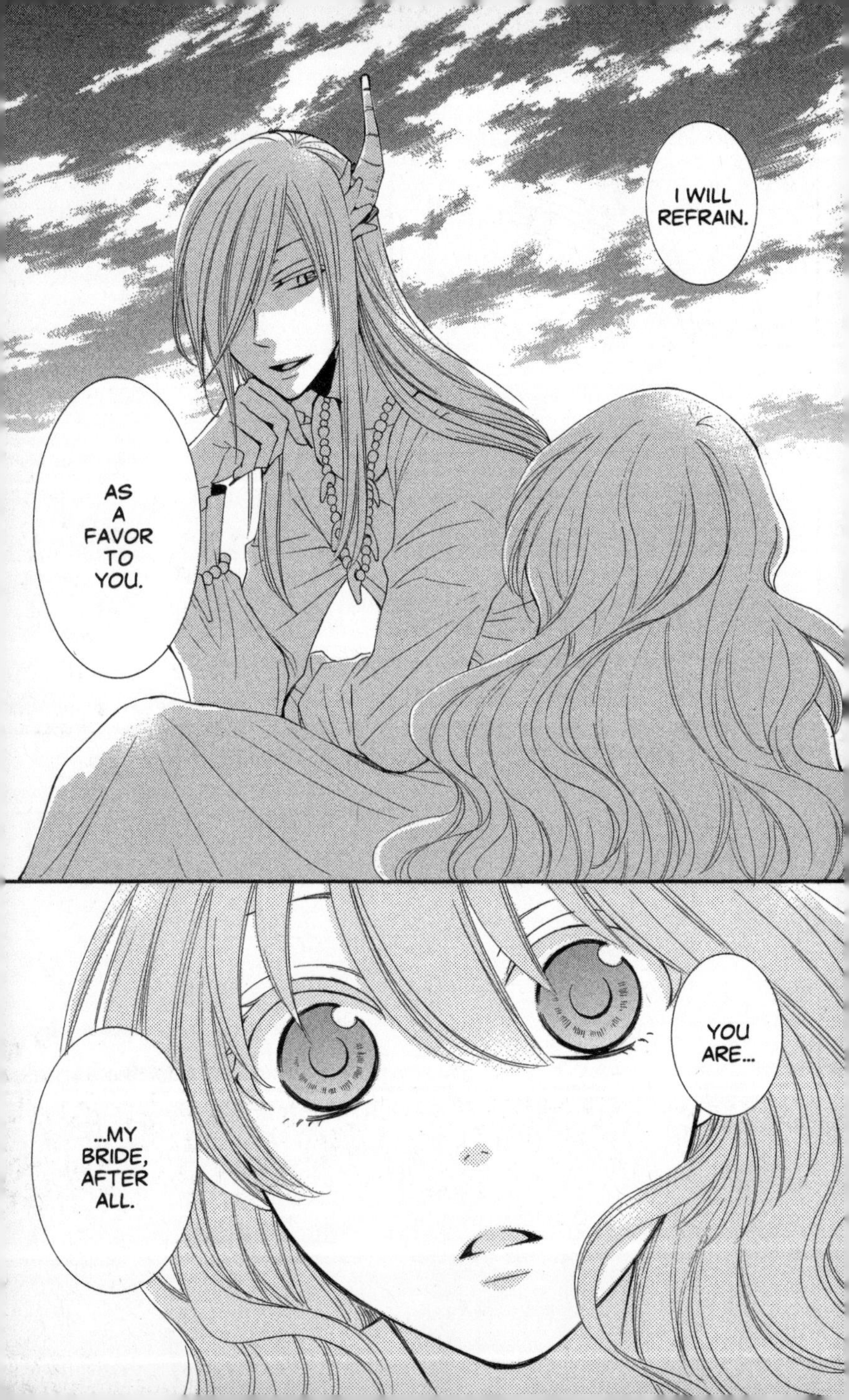
I WILL REFRAIN.
AS A FAVOR TO YOU.
YOU ARE...
...MY BRIDE, AFTER ALL.

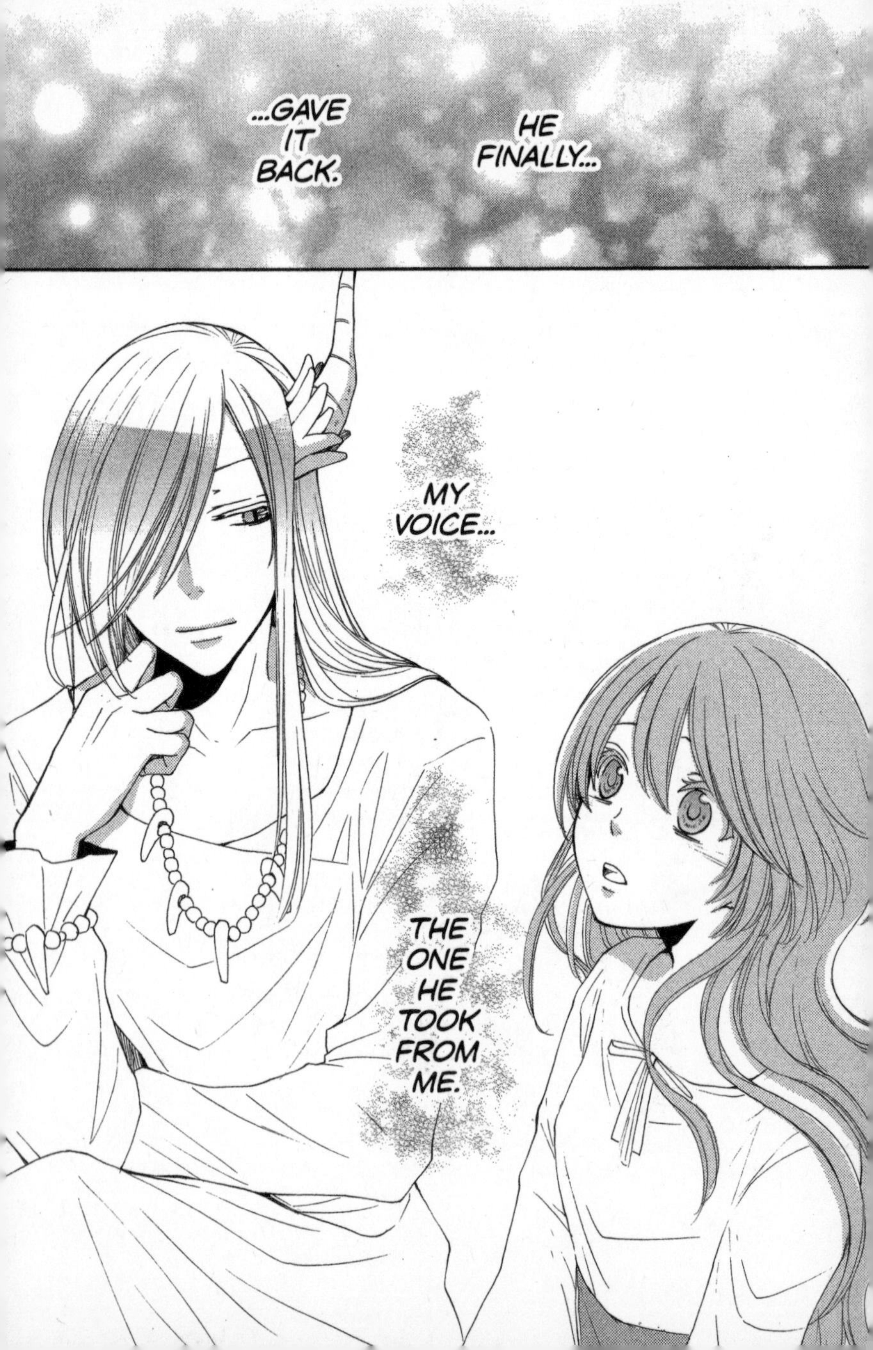
HE FINALLY...
...GAVE IT BACK.
MY VOICE...
THE ONE HE TOOK FROM ME.

CHAPTER 12

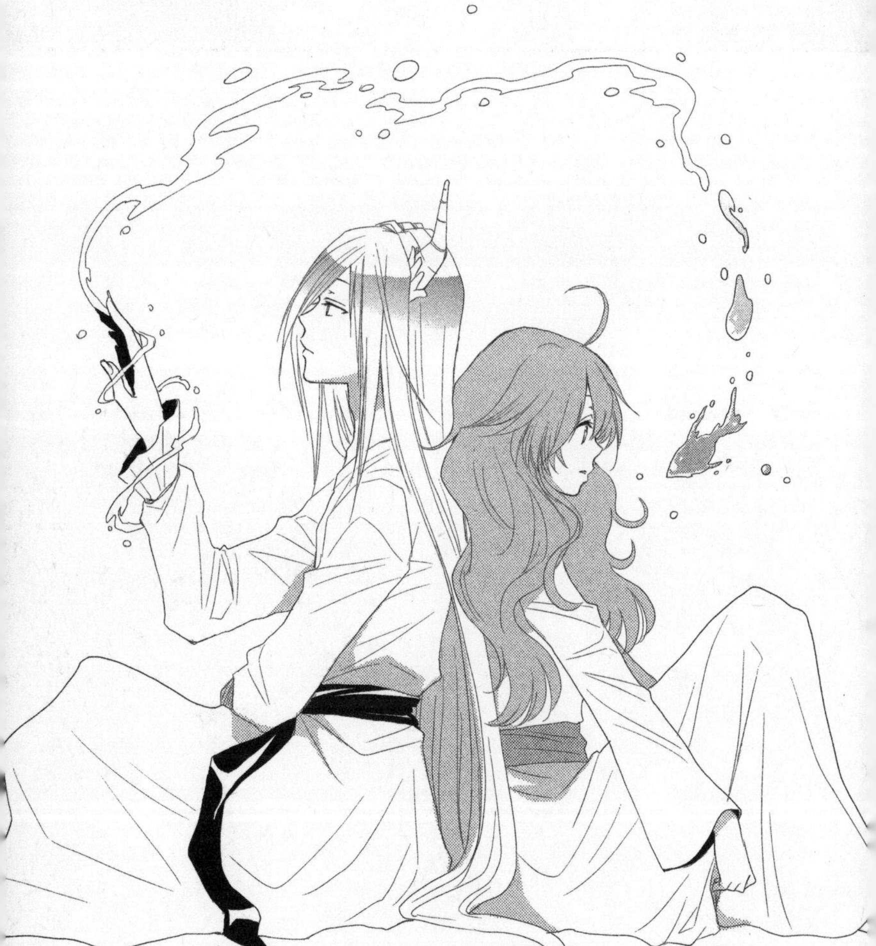

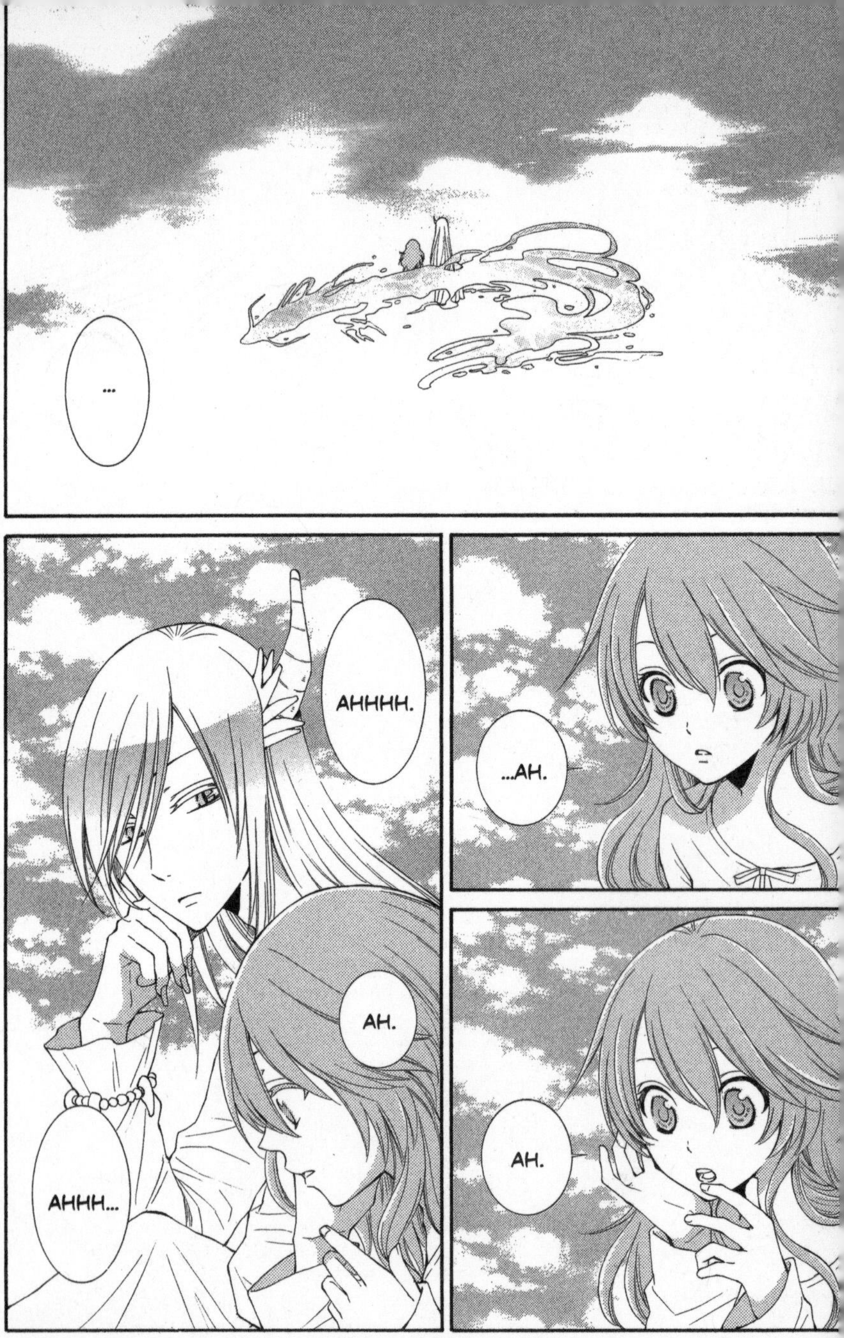
...
...AH.
AH.
AHHHH.
AH.
AHHH...

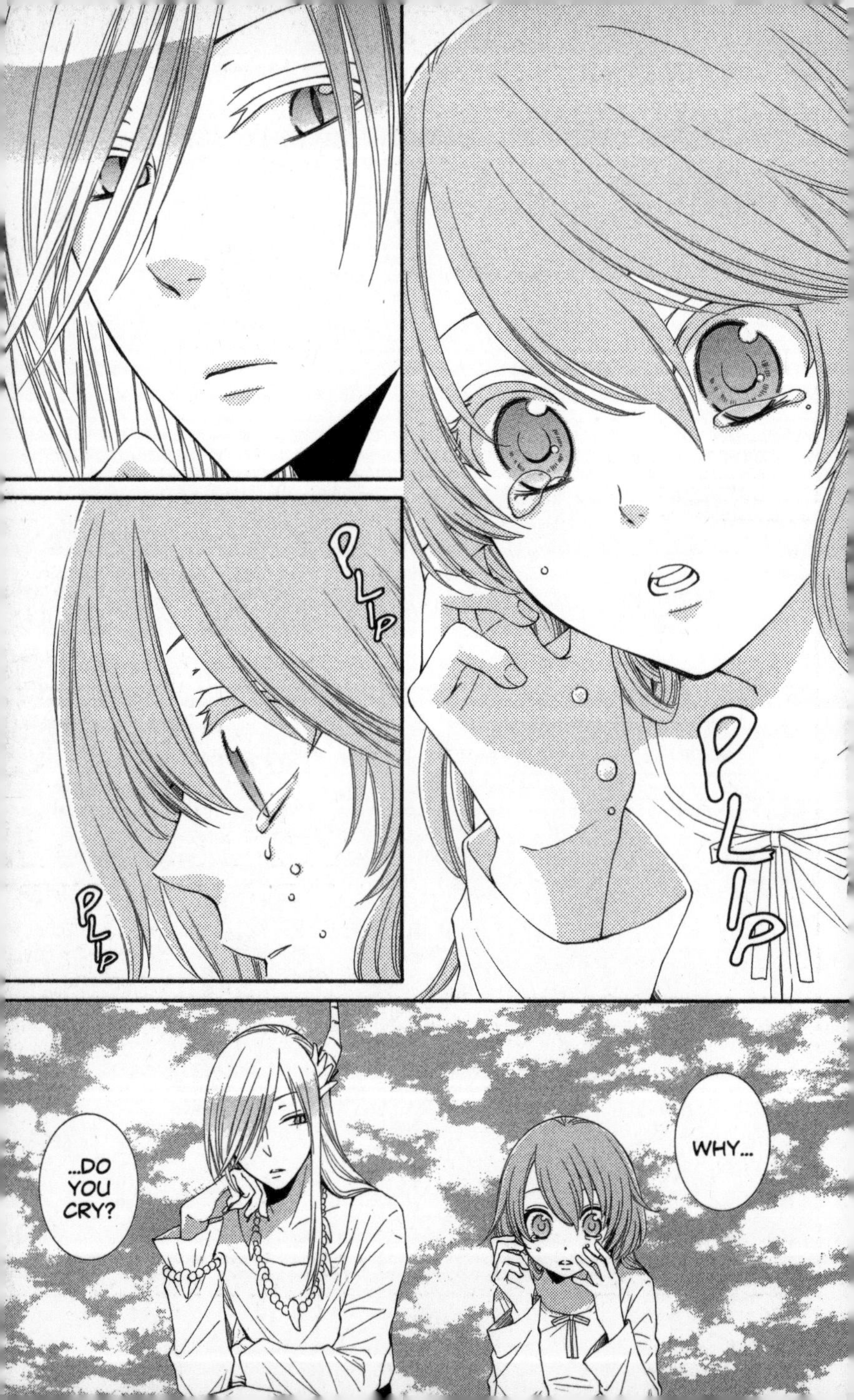
PLIP
PLIP
PLIP
WHY...
...DO YOU CRY?

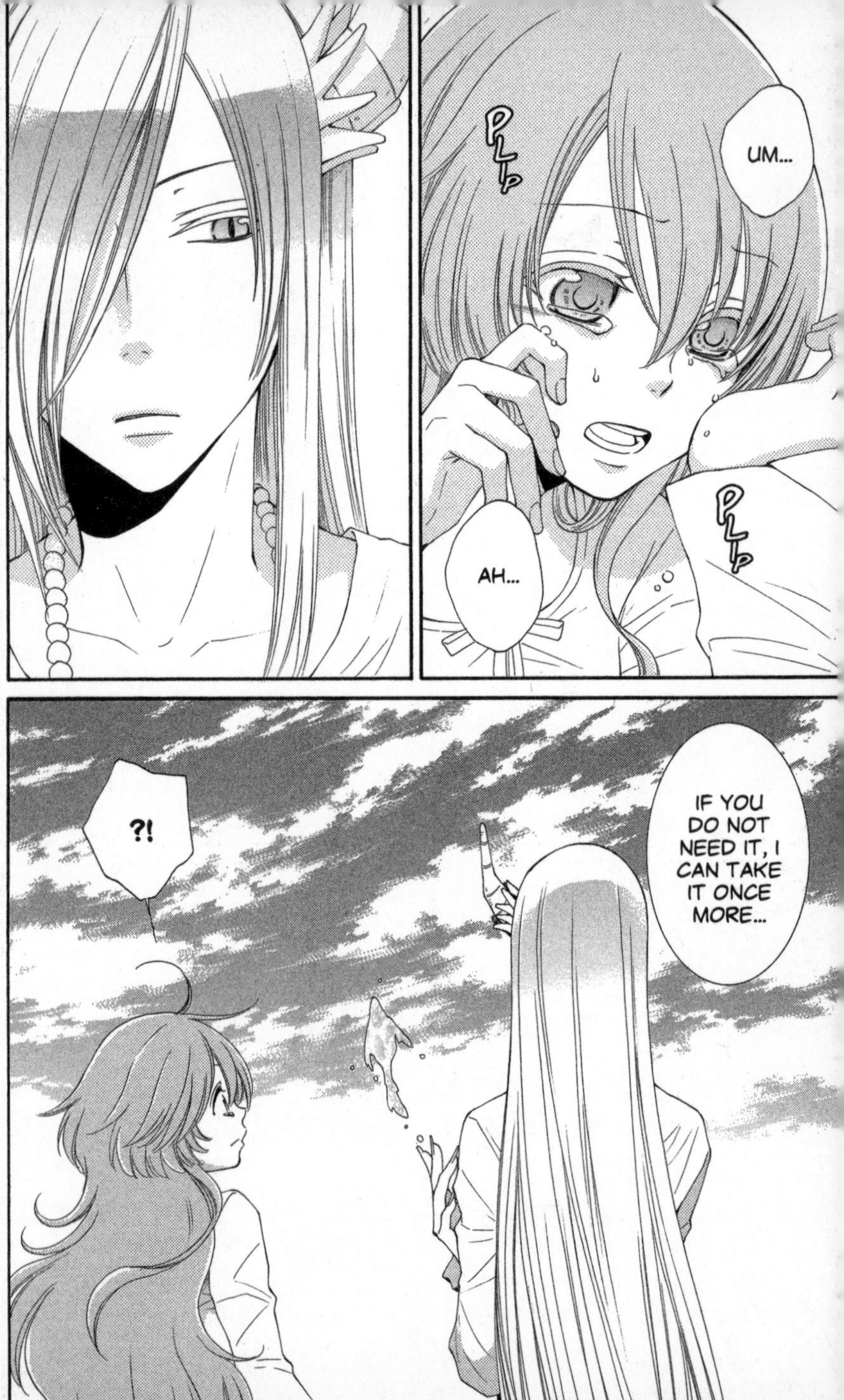
UM...
PLIP
PLIP
AH...
IF YOU DO NOT NEED IT, I CAN TAKE IT ONCE MORE...
?!

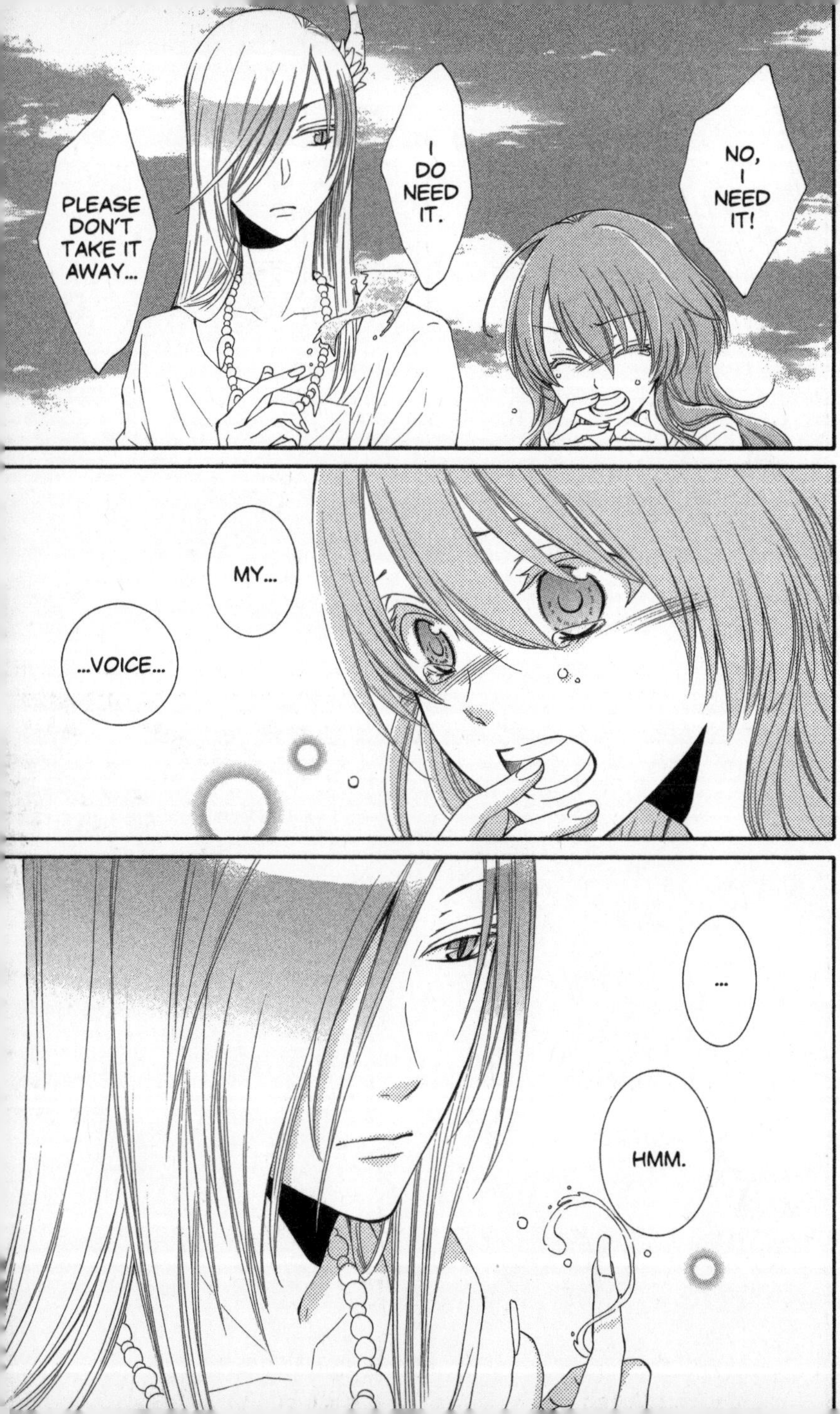
NO, I NEED IT!
I DO NEED IT.
PLEASE DON'T TAKE IT AWAY...
MY...
...VOICE...
...
HMM.

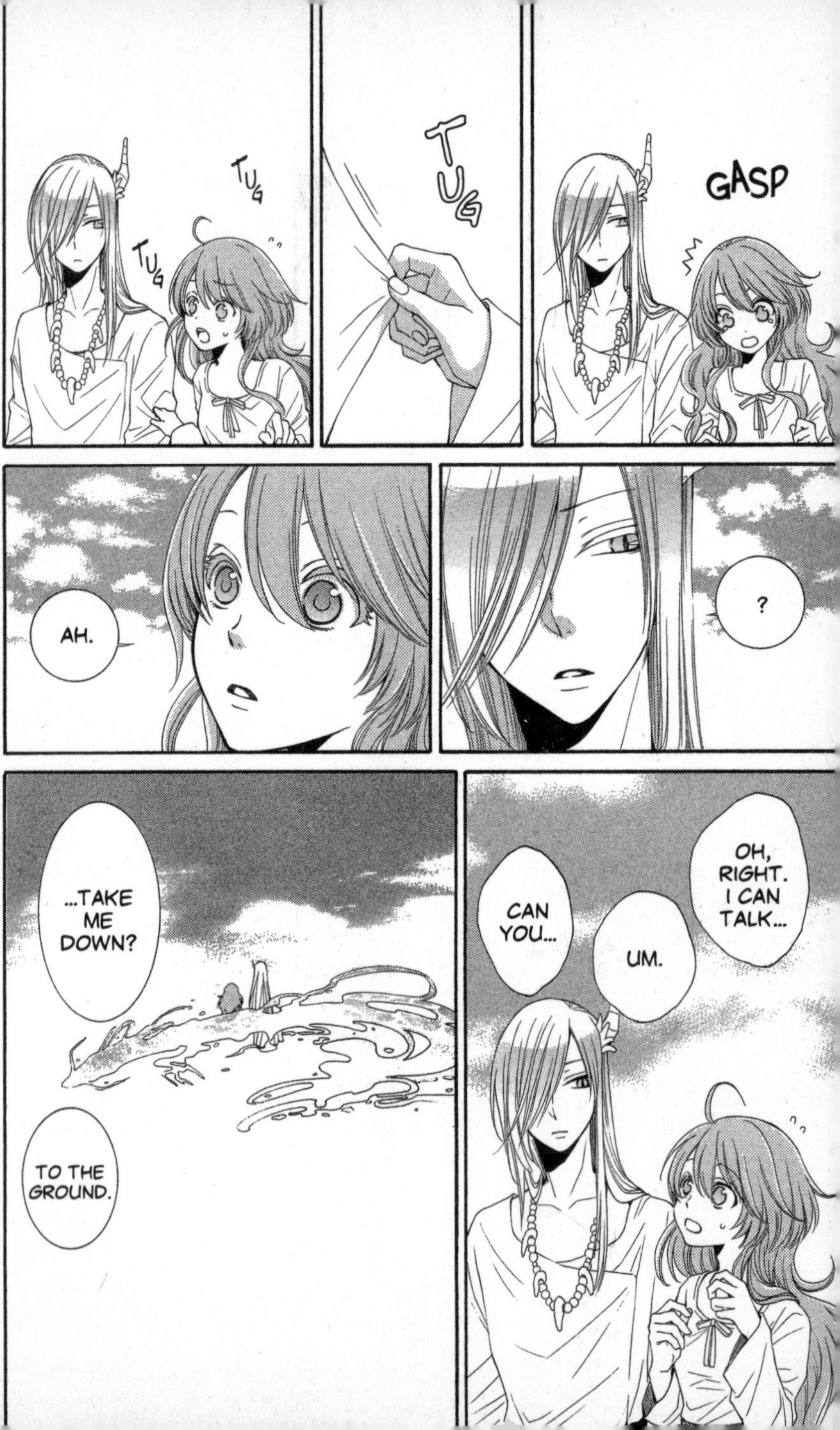
GASP
TUG
TUG
TUG
TUG
?
AH.
OH, RIGHT. I CAN TALK...
UM.
CAN YOU...
...TAKE ME DOWN?
TO THE GROUND.

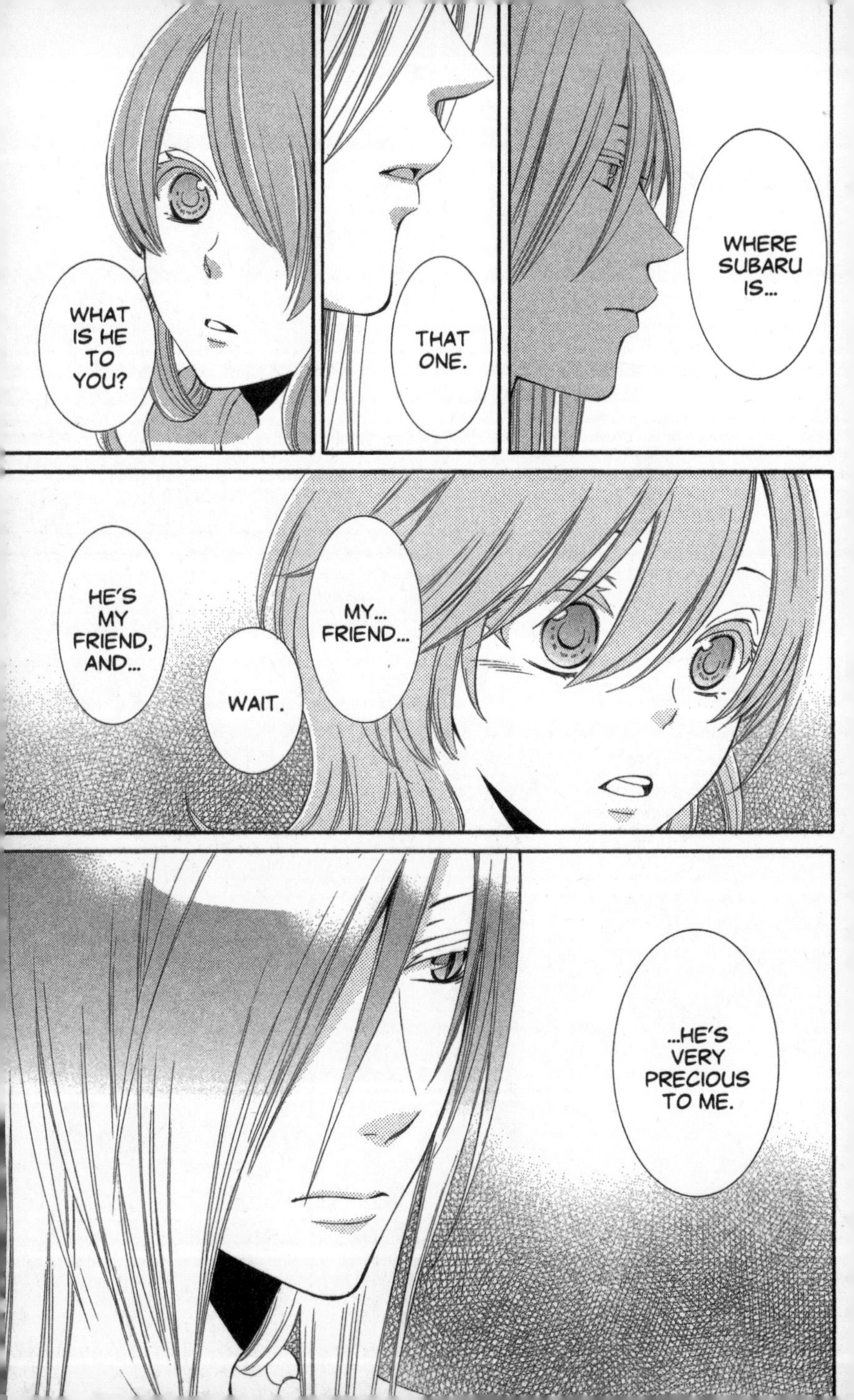
WHERE SUBARU IS...
THAT ONE.
WHAT IS HE TO YOU?
MY... FRIEND...
WAIT.
HE'S MY FRIEND, AND...
...HE'S VERY PRECIOUS TO ME.

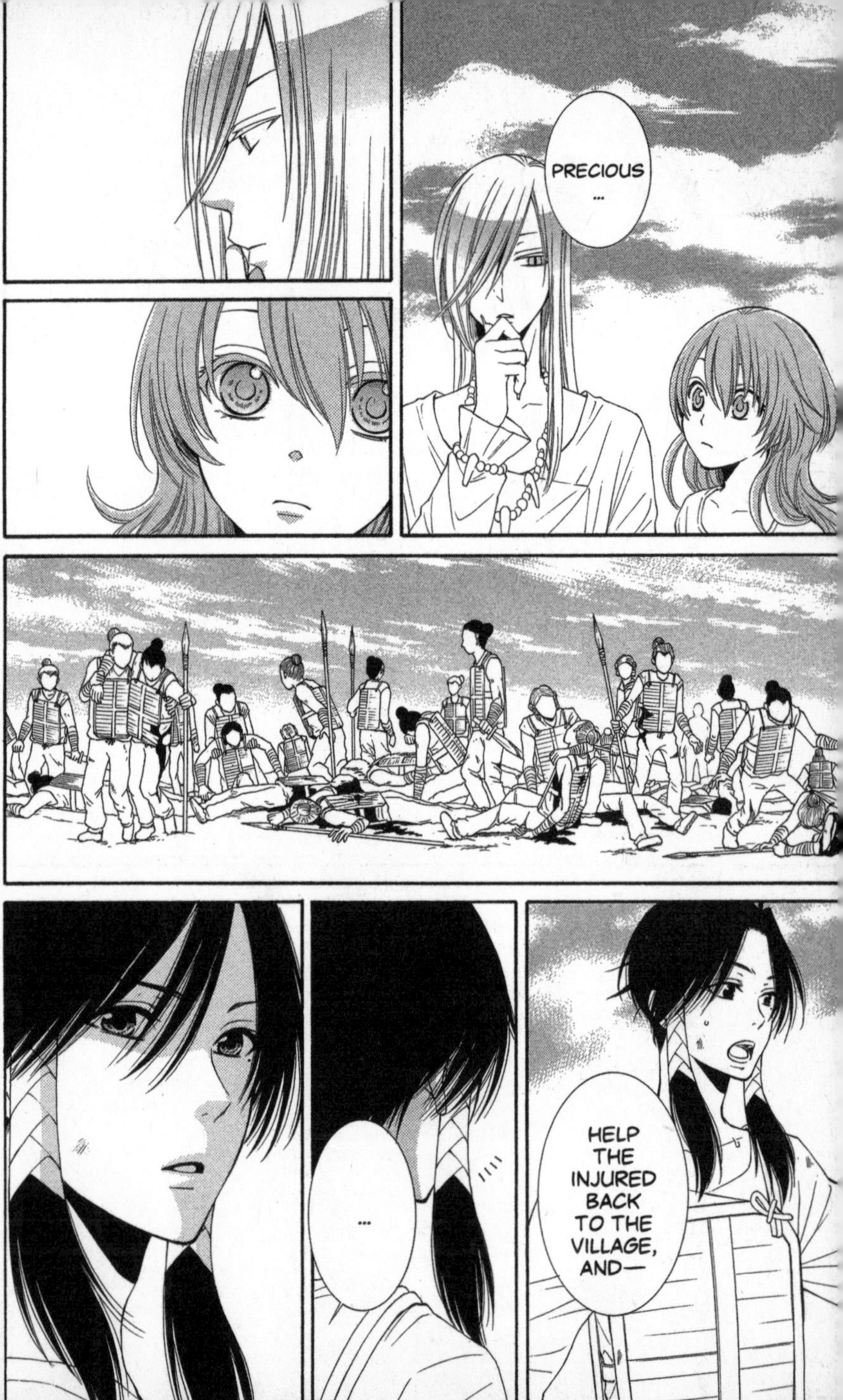

PRECIOUS ...
...
HELP THE INJURED BACK TO THE VILLAGE, AND—

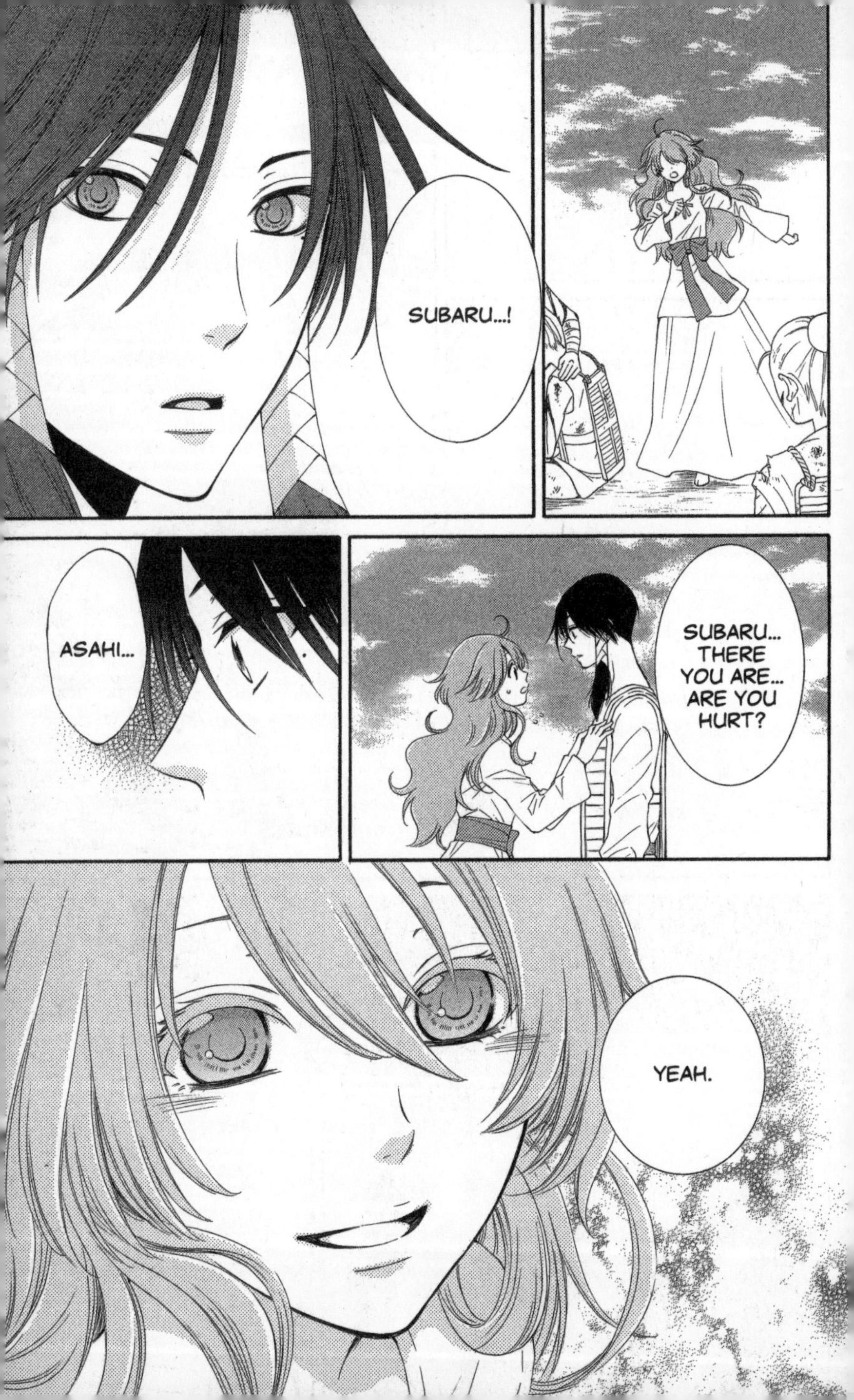
SUBARU...!
SUBARU... THERE YOU ARE... ARE YOU HURT?
ASAHI...
YEAH.

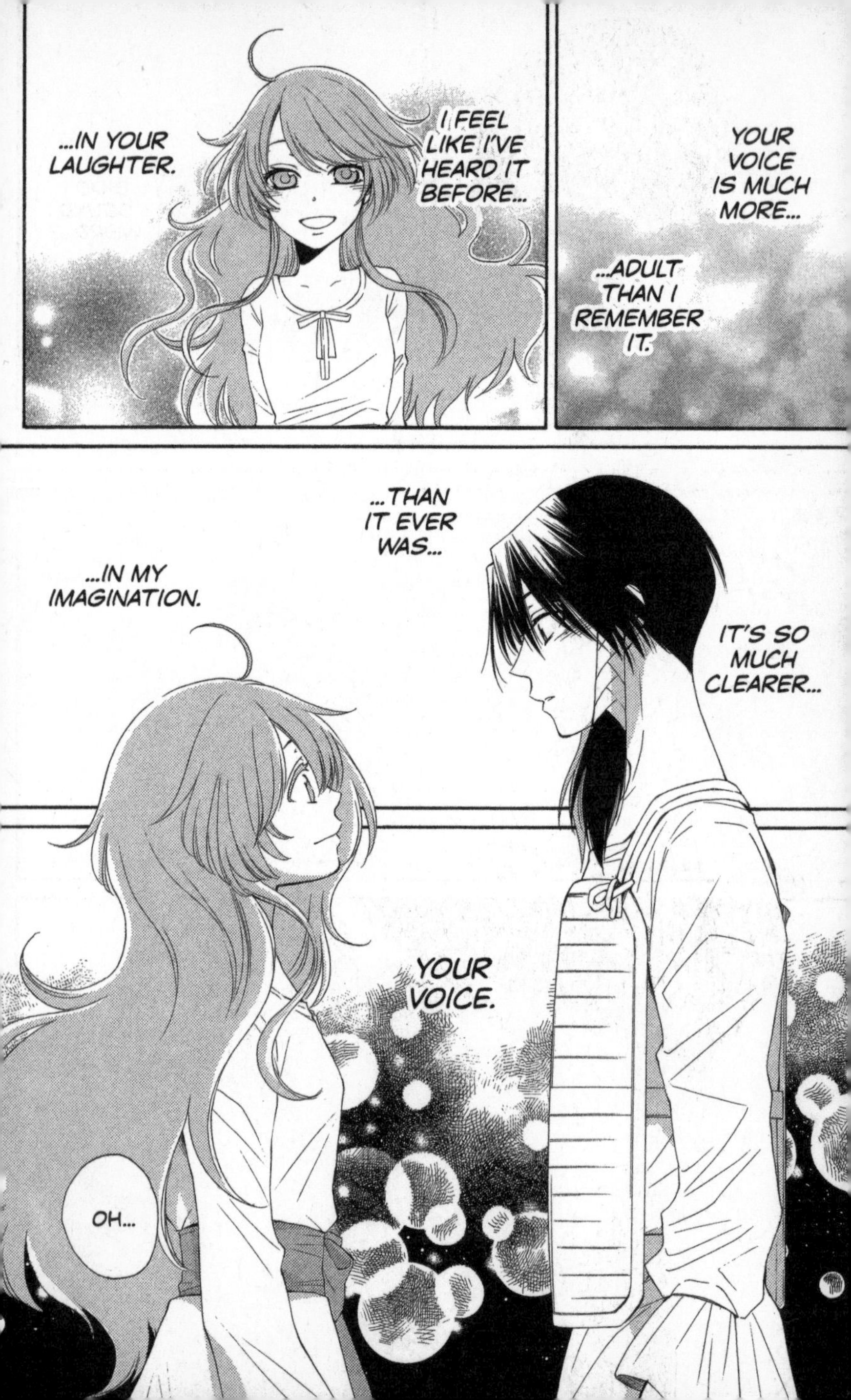
YOUR VOICE IS MUCH MORE...
...ADULT THAN I REMEMBER IT.
I FEEL LIKE I'VE HEARD IT BEFORE...
...IN YOUR LAUGHTER.
IT'S SO MUCH CLEARER...
...THAN IT EVER WAS...
...IN MY IMAGINATION.
YOUR VOICE.
OH...

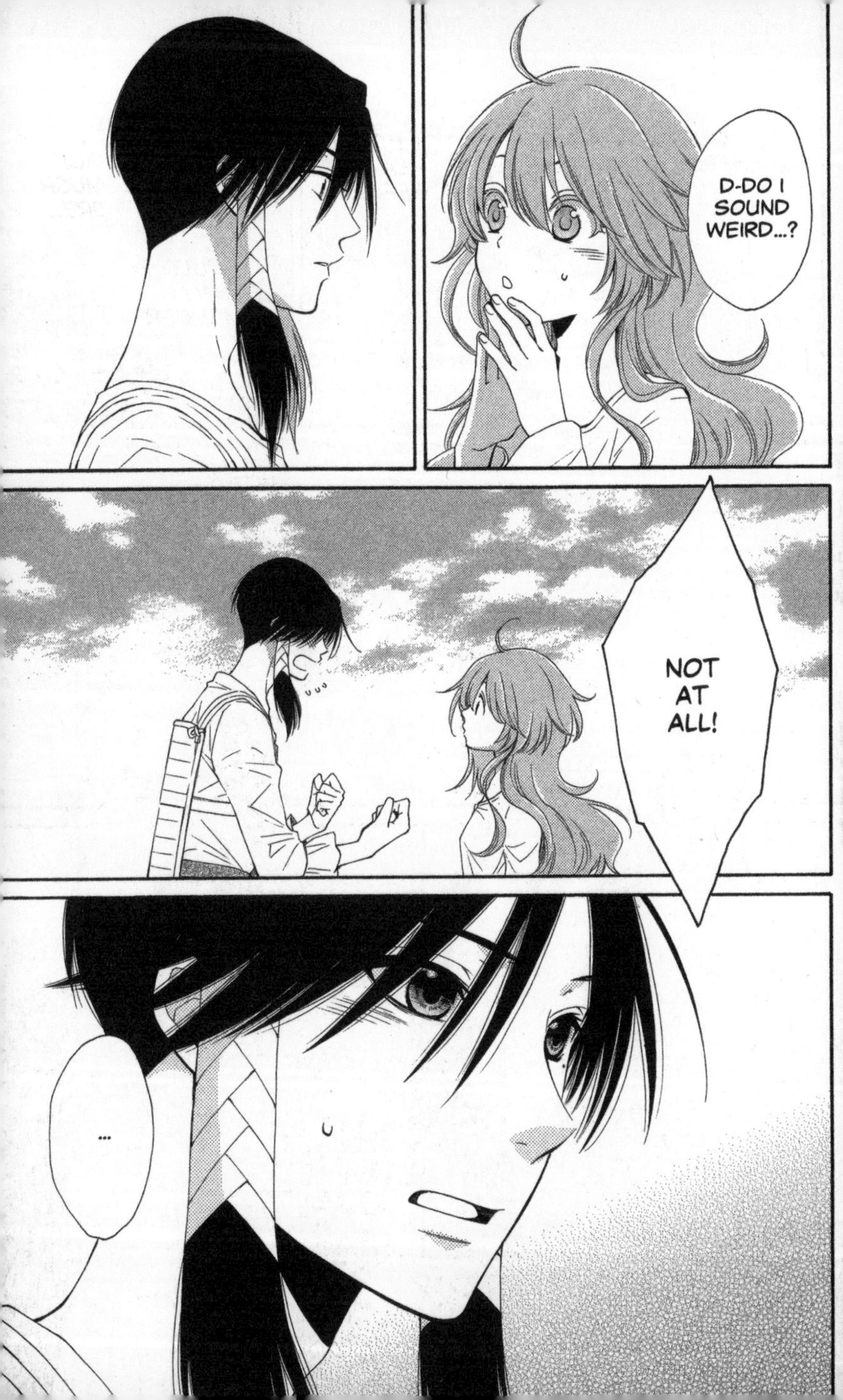
D-DO I SOUND WEIRD...?
NOT AT ALL!
...

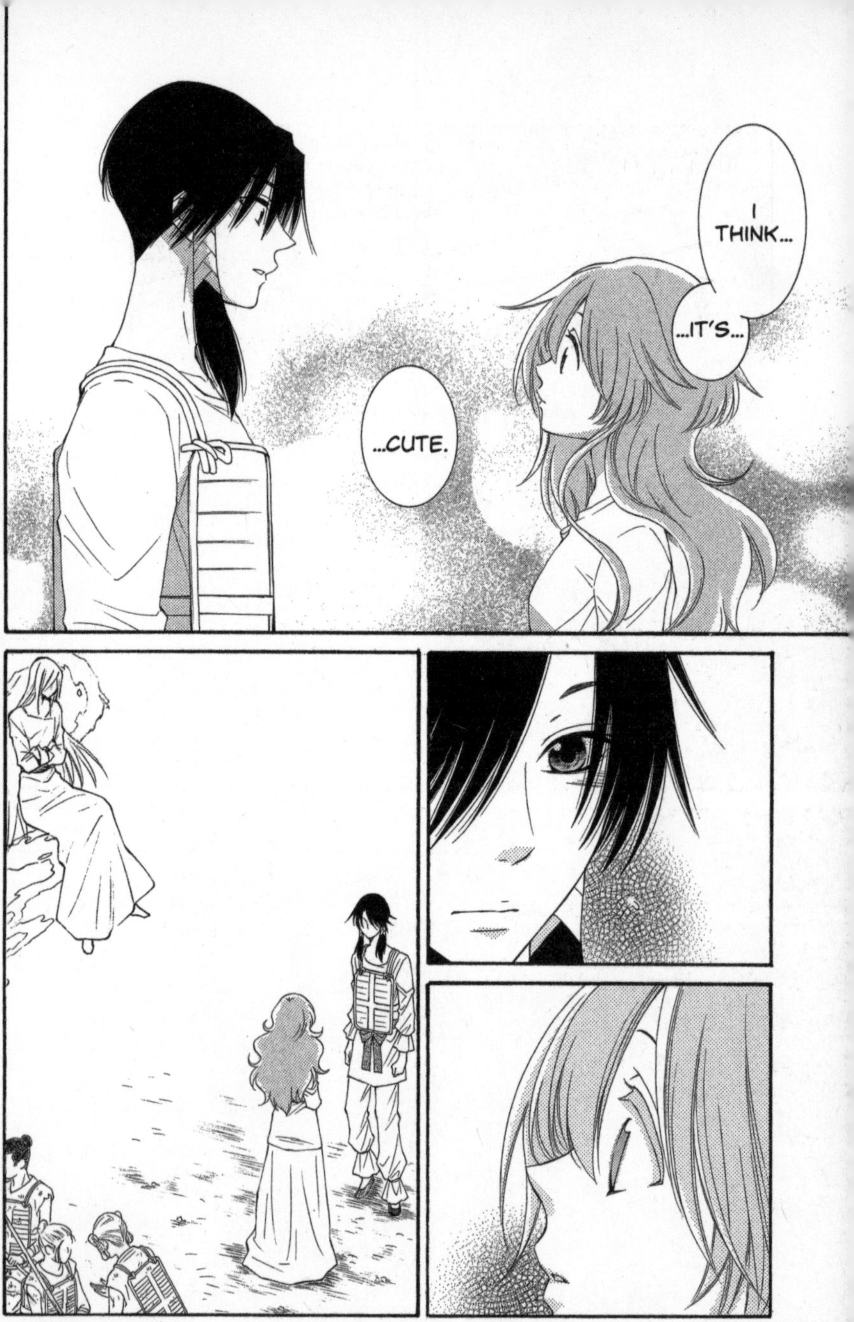
I THINK...
...IT'S...
...CUTE.

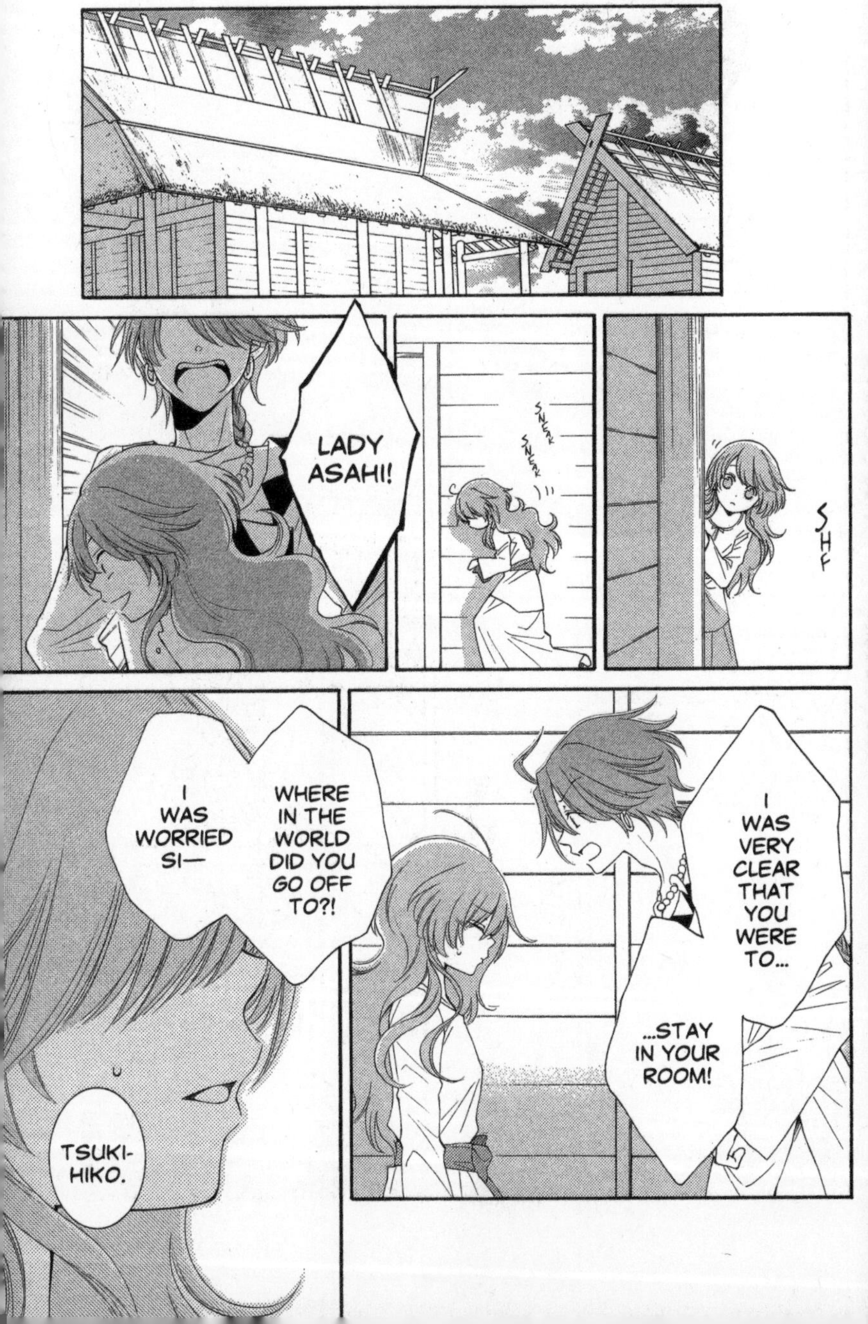
SHF
SNEAK SNEAK
LADY ASAHI!
I WAS VERY CLEAR THAT YOU WERE TO...
...STAY IN YOUR ROOM!
WHERE IN THE WORLD DID YOU GO OFF TO?!
I WAS WORRIED SI—
TSUKI-HIKO.

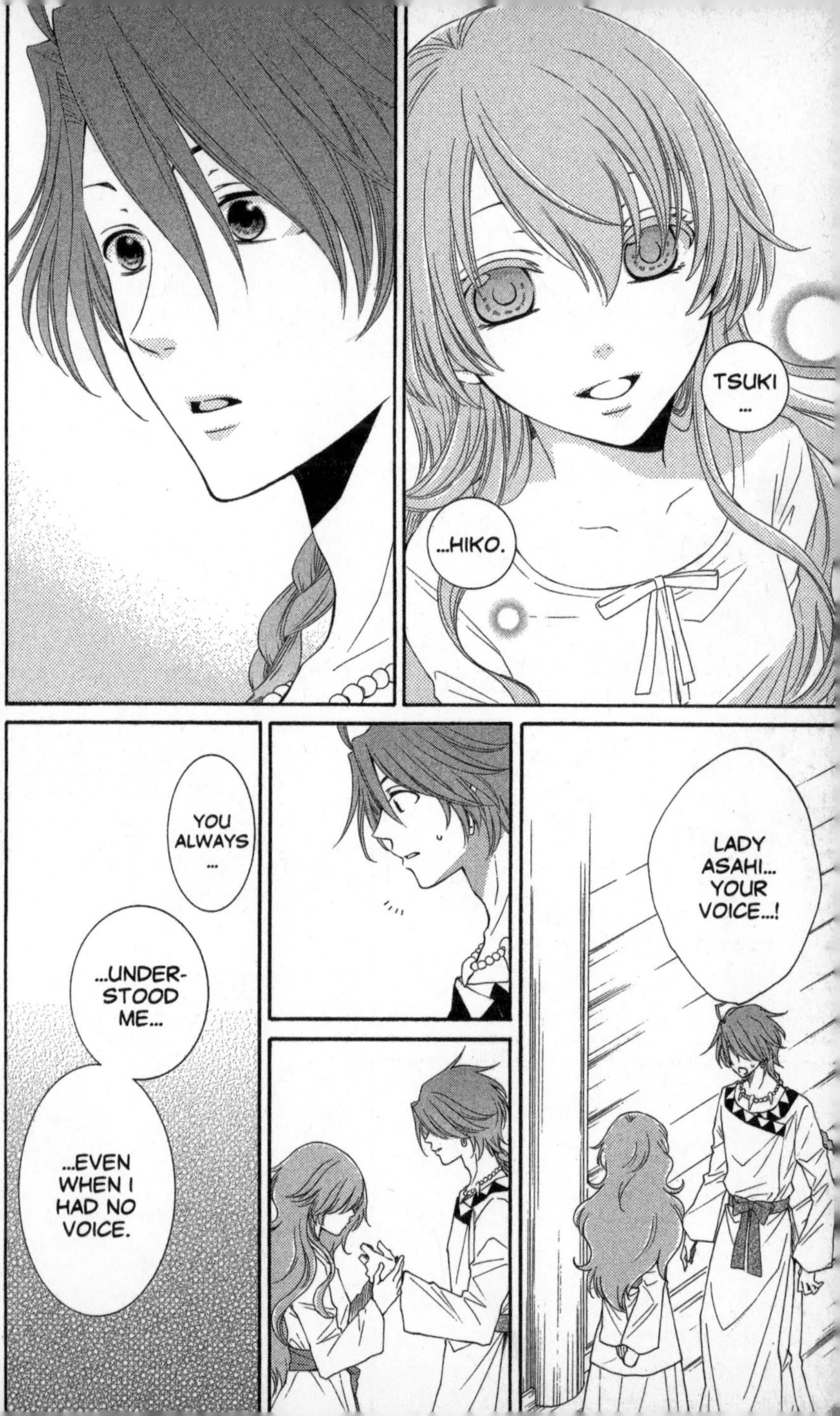
TSUKI ...
...HIKO.
LADY ASAHI... YOUR VOICE...!
YOU ALWAYS ...
...UNDER-STOOD ME...
...EVEN WHEN I HAD NO VOICE.

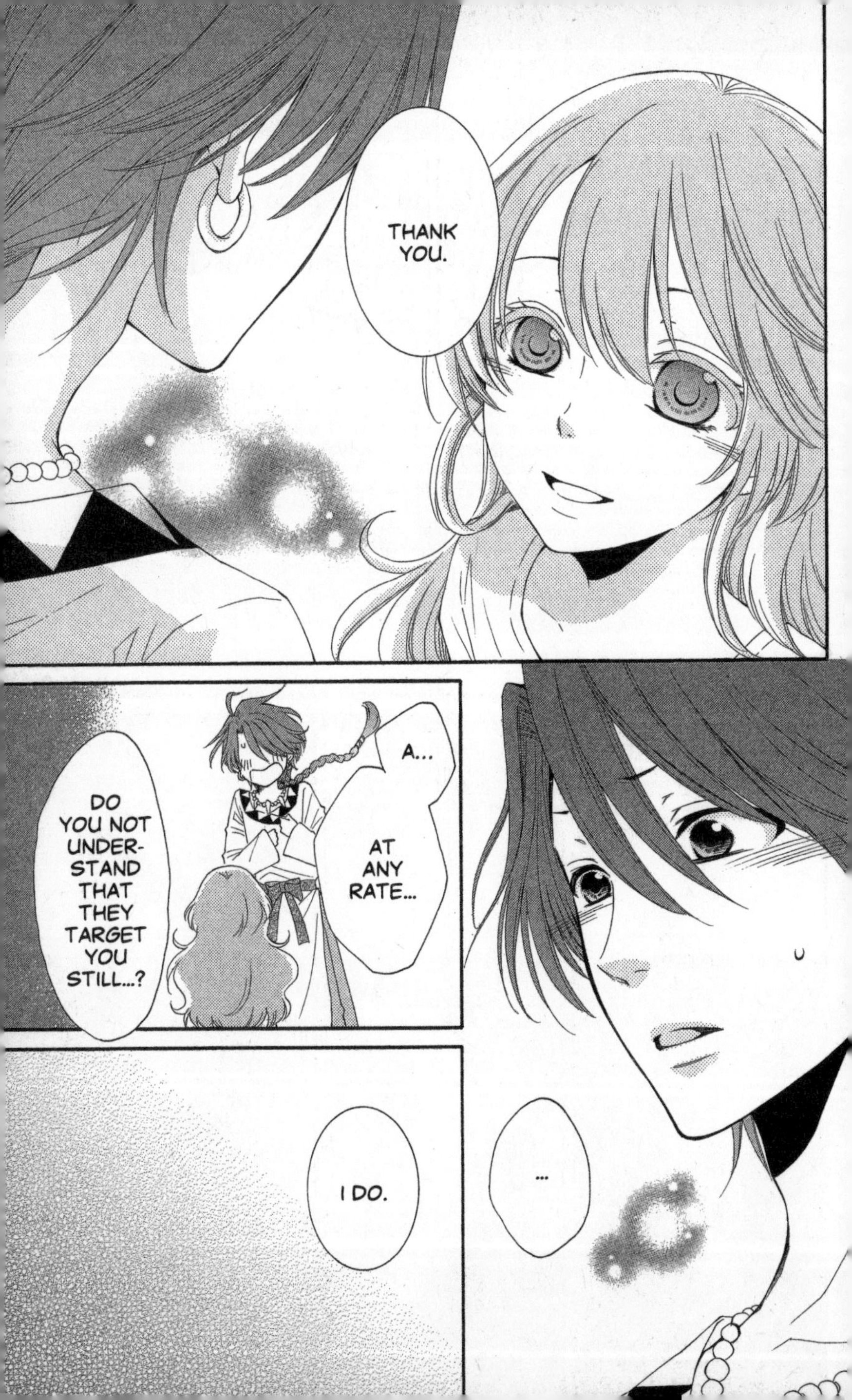
THANK YOU.
...
A...
AT ANY RATE...
DO YOU NOT UNDERSTAND THAT THEY TARGET YOU STILL...?
I DO.

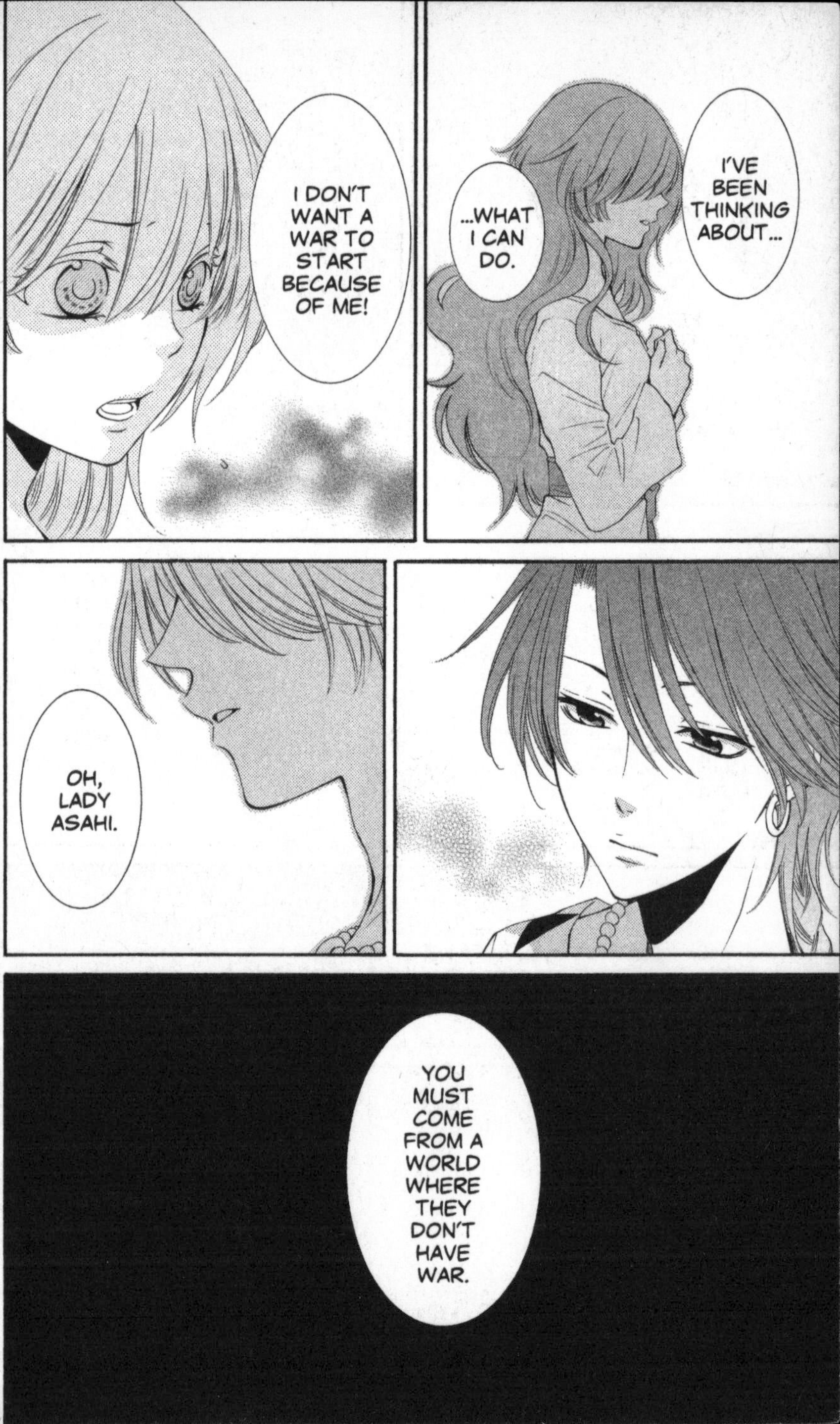
I'VE BEEN THINKING ABOUT...
...WHAT I CAN DO.
I DON'T WANT A WAR TO START BECAUSE OF ME!
OH, LADY ASAHI.
YOU MUST COME FROM A WORLD WHERE THEY DON'T HAVE WAR.

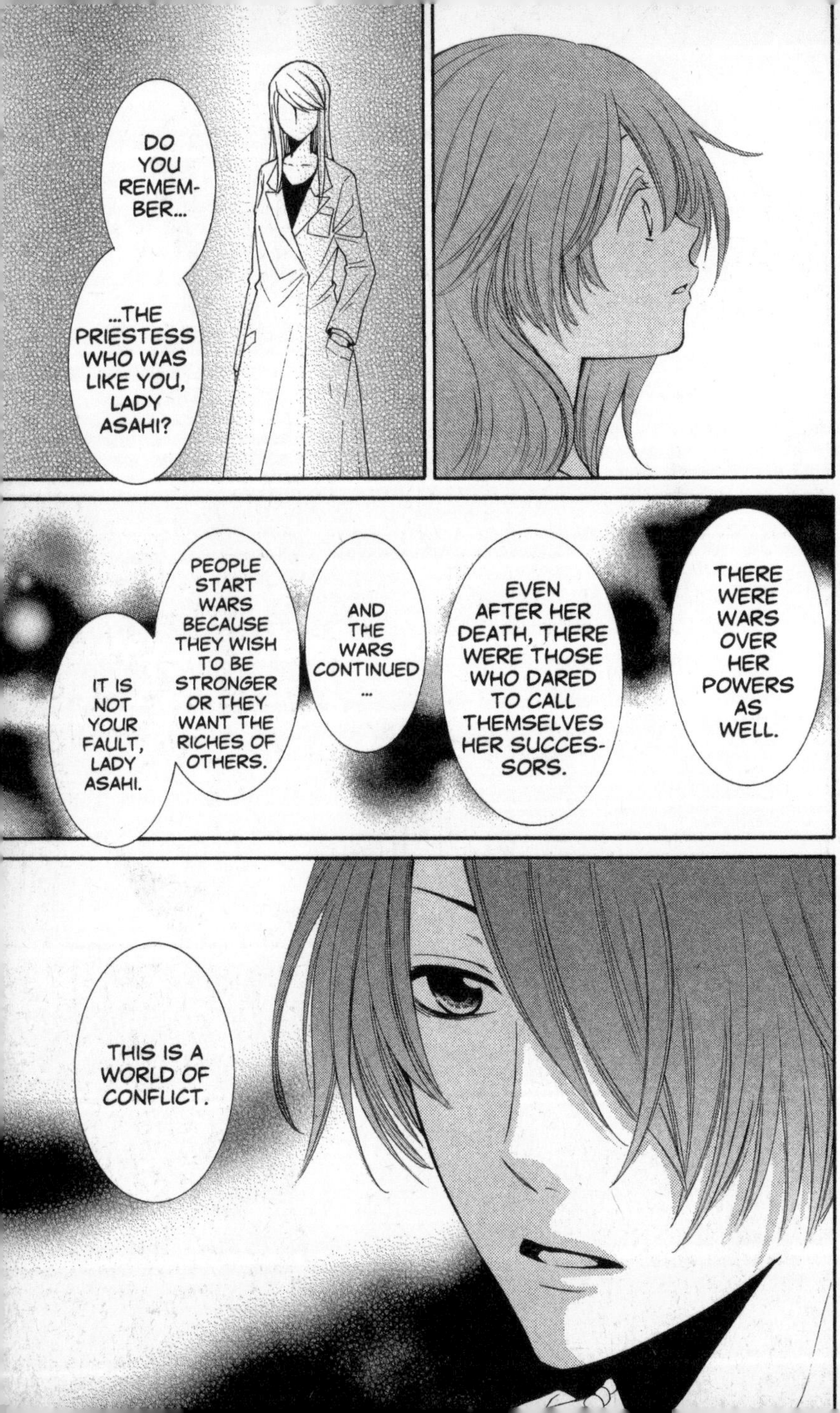
DO YOU REMEMBER...
...THE PRIESTESS WHO WAS LIKE YOU, LADY ASAHI?
THERE WERE WARS OVER HER POWERS AS WELL.
EVEN AFTER HER DEATH, THERE WERE THOSE WHO DARED TO CALL THEMSELVES HER SUCCESSORS.
AND THE WARS CONTINUED...
PEOPLE START WARS BECAUSE THEY WISH TO BE STRONGER OR THEY WANT THE RICHES OF OTHERS.
IT IS NOT YOUR FAULT, LADY ASAHI.
THIS IS A WORLD OF CONFLICT.

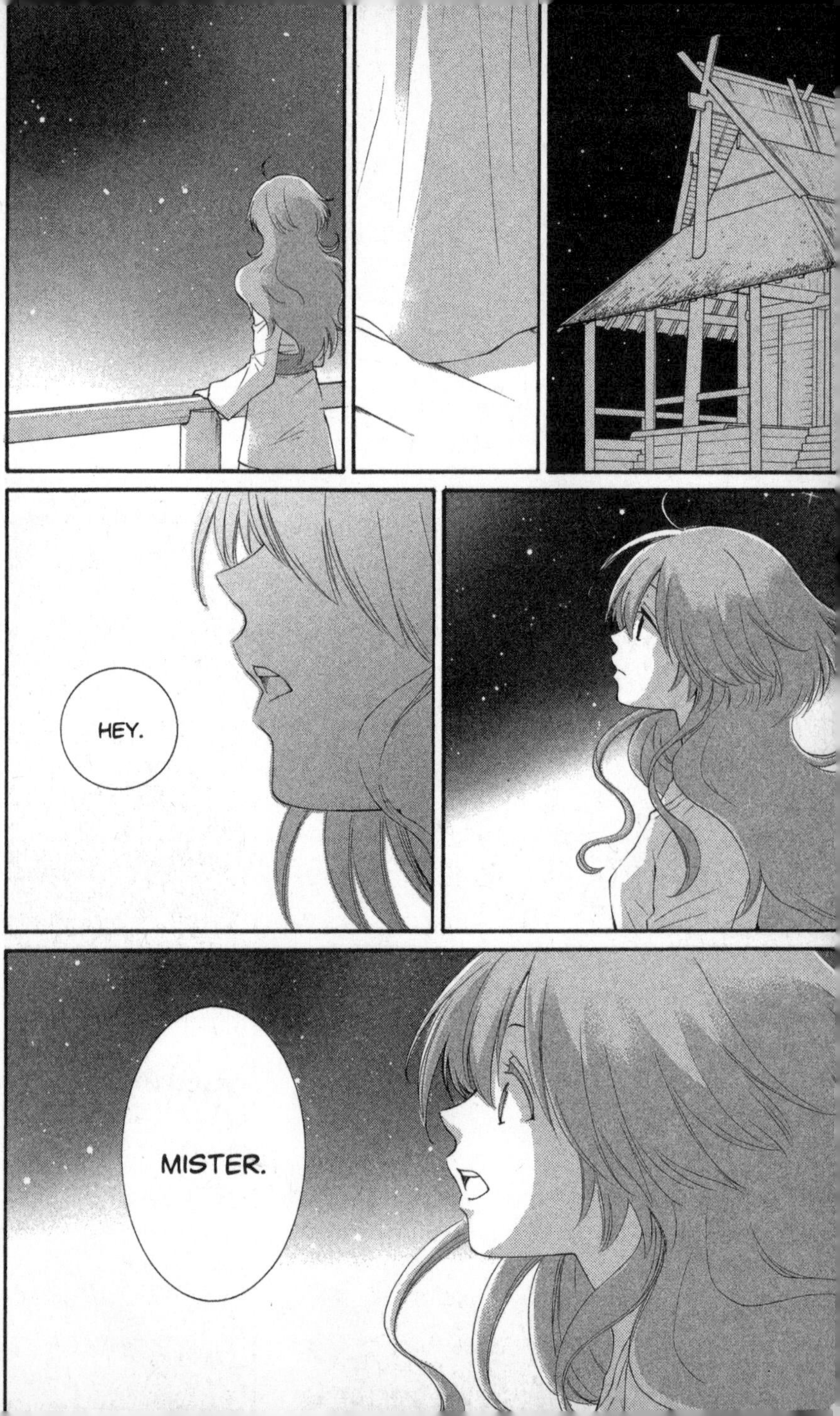
HEY.
MISTER.

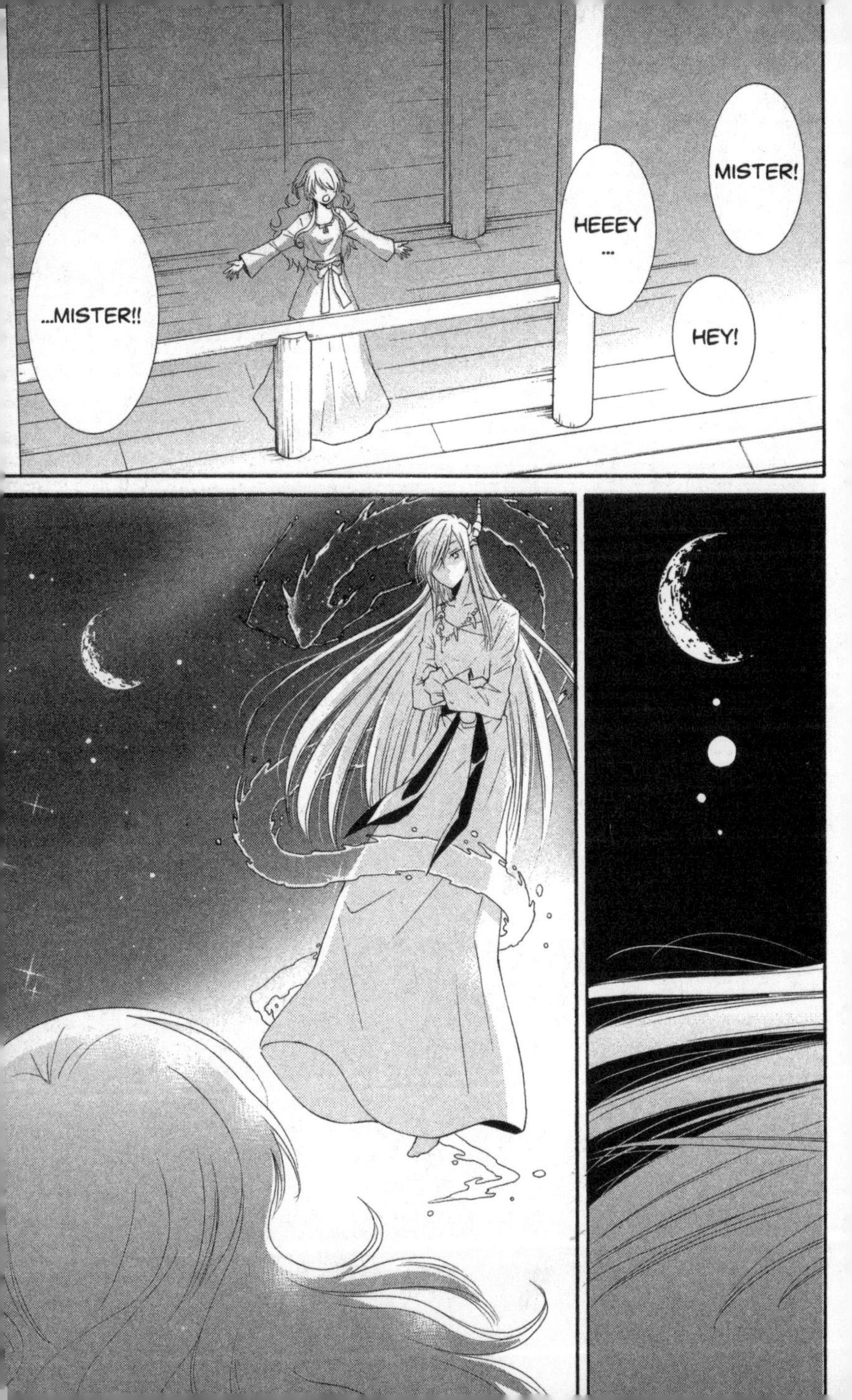
MISTER!
HEY!
HEEEY
...
...MISTER!!

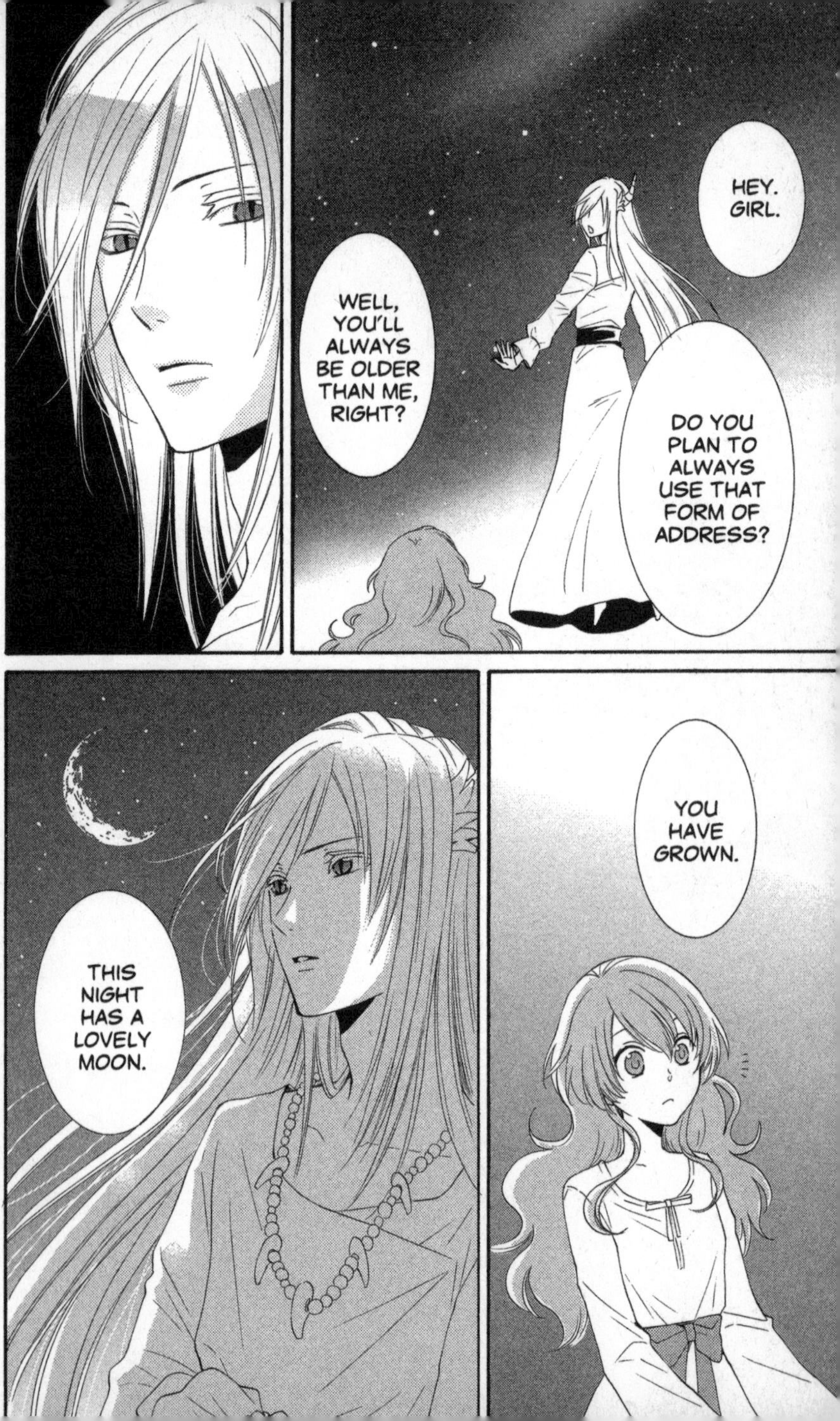
HEY. GIRL.
DO YOU PLAN TO ALWAYS USE THAT FORM OF ADDRESS?
WELL, YOU'LL ALWAYS BE OLDER THAN ME, RIGHT?
YOU HAVE GROWN.
THIS NIGHT HAS A LOVELY MOON.

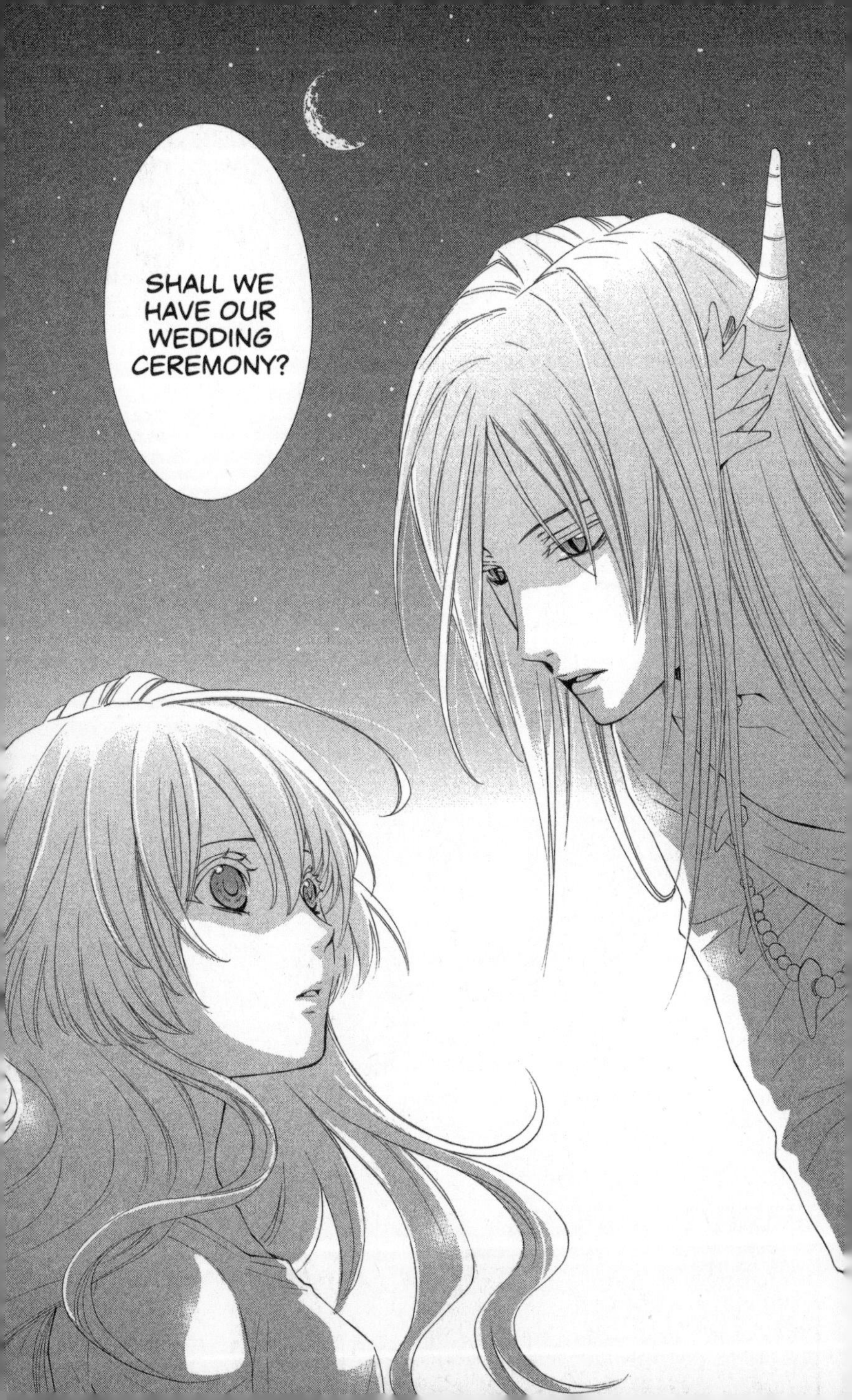
SHALL WE HAVE OUR WEDDING CEREMONY?

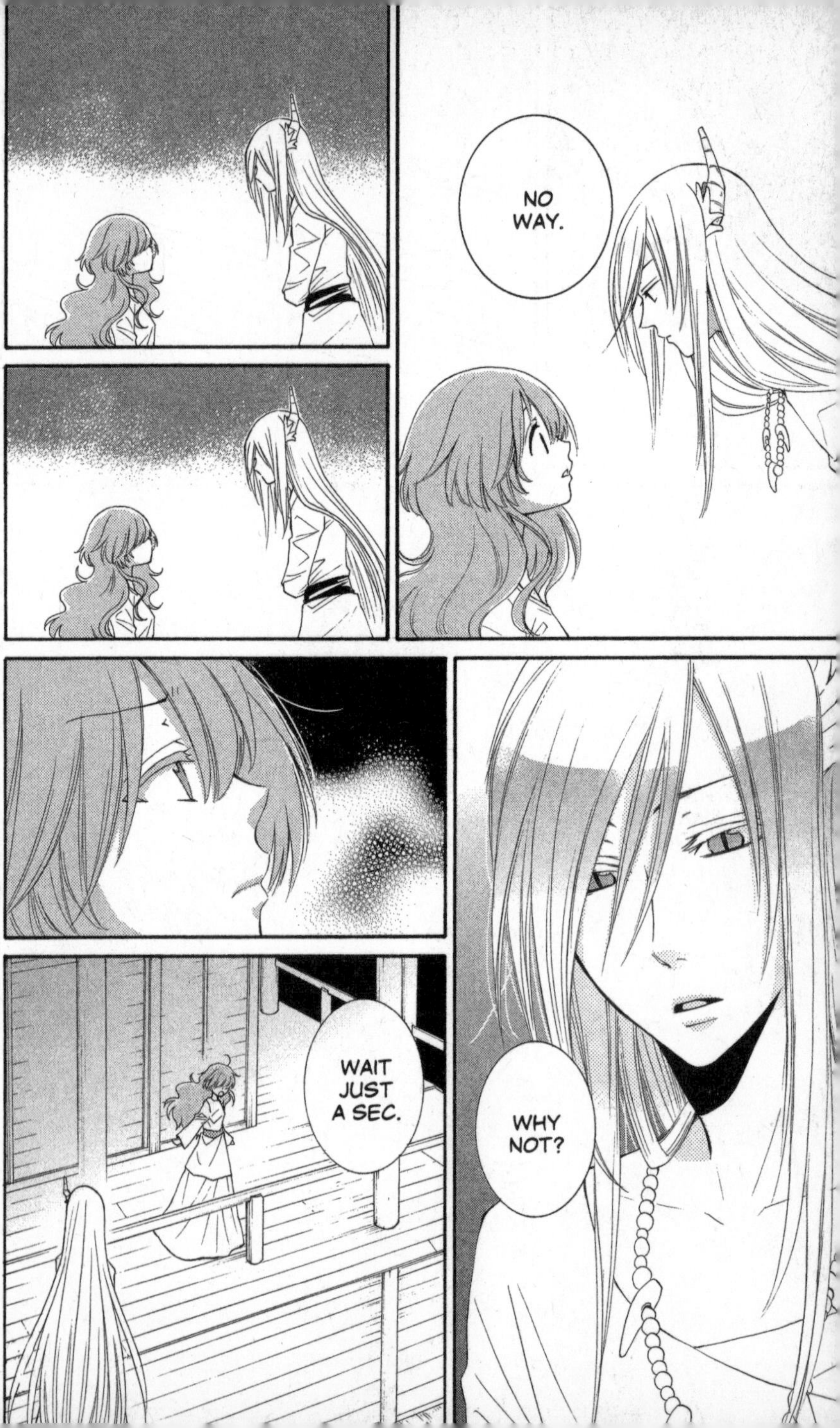
NO WAY.
WHY NOT?
WAIT JUST A SEC.

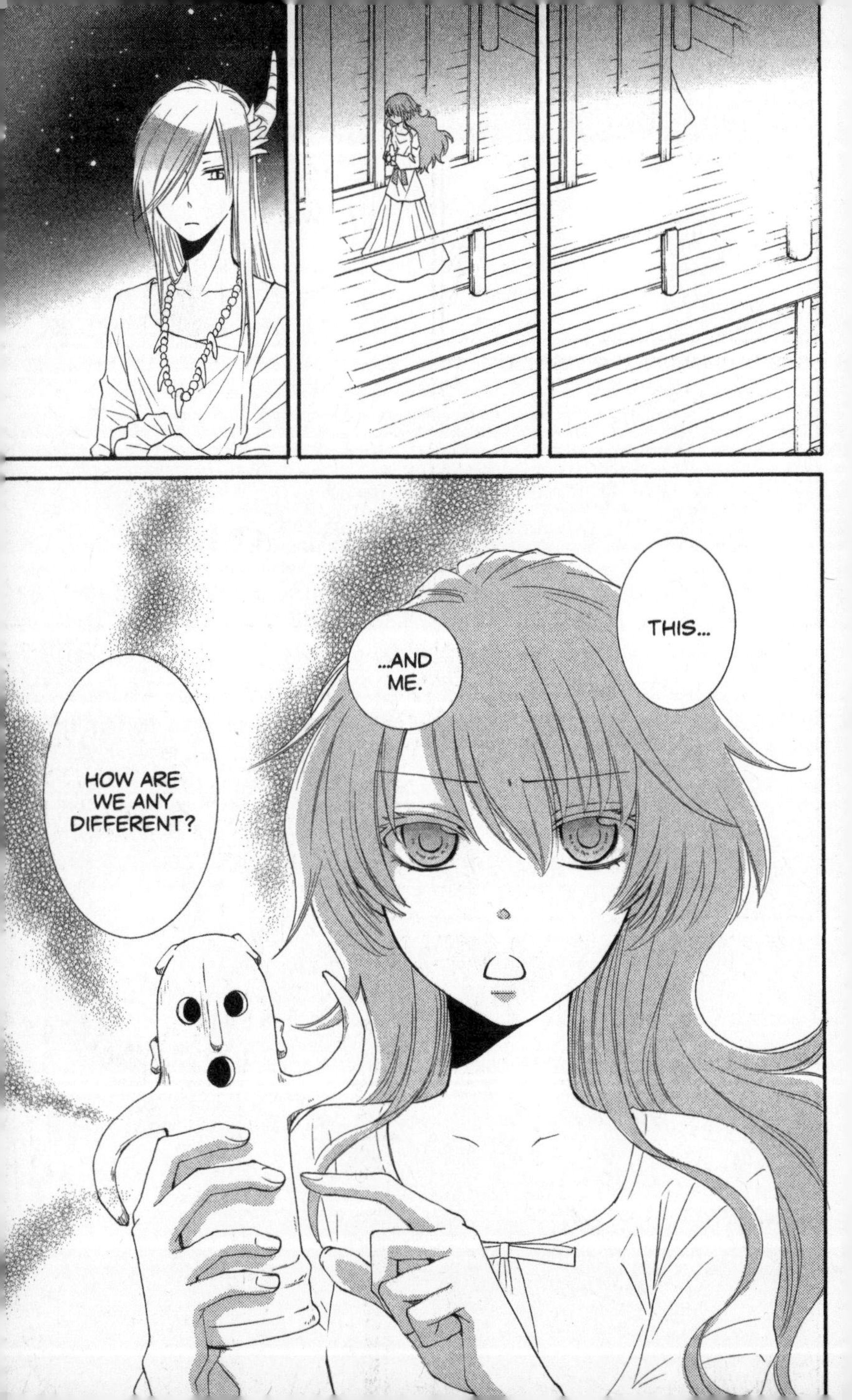
THIS...
...AND ME.
HOW ARE WE ANY DIFFERENT?

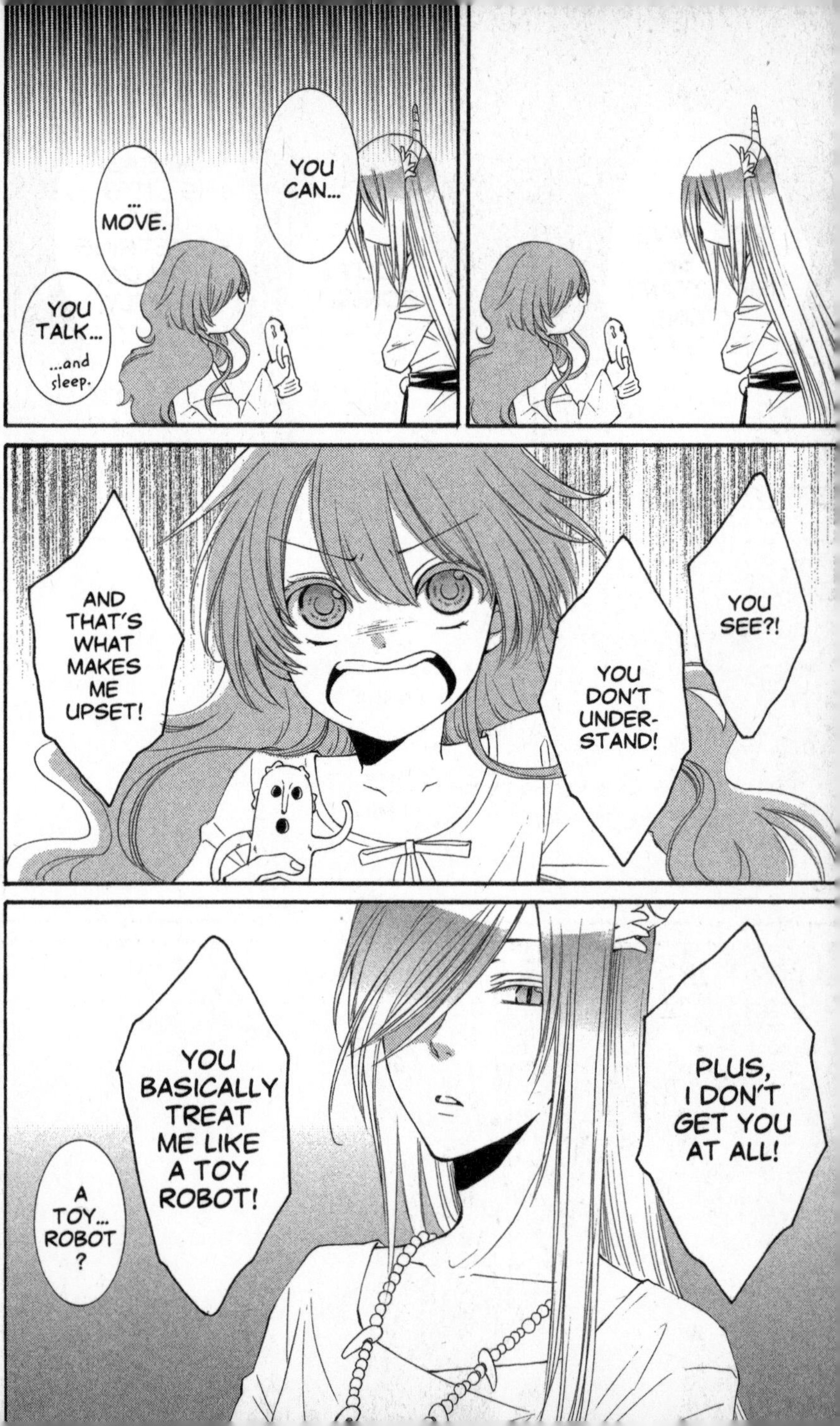
YOU CAN...
... MOVE.
YOU TALK...
...and sleep.
YOU SEE?!
YOU DON'T UNDERSTAND!
AND THAT'S WHAT MAKES ME UPSET!
PLUS, I DON'T GET YOU AT ALL!
YOU BASICALLY TREAT ME LIKE A TOY ROBOT!
A TOY... ROBOT?

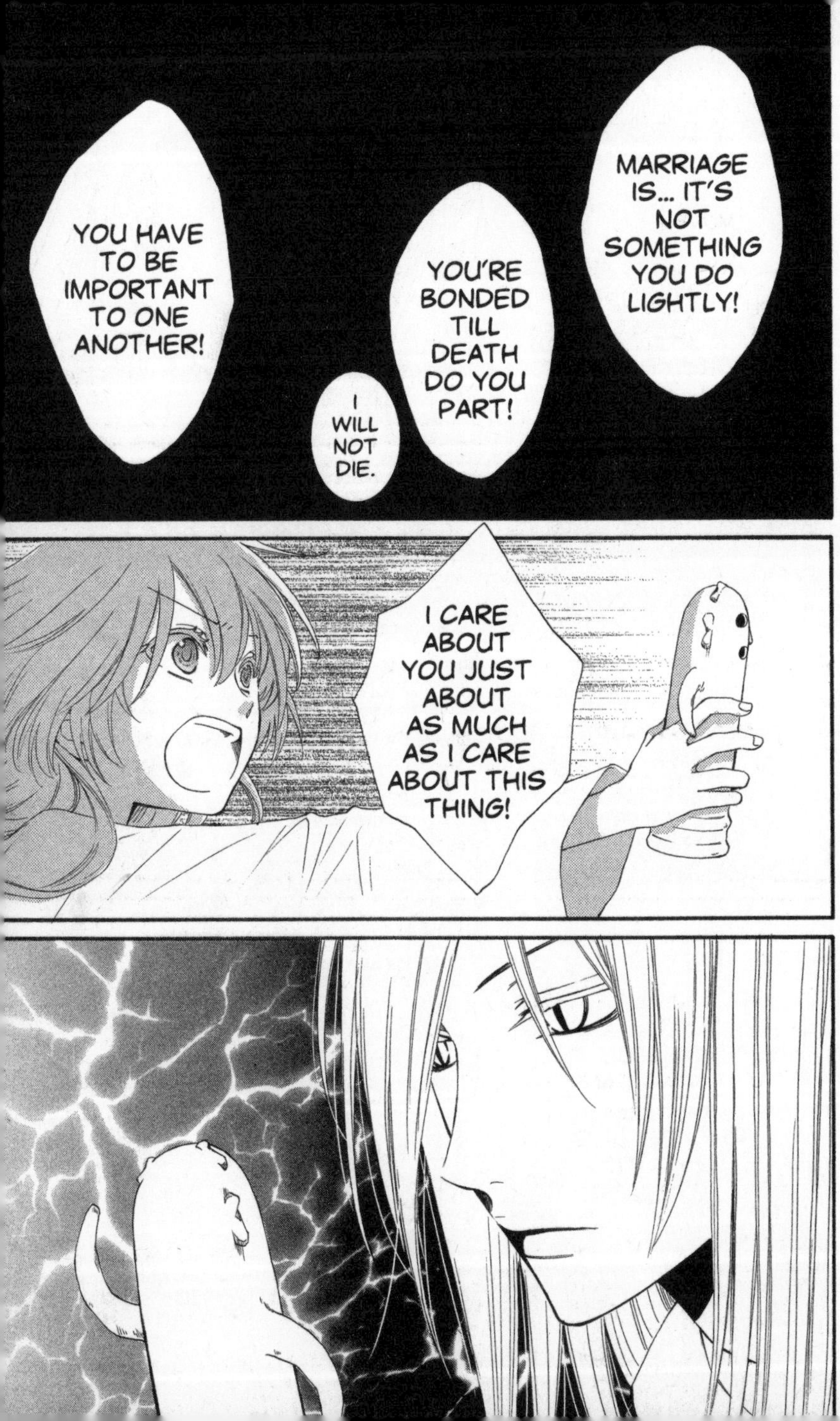
MARRIAGE IS... IT'S NOT SOMETHING YOU DO LIGHTLY!
YOU'RE BONDED TILL DEATH DO YOU PART!
YOU HAVE TO BE IMPORTANT TO ONE ANOTHER!
I WILL NOT DIE.
I CARE ABOUT YOU JUST ABOUT AS MUCH AS I CARE ABOUT THIS THING!

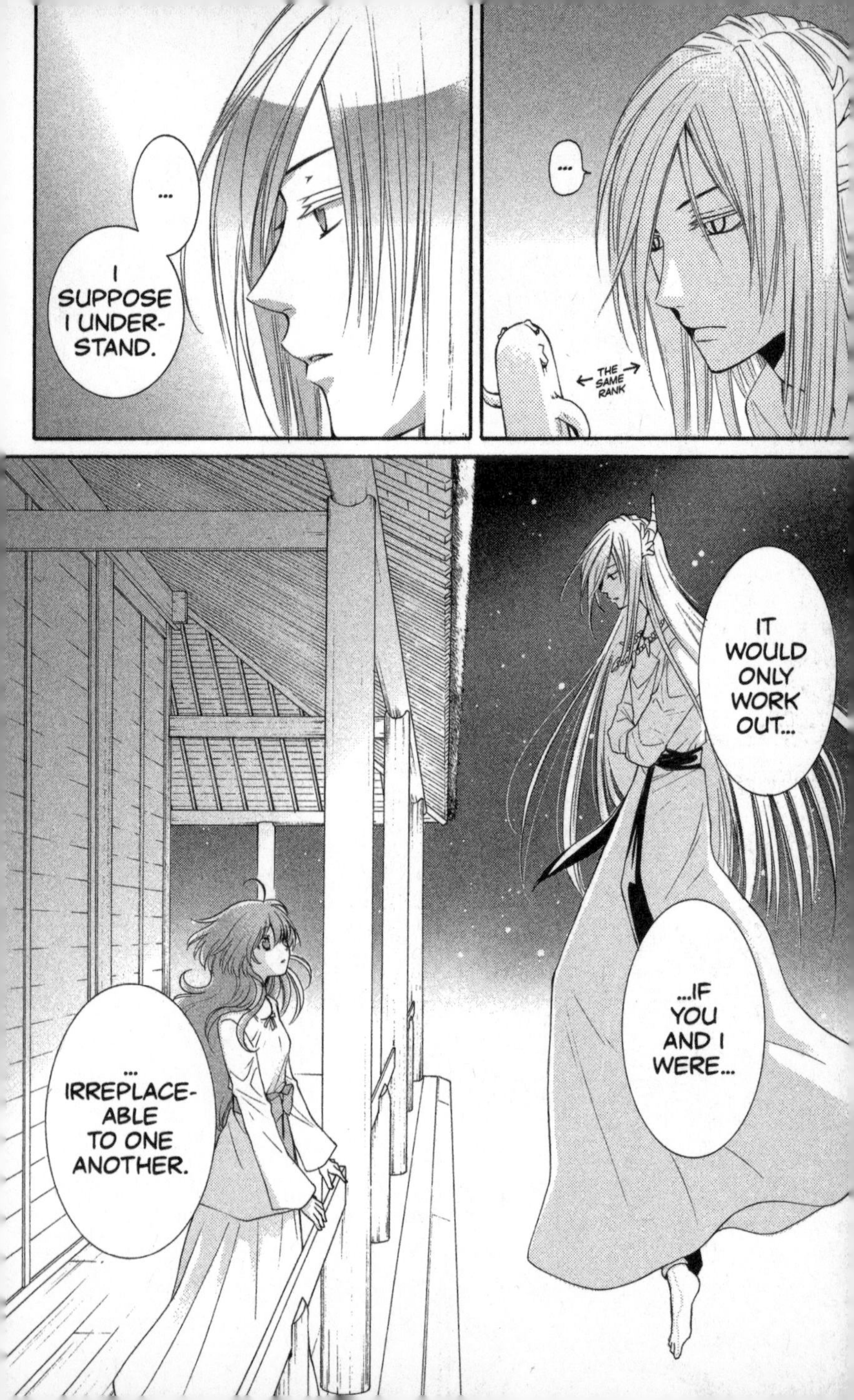
...
THE SAME RANK
...
I SUPPOSE I UNDER-STAND.
IT WOULD ONLY WORK OUT...
...IF YOU AND I WERE...
... IRREPLACE-ABLE TO ONE ANOTHER.

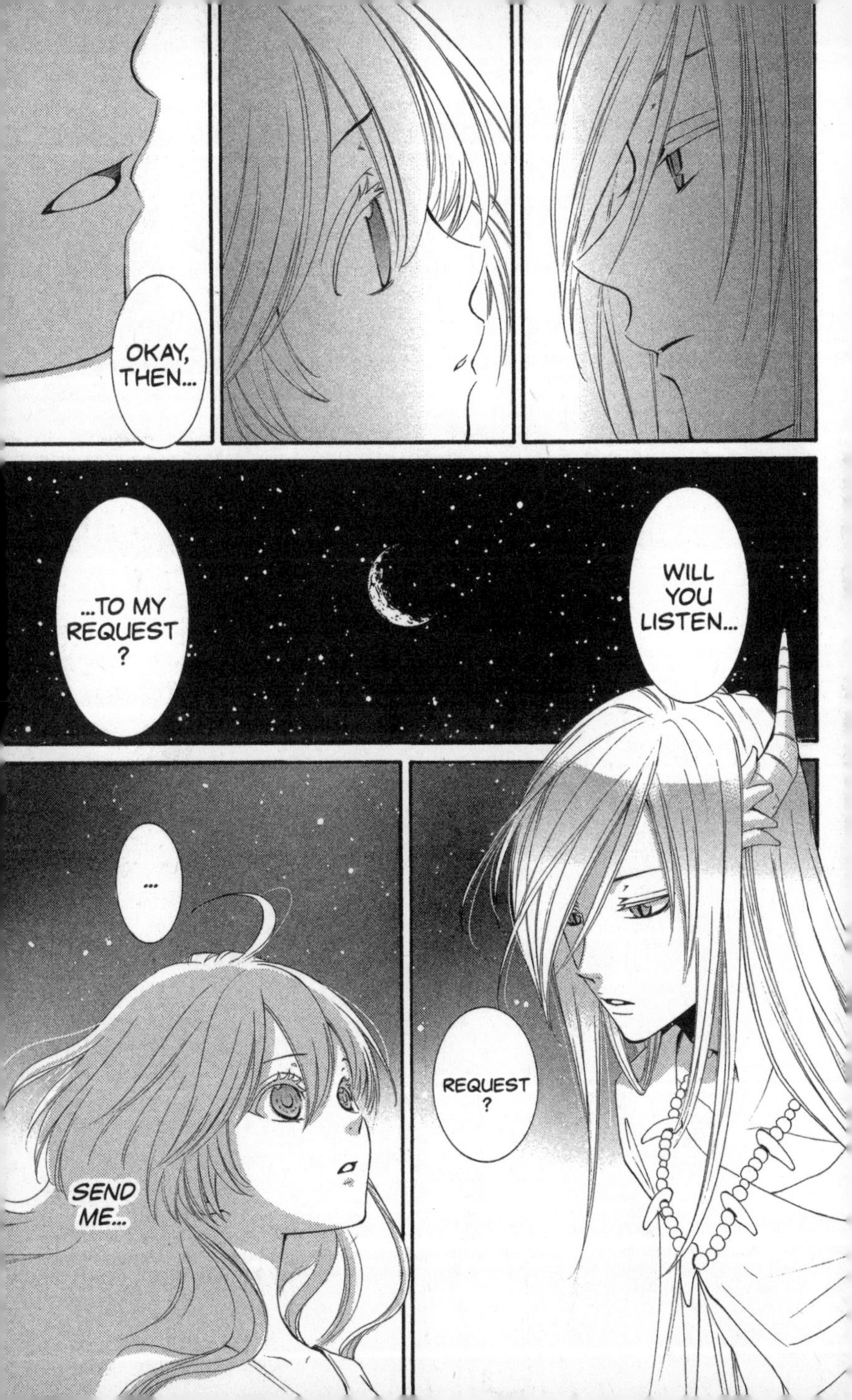
OKAY, THEN...
WILL YOU LISTEN...
...TO MY REQUEST?
REQUEST?
...
SEND ME...

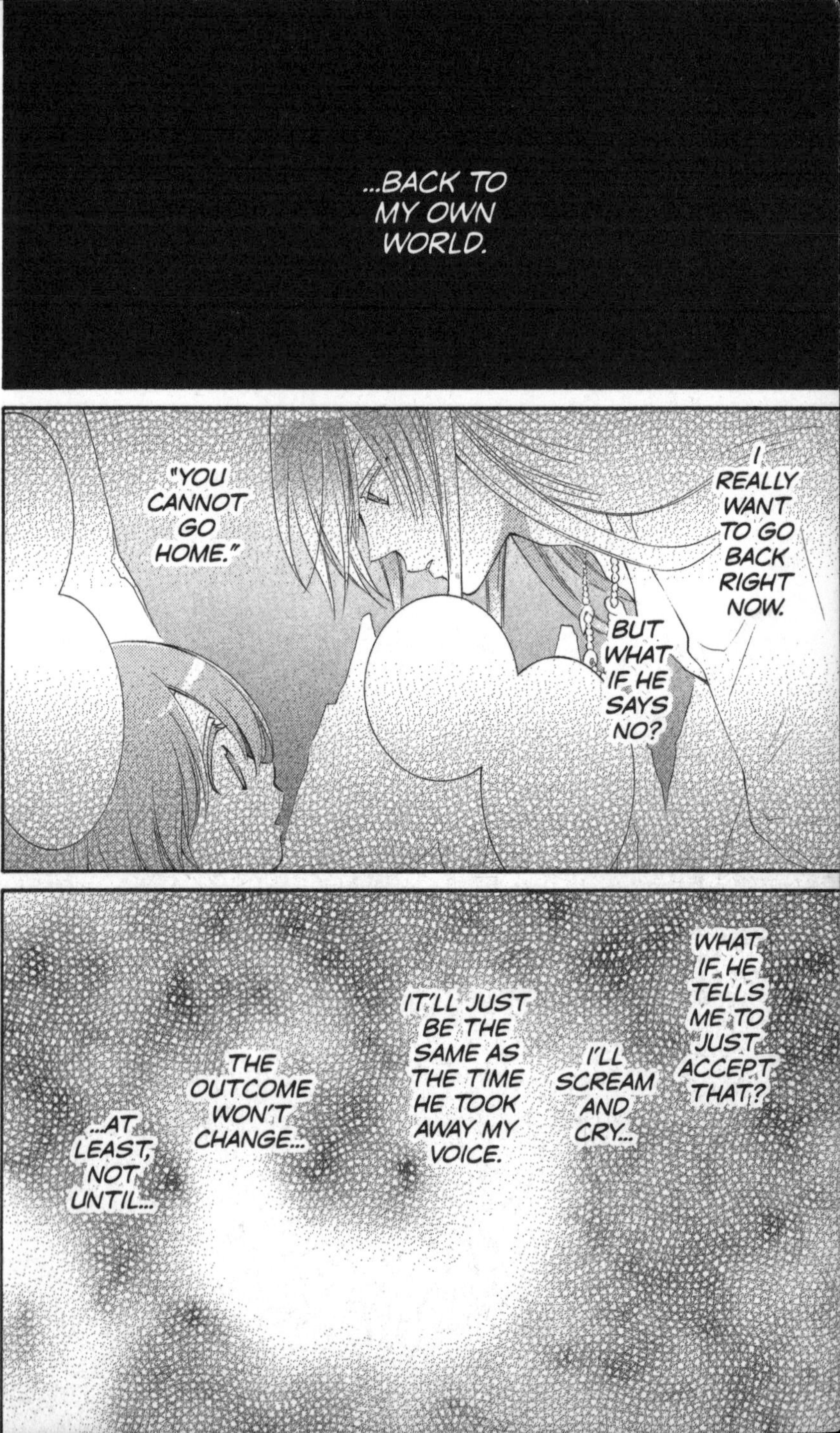
...BACK TO MY OWN WORLD.
I REALLY WANT TO GO BACK RIGHT NOW.
BUT WHAT IF HE SAYS NO?
"YOU CANNOT GO HOME."
WHAT IF HE TELLS ME TO JUST ACCEPT THAT?
I'LL SCREAM AND CRY...
IT'LL JUST BE THE SAME AS THE TIME HE TOOK AWAY MY VOICE.
THE OUTCOME WON'T CHANGE...
...AT LEAST, NOT UNTIL...

...HE THINKS OF ME AS...
...SOMEONE HE REALLY CARES ABOUT.
OR MAYBE THE TRUTH IS...
...I'M TERRIFIED...
...THAT HE'LL JUST TELL ME...
..."IT'S IMPOSSIBLE."

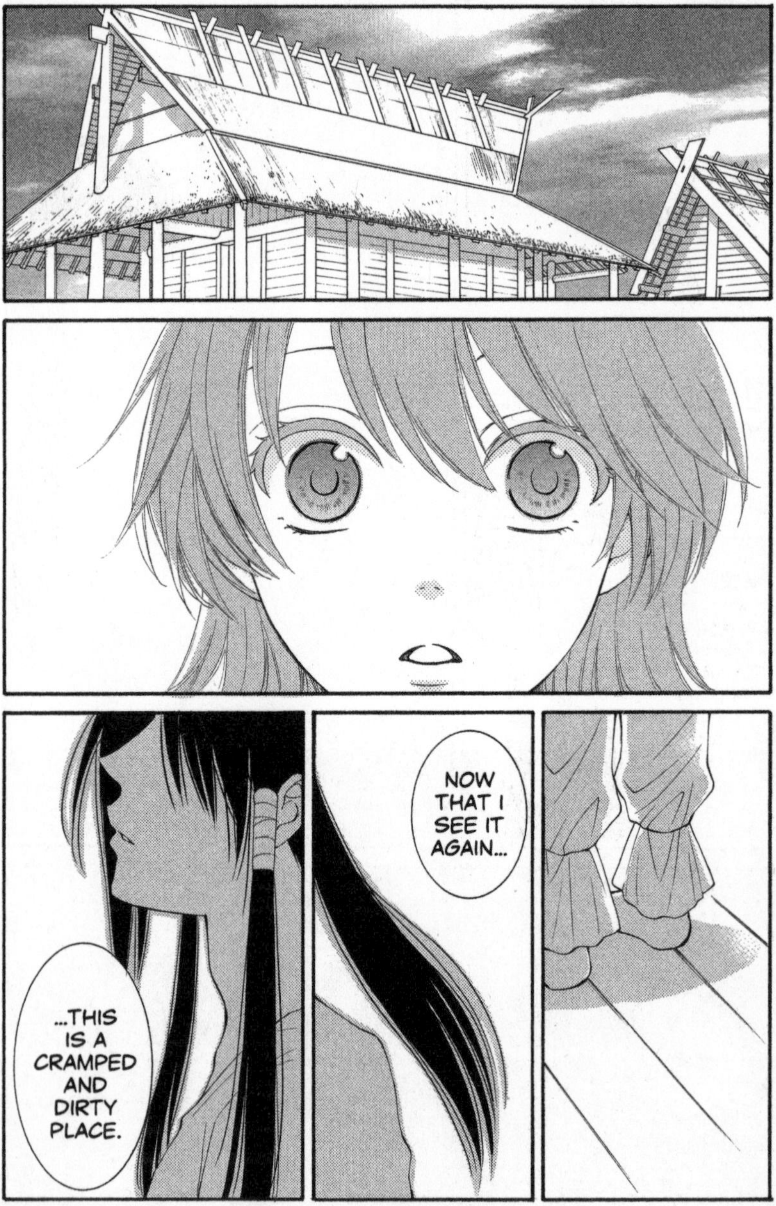
NOW THAT I SEE IT AGAIN...
...THIS IS A CRAMPED AND DIRTY PLACE.

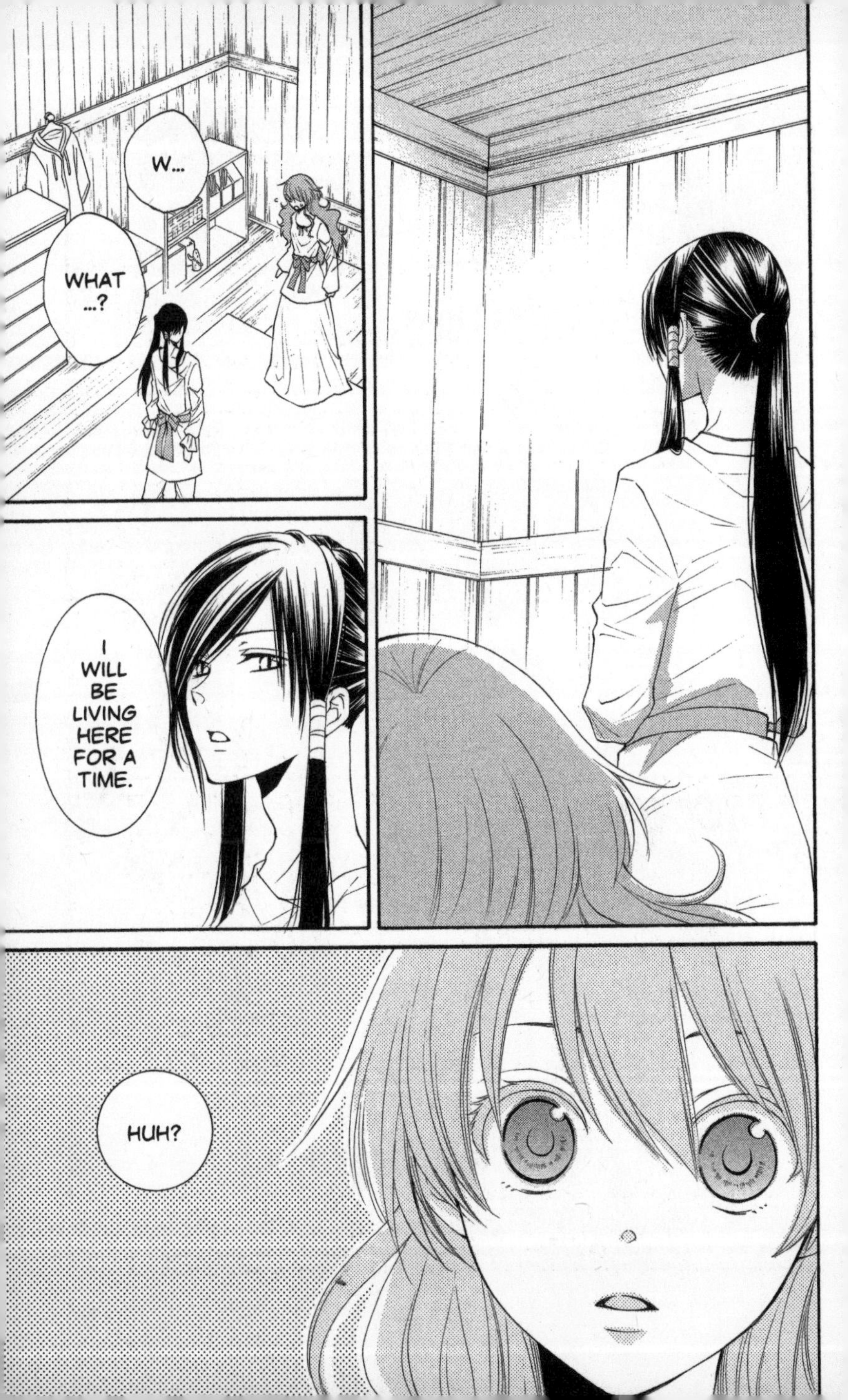
W...
WHAT ...?
I WILL BE LIVING HERE FOR A TIME.
HUH?

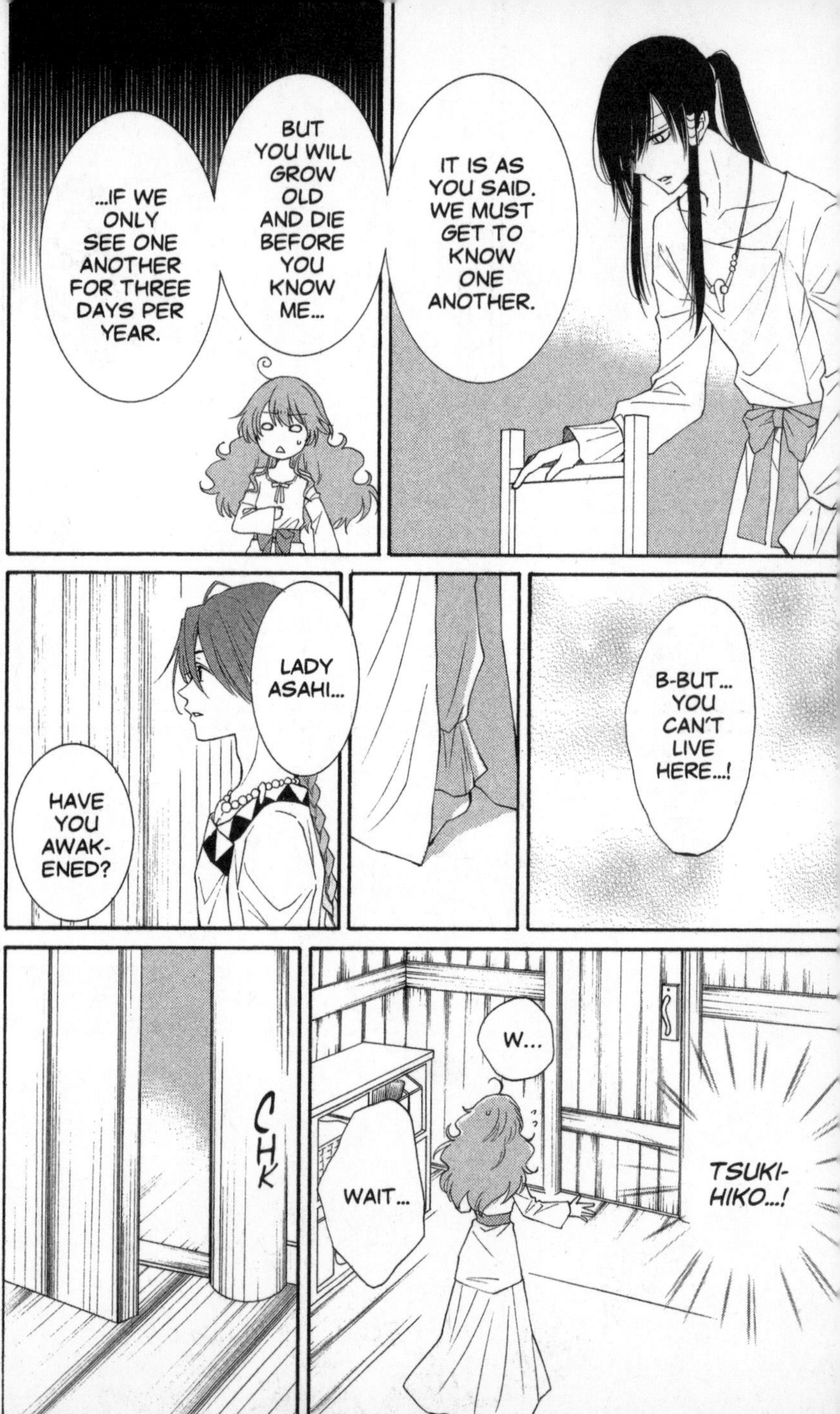
IT IS AS YOU SAID. WE MUST GET TO KNOW ONE ANOTHER.
BUT YOU WILL GROW OLD AND DIE BEFORE YOU KNOW ME...
...IF WE ONLY SEE ONE ANOTHER FOR THREE DAYS PER YEAR.
B-BUT... YOU CAN'T LIVE HERE...!
LADY ASAHI...
HAVE YOU AWAK-ENED?
TSUKI-HIKO...!
W...
WAIT...
CHK

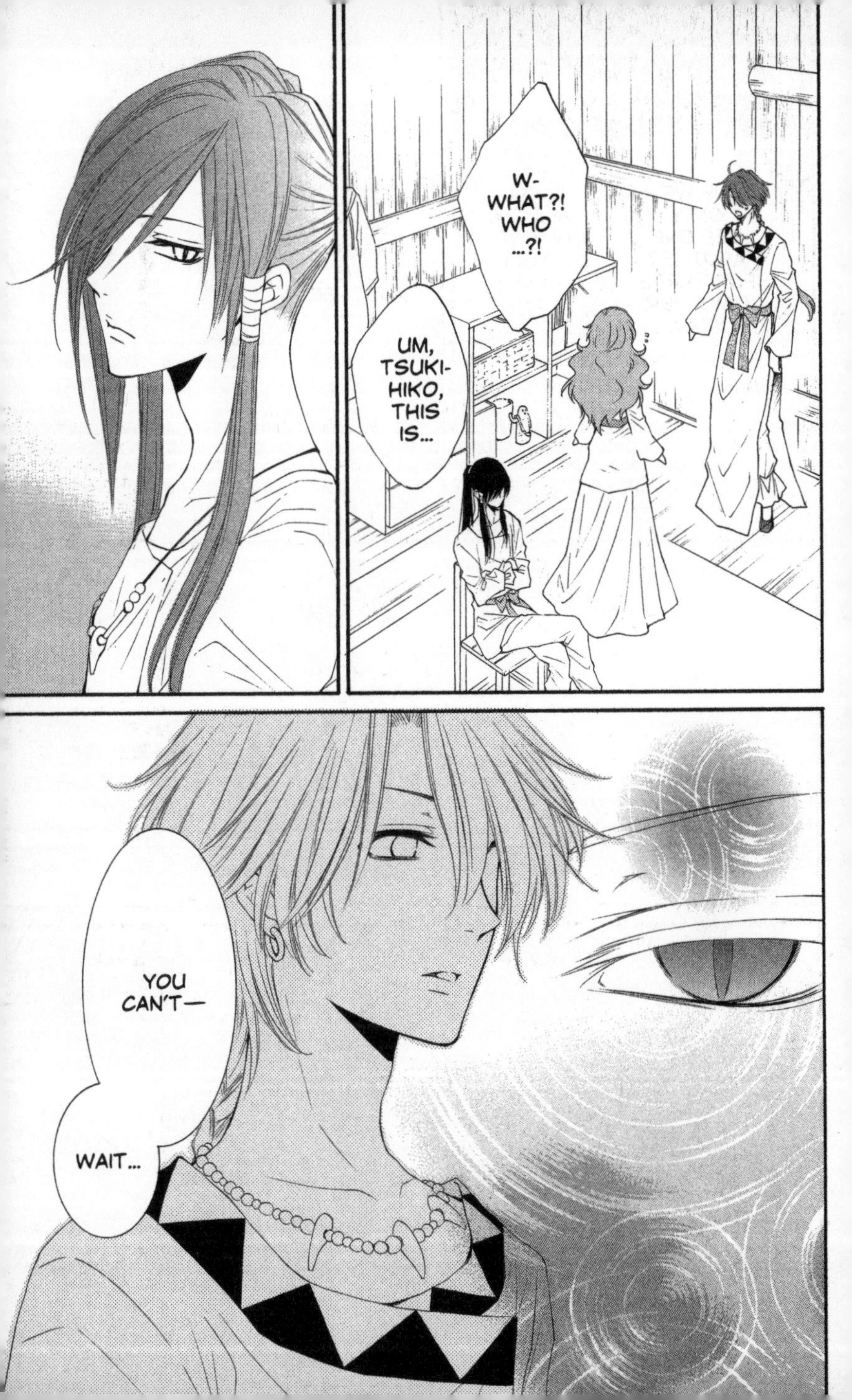
W-WHAT?! WHO ...?!
UM, TSUKI-HIKO, THIS IS...
YOU CAN'T—
WAIT...

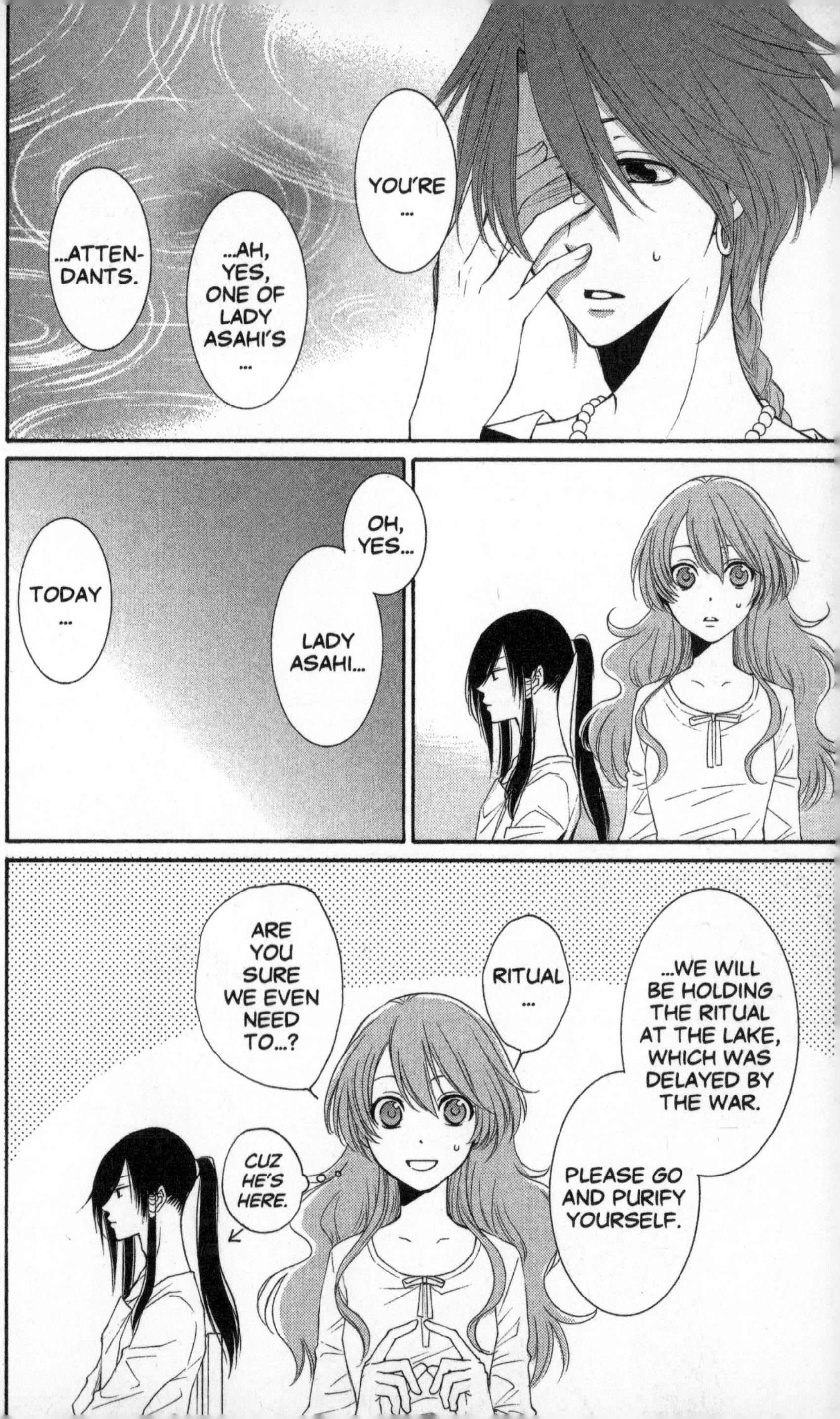
YOU'RE ...
...AH, YES, ONE OF LADY ASAHI'S ...
...ATTEN-DANTS.
OH, YES...
LADY ASAHI...
TODAY ...
...WE WILL BE HOLDING THE RITUAL AT THE LAKE, WHICH WAS DELAYED BY THE WAR.
PLEASE GO AND PURIFY YOURSELF.
RITUAL ...
ARE YOU SURE WE EVEN NEED TO...?
CUZ HE'S HERE.

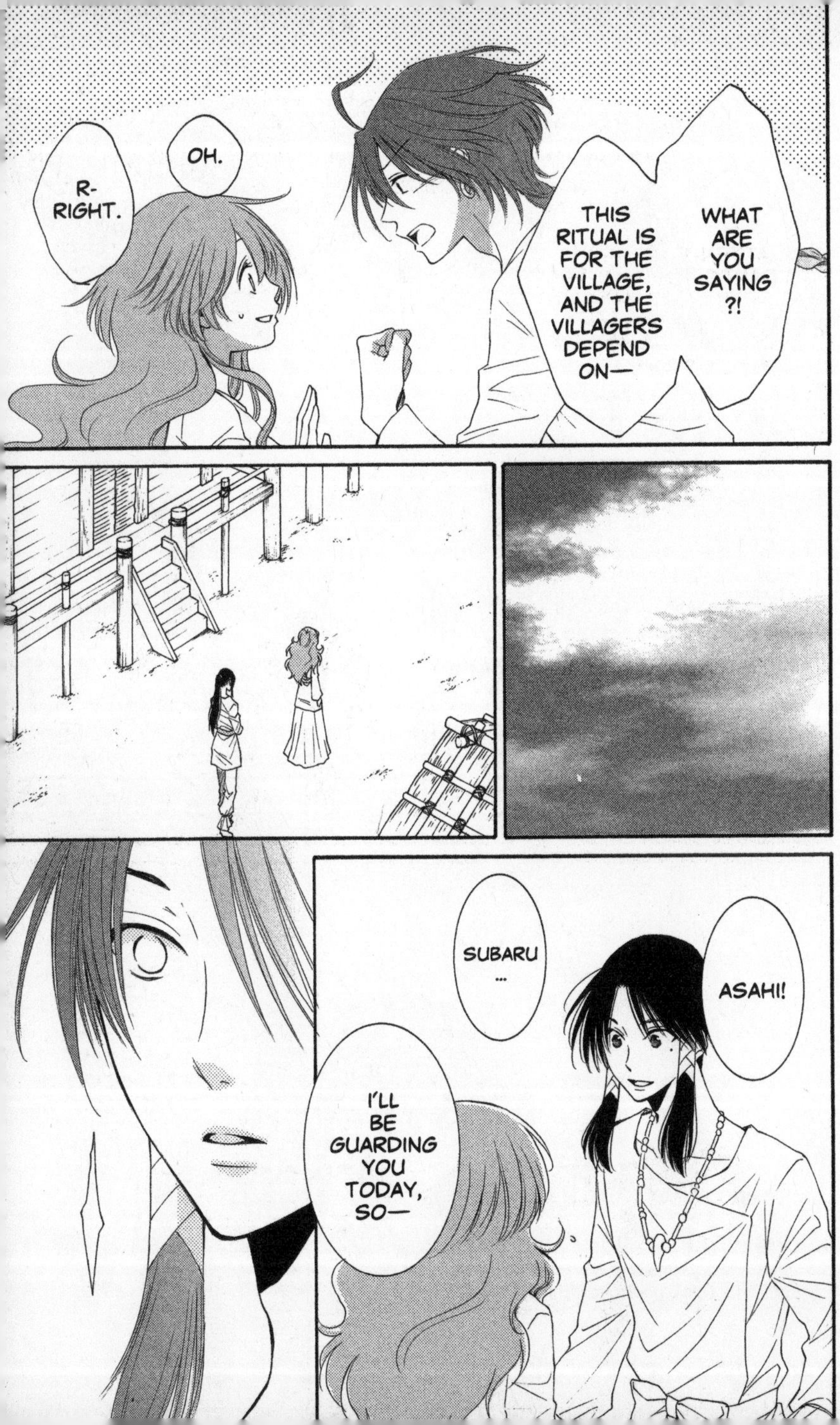
WHAT ARE YOU SAYING?!
THIS RITUAL IS FOR THE VILLAGE, AND THE VILLAGERS DEPEND ON—
OH.
R-RIGHT.
ASAHI!
SUBARU...
I'LL BE GUARDING YOU TODAY, SO—

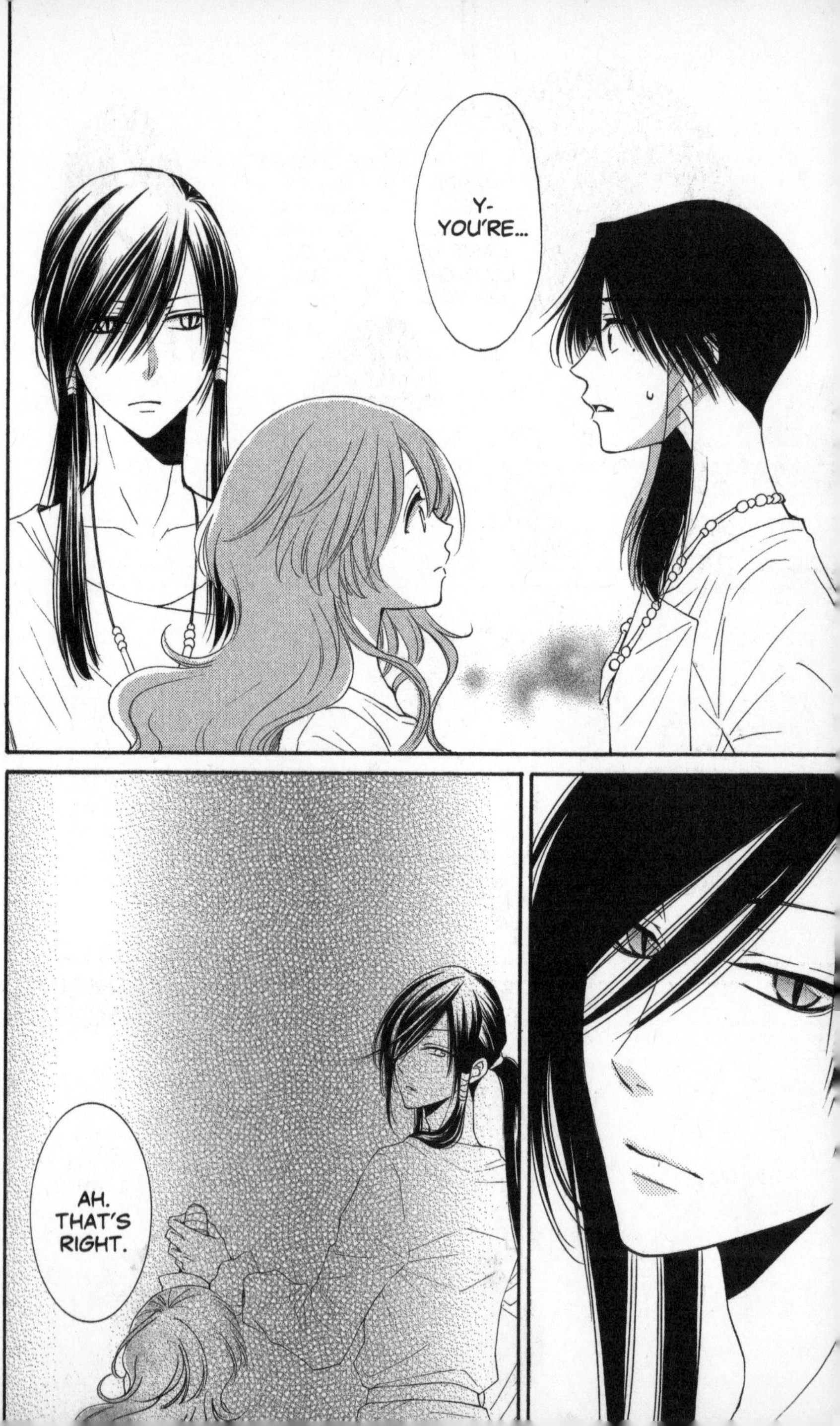
Y-
YOU'RE...
AH. THAT'S RIGHT.

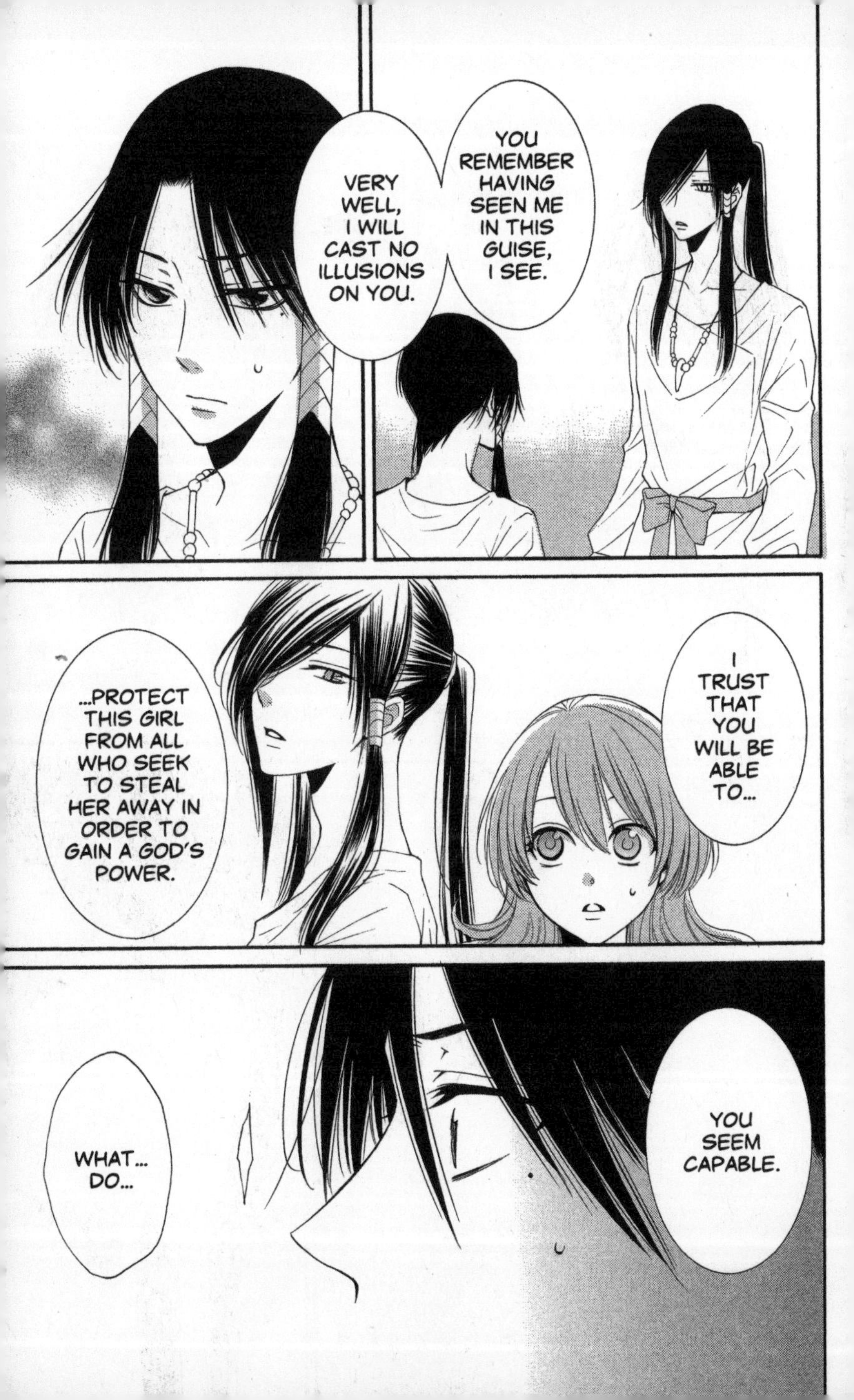
YOU REMEMBER HAVING SEEN ME IN THIS GUISE, I SEE.
VERY WELL, I WILL CAST NO ILLUSIONS ON YOU.
I TRUST THAT YOU WILL BE ABLE TO...
...PROTECT THIS GIRL FROM ALL WHO SEEK TO STEAL HER AWAY IN ORDER TO GAIN A GOD'S POWER.
YOU SEEM CAPABLE.
WHAT... DO...

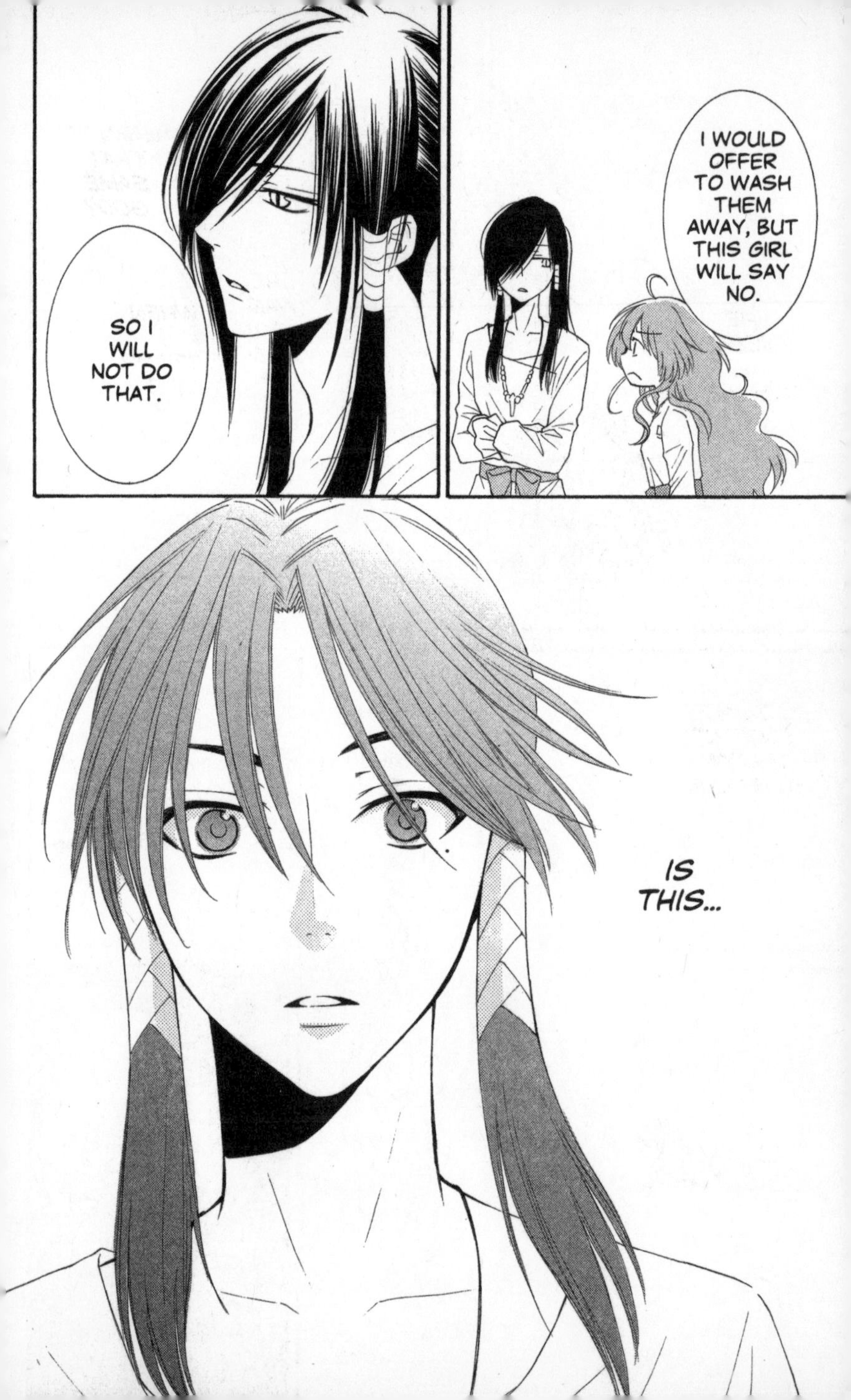
I WOULD OFFER TO WASH THEM AWAY, BUT THIS GIRL WILL SAY NO.
SO I WILL NOT DO THAT.
IS THIS...

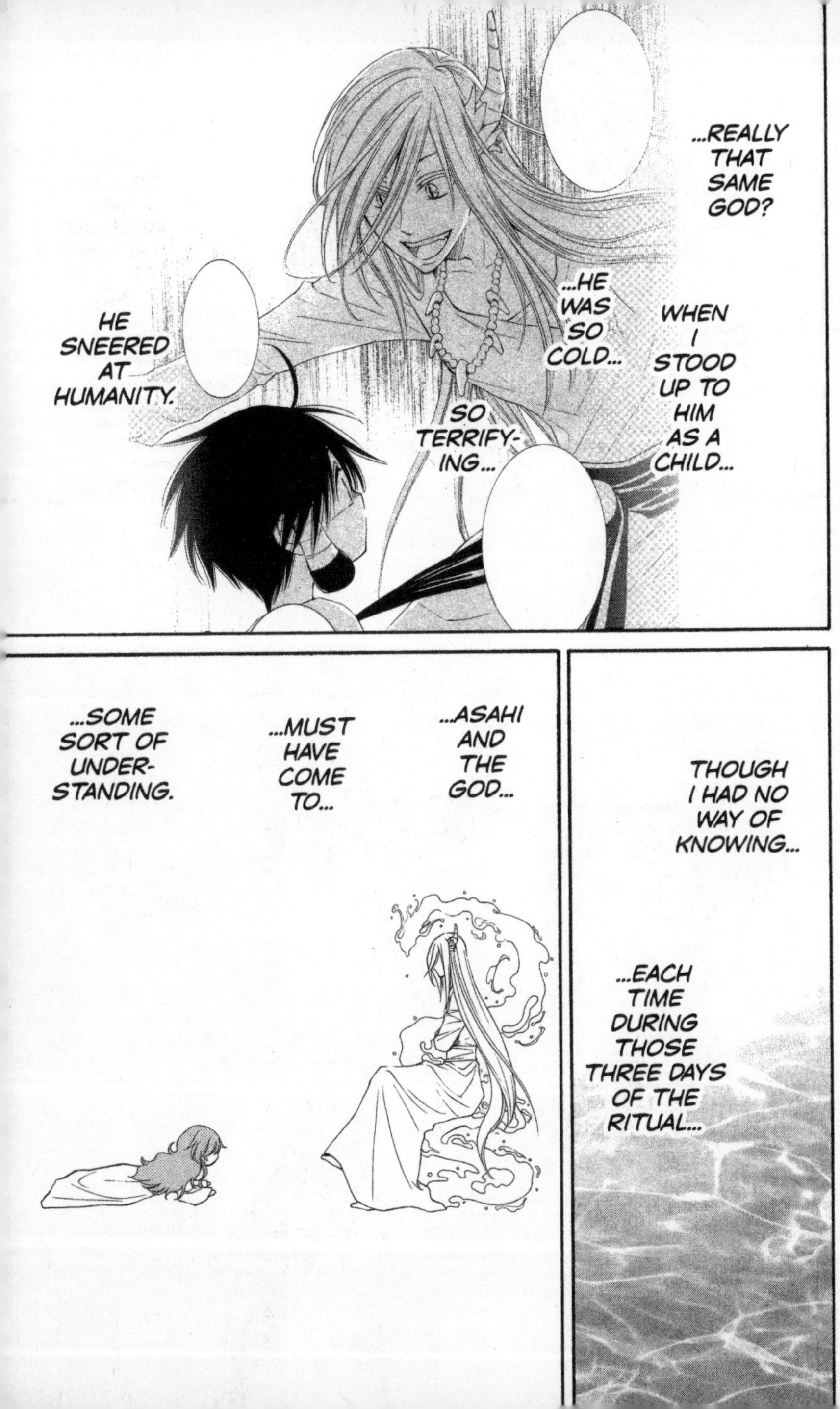
...REALLY THAT SAME GOD?
WHEN I STOOD UP TO HIM AS A CHILD...
...HE WAS SO COLD...
SO TERRIFYING...
HE SNEERED AT HUMANITY.
THOUGH I HAD NO WAY OF KNOWING...
...EACH TIME DURING THOSE THREE DAYS OF THE RITUAL...
...ASAHI AND THE GOD...
...MUST HAVE COME TO...
...SOME SORT OF UNDERSTANDING.

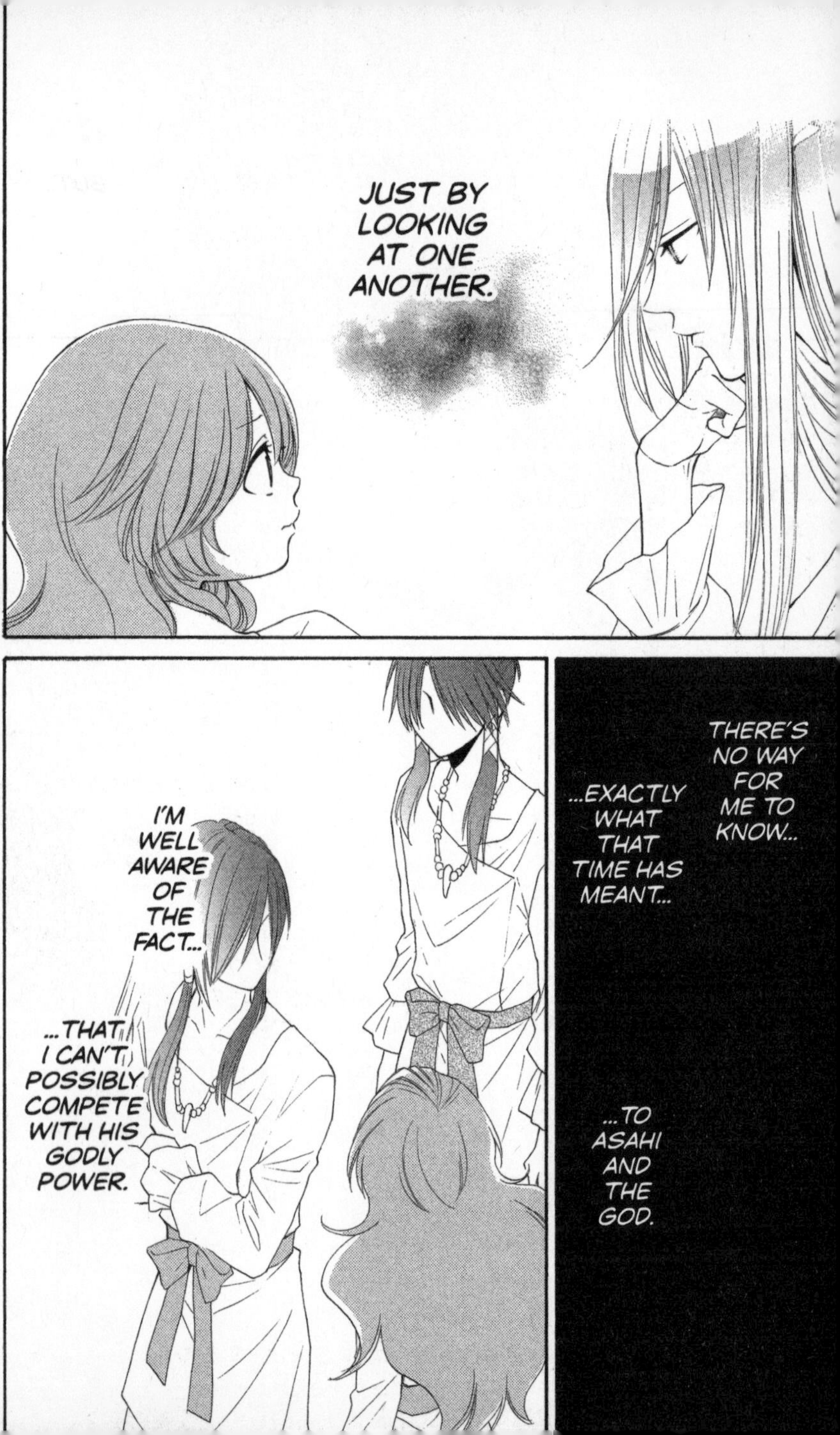
JUST BY LOOKING AT ONE ANOTHER.
THERE'S NO WAY FOR ME TO KNOW...
...EXACTLY WHAT THAT TIME HAS MEANT...
...TO ASAHI AND THE GOD.
I'M WELL AWARE OF THE FACT...
...THAT I CAN'T POSSIBLY COMPETE WITH HIS GODLY POWER.

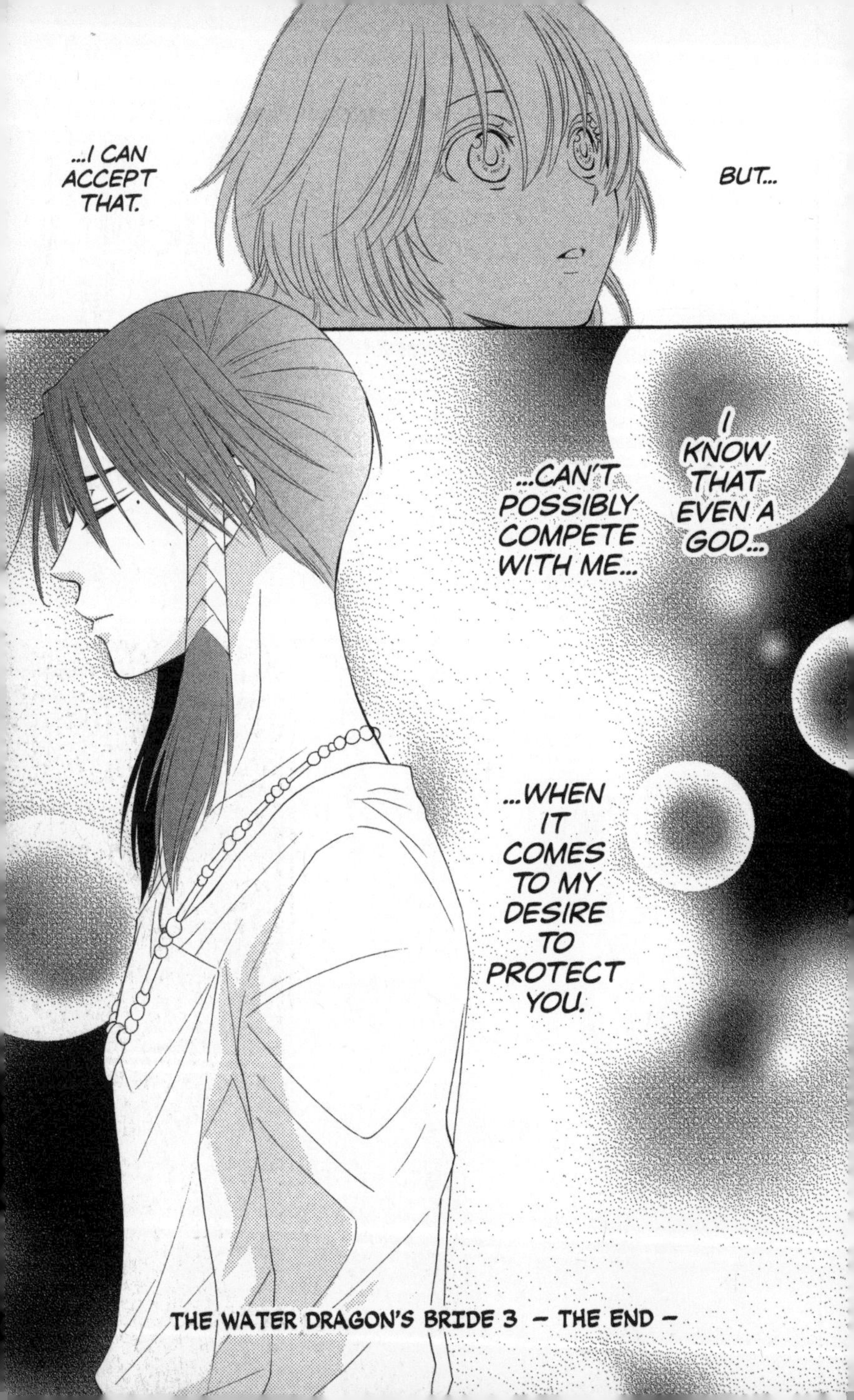
BUT...
...I CAN ACCEPT THAT.
I KNOW THAT EVEN A GOD...
...CAN'T POSSIBLY COMPETE WITH ME...
...WHEN IT COMES TO MY DESIRE TO PROTECT YOU.
THE WATER DRAGON'S BRIDE 3 – THE END –

The Water Dragon's Bride

Bonus Comics

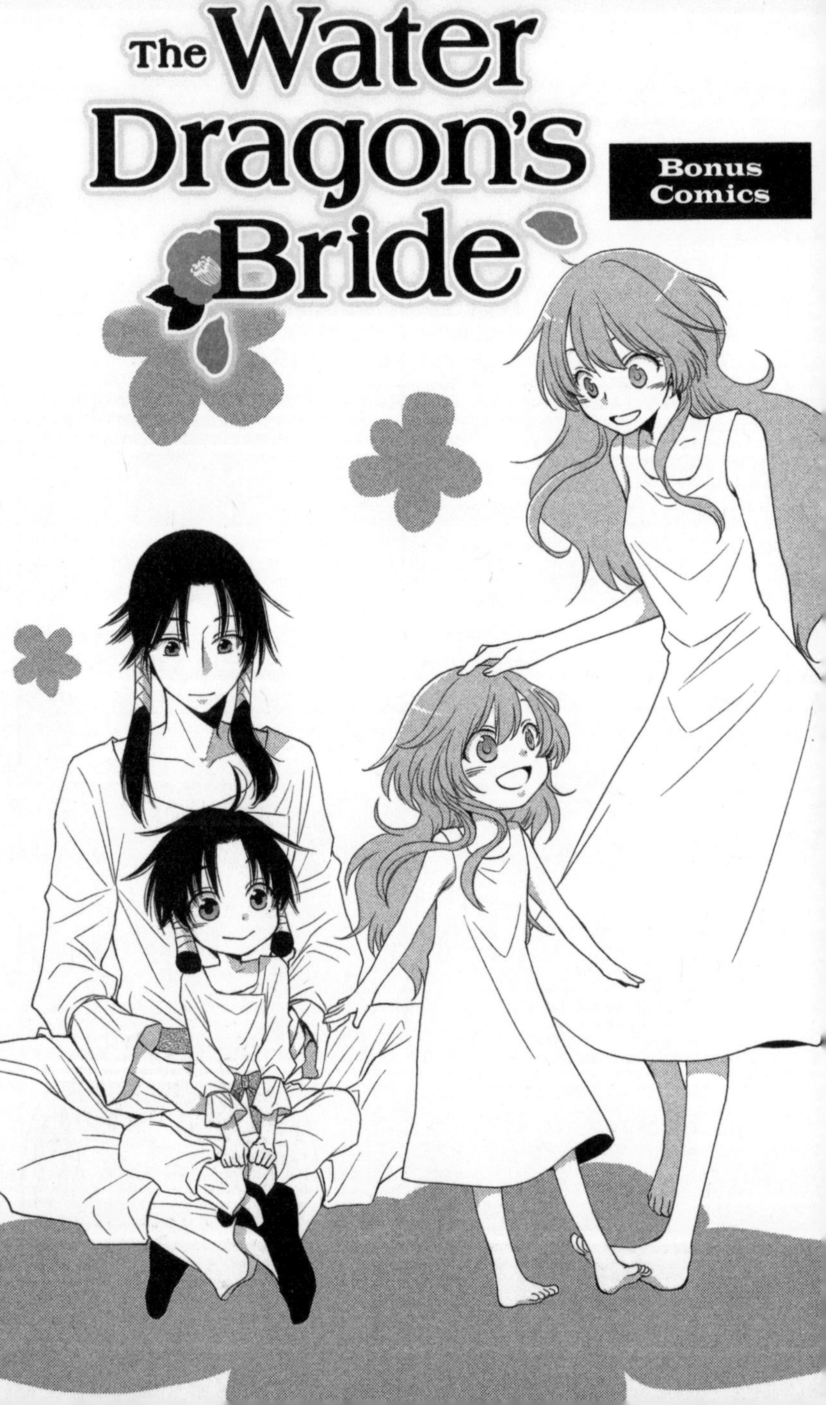

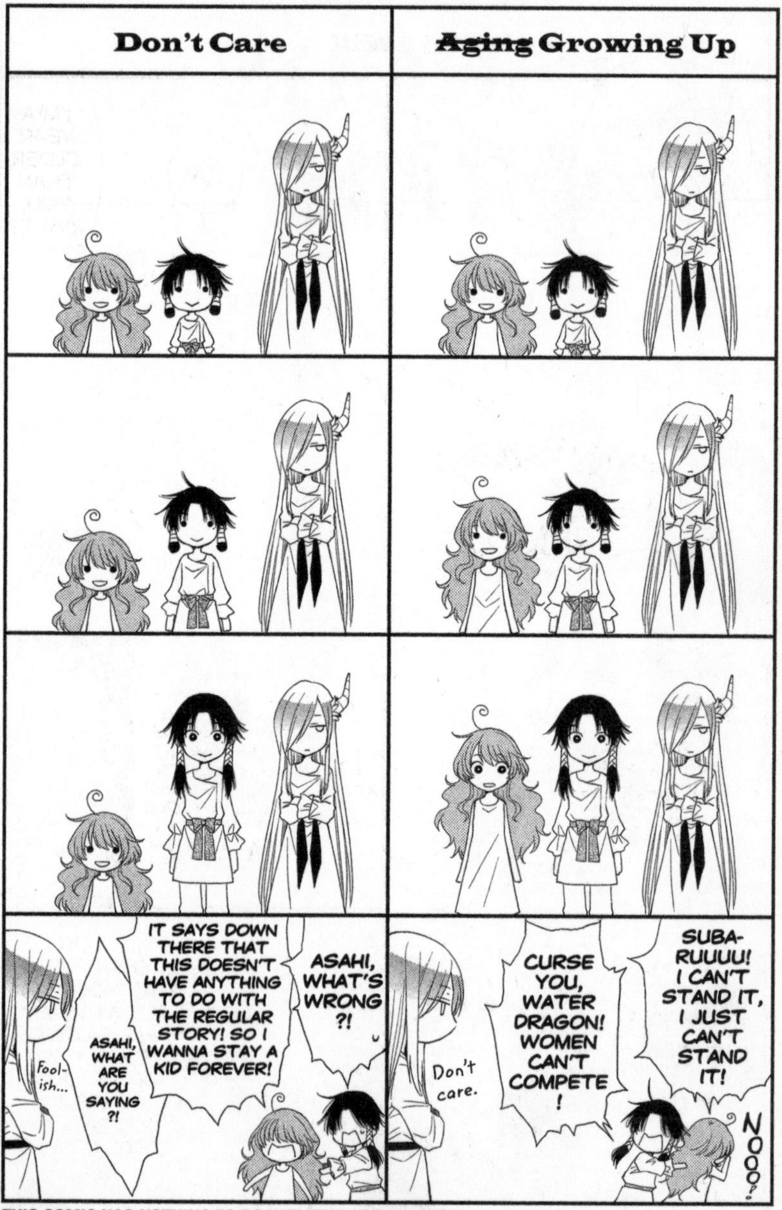
~~Aging~~ Growing Up
SUBA-RUUUU! I CAN'T STAND IT, I JUST CAN'T STAND IT!
NOOO?!
CURSE YOU, WATER DRAGON! WOMEN CAN'T COMPETE!
Don't care.
Don't Care
ASAHI, WHAT'S WRONG?!
IT SAYS DOWN THERE THAT THIS DOESN'T HAVE ANYTHING TO DO WITH THE REGULAR STORY! SO I WANNA STAY A KID FOREVER!
ASAHI, WHAT ARE YOU SAYING?!
Fool-ish...

THIS COMIC HAS NOTHING TO DO WITH THE ACTUAL STORY.

At Will

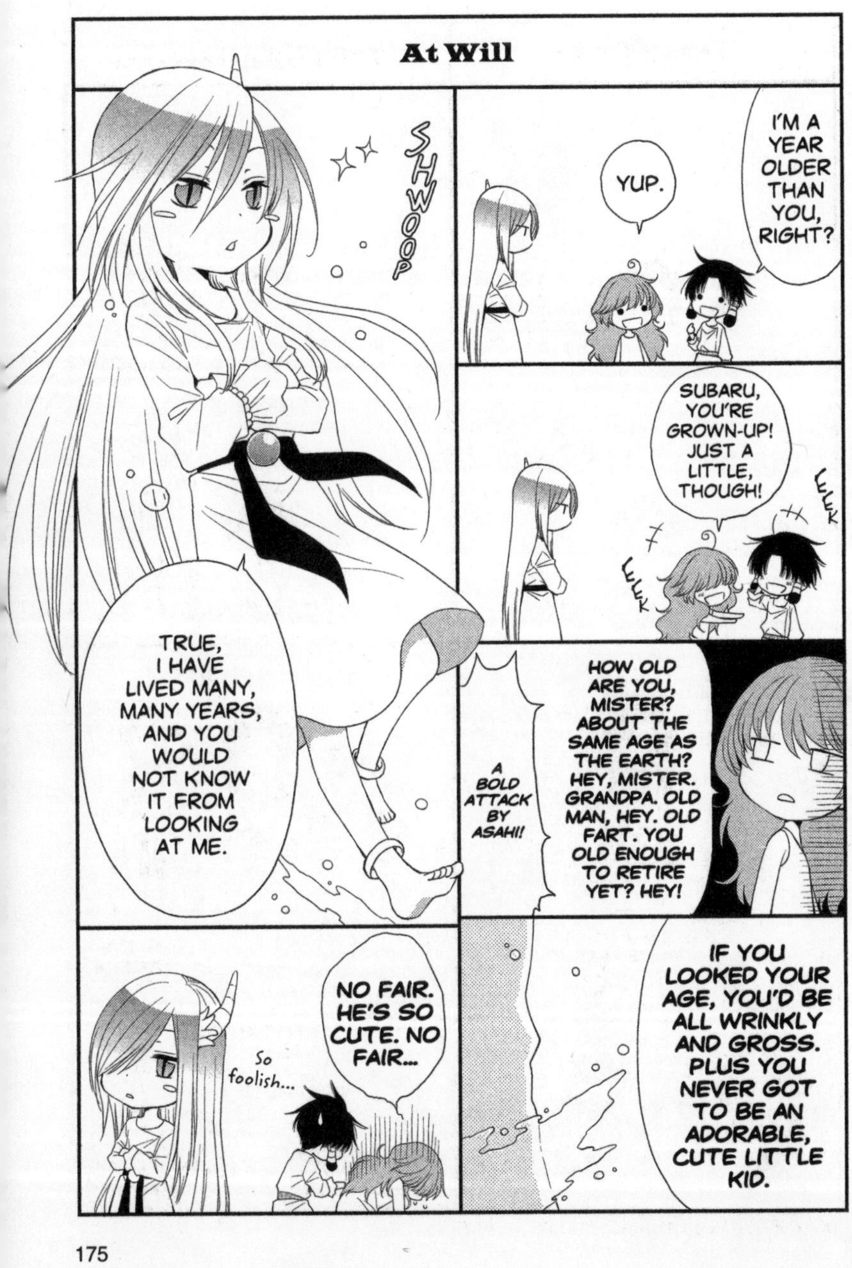
I'M A YEAR OLDER THAN YOU, RIGHT?
YUP.
SUBARU, YOU'RE GROWN-UP! JUST A LITTLE, THOUGH!
HOW OLD ARE YOU, MISTER? ABOUT THE SAME AGE AS THE EARTH? HEY, MISTER. GRANDPA. OLD MAN, HEY. OLD FART. YOU OLD ENOUGH TO RETIRE YET? HEY!
A BOLD ATTACK BY ASAHI!
SHWOOP
TRUE, I HAVE LIVED MANY, MANY YEARS, AND YOU WOULD NOT KNOW IT FROM LOOKING AT ME.
IF YOU LOOKED YOUR AGE, YOU'D BE ALL WRINKLY AND GROSS. PLUS YOU NEVER GOT TO BE AN ADORABLE, CUTE LITTLE KID.
NO FAIR. HE'S SO CUTE. NO FAIR...
So foolish...

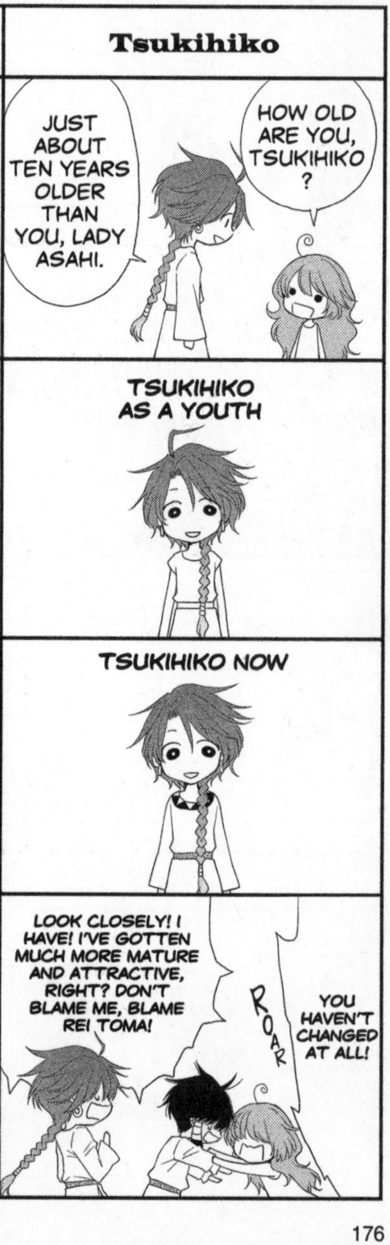
Tsukihiko
HOW OLD ARE YOU, TSUKIHIKO?
JUST ABOUT TEN YEARS OLDER THAN YOU, LADY ASAHI.
TSUKIHIKO AS A YOUTH
TSUKIHIKO NOW
YOU HAVEN'T CHANGED AT ALL!
ROAR
LOOK CLOSELY! I HAVE! I'VE GOTTEN MUCH MORE MATURE AND ATTRACTIVE, RIGHT? DON'T BLAME ME, BLAME REI TOMA!

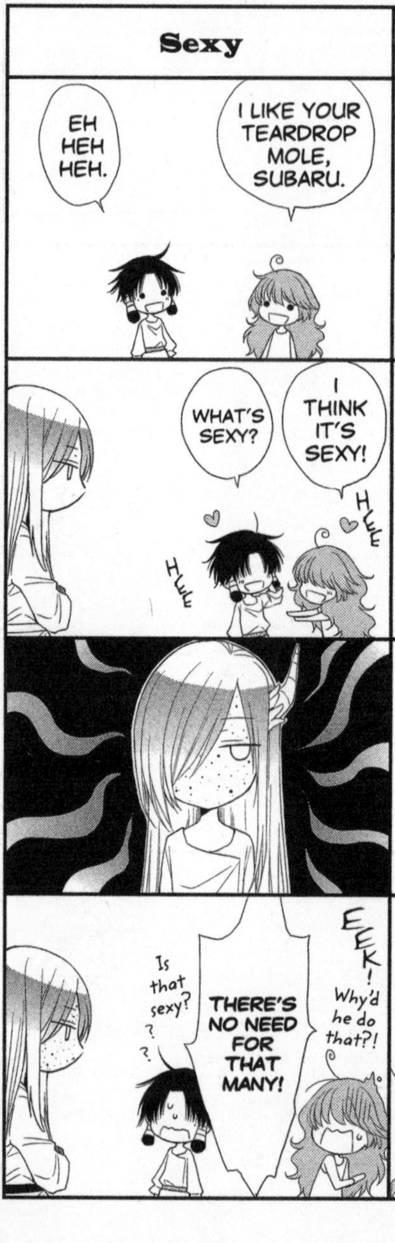
Sexy
I LIKE YOUR TEARDROP MOLE, SUBARU.
EH HEH HEH.
I THINK IT'S SEXY!
WHAT'S SEXY?
HEE
HEE
EEK!
Why'd he do that?!
THERE'S NO NEED FOR THAT MANY!
Is that sexy? ? ?

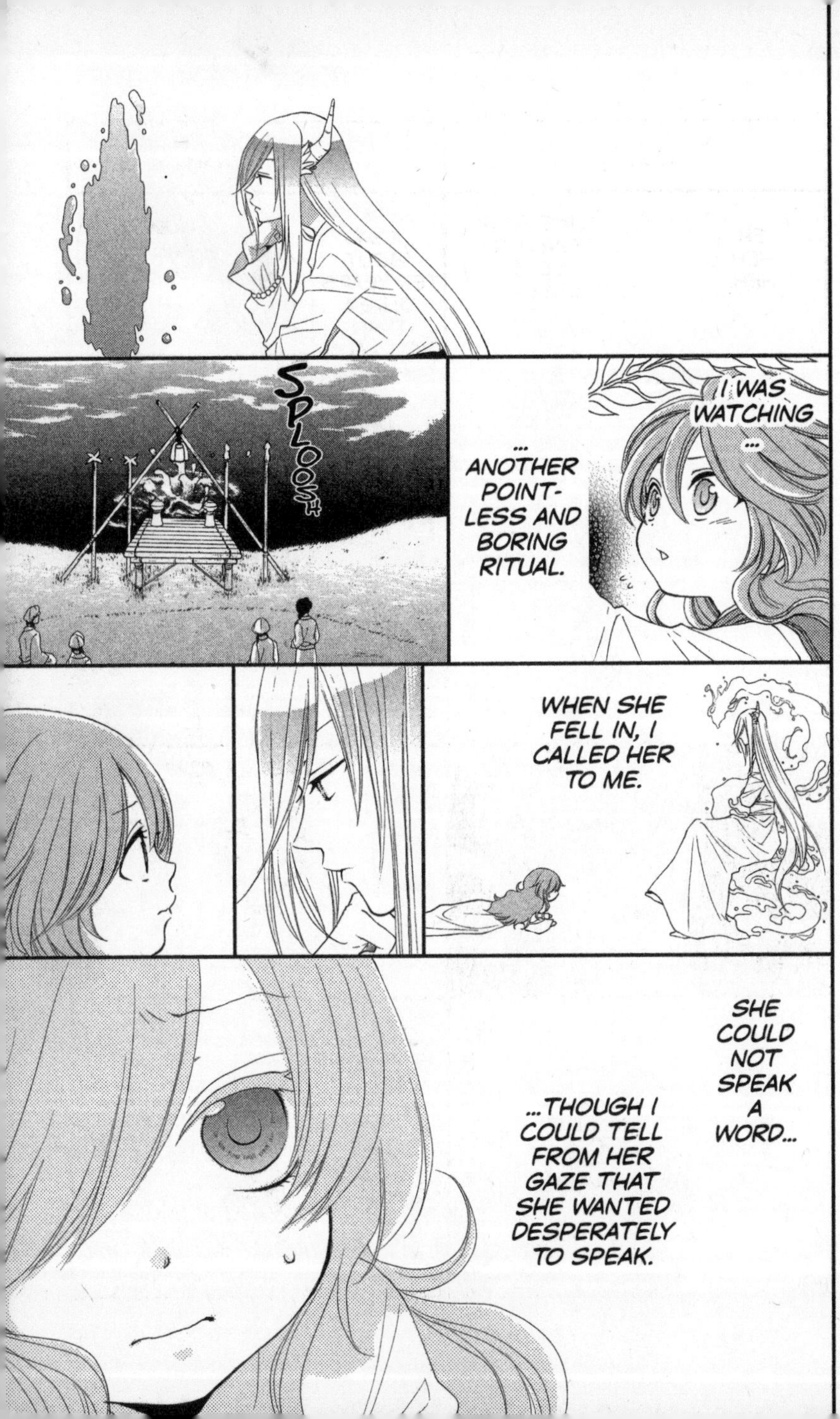
I WAS WATCHING ...
... ANOTHER POINTLESS AND BORING RITUAL.
SPLOOSH
WHEN SHE FELL IN, I CALLED HER TO ME.
SHE COULD NOT SPEAK A WORD...
...THOUGH I COULD TELL FROM HER GAZE THAT SHE WANTED DESPERATELY TO SPEAK.

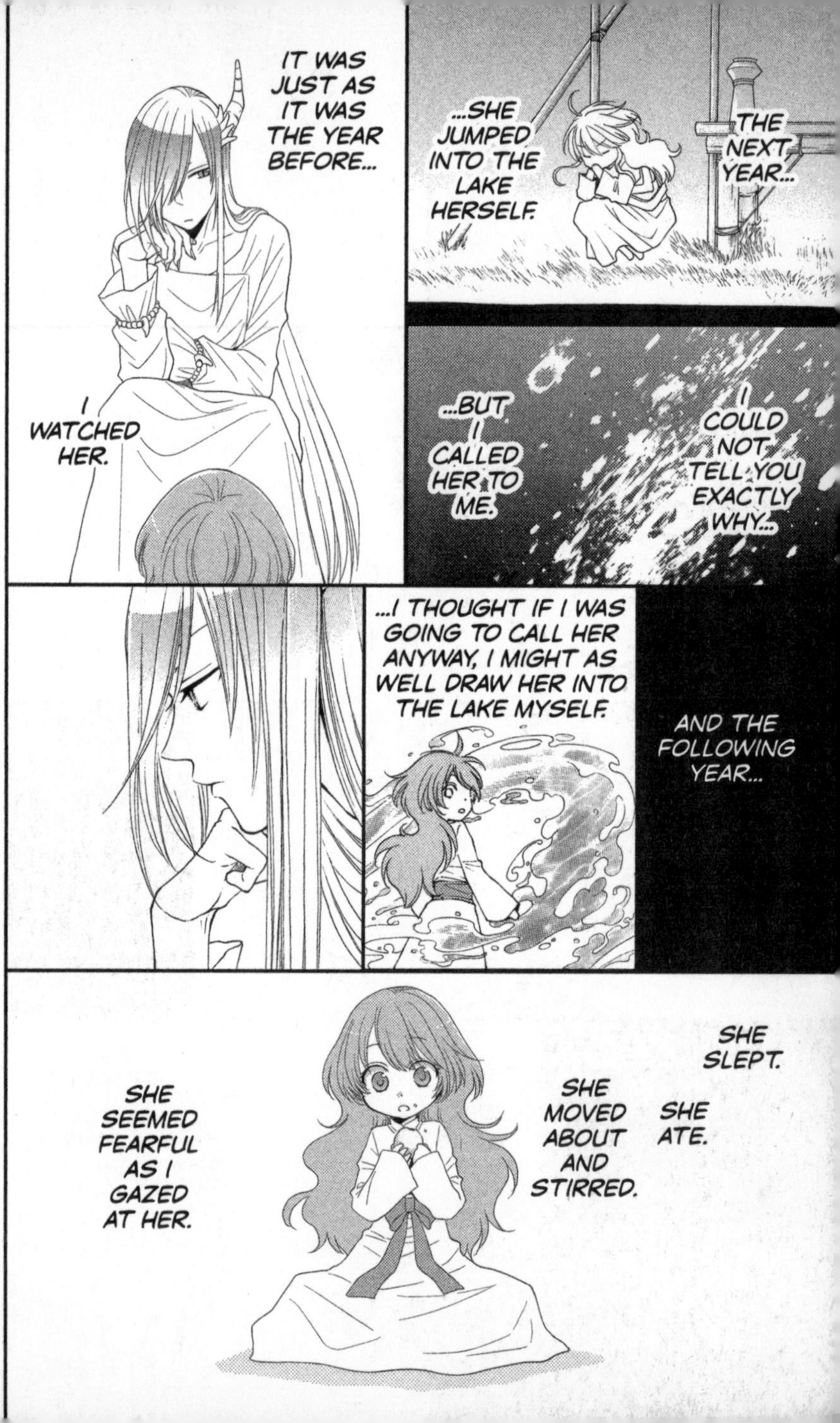
THE NEXT YEAR...
...SHE JUMPED INTO THE LAKE HERSELF.
I COULD NOT TELL YOU EXACTLY WHY...
...BUT I CALLED HER TO ME.
IT WAS JUST AS IT WAS THE YEAR BEFORE...
I WATCHED HER.
AND THE FOLLOWING YEAR...
...I THOUGHT IF I WAS GOING TO CALL HER ANYWAY, I MIGHT AS WELL DRAW HER INTO THE LAKE MYSELF.
SHE SLEPT.
SHE ATE.
SHE MOVED ABOUT AND STIRRED.
SHE SEEMED FEARFUL AS I GAZED AT HER.

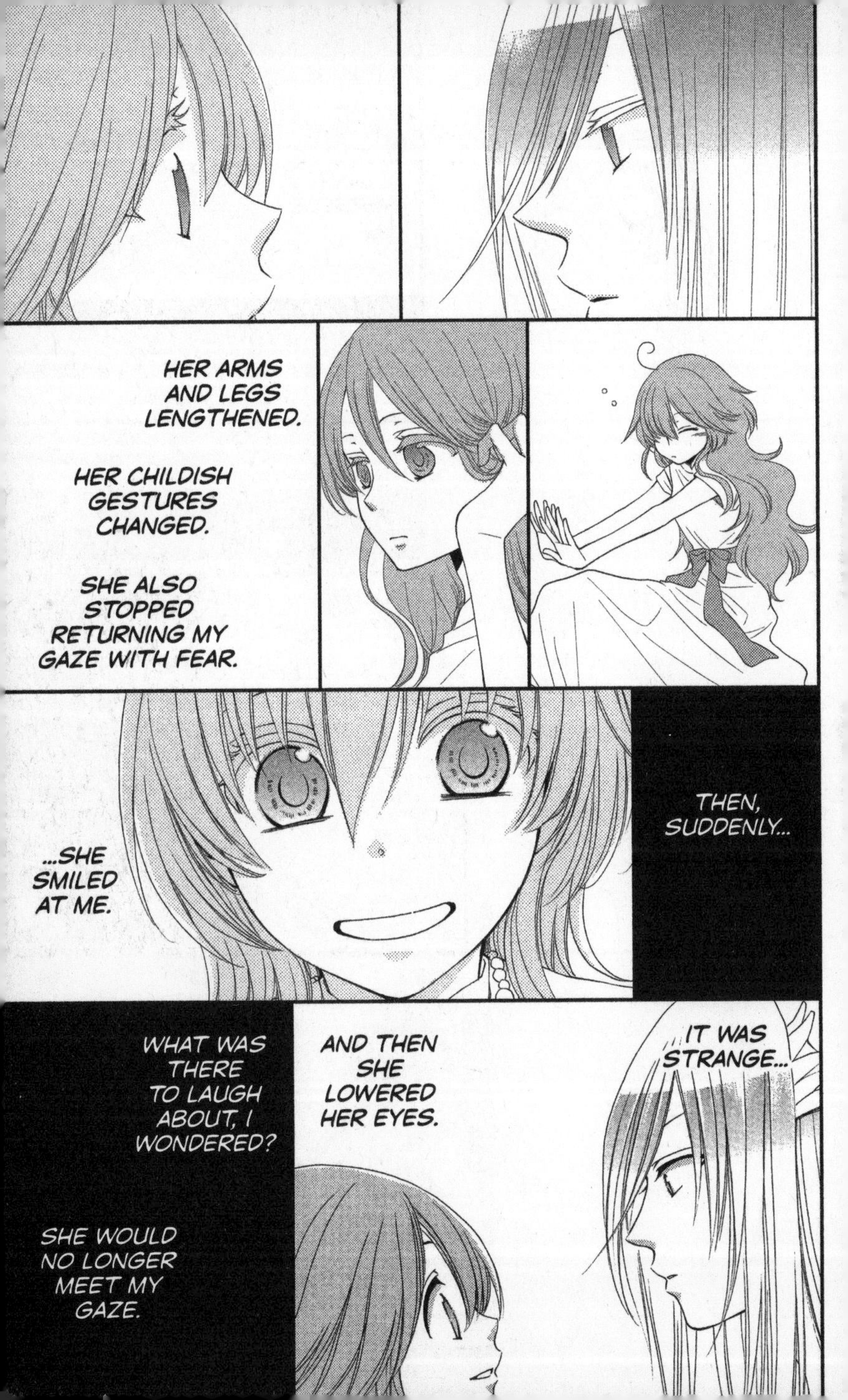
HER ARMS AND LEGS LENGTHENED.
HER CHILDISH GESTURES CHANGED.
SHE ALSO STOPPED RETURNING MY GAZE WITH FEAR.
THEN, SUDDENLY...
...SHE SMILED AT ME.
...IT WAS STRANGE...
AND THEN SHE LOWERED HER EYES.
WHAT WAS THERE TO LAUGH ABOUT, I WONDERED?
SHE WOULD NO LONGER MEET MY GAZE.

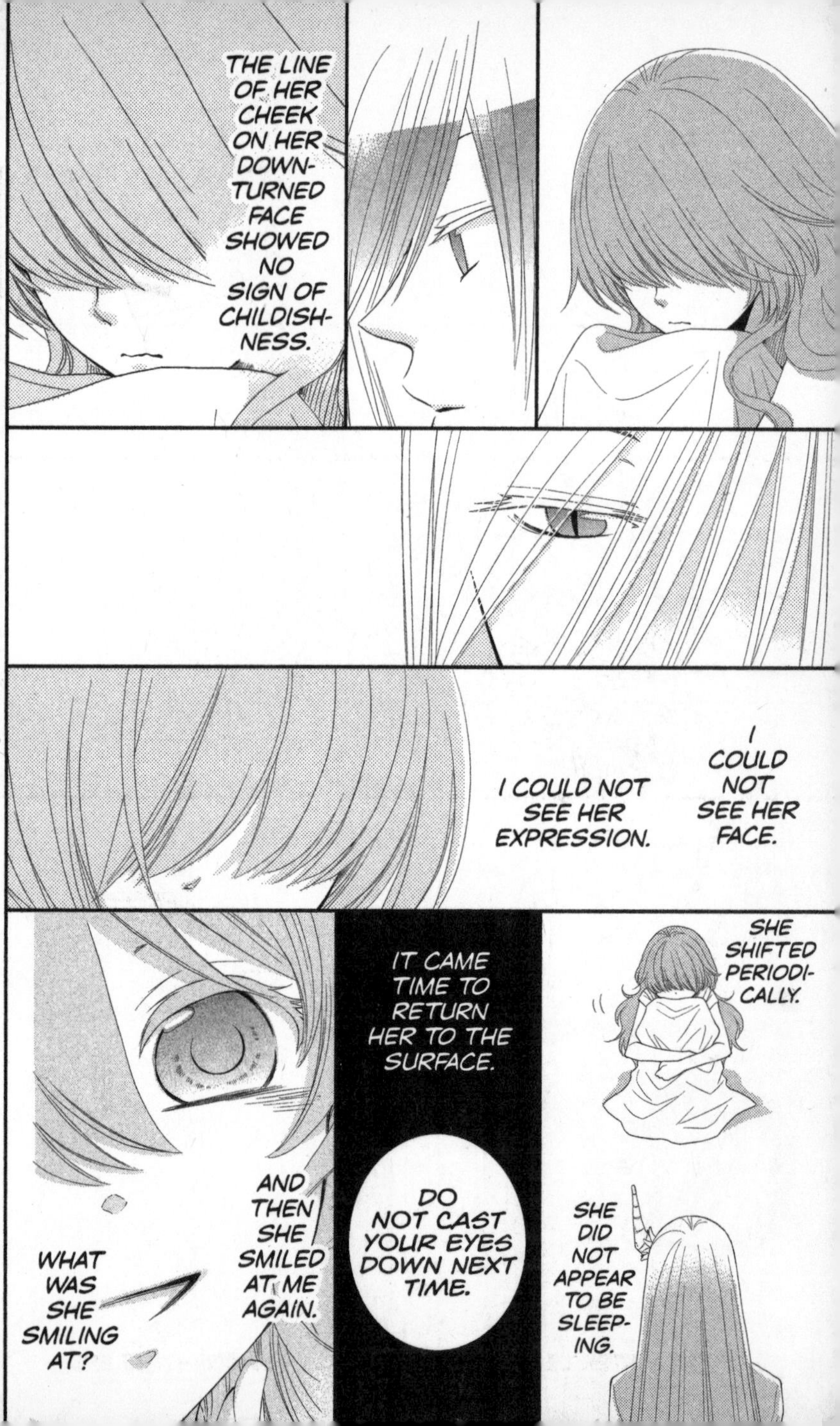
THE LINE OF HER CHEEK ON HER DOWN-TURNED FACE SHOWED NO SIGN OF CHILDISHNESS.
I COULD NOT SEE HER FACE.
I COULD NOT SEE HER EXPRESSION.
SHE SHIFTED PERIODICALLY.
SHE DID NOT APPEAR TO BE SLEEPING.
IT CAME TIME TO RETURN HER TO THE SURFACE.
DO NOT CAST YOUR EYES DOWN NEXT TIME.
AND THEN SHE SMILED AT ME AGAIN.
WHAT WAS SHE SMILING AT?

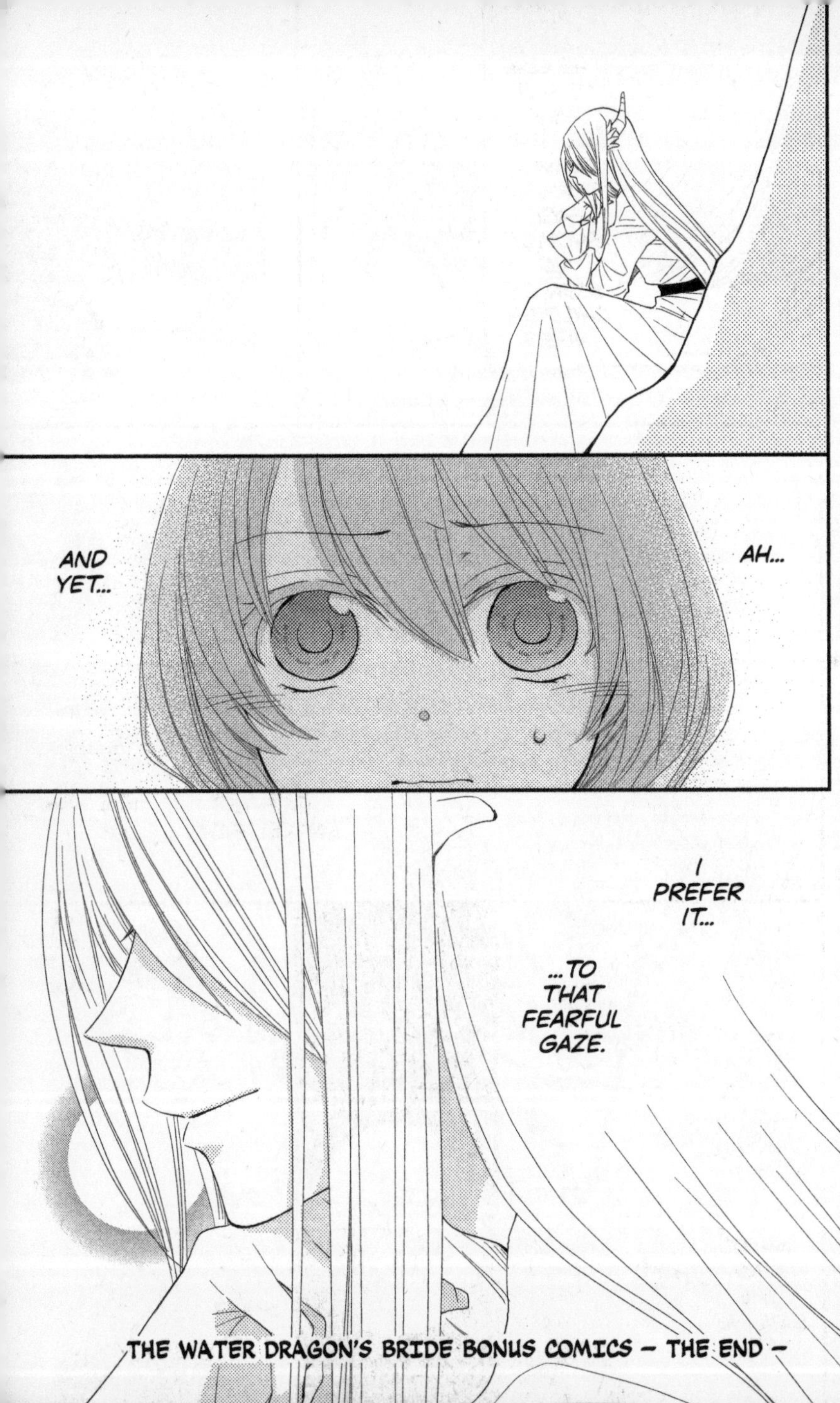
AH...
AND YET...
I PREFER IT...
...TO THAT FEARFUL GAZE.
THE WATER DRAGON'S BRIDE BONUS COMICS – THE END –

It's volume 3.

Hello, it's Rei Toma. We're already at volume 3. This time, the cover is the water dragon god and the all-grown-up Asahi. Who's going to be on the next one??

Well, then... The truth is, I can never figure out what to write in these spaces. So if you have any questions, feel free to write me a letter. (Please let me use your letters.)

Rei Toma
c/o The Water Dragon's Bride Editor
VIZ Media
P.O. Box 77010
San Francisco, CA 94107

Each of your letters is precious to me! They'll give me strength as I work on my next chapter.
Thank you so very much.